Getting the Most
for your
MEDICAL
DOLLAR

More books from Wings Books and the People's Medical Society

150 Ways To Be A Savvy Medical Consumer

Take This Book To The Hospital With You

Your Blood Pressure

Your Heart

A PEOPLE'S MEDICAL SOCIETY BOOK

Getting the Most
for your
MEDICAL DOLLAR

CHARLES B. INLANDER
President
People's Medical Society

KARLA MORALES
Vice President of Communications
People's Medical Society

WINGS BOOKS
New York • Avenel, New Jersey

The People's Medical Society is a nonprofit consumer health organization dedicated to the principles of better, more responsive, and less expensive medical care. Organized in 1983, the People's Medical Society puts previously unavailable medical information into the hands of consumers, so that they can make informed decisions about their own health care. Knowing that consumers, as individuals or in groups, can make a difference, the society is involved in the debate over the future of the medical care system.

Membership in the People's Medical Society is $20 a year and includes a subscription to the *People's Medical Society Newsletter*. For information, write to the People's Medical Society, 462 Walnut Street, Allentown, PA 18102, or call (215) 770-1670.

Copyright © 1991 by The People's Medical Society

This 1993 edition is published by Wings Books, distributed by Outlet Book Company, Inc., a Random House Company, 40 Engelhard Avenue, Avenel, New Jersey 07001, by arrangement with The People's Medical Society.

Random House
New York • Toronto • London • Sydney • Auckland

Printed and bound in the United States of America

Library of Congress Cataloging-in-Publication Data
Inlander, Charles B.
    Getting the most for your medical dollar / Charles B. Inlander,
Karla Morales.
        p.   cm.
    "A People's Medical Society book."
    Originally published: New York : Pantheon Books, 1991.
    Includes index.
    ISBN 0-517-08911-4
    1. Medical care—United States—Handbooks, manuals, etc.
  2. Consumer education—United States—Handbooks, manual, etc.
  I. Morales, Karla.   II. Title.
    RA410.53.I56   1993
    362.1'029'673—dc20   92-38765
                                                         CIP

8 7 6 5 4 3 2 1

CONTENTS

Acknowledgments

Many people have contributed to the development and publication of this book.

Special thanks to our literary agent Gail Ross. She makes it all happen with her ideas, suggestions, friendship, and hard work. In just six years she has been responsible for our having fourteen major books published with a whole lot more to come. She is wonderful.

On the home front there are some very special people who must be recognized. Michael Donio, our director of projects, put in many hours of intensive research for this book. His contribution is invaluable and there would be no book without him. Gayle Ebert and Linda Swank, who supported us by putting lists and data into our word processors, deserve special recognition. Bill Bauman's assistance in coordinating the checking of phone numbers and addresses found throughout the book was essential to the accuracy and usefulness of the material. Paula Brisco and Miriam Flexer have our eternal gratitude for their work and support. Thanks to Paula for letting us use her printer so freely, and thanks to Miriam, who labored at the copying machine for hours.

The Board of Directors of the People's Medical Society deserve an honorable mention. Since the People's Medical Society was formed in 1983, the board has guided the organization with a sincere commitment to ensuring that the health care system is responsive to, and ultimately driven by, the consumer. Our special thanks to the board, chaired by Lowell S. Levin, Ed. D., for its unswerving support of this project.

And special thanks to our respective spouses for putting up with us during the writing of the manuscript. In fact, it's pretty amazing they put up with us at all.

Finally, our thanks to the more than 150,000 citizens who have joined the People's Medical Society since its founding. Their input and needs are the reason the society exists and are the underlying cause for a book such as this. We thank them and acknowledge their ultimate contribution to making the health care system work better for all of us.

INTRODUCTION

You can save money on your health care. Big money! And you can start saving today. This book will show you how.

It's like the old "good news/bad news" joke; it's all in how you look at something. In this book we choose to look at the good news. That's because we know the good news can work.

Of course, the good news is that you can beat the health care system by getting high-quality health care at a cost much lower than you currently pay. The trick is knowing what you are buying. In *Getting the Most for Your Medical Dollar* we show and teach you everything you need to know to get the maximum benefit out of every dollar you spend.

Obviously, you know the bad news. Or at least you think you do. But let's take a quick look at what the American medical consumer is up against when confronting the health care system. After this short journey it should be crystal-clear why this book is so important.

Most Americans think they are getting good health care. Some are, some aren't. The trouble is most people have no basis to judge if the benefit of their care is really worth the money that is being expended. That's because they have virtually no information about the practitioners, services, and products they use.

And when you compare America's health statistics with most other Western industrialized countries, the numbers tell a startling story.

America spends more per capita on health and medical services than any other country in the world. Yet a score of other nations have a longer average life span. We have one of the worst infant mortality rates of any industrialized country, despite having the highest overall standard of living. We have more heart disease, cancer, and other degenerative diseases per capita than most of our allies, even though we spend more on occupational and public safety.

Forget disease for a moment and look at medical procedures. Some 25 percent of the babies born in America are born by cesarean section. In England the rate is 11 percent. The British consider that rate a crisis and are trying to lower it. And, tellingly, more British babies survive their first year of life than American babies.

We give more medical tests, perform more operations, and dispense more medications in one year than over half of the world's population consumes in a lifetime.

But that in itself is not necessarily bad. What is bad is that many American consumers, as well as a significant number of businesses, are on the verge of bankruptcy as a result of their efforts to pay for health care services and benefits.

In 1991, 13 percent of America's gross national product was spent on health care. That is almost $750 billion. By comparison, the nation spent half that amount on national defense and a fraction of it on education.

In 1991 the average family of four spent $4,296 on health care, including health insurance premiums, or $1,074 for every man, woman, and child. Business spending during this same period averaged $2,234 per family. Combined family and business spending for health care in 1991 totaled some $6,530.

Medical inflation during the 1980s ran more than three times that of overall inflation. The picture for the 1990s does not look much better. In fact, it will probably be worse.

Health insurance rates are also skyrocketing. It is not unusual for employers to see enormous jumps in their premiums from year to year. In fact, some companies have seen annual increases of over 100 percent! As a result, most companies have passed some of their increased costs on to their employees in the form of higher contributions to premiums, higher copayment provisions, and larger deductibles. Some companies have even dropped health insurance as a benefit.

Somewhere between 31 million and 37 million Americans are without any form of health insurance. More than half of these work full-time. Either their employers do not offer health insurance as a benefit, or the premium contributions they must make from their paychecks are so high that they cannot afford to buy in without sacrificing food, shelter, or transportation dollars.

No one is spared from the medical cost crunch. Senior citizens, most of whom qualify for and use Medicare, are being bankrupted.

The Medicare premium rises every year. In fact, in 1988 the Part B portion of it rose an astounding 35 percent. Since then the premium has continued to rise and the benefit has not necessarily kept pace. An added dilemma is the fact that Medicare pays less than half of the beneficiaries' bills over the course of their enrollment, thus seniors are required to carry ever more costly supplemental "medi-gap" insurance.

During the 1980s the prices of pharmaceuticals rose an average of 12 percent. Physician office fees consistently have risen 8 to 10 percent, and hospital costs are going up at double-digit rates.

The average physician in this country in 1990 earned $164,300 a year before taxes. That is not indictment, but rather fact. And with more than half a million physicians, tens of thousands of other practitioners, and many more allied health providers, the business of health care is enormous. In fact, in most metropolitan areas, the local health care industry is the largest employer.

Thus, in order to keep the health care machine well-oiled (some might say well-heeled), a steady flow of customers and cash must be present. And every conceivable trick in the book is employed. Hospitals, physicians, chiropractors, fitness centers, and just about every other type of provider of health care services today advertise in newspapers, on radio and television, and through the mail. Medical specialties that a decade ago were not even heard of are now popping up in every city. Even the traditional doctor's office is changing. Today we have outpatient settings for services that used to be performed only in hospitals.

How easy it is for the consumer to be confused—and how easy just to give up and figure you have to live with whatever is served up, like it or not.

But that is not the case. In fact, the more you know about how the health care system works, who the cast of "characters" are, and what your choices are, the better off you will be from both a health and a wealth standpoint.

Getting the Most for Your Medical Dollar is your key to the health care system. We cover just about every type of setting, practitioner, issue, and topic you will have to deal with in your travels through Medical Land. We know you can save at your doctor's office, in the hospital, on your health insurance, at the pharmacy, and in just about every place you find yourself doling out hard-earned cash for medical services.

The more knowledgeable you are about the health care system, the better your health care will be. And that is a fact borne out by many studies. Consumers who know how the system works, the questions to ask, and the tricks of the trade get far better care than those who passively accept what is put on their medical plate.

Getting the Most for Your Medical Dollar compresses many lifetimes of experience into a book. The tens of thousands of People's Medical Society members who have given us their insights into, and successes with, the health care system have served as a testing ground for everything we publish between these covers.

As consumers, we can't wait for the government to take action or our employer to buy a better health insurance policy. That's the route most of us have taken for too long and as a result we have been shortchanged by the medical world.

But now you have a tool that can help guarantee that your health care is the most appropriate at the right price. We think *Getting the Most for Your Medical Dollar* may be the most useful and important health book you ever read.

Getting the Most
for your
MEDICAL
DOLLAR

THE RIGHT PRACTITIONER FOR YOUR NEEDS

Looking for Dr. Right

Your doctor may someday hold your life in his or her* hands.

Across the country as many as 28,000 people may be practicing medicine and treating tens of thousands of patients each year, even though they do not hold physicians' licenses and in many cases have little or no medical training, according to a report in the May 5, 1986 New York Times.

In 1987 Americans spent $1,900 per capita on health care expenses, up from $500 in 1970, and the annual bill is expected to triple by the year 2000.

These are just a few of the multitude of reasons to shop carefully for a doctor, but the fact of the matter is that most consumers spend more time selecting a roofer than they do choosing someone to look after their health. True, with the growth of consumerism in medicine over the past few years, this is changing, but there is still more progress to be made.

Choosing a doctor isn't easy. It's a process filled with questions, both for the prospective doctor and for yourself, but the right choice can save you money. After all, bad medical care costs a lot more than

*We have tried to use male and female pronouns in an egalitarian manner throughout this book. Any imbalance in usage has been in the interests of readability.

good care and takes its toll on your health and your family, as well as your pocketbook.

The time to find the right practitioner is *before* you need one. Don't wait until you have a medical problem or, worse yet, a medical emergency. Not always the best choice, spur-of-the-moment decisions can be costly too.

Begin your search by getting a few good recommendations from family members, friends, and neighbors. Word of mouth is still one of the best methods of finding out which doctors are taking new patients and what others think of these doctors. The old adage of "If you want to find a good doctor, ask a nurse" is probably a good one, but not always practical.

Don't overlook your present doctor, especially if your relationship with this doctor is ending because he or she is leaving practice or retiring. Other sources to consider are:

Doctor referral services operated by a local medical society (usually county-based). Not necessarily our first choice, such services will refer only those doctors who are members of the society. And, to become a member of the society, all a licensed physician has to do is pay dues—not particularly reassuring, nor an endorsement of the doctor's competence. But these services at least give you a list of names to contact in your search.

Hospital-sponsored physician referral services. Similar to medical society referral services, in this case a local hospital refers you to a list of physicians who are either on their staff or have privileges at their facility. Lest you attach altruistic motives to the physician referral services that two-thirds of all community hospitals run (according to a March 6, 1989 *Medical Economics* article), just remember that hospitals, now more than ever, need doctors to send patients to fill their beds. And a big chunk of hospitals' ever-growing marketing budgets (according to the American Hospital Association, an average of $407,000 per hospital, with almost one in five going over the $1 million mark) is spent on this marketing strategy. Like their medical society counterparts, they will not comment on the ability of referred physicians other than to perhaps mention their board certifications.

Newspaper advertisements of doctors announcing the opening of a new practice. A caveat emptor is appropriate here too—ask yourself why the doctor is advertising. To attract patients because he is just out of medical school? Or is in a highly competitive and glutted market? Or has he just moved in from a state where his license was revoked? (There is more on other types of advertising elsewhere in this chapter.)

Your company personnel office. Companies sometimes use certain doctors for employment physicals and disability claims.

Your health insurance company. Companies can sometimes be helpful when you require a specialist for a second opinion.

Listings in the telephone directory. Doctors' names are usually arranged according to practice or specialty, but again be wary. Just because a doctor says he specializes in a certain area of medicine does not mean the doctor actually took any advanced training in it; a doctor can practice in any specialty area he chooses. Look for board certification. (We have more to say on this in the section on medical specialties.)

Senior centers. Some have lists of doctors either affiliated with or recommended by the center. Also, other senior citizens who have had good or bad experiences with doctors can pass along that information to you.

WHERE HAVE ALL THE PATIENTS GONE?

Some years ago reports began to circulate about an impending surplus of doctors, fueled in part by a 1980 study by the Graduate Medical Education National Advisory Committee that predicted a glut of some 150,000 doctors by the end of the century. In the years since, various surveys have disputed the exact figures if not the very idea of a doctor glut. But the fact remains that for several years the numbers of practicing physicians have grown faster than the population as a whole, according to a February 10, 1986 *Forbes* article. And in fact, studies show that in most urban areas a glut now exists.

Doctors suddenly find themselves in a situation in which there is more health care available than demand for it. While this may not spell complete economic catastrophe for the profession, unquestionably the doctor-patient ratio puts the medical consumer smack in the middle of a buyer's market, and the medical consumer who plays the market to the best advantage will get the most for his or her money.

How do you do that? Shop around, for starters. And refuse to abide the autocratic, chauvinistic, or paternalistic doctor of yesteryear.

WHEN SHOULD YOU
SWITCH DOCTORS?

The ready answer to this question is when you are no longer getting the best care for your dollar, but that's not easy to evaluate. Sure, every once in a while something goes so wrong with the doctor-patient relationship that it comes to an abrupt end, but more often than not the relationship drags out until you've spent too much time and money and received too little in return.

How can you prevent such a protracted but inevitable farewell? First, know the legal aspects of the doctor-patient relationship. Once established, this relationship becomes a legal arrangement, which only four conditions can end:

1. Both parties agree to end the relationship

2. It is ended by the patient

3. The doctor is no longer needed

4. The doctor gives reasonable notice that he or she is withdrawing from the relationship

If these procedures are not followed, a patient could make a case for abandonment by the doctor.

Now, back to how to keep the reins of control in your hands. When things are going wrong with the doctor-patient relationship, certain signs should serve as warnings to you that all is not well:

Overcrowded waiting rooms. You and twenty-two others show up for the first appointment at 8 A.M. Overbooking may be fine for the airlines, but it won't fly in your doctor's office. Besides, the doctor who crowds too many appointments into the day is going to leave at least one person waiting too long and/or have to whisk people in and out of examinations and consultations.

Excessive waiting time. You may be willing to accept the explanation that the doctor had an emergency, but not if it happens every time. (To save you time and money, try telephoning ahead to ask if the doctor is on schedule or what the approximate wait is.)

Hurried Consultation. A doctor who does not permit you sufficient time to explain your symptoms or complaints and ask questions and who eyes the door or jiggles the doorknob as he or she talks with you may not be providing the best of care. You stand a good chance of getting more for your money elsewhere.

Unavailability. You want to ask the doctor some questions but don't want to schedule an appointment. Will the doctor accept your telephone call? If he or she does not set aside a "telephone hour" once or twice a week to take calls, it may be time to switch to a doctor who does. After all, if the question can be answered briefly at such a time, you have saved yourself the time and expense of an office visit. Be aware, however, that it is not uncommon—or even unreasonable—for a doctor to charge for a telephone consultation, but the fee should be less than that of a regular office visit.

Lack of communication. How well does the doctor explain the medical problem and any proposed tests and/or treatments? If the doctor does not engage in effective dialogue with you, preferring instead to issue orders or pronouncements, and if he or she shows little interest in what you have to say or shows annoyance when you raise questions, then what you have is a failure to communicate—your doctor's, that is. Shop around.

Fee increases. If you're like most people, you can accept an increase in fees when the increase is justified by better service or a legitimate claim of higher overhead. But paying more money for the same old service does not set well with you, a problem that may be compounded by your insurance company's unwillingness to pay the higher fee. In this case you're stuck with an out-of-pocket expense.

Refusal of access to medical records. Treating your medical record with confidentiality is one thing; denying you rightful access is another. How can you develop an equal partnership with a doctor who does not trust you enough to share copies of *your own* health history and medical record with you? Laws and regulations in many states allow patient access to doctors' records, and even in the absence of specific laws there are ways to obtain your record. Of course, all states allow patients (or at least their attorneys) access to their medical records in the context of a lawsuit. We have more to say about this in chapter 7.

SKELETONS IN THE CLOSET

Sadly, not all doctors are clones of the fictional Marcus Welby. The percentage of physicians who are alcoholics equals that of the general population. Some studies report that drug addiction among physicians is higher than in the rest of society. As in any other profession, there are practitioners more competent than others and some who are fatally incompetent.

The problem (the "challenge" if you are a total optimist) is finding the doctor whose record is clean. And a problem it is.

As if a remnant of pre-*perestroika* Russia, a physician's record of misconduct is almost as difficult to get as the annual KGB recognition awards dinner invitation list. For example, the names of doctors who are in drug or alcohol rehabilitation programs are kept secret. The rationale is that the individual's privacy must be protected. Of course, the fact that that individual has violated his license does not seem to matter. Unless a physician has had his license revoked or suspended, state medical licensing boards will give out little if any information. And historically in most states, courts have not automatically reported verdicts of guilt against a doctor in a malpractice action to the licensing authority.

Probably the most publicized dilemma consumers have long faced has been the fact that physicians who had lost, or were on the verge of losing, their license in one state merely went to another one, applied for a license, and received it without the new state checking the past history of the applicant. This problem became so significant that the federal government passed a law in 1986 that created a National Practitioner Data Bank. In the bank, administered by the federal government, a record is kept of every doctor who has had his or her license revoked or suspended, or has been otherwise sanctioned by a state medical board; has had a verdict of guilty brought against him or her in a malpractice suit; has settled a lawsuit in favor of the plaintiff; or has been sanctioned for more than thirty days by a hospital.

As of 1990, every state medical licensing board must check the data bank when a physician files an application for a license. In addition, every hospital must consult the data bank when a physician seeks privileges. Hospitals must also recheck the data bank every two years for all current staff.

As important as the National Practitioner Data Bank is, there is a dark, anticonsumer side. Due to pressure from organized medicine, Congress capitulated and exempted the data bank from the mandates of the Freedom of Information Act. In so doing, it prevented any citizen from having access to the information.

While there is heavy consumer pressure being put on Congress to amend the law, for the time being the data bank remains a secret file, reserved for the same foxes who have always guarded the chicken coop.

Yet even with these barriers, there are a number of steps you can take to find out if your doctor has any black marks on his record:

▶ Contact your state medical licensing agency and ask if the doctor has had any actions taken against him.

▶ If you know the practitioner has practiced in another state, contact that state licensing agency and ask the same question. If you are not sure where the doctor has practiced previously, ask him for a list of the locations.

▶ Check with your local courts to see if any malpractice suits were filed against the doctor in that jurisdiction. Ask what the dispositions of those cases were.

▶ Call local hospitals and ask if the doctor has privileges at those facilities. If the answer is yes, ask if any sanctions have ever been taken against the practitioner. Even if the doctor does not have privileges, ask if he had them in the past. If he did, find out why he no longer has them.

▶ Don't be afraid to ask the doctor these above questions directly. As intimidating as it may be, good practitioners will answer with candor. But watch out for the "hemmers" and "hawers." Their reluctance may be a sign of trouble.

▶ Many good physicians have settled lawsuits in favor of the plaintiff simply to expedite the case. So remember, even a blotch on a practitioner's record does not necessarily mean the doctor is incompetent. However, it is a red flag that should cause you to pause and consider and possibly ask more questions.

THE GET-ACQUAINTED VISIT

Doctor shopping should include a get-acquainted visit, the object of which is to determine if you and the doctor are right for each other. Many problems do not arise until the first face-to-face encounter with the practitioner, the office, and the office staff.

When you telephone for an appointment, be sure to tell the receptionist that you want to arrange a get-acquainted visit. If the doctor refuses, go on to the next doctor on your list. You should be aware that some doctors charge for a get-acquainted visit and some do not. For instance, some busy, established doctors prefer not to give their time away, while other doctors are eager for new business and willing to waive even a nominal charge for a get-acquainted visit. As competition continues to heat up between doctors and other health plans, the get-acquainted visit becomes even more of a selling point. As one practice management consultant tells doctors wondering whether or not to charge, "Count the holes in your appointment calendar."

On the other hand, the doctor who agrees to a get-acquainted visit may be more consumer-oriented than other doctors, but you should not let this gesture completely color your view of the doctor since he or she may also be motivated solely by economic considerations.

The first thing you want to notice is the doctor's office and staff. Most offices will have a receptionist who will greet you and ask you to complete a few forms for their records. Ask the receptionist to orient you to the particulars regarding making appointments, telephoning the doctor, getting prescription refills, and obtaining copies of your medical records. Be sure to let them know, especially the doctor, that you have not yet decided on becoming a patient.

Sometimes the surroundings can give some clues to the way the doctor practices. Certainly, the waiting room should not be a bench, three hooks on the wall, and a 1922 issue of the *Old Farmer's Almanac.* But neither should it look like Queen Elizabeth's sitting parlor. A fancy office is not an indication of the doctor's competence, merely his or her income. Often that income is derived from excessive fees, unnecessary tests and treatments, or the sale of last year's luxury yacht. So beware of a medical Taj Mahal and keep a tight grip on your wallet or purse.

A first-time visit will probably run ten to fifteen minutes, so you need to have your questions ready and make the minutes count. When you meet the doctor, concentrate on his credentials—medical degree, board certification, and other specialized or postgraduate education—and hospital affiliations. If the doctor is not on the staff of any hospital, or at least the hospital of your choosing, then the doctor may not be able to serve you when you need him most. Ask about the doctor's fee schedule and payment plans. A doctor who

THE RIGHT PRACTITIONER FOR YOUR NEEDS 11

will openly discuss his fees may be more willing to discuss other aspects of your medical care. If you are on Medicare, find out if the doctor accepts assignment. If not, ask if he will in your case. It's negotiable:

LET'S TALK

Most people never think of negotiating with a doctor. Negotiating is something we do with a car dealer or a flea-market vendor. We forget that medicine is a business—in fact, the biggest business in America—and therefore, normal business practices apply, including negotiation.

So what's to negotiate? Here's a list of some items every consumer can negotiate with his practitioner:

Medicare Assignment. For the Medicare beneficiary this is probably the most important item you can negotiate with your doctor. A doctor who accepts Medicare assignment agrees to accept what Medicare pays for the treatment provided, less the deductibles and your 20 percent copayment, and agrees to do most of the paperwork. Nothing more. Only about 40 percent of doctors accept assignment for all their Medicare patients, so it is up to you to negotiate with your doctor to accept it in your case. Ask if he or she accepts assignment. If the response is negative, say: "I believe Medicare pays you a very fair rate for the services you provide. I cannot afford to pay more than the 20 percent copayment and hope that you will respect my wishes in this matter. If you will not, I will have to find another practitioner and tell my friends of your unwillingness to accept assignment."

Since the People's Medical Society was created in 1983, we have advised people to negotiate assignment and have found that in the majority of cases they have been successful.

All Fees. Doctors tend not to publish or post their fees for a variety of reasons. The primary one is that they do not have a set fee for a given procedure. For example, assume that a doctor has a wide variety of patients. Some are covered by Medicare, others by a number of private insurers, and still others pay cash out of pocket. Now let's take four different patients who come to see the doctor on the same day, with the same symptoms, and who receive the same services. Depending on who is paying, the doctor will receive a different amount of money for identical services. This is because Medicare has a predetermined rate that the doctor has agreed to accept, each of the insurers has negotiated a payment rate for the services provided, and there is still another charge that the physician quotes to the cash customer. Simply put, Medicare and the insurance companies have negotiated rates with the doctor. And so can you.

Each time you visit the doctor, ask what the charges will be for the procedures, tests, and treatments the doctor will perform. Ask the doctor directly; don't let him push you off to an accounting clerk or office manager. If the doctor does not know what his fees are (it may surprise some

---

folks, but often the physician has no idea what he charges for services he renders), insist that the person who does know come into the room with you *and* the doctor.

If the fee seems excessively high, or is more than you can pay, tell the doctor. Indicate that you feel this is wrong or that you cannot afford such a cost. Ask if the fee can be lowered in your case or if some other payment scheme can be devised. If you have been using the physician for many years, call upon your loyal patronage. Remember, doctors' services are like airline fares: no two people are necessarily paying the same amount for the same class of service to the same destination. And just like the airlines, a doctor's financial security over the long haul is based on your repeat business. So do not hesitate to negotiate your fee.

Treatment Options. Fees are not the only items negotiable at the doctor's office. Treatments are also negotiable.

A good consumer-physician relationship is a partnership. In this case the doctor has the skill and technical knowledge and you bring the body and the cash. Without you he cannot work and without him you may not get better. So the key is to come to a logical and well-supported agreement on what should be done to solve the problem you present. Here again, negotiation is important and practical.

Most practitioners do not discuss treatment options with their customers in the thorough manner necessary for the consumer to make a truly informed decision. For example, many consumers have reported that their doctor only gave them one treatment option for chest pains, later to discover that there were three or more other options that could have been considered in making the ultimate treatment decision.

To some extent, this failure to communicate options on the part of the doctor is understandable. In this era of microspecialization, it has gotten to the point where some physicians do only a single procedure. In so doing they fail to even consider what other options might be available, as long as they think theirs will work.

For the consumer, however, this mandates taking control. The important point is not knowing the answers when you walk in the door, but rather knowing the questions. And the questions are the basis of negotiation.

Let's assume the doctor recommends a particular test. Here's how to negotiate whether it is the most appropriate one for your current situation.

Begin by asking the practitioner why this particular test. Ask if there is a more comprehensive test that will answer more questions. (This is important, for many doctors are now recommending a series of tests, with the last one covering all the ground the earlier tests examined. While the last test may be more expensive, if this were the only test administered, it might ultimately be cheaper, not to mention more medically comprehensive). Ask the doctor to explain the risks associated as well as matters like pain or time involved with the procedure. Of course, ask the price and be prepared to pinpoint whether that price is all-inclusive. (Sometimes the fee stated includes only the doctor's charge and not those of the laboratory, hospital, etc.

When you get all the information, sit down with the doctor and negotiate what you want. Don't be afraid to ask more questions or make decisions that are not necessarily what the doctor might have originally recommended. **Make sure this is a give-and-take situation. Ask the doctor, "If I do X, what are my chances that Y will occur?" In other words, come to an agreement.**

Remember, negotiating is designed to bring two or more parties together on the best course for both sides. In the case of doctoring, negotiating is especially important to the consumer because the potential downside is far worse for those being treated than it is for those providing the care.

Determine what importance the doctor places on preventive health measures and what the doctor's philosophy of practice is— whether she sees the patient as a full partner in health care. An excellent point of reference is the People's Medical Society Code of Practice (see box on pp. 14–15).

Pay particular attention to the doctor's manner and attitude as she answers your questions. Is the doctor addressing the heart of your questions and answering in a forthright manner?

You should also notice a few other things:

▶ Is the practice solo or group? The lone practice is almost a vanishing breed. While a group practice offers the advantage of someone always covering the office, even during weekends, the possible downside is an overcrowded waiting room and the feeling that you are receiving assembly-line medical care. The doctor may be part of a one-specialty group or a multispecialty group where there is a mix of primary care doctors and specialists. The latter can be helpful when, needing a second opinion and having to find a specialist, you can be referred to another doctor in the group. But the multispecialty group works against your best interests when the doctors refer only to the specialists in the group and not necessarily to the best specialist for you.

▶ Does the office appear neat and clean? Are there current magazines? A telephone for patient use?

▶ Does the staff maintain a professional, friendly attitude?

▶ Is your insurance coverage accepted?

▶ Was your appointment kept on time?

A CHECKLIST OF POINTS TO NOTE DURING YOUR GET-ACQUAINTED VISIT

1. Doctor's name

2. Medical degree(s)

3. Educational background

4. Type of practice

5. Specialty or specialties

6. Board certification

7. Admitting privileges at what hospitals

8. Doctor's manner and appearance

9. Office appearance

10. Office staff manner and attitude

11. Your general impressions

In 1983 the People's Medical Society created the Code of Practice as a statement we believe each doctor should subscribe to. Ask your doctor to review it and tell you whether he or she will apply it to your care.

THE PEOPLE'S MEDICAL SOCIETY CODE OF PRACTICE

I will assist you in finding information resources, support groups, and health care providers to help you maintain and improve your health. When you seek my care for specific problems, I will abide by the following Code of Practice:

I. Office Procedures

1. I will post or provide a printed schedule of my fees for office visits, procedures, tests, and surgery, and provide itemized bills.

2. I will provide certain hours each week when I will be available for nonemergency telephone consultation.

3. I will schedule appointments to allow the necessary time to see you with minimal waiting. I will promptly report test results to you and return phone calls.

4. I will allow and encourage you to bring a friend or relative into the examining room with you.

5. I will facilitate your getting your medical and hospital records, and will provide you with copies of your test results.

II. Choice in Diagnosis and Treatment

1. I will let you know your prognosis, including whether your condition is terminal or will cause disability or pain, and will explain why I believe further diagnostic activity or treatment is necessary.

2. I will discuss with you diagnostic, treatment, and medication options for your particular problem (including the option of no treatment), and describe in understandable terms the risk of each alternative, the chances of success, the possibility of pain, the effect on your functioning, the number of visits each would entail, and the cost of each alternative.

3. I will describe my qualifications to perform the proposed diagnostic measures or treatments.

4. I will let you know of organizations, support groups, and medical and lay publications that can assist you in understanding, monitoring, and treating your problem.

5. I will not proceed until you are satisfied that you understand the benefits and risks of each alternative and I have your agreement on a particular course of action.

CHOOSING A DOCTOR
WHO ACCEPTS
MEDICARE ASSIGNMENT

Probably the least-known yet most significant cost-saving strategy for the consumer eligible for Medicare is to find a doctor who accepts Medicare assignment.

A doctor who "takes assignment" on all or part of your treatment accepts what Medicare pays, less the deductibles and your 20 percent copayment, and agrees to do most of the paperwork. In other words, the doctor agrees to accept the payment that Medicare has decided is appropriate for the service the doctor rendered. Your out-of-pocket expenses are limited to the deductibles and 20 percent copayment. Doctors who accept assignment for all their Medicare patients are called Medicare-participating physicians.

Let's compare the effects of taking and not taking assignment to illustrate just how substantial the savings can be:

COMPARISON OF EFFECTS OF
TAKING AND NOT TAKING ASSIGNMENT

	Doctor Takes Assignment	Doctor Does Not Take Assignment
Actual charge:	$3,000	$3,000
Medicare approved charge:	$2,000	$2,000
Balance billing limit:	N/A	$2,300 *
Medicare pays 80% of approved charge:	$1,600	$1,600
You pay:	$ 400	$ 700

If you have not met any of your Part B $100 deductible the effect on your payment and Medicare's would be as follows:

Medicare approved charge:	$1,600	$1,600
Minus $100 deductible:	- 100	- 100
Medicare pays:	$1,500	$1,500
You pay	$ 500	$ 800

* The balance billing limit for 1993, 1994, and 1995 is set at 115 percent of the Medicare-approved charge, which means no doctor may charge more than 15 percent above the approved amount.

By becoming a Medicare-participating physician, a doctor has agreed to absorb the $1,000, shown in the example. Participating physicians agree to accept assignment for *all services* they render to Medicare beneficiaries. But the snag in the scheme is that Medicare does not *require* doctors to accept assignment—to agree to take what Medicare decides is fair payment for their services. Only in Massachusetts are all doctors, as a condition of licensure, required to accept what Medicare pays. But thanks in part to the above-mentioned "balance billing limit," you now have some protection against excessive charges over and above the Medicare-approved amount.

Nevertheless, the best strategy is to find a doctor who is a Medicare-participating physician or to get your doctor to accept assignment in your case.

First, how do you know if a doctor is participating? The *Directory of Participating Doctors in Your Area* is available to you free of charge. You should receive an annual notice of the availability of this directory, and you can obtain one at any time by writing to the Medicare carrier for your state (see appendix L, pp. 448-56). (Medicare carriers are private organizations, usually insurance companies, that have contracts under the Health Care Financing Administration to process claims under Part B of Medicare.) Copies of the directory also are available for review at Social Security offices nationwide. Medicare-participating doctors may elect to display emblems or certificates that show they accept assignment on all Medicare claims. Or, of course, you can ask the doctor outright.

GETTING YOUR DOCTOR TO ACCEPT ASSIGNMENT: NEGOTIATING FEES

There may be reasons for not using a Medicare-participating doctor:

▶ You may not be able to find one in your area.

▶ You may have been getting genuinely good service from your family doctor, who for whatever reason does not participate.

▶ A specialist your family doctor refers you to may be the only one in town, or a good one, and may not participate.

While all are valid reasons, they do not have to apply to your situation. Remember, a doctor does not have to be "participating" to accept assignment. You can negotiate it with the doctor. And *now* is the time to negotiate. Medicine is a business. Doctors need customers these days, and that need will grow. And it is just good business—for both of you—to bargain, whether you are eligible for Medicare or not.

If you persuade your doctor to accept assignment in your case (the best outcome), the doctor is giving up the right to charge you more than 20 percent of the Medicare-approved price. Further, as mandated by law, he is required to handle the paperwork for Part B claims—whether or not he is a participating physician. An obvious advantage is that beneficiaries are relieved from cumbersome paperwork associated with Medicare filings and claims.

MEDICAL ADVERTISING:
WOULD YOU BUY A
NOSE JOB FROM
THIS DOCTOR?

For many years promotional advertising by physicians was unheard of, mainly because the American Medical Association's "Principles of Medical Ethics" banned all advertising by doctors. But a 1975 Supreme Court ruling that the prohibition of professional advertising was restraint of trade and a subsequently successful action by the Federal Trade Commission (FTC) against the AMA's position in 1982 changed all that. Since then any physician who wants to advertise has been free to do so, as long as the claims made are not deceptive or fraudulent in intent.

And advertise they do. A 1987 AMA survey found that approximately one in five physicians advertises somewhere: in the yellow pages, in newspapers and magazines, and/or on television and radio. Given the growing sophistication in what doctors call practice management, chances are good that these numbers have grown in the years since the survey, at which time physicians who advertised spent an average of $8,000 annually on advertising.

Critics of medical advertising contend that the mechanisms of control envisioned by the FTC just are not in place and that, rather than being better informed, consumers are being misled. Some of the general issues the critics raise are:

▶ Claims of board certification—not only whether the doctor is truly board-certified but also whether the board is legitimate (that is, one of the twenty-three recognized by the American Board of Medical Specialties)

▶ Ads that omit information about risks

▶ Unsupported claims of surgical results

Where the consumer stands in all of this is in the middle of shifting sands. The FTC has been relying on the local medical societies to ferret out potentially deceptive or fraudulent ads, something the societies have been loath to do. Meanwhile, today's competitive environment is prompting more and more doctors, especially the younger ones with less-established practices, to use advertising and other marketing tactics to attract patients. And the more lucrative the specialty, the more advertising being done, especially in services where consumers have more of a choice or where elective procedures prevail. The plastic or reconstructive surgery business is a prime example.

How much stock should you place in medical advertising? Treat the ad the way you would any other advertised product, be it a lawn mower, a refrigerator, a car, or whatever. *Compare* and *verify* are the watchwords. Talk credentials (and confirm on your own.) Talk money, including all costs associated with the service and whether your insurance plan will be accepted.

SPECIALISTS MAY BE JUST WHAT THE DOCTOR ORDERED, BUT DO YOU NEED THEM?

Generalist versus Specialist

Years ago the problem of generalist-versus-specialist did not even come up in the search for a good doctor. Doctors were generalists—able to deliver babies, set broken bones, and perform surgeries—and that was that. Kindly Marcus Welby, the popular representation of an old-time general practitioner, or G.P., was a man who moved confidently from examining room to operating room to his patients' living rooms as he cared for entire families. But that warm and glowing picture began to change by the 1950s with the decline of general practice. Since then, the numbers of all-around physicians have been decreasing and specialists proliferating.

Although there is a bewildering array of medical specialists administering to every nook and cranny of the human body, the primary need of each and every one of us remains the same: a personal physician for self and family who can provide routine care for a wide range of medical problems—if for no other reason than that a primary physician generally comes cheaper than a specialist. Using a gynecologist or cardiologist for basic medical care will cost you a whole lot more than having your family physician handle the problem. That's not to say that specialists are not needed, just that the first line of defense is what's called a primary care physician. *Remember, one physician for an entire family is far less costly than several doctors.*

Adults have three types of primary care physicians from which to choose:

General practitioners. Though dwindling in numbers—the tally of G.P.'s fell from 112,000 in 1910 to a little more than 50,000 in 1975—some G.P.'s still practice today. The *University of California-Berkeley Wellness Letter* describes them as "usually older men who went into practice after only a year of postgraduate residency, and who often make up in clinical experience what they lack in formal training." They usually treat a whole range of medical problems.

Family practitioners. Unlike the general practitioner of old who began to practice as soon as he finished his internship, doctors today who intend to become family practitioners take additional training beyond medical school. Since 1969, when the American Medical Association recognized family practice as a specialty, any doctor wishing to qualify must take a three-year residency that covers certain aspects of internal medicine, gynecology, minor surgery, obstetrics, pediatrics, orthopedics, and preventive medicine, and then pass a comprehensive examination.

Internists. Like family practitioners, these specialists in internal medicine complete a three-year residency and must pass a comprehensive examination. Unlike family practitioners, however, these doctors do not normally take training in pediatrics, orthopedics, and child delivery, but instead have more advanced training in the diagnosis and management of problems involving such areas as the gastrointestinal system, the heart, the kidney, the liver, and the endocrine system. While internists may set up practices in which they act as highly trained family doctors, they often subspecialize in other areas, such as any of the ones listed above.

As to the question of how the differences between family or general practitioners and general internists can affect *your* pocketbook, all that can be said for certain is that their respective practice styles do differ. An important study published in the January 3, 1980 *New England Journal of Medicine* found that family and general practitioners spend less time examining and instructing patients than internists, and they order fewer laboratory and X-ray studies.

SELF-REFERRAL TO A SPECIALIST—THINK TWICE!

Self-referral to a specialist has potential problems. Sure, at some time or another any of us may need a specialist to perform procedures to help discover the cause of a troublesome problem or to manage an uncommon or complicated disease; however, this age of specialization has its down side. Out of the obvious need for experts in fields of medicine has come an overspecialized, fragmented system of medical care. And out of this has sprung the phenomenon of, for example, the orthopedist who sees "the back problem" and not the person as a whole, the urologist who sees "the bladder infection" and not the person's complete medical condition, and so on.

The bottom line is that fragmented medical care gets expensive. It's bad enough when your very own family physician sends you ping-ponging from one specialist to another, each of whom at great expense reassures you (or not, whichever is the case) that nothing is wrong with the specific organ system in which he or she is interested. (You would do well, however, to keep in mind that a good primary care physician does not abandon you to a specialist or fragment your care. Rather, she does refer you if you have special, unusual problems beyond her ability or purview.)

On the other hand, self-referral to a specialist may be more of a menace to your health and pocketbook since there are no "checks and balances" such as you have with a good family doctor. If you act too hastily and choose the wrong one, you may find yourself making the rounds from specialist to specialist. Of course, the problem is moot if the specialist will not see you "off the street"—that is, without a referral from another doctor—which is the case with many.

Self-refer if you must and if you feel that you, alone or preferably with an advocate by your side, can maintain control over any decisions regarding tests, procedures, and so on. It's best not to fragment your care by going to a specialist at the outset. Don't make the mistake of referring yourself before you determine what type of specialist you need, or if you even need one. This could be a rather costly lesson when you find yourself several thousand dollars poorer and no diagnosis in sight.

QUESTIONS TO ASK
YOUR DOCTOR BEFORE
YOU SEE A SPECIALIST

You usually encounter a specialist when your primary care doctor wants to confirm a diagnosis or wants a second opinion. *If your family physician recommends a specialist or you seek one on your own, then here are questions that need to be answered:*

"Why do I have to see a specialist?" Or, put another way, "I'd like a good explanation of what you think is wrong with me." Ask for—demand, if necessary—a complete and understandable point-by-point diagnostic portrait. Maybe your doctor can't or won't explain things clearly to you. Or he or she might respond resentfully to your questions with "If you don't trust my judgment, then perhaps you should find yourself another doctor." Take that advice. Find yourself another doctor who can and wants to explain things, one you can trust, and who trusts *you.* Going to a specialist should not be a casual next step routinely taken in every medical situation.

"Why this kind of specialist?" Again, it's information you're after. You need to know about the specialist's areas of expertise, and what is involved with the performance of that specialty. Knowing this will help you determine whether you want to see the specialist at all. That is an option. You don't have to see a specialist (or see that particular specialist) immediately if you are not convinced that consultation is justified. Let your doctor know that he or she must make a very good case for every step taken in your medical care.

"Why this particular specialist?" Why Dr. Jones and not Dr. Smith? Is Dr. Jones the best person for the job? Are you being sent to Dr. Jones because he is an excellent representative of his profession? Or is it because Dr. Jones and your doctor are country club buddies or old college friends who have an arrangement, each recommending the other? While there is nothing wrong with friends referring patients to each other, you want to feel confident that competence is the basic reason for the referral.

WHAT IS A SPECIALIST?

A specialist is a doctor who concentrates on a specific body system, age group, or disorder. After obtaining an M.D. or D.O. degree, a doctor then undergoes two to three years of supervised specialty training (called a *residency*). Many specialists also take one or more years of additional training (called a *fellowship*) in a specific area of their specialty, called a *subspecialty*.

How can you tell if a doctor is a trained specialist? A doctor who has taken extra training in his or her field often chooses to become what is called *board-certified.* In addition to the extra training, the doctor must pass a rigorous examination administered by a specialty board, a national board of professionals in that specialty field. A doctor who passes the board examination is given the status of *Diplomate.* Plus, most board-certified doctors become members of their medical specialty societies, and any doctor who meets the full requirements for membership is called a *Fellow* of the society and may use the designation. For instance, the title "FACOG" after a doctor's name denotes that he or she is a Fellow of the American College of Obstetricians and Gynecologists.

In its most basic sense, board certification indicates that a physician has completed a course of study in accordance with the established educational standards of one or more of the twenty-three member boards of the American Board of Medical Specialties, a Chicago-based independent regulatory body. Board certification has been called a minimum standard of excellence and nothing more. Paper certification does not produce professional excellence. On the other hand, although there are some inferior doctors who somehow manage to become board-certified, and there are some excellent doctors without board certification, board certification is a good sign that the person is up to date on the procedures, theories, and success-failure rates in the specialty.

Just bear in mind that specialization profoundly influences the way medicine is practiced. Patients are referred from doctor to doctor to be reassured that nothing is wrong with the organ system of the doctor's field of interest or specialty. Although not all bad, the proliferation of specialists has become confusing and expensive. Therefore, the choice of the type of doctor to consult requires an understanding of the training, orientation, and special skills of each type of physician.

Below is a list of what the American Medical Association calls "self-designated [medical] specialty classifications." Translated, this means that these specialties are those the physicians use to describe themselves and their primary and secondary fields of practice. The American Medical Association is quick to point out that this list does not imply "endorsement" or "recognition" (their quotes) by the AMA; it is merely a catalog of the myriad possible areas of "expertise" a physician may claim.

> *You should be aware that a licensed physician may practice any specialty and call himself or herself a specialist in a particular field, whether or not the physician is actually board-certified in that specialty.*

Abdominal surgery. A subspecialty of surgery involving the abdominal organs.

Adolescent medicine. A subspecialty of pediatrics dealing with the medical needs of young people between the ages of fourteen and nineteen.

Allergy and immunology. A subspecialty of internal medicine or pediatrics involving the diagnosis and treatment of all forms of allergy and allergic disease and other disorders potentially involving the immune system.

Anesthesiology. The administration of drugs (anesthetics) to prevent pain or induce unconsciousness during surgical operations or diagnostic procedures. Anesthesiologists may further specialize in critical care medicine as practiced in critical care and intensive care units, postanesthesia recovery rooms, and other settings.

Cardiovascular diseases (Cardiology). A subspecialty of internal medicine that deals with the heart and blood vessels.

Cardiovascular surgery. A subspecialty of cardiology involving surgery on the heart and associated vascular system. Cardiovascular surgeons perform open-heart surgery, which may include heart transplants.

Child neurology. The branch of psychiatry and neurology involving the diagnosis and treatment of nervous system disorders in children.

Child psychiatry. A subspecialty of psychiatry that deals with emotional problems of children.

Colon and rectal surgery (Proctology). The diagnosis and treatment of diseases of the intestinal tract, rectum, and anus.

Cosmetic surgery. Surgery to reshape normal structures of the body in order to improve a person's appearance and self-esteem.

Dermatology. The diagnosis and treatment of benign and malignant disorders of the skin and related tissues. The dermatologist also diagnoses and treats a number of diseases transmitted through sexual activity.

Diagnostic radiology. A subspecialty of radiology employing the use of ionizing, electromagnetic, or sound wave imaging devices to diagnose medical problems.

Emergency medicine. That aspect of medical practice that focuses on the immediate decision-making and action necessary to prevent death or further disability. It is based primarily in the hospital emergency department.

Endocrinology. A subspecialty of internal medicine that deals with disorders of the internal (or endocrine) glands such as the thyroid and adrenal glands. Endocrinology also deals with disorders such as diabetes, pituitary diseases, and menstrual and sexual problems.

Family practice/General practice. Medical practice concerned with the total health care of the individual and the family. The scope of family practice is not limited by age, sex, organ system, or disease entity.

Gastroenterology. A subspecialty of internal medicine that involves disorders of the digestive tract: stomach, bowels, liver, gallbladder, and related organs.

General surgery. Surgery of the parts of the body that are not in the domain of specific surgical specialties (some areas do overlap, however).

Geriatrics. A subspecialty of family practice and internal medicine that deals with the diseases of the elderly and problems associated with aging.

Gynecology. The diagnosis and treatment of problems associated with the female reproductive organs.

Hand surgery. A subspecialty of orthopedic surgery, general surgery, or plastic surgery that is limited to the musculoskeletal structure of the hands, including bone, muscle, and ligaments.

Head and neck surgery. A subspecialty of otolaryngology that deals with surgery of the head and neck, excluding the brain and eyes.

Hematology. The diagnosis and treatment of diseases and disorders of the blood and blood-forming parts of the body.

Immunology. The study and treatment of problems of the body's immune system, which may include allergies, infections, and life-threatening diseases such as AIDS (acquired immune deficiency syndrome).

Infectious diseases. A subspecialty of internal medicine involving the diagnosis and treatment of life-threatening infectious illnesses.

Internal medicine. The diagnosis and nonsurgical treatment of diseases, especially those of adults. While internists may set up practices in which they act as highly trained family doctors, they often subspecialize in many other areas.

Laryngology. The branch of medicine that involves the throat, pharynx, larynx, nasopharynx, and tracheobronchial tree.

Maxillofacial surgery. A subspecialty of dentistry that deals with problems of the mouth and jaw.

Neonatal-perinatal medicine. A subspecialty of pediatrics that deals with disorders of newborn infants, including premature ones.

Nephrology. A subspecialty of internal medicine concerned with disorders of the kidney.

Neurology. The diagnosis and nonsurgical treatment of diseases of the brain, spinal cord, and nerves.

Neurological surgery (Neurosurgery). The diagnosis and surgical treatment of diseases of the brain, spinal cord, and nerves.

Nuclear medicine. The use of radioactive substances for diagnosis and treatment.

Nuclear radiology. A subspecialty of radiology that involves the use of radioactive materials in the diagnosis and treatment of disease.

Obstetrics and gynecology. The care of pregnant women and the treatment of disorders of the female reproductive system.

Occupational medicine. A subspecialty of preventive medicine that deals with the special physical and psychological risks in the industrial workplace.

Oncology. A subspecialty of internal medicine concerned with the diagnosis and treatment of all types of cancer and other benign and malignant tumors.

Ophthalmology. The diagnosis, monitoring, and medical-surgical treatment of vision problems and other disorders of the eye, including the prescription of glasses and contact lenses.

Orthopedic surgery (Orthopedics). The care of diseases of the muscles, and diseases, fractures, and deformities of the bones and joints.

Otolaryngology. The medical and surgical care of patients with diseases and disorders that affect the ears, respiratory and upper alimentary systems, and related structures: in general, the head and neck.

Otology. A subspecialty of otolaryngology that deals with the medical treatment of and surgery on the ear.

Pathology. The examination and diagnosis of organs, tissues, body fluids, and excrement.

Pediatrics. The branch of medicine concerned with the physical, emotional, and social health of children from birth to young adulthood.

Pediatric allergy. A subspecialty of pediatrics that involves the diagnosis and treatment of allergies in children.

Pediatric cardiology. A subspecialty of pediatrics that deals with diseases of the heart.

Pediatric endocrinology. A subspecialty of pediatrics that deals with diseases resulting from an abnormality in the endocrine glands (glands that secrete hormones).

Pediatric hematology-oncology. A subspecialty of pediatrics that treats blood disorders and cancers.

Pediatric nephrology. A subspecialty of pediatrics that deals with kidney disorders.

Pediatric pulmonology. A subspecialty of pediatrics that deals with the prevention, diagnosis, and treatment of all respiratory diseases affecting infants, children, and adolescents.

Pediatric radiology. A subspecialty of pediatrics that utilizes radiant energy to diagnose and treat childhood diseases.

Pediatric surgery. A subspecialty of surgery that deals with the surgical problems of premature and newborn infants, children, and adolescents.

Physical medicine and rehabilitation (Physiatry). The diagnosis, evaluation, and treatment of patients with impairments and/or disabilities involving musculoskeletal, neurologic, cardiovascular, or other body systems.

Preventive medicine. Medical practice that focuses on the health of individuals and the prevention of disease through immunization, good health practice, and concern with environmental and occupational factors.

Psychiatry. The diagnosis, treatment, and prevention of mental, emotional, and behavioral disorders. (Do not confuse the psychiatrist with the nonphysician psychologist.)

Psychosomatic medicine. More a way of practicing medicine than a specialty as such; a concept of total medical care that considers the emotional needs of the patient by taking into account the mind-and-body interactions of the patient.

Public health. The branch of medicine that deals with the protection and improvement of community health by organized community effort, and includes the monitoring and screening of populations to prevent the spread of communicable diseases. Many consider public health to be allied with, if not actually a subspecialty of, preventive medicine.

Pulmonary diseases. A subspecialty of internal medicine concerned with diseases of the lungs and other chest tissues, including pneumonia, cancer, occupational diseases, bronchitis, emphysema, and other complex disorders of the lungs.

Radiology. The study and use of various types of radiation, including X rays, in the diagnosis and treatment of disease.

Reconstructive surgery. Surgery on abnormal structures of the body, caused by congenital defects, developmental abnormalities, trauma, infection, tumors, or disease, and generally performed to improve function but may also be done to approximate a normal appearance.

Rheumatology. A subspecialty of internal medicine that deals with diseases of the joints, muscles, and tendons, including arthritis.

Rhinology. See Otolaryngology.

Surgical critical care (Traumatic surgery). A subspecialty of surgery that deals with the treatment of the critically ill patient, particularly the trauma victim, and the postoperative patient in the emergency department, intensive care unit, trauma unit, burn unit, and other similar settings.

Therapeutic radiology (Radiation oncology). A subspecialty of radiology that deals with the therapeutic applications of radiant energy, especially in the treatment of malignant tumors.

Thoracic surgery. Operative, perioperative, and critical care of patients with disease-causing conditions within the chest, including coronary artery disease, cancers of the lung, esophagus, and chest wall, abnormalities of the great vessels and heart valves, and injuries to the airway and chest.

Urology. The diagnosis and treatment of diseases of the urinary system, as well as the organs of reproduction in men, such as the prostate.

Urological surgery. A subspecialty of urology that deals with the surgical treatments of the adrenal gland and genitourinary system.

Vascular surgery. A subspecialty of surgery that deals with medical disorders affecting the blood vessels, excluding those of the heart, lungs, and brain.

More information can be obtained from the American Board of Medical Specialties, which will send its publication *Which Medical Specialist For You?* free of charge to anyone who accompanies his request with a self-addressed and stamped return envelope. The board's address is:

American Board of Medical Specialties
1 Rotary Center, Suite 805
Evanston, IL 60201-4889

MORE QUESTIONS
BEFORE YOU GO

There are many reasons for your family doctor to refer you to a specialist: additional testing that he does not have the equipment or expertise to do; the confirmation or ruling out of a specific diagnosis; failure of standard treatment; and new or experimental treatment. The questions that we earlier suggested you ask your family doctor are designed to get at the heart of his *reasons* for referral. Just bear in mind, however, that the simplest reason for referral is to have tests or procedures done that a general practitioner does not have the equipment or expertise to do.

For you to get the most out of this specialist consultation—and the most for your money, because highly technical and specialized tests and procedures can cost big bucks—your family doctor will have to answer *a few more* questions, these latter more specific to what he wants the specialist to do for or to you.

Instead of sending you to a specialist, your doctor might want to send you to a hospital lab or perhaps a private clinic to have tests performed requiring radiation or ultrasound or some type of invasive technique. A specialist might do so too. If so, ask all these questions:

"What will you be looking for in the results of these tests?"
This is a key question because it requires your doctor to let you in on the process, diagnosis, and prognosis, and to justify the need for further testing.

"Will the procedure be painful, and is it dangerous?"   Don't hesitate to ask this question because if the test might cause more pain (or might lead to complications more dangerous) than the condition itself, you should think twice about having the test.

"How much will it cost?"   This is an important question because you will want to shop around for the best doctor at the best price.

"How much time will it take?"   This is not as selfish and trivial a question as it may sound at first glance. Certainly, to decide against having essential medical care simply because you don't want to juggle your schedule would be foolish. However, if an examination or testing procedure is of questionable diagnostic value and to have it performed means losing work time, some much-needed pay, and maybe even your job itself, then the matter of time—how long, what time of day, and whether multiple visits are involved—is a consideration. When you have the information, discussions with your family doctor and employer will help you to determine if you can afford to—or afford not to—pursue a certain medical course.

"Is this the most appropriate test?"   Tests are big money for doctors and facilities. Today any number of tests are used to diagnose or rule out a condition. Because of this, many doctors have fallen victim to "testitis"—they use all the tests available instead of the most comprehensive one. Watch out for the doctor who wants to move you up the test ladder. Ask why he or she is not recommending the most comprehensive one *in the first place.* Remember, one comprehensive test may be a lot cheaper than three lesser ones.

"What will happen if I don't have this procedure done?"   This is a question you must ask. It may be the single most important query anyone could pose at any and every level of dealings with the medical system, and it should be asked every time a procedure is recommended. You can't lose anything by asking—and you might gain a great deal.

"What is your relationship to the laboratory?"   Conflicts of interest are not good in anything. They are especially dangerous in medicine. Since laboratory results can vary significantly from lab to lab, it is important to make sure that your tests are being analyzed by the best lab available. However, that may not be the case, especially if your doctor owns, or has a financial stake in, the laboratory. To date, Arizona, California, Pennsylvania, and Virginia are the only states in the country that require a doctor to disclose any financial participation he or she might have in a lab or other entity to which you are referred. Everywhere else the onus falls on you to ask. So ask! And if the answer is yes, ask what assurances of quality his or her lab has over an independent or hospital-based facility.

MEDICAL SPECIALTY BOARDS

After you have found a specialist or determined that your family doctor's decision to refer you to a specialist is a sound one, what can you do to assure that you get the best care for your money? At this point you should check the specialist's credentials in her area of specialty. In short, find out whether or not she is board-certified. Remember what we said earlier: while not a guarantee of competence, board certification is a minimum standard of excellence—and many would say the minimum standard for choosing a doctor today.

A word of caution here: beware of "yellow pages professionalism." An insightful study reported in the May 31, 1987 *New England Journal of Medicine* compared specialty listings of physicians in the yellow pages of the 1983 Hartford, Connecticut, telephone directory with lists of physicians certified in specialties recognized by the American Board of Medical Specialties. Researchers found significant discrepancies: namely, of the nearly 1,200 listings by 946 physicians under 61 specialty headings, a mean of 12 percent of the specialists were not board-certified. And in plastic surgery 43 percent of doctors advertising themselves as specialists lacked board certification.

In 1989 the American Board of Medical Specialties announced that it would place ads in two thousand yellow-page directories across the country in 1990, listing only ABMS board-certified doctors. The ads would also include a toll-free hot line consumers can call to check credentials of unlisted doctors.

To verify the credentials of any physician claiming to hold board certification in a medical specialty, you also can call or write the appropriate board (see appendix D, pp. 411–13).

Or see if your public library or hospital library has a copy of the *American Medical Directory: Physicians in the United States.* This lists every doctor who is a member of the American Medical Association (270,000 out of 530,000 practicing physicians and surgeons) and gives his or her year of license, primary and secondary specialties, type of practice, board certification, and premedical and medical school education. There is also the *Directory of Medical Specialists,* published by Marquis Who's Who, Macmillan Directory Division.

MORE MEDICAL
SPECIALTY BOARDS: IS
MORE LESS?

Not all specialty boards fall under the American Board of Medical Specialties umbrella, however. An additional 105 medical specialty boards—often called self-designated specialty boards—don't have ABMS recognition. Some medicos see this sort of growth in specialty boards as a source of great concern, and they call for one standard of competency—in particular, the one established by ABMS. But others in the medical world believe that there should be competitive specialty boards. Michael Rask, M.D., head of the National Federation for Medical Accreditation, with thirty-two member boards and approximately six hundred members, says that many of the physicians who do not achieve certification still make adequate practitioners, and that even undistinguished M.D.'s deserve their own specialty boards (*American Medical News,* September 15, 1989).

Some of the so-called self-designated boards say they were formed to address "microspecialties" that have not yet been recognized by the medical mainstream. And some boards are competitors of ABMS boards.

Now competition may be a good thing, but it can make life more confusing for the consumer. Just as any physician can declare a specialty—whether or not he or she has any specialized training—so can any physician start a specialty board. And there's nothing to say that a board has to be demanding in its certification requirements. So, as always, it comes down to this: you can't necessarily equate certification with competency. Your mission, then? Question, question, question.

M.D.'S AND D.O.'S:
WHAT'S THE DIFFERENCE
TO YOU AND YOUR
WALLET?

Osteopathy is a sometimes forgotten branch of mainstream medical care. By no means insignificant in numbers of practitioners—28,000 in this country alone—osteopathy nevertheless is overshadowed by allopathic medicine and its more than 500,000 practitioners, and in part ignored as a result of the public perception that the M.D. is the sole torchbearer for traditional medicine. This is simply not true. Both osteopathy and allopathy claim scientifically accepted methods of diagnosis and treatment as their basis. Except for a notable difference in philosophy and, to a lesser extent, practice habits, D.O.'s and M.D.'s are essentially the same.

If traditional medicine can be neatly categorized in two basic approaches—focus on the patient versus focus on the patient's disease—osteopathy stresses the former. In brief, D.O.'s, or doctors of osteopathic medicine, are fully licensed physicians and surgeons who hold that the body is an interrelated system. The practitioners are called *osteo*paths because they emphasize the role of bones, muscles, and joints of the body—the musculoskeletal system—in a person's well-being.

Consequently, manipulation and hands-on diagnosis and treatment are mainstays of osteopathic practice and, in short, what distinguish D.O.'s from M.D.'s. In fact, whether such manipulations, used alone or in conjunction with other therapies, are indeed of any value is the crux of what remains of a once virulent M.D.-D.O. debate.

As a general rule, compared to M.D.'s, D.O.'s *tend* to be more holistic in their approach to care, *tend*—at least at first—not to order a full battery of tests for diagnostic purposes but instead to rely on a more selective range, and *tend* to utilize manipulation before drugs and surgery. D.O.'s employ two forms of hands-on contact, or manipulation: One is palpation (touch), literally a hands-on diagnostic procedure to detect soft-tissue changes or structural asymmetries. D.O.'s also use manipulative therapy, whereby muscles, bones, joints, nerves, and tissue are in some way manipulated or have pressure applied to them in order to effect some beneficial change in a patient's condition.

Let us say here that, while it is true that D.O.'s underscore the body's natural ability to heal itself (called *vis medicatrix naturae,* an ancient philosophy virtually banished from allopathy), they also utilize the usual bag of medical tricks—all the recognized procedures and modern technologies, including drugs, radiation, and surgery.

Whether one becomes a D.O. or an M.D., the route of complete medical training is basically the same. In matters of licensing, D.O.'s hold the same unlimited practice rights as M.D.'s in all fifty states and the District of Columbia and can admit patients to both osteopathic and allopathic hospitals and clinics and treat them there. (In the United States there are nearly two hundred designated osteopathic hospitals that provide special osteopathic care in addition to general medical-surgical services. But more likely than not, D.O.'s practice alongside M.D.'s in allopathic facilities, with referrals between the two professions common.) Osteopaths also participate in federal Medicare and Medicaid programs on an equal basis with their allopathic counterparts.

Most D.O.'s are generalists, but some have additional training and qualifications and work in specialized fields. Except insofar as the basic approach to care differs, osteopathic specialties resemble allopathic ones. The American Osteopathic Association (AOA), a trade organization similar to the American Medical Association, recognizes seventeen areas of certification: anesthesiology; dermatology; emergency medicine; general practice; internal medicine; neurology and psychiatry; nuclear medicine; obstetrics and gynecology; ophthalmology; orthopedic surgery; pathology; pediatrics; proctology; preventive medicine/public health; radiology; rehabilitation medicine; and surgery.

Within these broad categories are subspecialties. Under surgery, for example, are general surgery, neurological surgery, plastic and reconstructive surgery, and so on.

Bear in mind that, as with the M.D., the osteopathic practitioner can "self-designate" a specialty: without the benefit of additional training and without the benefit of certifying credentials from an AOA-sanctioned board. To check on the credentials of a D.O., you will want to contact the certifying board for his or her specialty (see appendix E, pp. 414–15).

For more information about the osteopathic specialists or the profession, contact:

American Osteopathic Association
142 East Ontario Street
Chicago, IL 60611
312-280-5800

D.D.S. VERSUS D.M.D.

Aside from your physician, your dentist probably is the practitioner you see on a regular or semiregular basis. And we recommend the same cautious, thorough approach in the selection of a dentist.

As you shop around for a good dentist with a pleasant chair-side manner and valid credentials, you will notice, if you have not already, that some dentists have the letters D.D.S. trailing after their names and others have D.M.D. What's the difference? And should you be impressed with one over the other?

Currently, the majority of dental schools in the United States award their graduates the D.D.S. degree, which stands for doctor of dental surgery. But more and more schools are adopting the other designation—doctor of medical dentistry, abbreviated D.M.D. The schools that award the latter degree claim that their curricula are more "medically oriented," and no doubt believe that the consumer will have more respect and reverence for the practitioner if given the impression that he or she has a medical degree.

Think again! In actuality, there is little or no difference between the two. According to the American Dental Association, all dental schools in the United States are accredited, with clearly stated requirements for graduation, and there is no difference in what is taught. D.D.S. or D.M.D.—one is just as good as the other, or just as bad, depending on the individual dentist.

DENTISTS AND 'DONTISTS—WHO'S WHO? AND WHEN DO YOU NEED ONE RATHER THAN THE OTHER?

Your family-practice dentist refers you to a dental specialist whenever he believes you have a problem beyond his own ability and purview as a general practitioner. As with your family doctor and a problematical medical condition, you should reassure yourself that a consultation with a specialist is absolutely necessary, since in almost all cases a specialist's fee is higher than a general practitioner's. That's because, ideally speaking, the procedures require more skill and specialized knowledge—the reason, after all, for needing a specialist in the first place. The questions we recommend you ask your family doctor concerning the need for a specialist are appropriate here as well (see pp. 30–31).

Now for a little background to make you a more informed consumer in any situations and decisions involving dental specialists. According to the American Dental Association (ADA), a specialist must have certain qualifications: two years of education beyond the general degree at an accredited dental school, *and/or* certification by an ADA-recognized certifying organization.

What is certification? A dentist who beyond dental school has continued his or her studies in depth in a chosen field may choose to become board-certified. First, the dentist must pass a qualifying examination administered by a specialty board (national board of professionals in that specialty field). While board certification is an achievement awarded by the dentist's colleagues and does require additional education, it is not necessarily an indicator of skill or higher-quality care. What it does indicate is a higher price tag for the services, so it's important to know who's who and what each does so that your money is well spent.

The American Dental Association has approved eight specialized areas of dental practice:

Endodontics. An endodontist performs root canal therapy. Although a general practitioner does too, a particularly complicated case may be referred to the specialist, whom you should reasonably expect to be more proficient and expert—and more expensive. One thing to bear in mind, however, is that with successful root canal therapy you may have avoided the expense of having the tooth extracted and a false tooth put in its place.

Oral and maxillofacial surgery. Sometimes called an exodontist, an oral and maxillofacial surgeon extracts teeth as well as performs surgery on the mouth, jaws, and related structures. While the general dentist can perform simple extractions, the specialist usually does the problem extractions—complications such as an impacted wisdom tooth (imbedded in the bone under the gum far back in the mouth) or the tip of a broken root. The "maxillofacial" designation, referring to the jaw and the face, is relatively recent, and requires some skilled surgical techniques such as those involved in cosmetic surgery and surgery on the temporomandibular joints, which connect the jawbone to the skull.

Oral pathology. The oral pathologist is involved in the diagnosis of disease through biopsy and other methods. Typically, when your general dentist is stymied by a particularly tricky problem and having difficulty identifying the cause of oral disease, then he or she consults an oral pathologist.

Orthodontics. The orthodontist corrects malocclusion (the improper position of the teeth) by wiring the teeth so that they move into the correct and most attractive positions. Although it was once true that older children and teenagers were the orthodontist's only customers, lately more adults are getting braces. As a general rule, your family dentist will not do orthodontics and instead will refer you to the specialist. Of course, you can choose an orthodontist yourself—preferably someone whose "success stories" you have personally seen. Considering that the therapy takes around two years, on the average, it pays to find an orthodontist you can trust for that length of time, not to mention one you can afford and who is willing to make financial arrangements you can live with.

Pedodontics. The pedodontist looks after children's teeth—not that the general practitioner cannot or does not, just that the specialist is supposed to know more about the psychological and emotional aspects of working with children. Usually children with behavioral problems, children with some disabilities, and children with unusual dental problems are referred to the pedodontist. Some pedodontists even do orthodontic work, and you may end up saving money by having both phases of your child's dental work done by one specialist. Check into it.

Selecting such a practitioner for your child is different from choosing one for yourself, since the process often relies on understanding the child's impressions of the practitioner—and a child's thoughts are not always easy to discover—and on determining the practitioner's attitude toward children, which may also require acute observation.

Periodontics. Probably known best for the treatment of gum problems, the periodontist also looks after the bones and supportive tissue that surround the teeth. Although the general dentist can treat some gum disease, only the periodontist does gum surgery, which involves various procedures, including the recontouring, tightening, or grafting of gum tissue. If your dental problems require this specialist's services, again choose carefully because much of the treatment calls for multiple visits and an extended series of checkups.

Prosthodontics. The prosthodontist replaces missing teeth with prosthetic (artificial) ones: caps, bridges, and dentures. Most general dentists do some prosthodontic work in their practices, so the specialist is reserved for the truly difficult cases that the dentist does not want to undertake.

Dental public health. In general, the public health dentist is concerned with the dental health education of the public, with the prevention and control of dental disease on a community-wide basis, and with the administration of group dental care programs. To check the credentials of dental specialists, contact the appropriate specialty board, listed in appendix F, pp. 416–17.

COSMETIC DENTISTRY: NEW KID ON THE BLOCK

Although it is not yet recognized by the American Dental Association as a separate specialty, cosmetic dentistry is becoming more and more popular. According to one estimate, cosmetic techniques accounted for more than half of all dental restorative work done in 1987, and signs are that the techniques are even more popular now. Cosmetic dentistry is the "artistic" side of the profession, in which new techniques such as bleaching, bonding, veneering, and resculpting have been developed to "brighten the smiles" of people with chronically stained, broken, or malformed teeth.

A word of caution: since cosmetic dentistry is not an approved specialty, and as such has no certifying board, there are no precise criteria, standards, and qualifications for becoming a cosmetic dentist. *What can you do to track down the credentials of such a practitioner?* Ask the dentist if he or she has taken classes in cosmetic dentistry—where and when? And make it a top priority to see examples of the dentist's work. Check and double-check before entrusting your smile to major cosmetic renovation—and paying through the nose for no improvement.

ALLIED HEALTH PROFESSIONALS

If you think the different types of medical, osteopathic, and dental practitioners comprise a hodgepodge of choices, in a quick glance through the medical services section of the *Dictionary of Occupational Titles* you'll be astonished to find hundreds *more* professional occupations concerned with treating and caring for sick and injured people. Some of these practitioners support and complement the services of doctors and dentists, while others practice independently, depending upon the laws of the particular state in which they are licensed. To find out whether you must have a doctor's referral to avail yourself of an allied health professional's services, call your state's health department (see appendix I, pp. 429–34). Below we have listed and briefly described the more common allied health professionals.

Audiologist. This professional assesses hearing problems and corrects them through the use of such mechanical devices as hearing aids. By conducting hearing tests and measuring the subject's reaction to a wide range of audible frequencies, the audiologist can detect where a problem exists. An audiologist must complete a graduate-level program in speech-language pathology or audiology and also must have a certain number of hours of supervised clinical experience. Licensure requirements vary from state to state.

Nurse-anesthetist. This professional is a nurse specialist involved in the administration of intravenous, spinal, and other anesthetics to surgical patients or people undergoing certain diagnostic procedures. During surgery the nurse-anesthetist monitors the patient, paying close attention to pulse, respiration, body temperature, blood pressure, and skin color. Nurse-anesthetists must complete an approved course of training and pass a qualifying examination before referring to themselves as certified registered nurse-anesthetists (CRNA). CRNAs are licensed in every state and generally work under the direction of licensed physicians.

Nurse-practitioner. This professional is a nurse specialist involved in providing primary health care services to both adults and children. With special skills and knowledge in the areas of personal health evaluation and assessment, interpretation of diagnostic tests, and health promotion activities, the nurse-practitioner participates in the design of treatment plans, including medications and other therapies. Nurse-practitioners are registered nurses who have completed an approved graduate program. In some states they are recognized as independent practitioners and do not require the direct supervision of a medical doctor.

Occupational therapist. This professional treats people who are mentally, physically, or emotionally disabled, the primary goal being to restore a degree of functioning. An occupational therapist usually works as a member of a team to design and plan programs involving such activities as manual arts and crafts, homemaking skills, and daily living tasks. An occupational therapist must have a bachelor's degree from an approved program. Certification may be obtained from the American Occupational Therapy Association. In addition, some states require a license for private practice.

Physical therapist. This professional employs physical means—including heat, water, massage, ultrasound, and electrical stimulation—to restore mobility, relieve pain, and prevent or limit permanent injury. A physical therapist must be knowledgeable in the areas of human anatomy and the function of muscles and tendons. Licensed in all states and independent providers in some states, a physical therapist must have at least a bachelor's degree.

Speech pathologist. This professional diagnoses and treats speech and language problems and assesses language skills on the basis of educational, medical, social, and psychological factors. A speech pathologist plans, directs, and conducts treatment programs to restore communication skills and provides guidance and counseling to language-handicapped people. Before starting to practice, a speech pathologist must complete at least a master's degree, and in addition, some states require a license before independent practice status can be given.

Options in Health Care

The search for the right practitioner for your needs may take you outside mainstream medical care and away from traditional allopathic or osteopathic therapies. And if so, you will not be alone. Even though ventures outside the medical mainstream may mean money out of pocket because of insurance-payment problems, more and more people are turning to alternative health care services and nontraditional therapies such as chiropractic, acupuncture, and biofeedback.

As always, the way to get the most for your medical dollar *and* steer clear of incompetent practitioners and questionable medical expenses is to know your options. As with mainstream medicine, there are a lot of alternative practitioners doing good work and a lot who don't know what they're doing. Arm yourself with knowledge about the principles of the approach, how it proposes to help, and what the practitioner does or does not do. Know what to expect.

What follows is background on many varied options in health care, including allopathy and osteopathy. Not every kind of practitioner described below may be licensed to practice in your state. If the state does license and regulate a particular practice, all this means is that minimum standards have been met, probably educational credentials. If particular practices are not licensed, it does not necessarily mean they are not legitimate, but that you need to be even more diligent about checking credentials yourself. To find out if any of these are licensed, call your state's department of occupational and professional licensing.

ACUPUNCTURE

Acupuncture is the ancient Chinese healing art in which very thin needles are inserted under the skin in order to treat illness and restore good health. A practitioner of this art is an acupuncturist.

Acupuncture reportedly dates from 1600 to 1500 B.C. It attracted renewed attention and interest in the West after the opening of China in the early 1970s.

A key element in understanding acupuncture is an acceptance of the Eastern belief in the poles or extremes of *yin* and *yang* (roughly corresponding to our ideas of negative and positive, or female and male, forces) and the flow of a life force known as *chi.* Chinese medicine teaches that in order to remain healthy the yin and yang forces must be perfectly balanced and that it is necessary to have a flow of chi throughout the body. The chi flows along paths known as meridians (sets of invisible lines) and covers the body in set patterns. While meridians are not identical to the nervous system or circulatory system, they are thought to resemble them. Each meridian has its own pulse, and these pulses provide information about any meridians that need to have their energy balance restored.

When illness occurs, the acupuncturist examines the meridians and carefully selects acupuncture sites. It is at these sites that acupuncture treatment is given.

Extremely thin needles made from gold, silver, or copper are placed in carefully selected sites just below the skin by the acupuncturist. A gentle twisting of the needle helps to ensure that it is properly placed and will correct the flow of chi along the meridians.

Acupuncturists believe that currents, or impulses, begin to flow along the meridians where the needles are placed. This current travels through the nervous system and goes to the organ that is out of balance. Once the obstruction or hindrance is removed, the life forces are free to circulate once again, and balance is restored.

Reports from China indicate that major surgery has been performed while using acupuncture as the only anesthetic. Acupuncture also includes herbal medicine, disease-specific and preventive nutritional measures, relaxation skills, exercise, and specific advice on health behaviors.

Western medicine, with its foundations in the scientific method, has been slow to show interest in acupuncture, but some physicians now use it, and their numbers are growing.

For more information, contact:

Traditional Acupuncture Institute
American City Building, Suite 108
Columbia, MD 21044
301-596-6006

ALLOPATHIC MEDICINE

Allopathic Medicine is a healing art founded on scientific principles in which diseases are treated with medications that produce conditions incompatible with the disease-causing agent. It is based on the philosophy that the physician must actively intervene to combat illness. An allopathic physician is a practitioner who has completed the prescribed course of study leading to the degree of doctor of medicine (M.D.) and who has a license to practice. Most physicians also complete a residency program in a specialty or subspecialty of their choosing.

Historically, allopaths trace their origins to Hippocrates, and to the surgeon-barbers of the Middle Ages who were known for their blood-letting technique. It was also during this latter period that the three so-called heroic remedies—bleeding, blistering, and purging— were developed. Often these cures were worse than the condition that prompted the need for treatment.

Allopathic medicine has been the dominant medical philosophy in the United States since the early 1900s. Its rise to predominance was hastened by the scientific discoveries that were made in the areas of bacteriology, pathology, organic chemistry, and surgery. During this time the scientific principle of double-blind study was introduced, a technique that enables doctors and medical researchers to evaluate the effectiveness of their methods using an experimental group and a control group.

Allopathic medicine has proven to be very effective against the acute infectious diseases that once ravaged humankind, such as smallpox, polio, pneumonia, whooping cough, and plague. Advances in surgery now permit transplantation of organs, reattachment of limbs, replacement of joints, and cosmetic applications.

An allopathic physician begins by taking a complete medical history and conducting a physical examination, often including a battery of diagnostic tests that may involve blood work, analysis of body specimens, X rays, ultrasound, or other sophisticated scanning devices. Once a diagnosis has been determined, the physician may administer medications, each selected on the basis of how well it combats or counteracts what is going on within the body. Other treatment modalities include chemotherapy, surgery, and ionizing radiation.

For more information, contact:

American Medical Association
535 North Dearborn Street
Chicago, IL 60610
312-645-5000

AYURVEDIC MEDICINE

Ayurveda is a system of holistic medicine that originated in India and is among the oldest of the healing arts. Ayurvedic medicine combines the mysticism of Eastern religion with the science of healing and serves as the basis for many Oriental healing methods.

Ayurveda is holistic in nature and views the person in terms of body, mind, and spirit. Ayurvedic physicians believe that disease is caused by imbalances in the body's five basic elements and the forces in those elements. Earth, fire, water, air, and ether are the basic elements, and they combine into three principles, or humors, known as the *tridosha.*

The first of these is *vata,* which is formed by air and ether, and the second is *pitta,* formed by fire and water. The third and last is *kapha,* formed by earth and water. These elements govern all the biological, psychological, and physiological functions of the body, mind, and spirit. When these elements are out of balance, disease occurs.

An Ayurvedic physician will take a complete history from the patient and conduct a thorough physical examination before determining what caused the particular imbalance. Fasting, baths, diets, and applications to the skin are used to cleanse the body before a specific treatment is recommended. A complete pharmacopoeia is consulted, and drugs to restore normal health and balance are given in the form of jellies, tinctures, powders, pills, or oils.

Other branches of Ayurvedic medicine include surgery, obstetrics, gynecology, pediatrics, and psychology.

For more information, contact:

Ayurvedic Institute
P.O. Box 23445
Albuquerque, NM 87192–1445
505-291-9698

BACH FLOWER REMEDIES

Bach flower remedies are a form of herbal medicine devised in the early 1930s by Dr. Edward Bach, a British bacteriologist who later became a pathologist. The doctor's interest in the healing powers of trees and plants had produced thirty-eight herbal remedies by the time of his death in 1936.

Bach's formula for devising a particular remedy involved collecting the flowering heads of wild plants, placing them in water, and then filtering the solution before bottling. Basically, he believed that the solutions he prepared contained the physical properties of the derivative plants. Much of what Bach devised depends upon discovering the emotional state of the person, and the remedies are supposed to quiet the disharmonies within the person and thus restore health.

Bach's remedies, best used for emotional rather than physical complaints, are divided into seven groups that cover the negative states of mind that affect most people: fear, uncertainty, lack of interest, despondency, overcare for others, loneliness, and oversensitivity. He was never able to fully describe how his solutions worked; rather, he claimed they had "the power to elevate our vibrations, and thus draw down the spiritual power which cleanses mind and body, and heals."

Although a few practitioners limit themselves exclusively to Bach remedies, most remedies are employed as complements to natural healing, especially in herbal medicine.

CHINESE MEDICINE

Chinese medicine consists of acupuncture, massage, and herbal medicine and includes an acceptance of the poles or extremes of *yin* and *yang* (roughly corresponding to our ideas of negative and positive, or female and male, forces) and the flow of a life force known as *chi*. Chinese medicine teaches that in order to remain healthy the yin and yang forces must be perfectly balanced and that it is necessary to have a flow of chi throughout the body.

In place of highly technological diagnostic and treatment equipment, practitioners of Chinese medicine rely upon looking, listening, smelling, asking, and touching to make their diagnoses.

Another theory in Chinese medicine, one basic to determining a particular illness and the prescribed treatment, is called Five Elements. The five elements are fire, wood, earth, metal, and water, which practitioners of Chinese medicine use when evaluating bodily functions, organs, acupuncture meridians, emotions, and external influences. As always, they are seeking to discover some disturbance in the flow of chi throughout the body.

As we said, touching is an important aspect of Chinese medicine, much more so than in Western medicine. By carefully taking the pulses of the body, the practitioner can detect slight imbalances that may indicate a condition of disease. These pulses flow along the meridians of the body, and since they connect to every organ system, it is possible to determine which organ or body part is affected.

When a diagnosis is made, the practitioner will decide upon one or all of the treatment methods available, specifically acupuncture, acupressure, or herbs. (See our discussions of each of these elsewhere in this section.)

For more information, contact:

American Association of Acupuncture and Oriental Medicine
1424 16th Street, N.W.
Washington, DC 20036
202-265-2287

CHRISTIAN HEALING

Christian healing is a paranormal therapy centered on the belief that a healer has the power to cure physical illnesses through the laying-on of hands. It is also called faith healing or therapeutic touch.

Healing without medicines and surgery has always been viewed with skepticism, not only by traditional medicine but also by mainstream religions. Many people find it hard to believe that someone who claims to possess an energy field can actually cure illness.

Miracles were always the province of religion, and their occurrences have been duly recorded in scripture. It was believed that only simpleminded people with limited education would have any interest in faith healing, and it was not until parapsychologists began investigating the claims of faith healers that serious attention was paid to this practice.

Christian healing involves belief, and specifically belief that a particular person for whatever reason is tuned into a source of power not of this world. The effectiveness of Christian healing depends upon the willpower of the person being healed. Research into the powers of the mind indicates that humans have the capacity to will physical changes, but it is necessary that the person wishing to be healed believe in the healing process.

In some medical schools today, medical students are being taught that touching patients may be just as important as writing a prescription or performing surgery. Some religiously affiliated medical centers are now permitting lay ministers to visit the sick and pray with them if the patient has no objections.

For further information, contact:

New Life Clinic
Mt. Washington United Methodist Church
Falls Road
Baltimore, MD 21209
301-561-0428

Healing Light Center
204 East Wilson
Glendale, CA 91206
818-244-8607

DENTISTRY

Dentistry is the healing art concerned with the care and treatment of teeth and the surrounding tissue and bone structure of the oral cavity. A dentist is a professional who has completed the prescribed course of study leading to the degree of doctor of dental surgery (D.D.S.) or doctor of dental medicine (D.M.D.) and who has a license to practice.

Early dentists were more tradesmen than professionals, since there really was not much available in the way of formal training. Aside from a few herbal remedies, the only treatment for an aching tooth was to remove it. The concept of modern dentistry, with its emphasis on prevention and restoration, was still many centuries away.

Today dentists treat tooth and gum problems with a wide array of materials and techniques. The filling of cavities can be done almost painlessly, and high-speed drills and improved anesthetics make it possible to save teeth that otherwise might be lost.

Cosmetic dentistry is the newest direction in the profession and becoming so popular that an array of cosmetic techniques—bleaching, bonding, veneering, and resculpting—are available to brighten the smiles of people with chronically stained, broken, or malformed teeth. These cosmetic techniques account for more than half of all dental restorative work currently being done.

For more information, contact:

American Dental Association
211 East Chicago Avenue
Chicago, IL 60611
312-440-2500

American Academy of Esthetic Dentistry
500 North Michigan Avenue, Suite 1400
Chicago, IL 60611
312-661-1700

HERBAL MEDICINE

Herbal medicine is a healing art that uses plants to prevent and cure illnesses. A person skilled in the art of herbal medicine who can compound herbal mixtures made from the various plants is an herbalist.

Herbology, the use of plants as medicine, is probably as old as humankind. According to historians, many ancient peoples, including the Chinese, Egyptians, Babylonians, and Aztecs, practiced herbal medicine. Some of the herbs used were elderberry, pomegranate bark, cinnamon, mustard, gentian, and rhubarb.

Humans probably learned how to use herbs to treat illnesses by watching animals and noting what plants they ate when they were sick. Herbalists claim that their remedies do not have the harmful side effects that are so common with modern medicines.

Before scientific medicine gained the upper hand early in this century, both herbology and allopathy existed side by side. Once the scientific faction won out, however, herbology was relegated to the status of folk medicine or just plain quackery. But the fact of the matter is that all early medicines were vegetable in origin since the elaborate process of making synthetic compounds did not exist. Once the use of organic and inorganic chemicals became dominant, the need for plant-derived medicines waned.

Herbs can be used as astringents, tonics, laxatives, and acidifiers. Nervines are another class of herbs that can either relax or excite the nervous system. Some people brew herbal teas to help them relax or sleep, with chamomile being the most popular herb for this. Garlic is another herb receiving renewed interest as an adjunct to traditional medications.

As with medications, the key to using herbs is to carefully research the claims for each one. Libraries and health food stores usually have books on herbal medicine.

For more information, contact:

American Botanical Council
P.O. Box 201660
Austin, TX 78720
512-331-8868

HOMEOPATHIC MEDICINE

Homeopathic medicine treats illnesses by using safe natural medicines that stimulate a person's own healing powers while avoiding harmful side effects. A practitioner skilled in the art of homeopathic medicine is a homeopathic physician. Most homeopathic physicians in practice today are M.D.'s or D.O.'s who have additional training in homeopathic principles.

The concept of homeopathy dates to Hippocrates, but it was a German physician, Samuel Hahnemann, who provided the scientific foundation. In 1810 he published the *Organon of Medicine,* which set forth the principles of homeopathy as he saw them.

Homeopathic medicine believes that like cures like and that medicines that cause symptoms of diseases in healthy people will bring about cures in sick people. Another basic tenet of homeopathy is that the whole person must be treated and not just the disease.

Allopaths treat the symptoms of diseases, for instance fever, with medication that will produce the opposite effect. The homeopath views the symptoms as indicating an imbalance in the person's life forces and strives to restore balance to the body, mind, and spirit.

Aside from the principle that like cures like, homeopathic medicine also believes in the use of a single remedy. Homeopaths will administer only one medicine at a time, and if the condition persists, then a second medication is used but never a combination of medications. Finally, because it is concerned with the body's ability to absorb the medication, homeopathic medicine encourages the smallest dose possible in order to prevent outright rejection or reactions from strong doses.

Homeopathic medications are extracted from naturally occurring substances such as plants, animal material, and natural chemicals. These preparations are somewhat unique in that they are taken by mouth, tend to be tasteless, can be stored for periods of time, and do not produce toxic side effects.

Homeopathic remedies usually indicate how many times they have been diluted from the original material, although a basic belief of homeopathy is that no matter how many times a solution has been diluted it will remain effective.

While homeopathic medical schools have been absorbed by their allopathic counterparts, many physicians today still abide by homeopathic principles.

For more information, contact:

National Center for Homeopathy
1500 Massachusetts Avenue, N.W., Suite 42
Washington, DC 20005
202-223-6182

HYDROTHERAPY

Hydrotherapy uses water, either internally or externally, to treat certain illnesses and bodily injuries. Hydrotherapy is most often associated with physical therapy.

Archaeological records suggest that ancient civilizations made great use of water as a healing therapy. Public baths were commonplace in the Roman Empire, with most early baths located adjacent to hot mineral springs whose therapeutic powers were widely known.

You may have used hydrotherapy already and not realized it. Have you ever soaked your aching feet in a basin of hot water? That's hydrotherapy.

Athletic trainers make extensive use of whirlpool baths to treat athletes who have strained or sore muscles. Water therapy has become so popular that many people have installed "hot tubs" in their homes. Not too long ago hydrotherapy was used for polio victims as a method to help them regain some use of their crippled limbs. Swimming, by far the most popular form of hydrotherapy, is done by millions of people around the world. In hydrotherapy the water may be hot, cold, or tepid, depending upon the particular need, and may be used in any one of three states: liquid, solid (ice), or gas (steam). Ice packs are a form of hydrotherapy used to prevent swelling associated with injuries.

Some other popular hydrotherapy techniques include:

Sitz bath. A sitting bath used to treat many abdominal and pelvic conditions.

Contrast baths. The alternative application of hot and cold to the body, which results in dilation and contraction of blood vessels to improve circulation.

Cold mitten friction. A mitten made from Turkish towel material is dipped in cold water, wrung out lightly and then rubbed briskly across the body.

Epsom salts bath. Magnesium sulphate is added to very hot bath water, which causes profuse sweating. After an epsom salts bath, the person showers and receives a brisk rubdown.

Colonic. The internal application of water to flush waste products and toxins from the body and cleanse the lower digestive tract.

MANIPULATIVE THERAPIES

Acupressure

Acupressure is a form of therapy in which the fingertips are used to apply pressure along meridians found on the body. By stimulating the acupressure points along the meridians, life forces are permitted to flow to various parts of the body. A practitioner skilled in the application of acupressure is an acupressurist.

Acupressure originated at about the same time as acupuncture and is an integral part of Chinese medicine. The major difference between acupressure and acupuncture is the use of the fingertips as opposed to very fine needles.

The fingers are used to rub or massage specific acupressure points along the body's meridians (invisible lines that crisscross the body) in order to promote the even flow of the life force known as *chi*. In a healthy person, chi flows evenly, maintaining a balance between the vigorous *yang* and the restraining *yin* elements. Practitioners of acupressure or any other Chinese therapy aim to correct any imbalances and encourage chi to flow freely again.

The acupressurist studies the meridians of the body and locates the acupressure points along these meridians. It is thought that all life force flows along these pathways. If there is some blockage or deficiency along the pathways, then the vital force cannot reach the organs or other parts of the body.

Through proper stimulation of the acupressure points, the flow of vital energy is restored and good health returns. Conversely, it is also possible to have too much life force or energy flowing in a particular organ or body part. Once again, the acupressurist would stimulate the correct acupressure points and redistribute the life force.

There's really nothing strange about rubbing a sore or aching spot, since most of us do it naturally. Acupressure may be an ancient healing method originating in traditional Chinese medicine, but it appears to have a place in today's world.

For more information, contact:

Acupressure Institute
1533 Shattuck Avenue
Berkeley, CA 94709
415-845-1059

Alexander Technique

The Alexander technique is classified as a manipulative therapy because it attempts to correct a range of disorders by improving posture. The technique was developed in the late 1800s by F. Matthias Alexander, an Australian actor who had experienced problems with his voice. In his efforts to discover the cause, he hit upon the idea of postural changes. By studying what he was doing with his posture when the problems arose, he learned that he was pulling his head downward and backward.

Alexander borrowed the theory of spinal integrity from chiropractic and osteopathy, but with two important distinctions: he believed that if the vertebrae were out of alignment, it was due to misuse. And he believed that the way we use our bodies, and the habits we develop—such as slumping, tensing, and slouching—influence function.

The Alexander technique is really one of relearning or learning what not to do. There are no formal exercises, so the technique will vary with the individual. The basic approach is for a teacher to evaluate and determine where postural changes are needed and where reconditioning must begin. Then the teacher manipulates various parts of the body, such as the head, neck, limbs, or pelvis, and the person is told to focus on the instructions given—for example, "neck free, head forward and out." Alexander believed very strongly in the mind and body connection. This technique is repeated until the problem is corrected.

For more information, contact:

American Center for the Alexander Technique
142 West End Avenue
New York, NY 10023
212-799-0468

Applied Kinesiology/Touch for Health

Applied kinesiology/Touch for Health is a form of healing that uses thera-
peutic touch to correct imbalances in the body's energy system and to restore
health. A practitioner who employs the principles of kinesiology and is trained
in the proper functioning of the body's muscle systems is a kinesiologist. (Chiro-
practors and massage therapists also may use the principles of kinesiology in their
practices.)

Applied kinesiology/Touch for Health is a branch of natural
healing that applies touch to transmit and arouse the healing forces.
It combines some of the manipulative practices of chiropractic and
massage with the concept of energy flow found in acupuncture and
shiatsu. At the core of applied kinesiology is a system of muscle
testing that enables the practitioner to identify the weaknesses in
the body's energy system. Once these weaknesses are corrected, the
body is restored to balance and good health.

A chiropractor, George Goodheart, established the basis for applied kinesiology while he was attempting to determine the cause
of taut muscles or muscles in spasm. During his investigation, he
determined that the tautness or spasms were caused by weak muscles on the opposite side of the body. He reasoned that the energy
flow to the muscles must be disrupted. By applying chiropractic
techniques and Eastern ideas of energy flow, he devised a system for
restoring muscle balance.

A practitioner looks for symptoms of muscle weakness by
examining the person's posture and testing specific muscles. The
patient lies flat on the examining table while the practitioner ro-
tates and flexes the arms and legs. The meridians of acupuncture
are used as reference points and to determine where energy is restricted or excessive. For example, a practitioner will test the relative strength of the hamstring muscles if he or she suspects an
intestinal problem. Treatment is started if these muscles are
found to be weak.

For more information, contact:

Touch for Health Foundation
1174 North Lake Avenue
Pasadena, CA 91104
818-794-1181

Chiropractic

Chiropractic is a healing art that emphasizes manipulation of the spinal vertebrae as a method of restoring bodily health. A chiropractor is a practitioner of the art of chiropractic who holds the degree of doctor of chiropractic (D.C.) and is licensed to provide chiropractic treatments.

Chiropractic in the United State can be traced to Daniel David Palmer, who in 1895 reportedly manipulated the spine of a deaf man and restored his hearing. Chiropractic is based upon the principle that the spinal column is central to a person's entire sense of well-being because it is instrumental in maintaining the health of the nervous system. Through chiropractic adjustments, or the manipulation of the vertebrae by a chiropractor, the nervous system is kept in or returned to good health.

Chiropractic is considered a drugless therapy since chiropractors generally believe the body's own healing forces can be utilized to combat disease. This view of health care requires acceptance of the flow of life forces through the body and the use of those forces to maintain health. Hence, if something interferes with the flow of these forces, then illness will occur.

Since chiropractors are concerned with the structure of the body, they are required to study anatomy, physiology, neurophysiology, biomechanics, and kinesiology. This training, as well as the use of certain diagnostic procedures, permits chiropractors to consider the body's entire neuro-musculoskeletal system when making a diagnosis.

Diagnostic procedures used by chiropractors include treadmills, temperature sensing, stationary bicycles, and devices to measure the distribution of the body weight. The X ray remains the staple for examination of the spinal column and its twenty-four vertebrae.

Chiropractic treatment generally consists of spinal adjustments in which the chiropractor pushes on the vertebrae to reposition them. When a chiropractor is making an adjustment, the patient may hear a "pop" or "click" sound as the vertebra goes back into place. Other joints also are manipulated and returned to their normal positions.

There are two main schools of thought in the practice of chiropractic today: One emphasizes traditional spinal manipulation and is called the "straight school." Chiropractors from this school adhere to the principles first set down by Dr. Palmer and, as such, do not use any adjunctive therapies such as heat, ultrasound, traction, vitamins, minerals, and exercise. On the other hand, chiropractors who supplement traditional spinal manipulation with adjunctive therapies are said to be from the "mixed school," which accounts for the majority of chiropractors in practice today.

Chiropractic adjustments have been successful for a number of people; however, chiropractors point out that adjustments may not work in every case. When a chiropractor detects a condition that is beyond his or her scope of practice, a referral is made to the proper medical specialists.

For more information, contact:

International Chiropractors Association ["straight school"]
1110 North Glebe Road
Arlington, VA 22201
800-423-4690

American Chiropractic Association ["mixed school"]
1701 Clarendon Boulevard
Arlington, VA 22209
703-276-8800

Feldenkrais Technique

The Feldenkrais technique was designed by Dr. Moshe Feldenkrais for the purpose of improving posture and general health. In some respects Feldenkrais owes his concept to the work done by F. Matthias Alexander in the development of the Alexander technique.

There are two facets to the Feldenkrais technique: awareness through movement, and private manipulative treatment. The first involves group-based classes where various exercises are performed while lying down in order to lessen the effects of gravity on the body. The purpose is to gently exercise the muscles and joints with as little strain as possible. A Feldenkrais teacher instructs pupils on the proper way to completely relax until they feel "that the body is hanging lightly from the head, the feet do not stomp on the ground, and the body glides when moving."

The second foundation of the Feldenkrais technique is private manipulative therapy, referred to as "functional integration." This is the person-to-person phase of the technique in which the teacher works with the pupil by using a series of gentle manipulative movements, but does not work directly on a problem in the belief that this could add to the pain and discomfort. For example, the legs and pelvis may be manipulated in order to relieve a problem in the shoulders.

Like the Alexander technique, the Feldenkrais technique strives to correct posture and break bad habits that lead to muscular and joint discomfort.

While there are Feldenkrais teachers, the most likely place to find the technique practiced is in other types of massage therapy.

For more information, contact:

Feldenkrais Center for Learning
48 North Pleasant Street, Suite 204
Amherst, MA 01002
413-253-3550

Feldenkrais Guild
14 Corporate Woods
8717 West 110th, Suite 140
Overland Park, KS 66210
913-492-1444

Massage Therapy

Massage therapy is the healing art in which hand manipulation of the body is employed to create a feeling of relaxation, ease mental and physical tensions, alleviate aches and pains, improve circulation, and generally reinvigorate and stimulate the body's systems. A massage therapist is trained in one or more of the following forms of massage therapy: Swedish massage, shiatsu, acupressure, Rolfing, reflexology, polarity, and bioenergetics.

The philosophy of massage is rooted in Eastern medicine and is based upon the *balance point* of the human body. It is believed that when this balance is tipped, one way or the other, illness can occur. Massage therapy can relax the body and improve circulation, which enables the body to regain its balance point and return to good health.

While an integral part of Chinese medicine, massage therapy generally has been avoided in Western medicine. When it is utilized, it is usually in connection with the conditioning of athletes and primarily to limber up joints and relieve aches and pains. However, today there is more interest in the use of massage therapy for a myriad of health care problems. In fact, two groups of medical practitioners already use a form of manipulation as part of their treatment. Osteopaths and chiropractors manipulate joints of the body to treat certain conditions.

Massage therapists claim it is effective in treating stress and fatigue, headaches, insomnia, lower back pain, muscle fatigue, and pregnancy and postpartum problems, as well as in aiding digestion and circulation.

Most massages begin at the head or feet, then gradually work toward the heart, since this is believed to be the body's natural circulatory path. Each massage is composed of a series of strokes or movements done with different pressure. The basic massage strokes are kneading, tapping or striking, and gliding. Swedish massage makes use of two additional motions: vibration and friction.

Since massage therapy is noninvasive and involves no drugs, just about anyone can enjoy its benefits. And, if nothing else, massage makes you feel good.

For more information, contact:

American Massage Therapy Association
1130 West North Shore Avenue
Chicago, IL 60626
312-761-2682

Myotherapy

Myotherapy is a method of pain relief that is based upon locating "trigger points" in muscles that cause the muscles to go into spasm. Using the fingers, knuckles, or elbows, pressure is applied to these trigger points. A person certified in the use of myotherapy techniques is a myotherapist.

Trigger points are difficult to explain, but can best be described as sensitive spots that contribute to pain. The pain occurs when these points "fire," thus causing the muscles to react.

Trigger points occur because muscles are subjected to bumps, sprains, blows, and strains. Many of these points can be located in a single muscle, and during a lifetime it's possible to accumulate a large number of them. Not limited only to the large muscles of the body—legs, back, shoulders, chest, and so on—trigger points also occur in the muscles of the face, hands, and feet.

Very familiar with anatomy and the complete muscle structure of the body, a myotherapist searches for trigger points by pushing on or putting pressure on the muscles. Since myotherapy is a drugless therapy, the only tools are fingers, knuckles, and elbows, and something called a *bodo.* Basically, this is a wooden dowel used to apply pressure.

The whole point of myotherapy is that trigger points can be released or neutralized by applying pressure for at least seven seconds, a rule that works fine for most muscles; however, smaller muscles respond to as little as four seconds of pressure. Myotherapists also go easier when working on children or the elderly.

While there is no scientific basis per se for myotherapy, it has received favorable notice from the media and is looked upon as a form of physical therapy.

For more information, contact:

Bonnie Prudden Workshops
P.O. Box 59
Prospect Hill
Stockbridge, MA 01262
413-298-5129

Reflexology

Reflexology is the practice of stimulating certain areas of the feet that correspond to various organs and other parts of the body. Proper stimulation of these points can aid in maintaining good health. A person who practices reflexology is a reflexologist. Some reflexologists are also certified, which indicates they have completed a formal course of instruction in reflexology.

Reflexology has its proponents, as well as its detractors. With origins in Chinese medicine, reflexology is considered a cousin of acupuncture but uses the hands to massage the toes and bottom of the feet. Both approaches believe in the flow of life force to every part of the body, and both attempt to improve that flow as a way to ward off disease.

The first known writings on reflexology in the United States were done by Eunice D. Ingham in the 1930s. A booklet entitled *Stories the Feet Can Tell* set forth the principles of reflexology and described how various organs and body parts correspond to specific locations on the feet.

Surprisingly complex, the foot contains twenty-six bones, fifty-six ligaments, and thirty-eight muscles. Reflexologists knead, rub, stroke, and pry at the muscles and toes of the feet to improve circulation of the life force to the organs and joints in the body.

A reflexologist will "read" the foot for symptoms of illness, which usually are indicated by a gritty or sandy feeling. These are often referred to as crystals, which represent waste products that are impeding normal circulation. The location of these crystals enables the reflexologist to determine which organ or body system is experiencing a problem. The reflexologist uses the thumb and fingers to break up the crystals and thus restore normal circulation.

Reflexologists seldom claim that their therapy cures. Rather, reflexology is looked upon as a preventive method for maintaining good health. Some sources indicate that reflexology can be effective in helping to relieve headaches, stress, sinus problems, constipation, and other functional disorders.

There is still considerable debate as to how or why reflexology works. To Western medicine the concepts of life forces and energy fields are difficult to comprehend, so it has not readily accepted the philosophy of its Eastern counterpart.

For more information, contact:

International Institute of Reflexology
P.O. Box 12642
St. Petersburg, FL 33733
813-343-4811

Rolfing

Rolfing is a therapy in which very deep massage is used to correct improper structural or postural positions. A practitioner skilled in the use of this deep muscle massage to bring about structural balances is a Rolfer.

Rolfing was developed in the 1930s by Ida Rolf and grew in

popularity when people began exploring healing methods outside of traditional medicine. As with any manipulative therapy, Rolfing owes its philosophical and physical tenets to healing methods developed in the East, such as acupressure.

Rolfing involves the manipulation of muscles and fascia (connective tissue of the body, including tendons, lymph nodes, and ligaments) to permit freer movement of the body. As the muscles and fascia are manipulated, the body returns to its natural posture. Rolfing usually consists of ten sessions conducted over a five- or ten-week period. These sessions are divided into three distinct parts in which the Rolfer has very specific objectives to achieve.

Rolfers are interested in freeing the body from the constraints imposed by stress, poor living habits, and bad posture. Since part of the problem is related to breathing, the Rolfer works to loosen the chest and pelvic muscles. The second group of sessions concentrates on the ankles and feet.

The final sessions concentrate on establishing new patterns of movement, and once these are developed, the person should notice an improvement in both physical and mental energies.

Some massage therapists, kinesiologists, and chiropractors may be familiar with the technique of Rolfing.

For more information, contact:

Rolf Institute
P.O. Box 1868
Boulder, CO 80306
303-449-5903

Shiatsu

Shiatsu is a form of Japanese massage in which the fingers are used to apply pressure to specific points on the body known as meridians. The philosophy behind shiatsu is to promote better health by stimulating the meridians and improving the flow of chi energy throughout the body.

(See also Acupressure.)

MIDWIFERY

Midwifery is the practice of assisting in childbirth. A person who practices midwifery is a midwife, usually a certified nurse-midwife.

In large measure due to changes in conventional medicine and the desire of women to control the circumstances of giving birth, midwifery has reemerged as a force in maternity care.

Having supplanted the lay midwife, the certified nurse-midwife is the predominant practitioner. This is a registered nurse who has taken additional training in obstetrics and gynecology and newborn care and who has passed an extensive credentialing examination administered by the American College of Nurse-Midwives.

Nurse-midwives practice in a variety of settings: hospitals, birthing centers, health maintenance organizations, public health departments, and public and private health clinics. Although nurse-midwives independently manage maternity and newborn care, they are affiliated with physicians—an aspect of independent practice recognized by many insurance companies that now reimburse for nurse-midwife services.

Nurse-midwives provide care before, during, and after pregnancy. Women are advised of family-planning methods, normal gynecological care, diet and nutrition, birthing methods, and newborn care. During labor the nurse-midwife monitors progress and offers emotional and physical support, and also monitors the presence or absence of fetal distress and whether physician services are required. At birth the nurse-midwife assists the delivery and examines the newborn.

For more information, contact:

American College of Nurse-Midwives
1522 K Street, N.W., Suite 1120
Washington, DC. 20005
202-347-5445

NATUROPATHIC MEDICINE

Naturopathic medicine is a healing art that emphasizes the body's natural healing forces. It is a drugless therapy that makes use of massage, light, heat, air, and water.

A person schooled in the art of naturopathic medicine who has earned the degree of doctor of naturopathic medicine (N.D.) is a naturopathic physician. Students enrolled in naturopathic medical schools complete courses that are a balance of traditional naturopathic philosophy, medical science, and the effectiveness of natural therapeutics.

Naturopathic medicine is rooted in the concept of *vis medicatrix naturae,* the healing power of nature. Naturopaths trace their origins to Hippocrates, who is said to have believed in the ability of nature to cure illnesses. One explanation given for the emergence of naturopathic medicine is disenchantment with the heroic remedies of orthodox medicine: bleeding, blistering, and purging. Very often they proved worse than the illness and did little to relieve the underlying health problem.

Naturopathy is practiced throughout the world, yet little is known in the West because of the bias against any healing art that is not founded in allopathic philosophy. Naturopathy is concerned with removing the root cause of disease whether it be psychological, chemical (faulty eating, drinking, breathing, or elimination), or mechanical (bad posture or muscular tension).

To the naturopath, a person's medical history is the most important piece of information used to make a diagnosis. Naturopaths also rely on laboratory tests and other diagnostic techniques such as X rays, scans, physicals, and so on. Once the diagnosis is made, the naturopath sets about restoring health by taking the whole person into account and not just the symptoms.

Naturopaths consider diet and nutrition essential to good health, and will advise patients on proper nutrition, including the types of food which should be eaten as well as those to avoid. In some cases, naturopaths will recommend fasting as one method for detoxifying the body before beginning a new regimen of diet and nutrition. The fasting process is not designed to be starvation; rather, it is an attempt to permit the body's metabolic functions to rest, thus enabling the body to eliminate waste and toxic products and thereby cleanse itself.

For more information, contact:

John Bastyr College of Naturopathic Medicine
11231 Southeast Market
Portland, OR 97216
503-255-4860

OPTOMETRY

Optometry is the practice of examining, diagnosing, and treating visual defects through the use of lenses, other visual aids, and visual therapies. A professional who practices optometry, an optometrist, must complete a four-year course of study before receiving the degree of doctor of optometry (O.D.), and must obtain a license before opening a practice.

Vision is one of the most important senses that humans possess. It is estimated that over 90 percent of all we know and learn has been acquired through the visual sense. When vision problems do arise, a visit to any eye care specialist is usually in order.

Optometrists study the manner in which the eyes receive light rays and the way the lenses focus that light upon the retina. They are concerned with the general health of the eye and the surrounding structure, including the eyelids, eyelashes, tear ducts, muscles, and so forth.

Optometrists measure the visual power of the eyes by using various instruments. They also test for color blindness, glaucoma, and other eye disorders.

Optometrists use lenses to correct the two more common visual problems: myopia (nearsightedness) and hyperopia (farsightedness). Optometry also makes use of prisms and other visual aids to correct other eye disorders such as crossed eyes (strabismus) and "lazy eye" (amblyopia).

Optometrists also do vision therapy, exercises, and other techniques that enable people to maintain or improve their vision without the use of mechanical aids such as eyeglasses or contact lenses.

When optometrists detect conditions beyond their scope, such as a disorder that may require surgery, they refer the patient to an ophthalmologist, an M.D. who specializes in the medical or surgical treatment of eye diseases.

For more information, contact:

American Optometric Association
243 North Lindbergh Boulevard
St. Louis, MO 63141
314-991-4100

OSTEOPATHIC MEDICINE

Osteopathic medicine is a healing art founded by Dr. Andrew Taylor Sill, based on the theory that the entire body must be considered when treating disease. An essential part of osteopathic practice is the belief in the relationship between disease and the body's structure. One schooled in the art of osteopathic medicine is an osteopathic physician, or osteopath. To be granted the degree of doctor of osteopathy, a person must complete four years of study at an approved school of osteopathic medicine.

Osteopathy has much the same scientific foundations as allopathic medicine, but does have certain philosophical differences. Osteopaths believe in treating the whole person and not just the symptoms of a particular illness. Another major difference is that osteopaths use manipulative therapy to reposition the joints in the body or the vertebrae of the spine. Otherwise, they use the same methods of diagnosis and treatment as allopathic practitioners, namely examinations, tests, X rays, medications, and surgery.

Because of the osteopathic philosophy of treating the whole person, many practitioners are in general or family practice. However, osteopaths also have developed specialties and are board-certified by the American Osteopathic Association (AOA). Specialties currently certified by the AOA include anesthesiology, dermatology, internal medicine, neurology, obstetrics-gynecology, ophthalmology, pathology, pediatrics, psychiatry, physical medicine, proctology, radiology, and various surgical specialties.

To be certified in a specialty, an osteopath must complete a residency program that usually requires an additional two to five years of study.

Because of past biases, osteopaths were forced to establish their own hospitals, since they were not permitted in the M.D.-dominated hospitals. However, as osteopathy has gained acceptance, some hospitals now grant privileges to both M.D.'s and D.O.'s.

For more information, contact:

American Osteopathic Association
142 East Ontario Street
Chicago, IL 60611
312-280-5800

PODIATRY

Podiatry is the field of medical care that deals with the diagnosis and treatment of diseases, injuries, deformities, and other conditions of the foot. A podiatrist is a practitioner of podiatry who has completed a four-year course of study for the degree of doctor of podiatric medicine (D.P.M.). Licensure is required before a practice can be established.

Once known as chiropodists and considered tradesmen as opposed to medical professionals, podiatrists now treat foot conditions ranging from simple corns to infectious diseases. They also perform surgery to correct deformities of the foot and toes, including the removal of bone spurs, warts, and tumors. Podiatrists set fractures and prepare *orthoses* (devices to rearrange the weight-bearing structure of the foot).

Preventing injuries is also a major concern of podiatrists. Many athletes consult with podiatrists to determine the best methods for preventing injuries to the foot, ankle, and connective muscles and tendons. Podiatrists rely upon physical examinations, tests, and X rays to aid in making a diagnosis.

Treatment modalities include medications; surgery on bones, muscles, and tendons; ultrasound; diathermy; and physical therapy.

For problems of the feet the most obvious choice is between a podiatrist and an orthopedic specialist (an M.D. who specializes in bone disorders). Many people choose podiatrists because they believe this practitioner is more likely to recommend a conservative approach.

Podiatrists are becoming more involved with screening the lower extremities for signs of other systemic disorders such as diabetes and hardening of the arteries. When such problems are found, podiatrists will make referrals to the appropriate medical specialists. While there is still some controversy over the proper role of the podiatrist in the medical world, organized medicine has not been able to prevent podiatrists from gaining hospital admitting privileges.

For more information, contact:

American Podiatric Medical Association
9312 Old Georgetown Road
Bethesda, MD 20814
301-571-9200

PSYCHOLOGICAL
THERAPIES

Biofeedback

Biofeedback uses the conscious mind to control the involuntary body functions, such as respiration, heartbeat, and body temperature. It can be learned by anyone and utilized when needed for specific conditions.

While there may not be a precise definition of biofeedback, the following example demonstrates how we all use biofeedback at one time or another.

You may not have given much thought to how you learned to ride a bicycle, yet you employed a form of biofeedback in the learning process. If you had to think consciously of all the steps it takes to ride a bicycle, you may not have gotten past the first one. As you pedaled the first few shaky feet, your brain was processing the feedback it was getting from your body as it sought to make automatic adjustments to achieve the balance necessary for you to keep pedaling and stay on the bike.

The application of biofeedback to health disorders is not new. For many years, especially in Eastern cultures, yogis have been able to control involuntary body reflexes such as respiration and heartbeat. By slowing down body functions, they are able to induce conditions that a more active or conscious body cannot.

Biofeedback has found acceptance in the psychological profession as practitioners seek alternative methods to drug therapies. For many people, living with pain and stress has become the price for living in the modern world. And while drug therapy may be effective, many people are concerned about drug side effects. Biofeedback holds some promise as being one way to help people cope with chronic pain and deal with stress. It should be pointed out, however, that biofeedback is not a cure, but is a method for dealing with symptoms.

The techniques used to train someone in the use of biofeedback have become very sophisticated. It is now possible to monitor brain impulses and make them audible to the person who is using biofeedback. By monitoring this electrical activity and listening to the series of "beeps," the person will learn how to control the situation.

Some people use biofeedback to control their body temperature or increase the flow of blood to certain body parts. Biofeedback has also been employed for stress headaches, migraine headaches, back pain, temporomandibular joint pain, and nerve damage.

The concept of using biofeedback to control the involuntary workings of the body is new to Western medical thought; therefore, you may not find every practitioner open to discussing its use. A good starting point is a certified biofeedback instructor.

For more information, contact:

Biofeedback Society of America
10200 West 44th Avenue
Wheat Ridge, CO 80033
303-422-8436

Hypnotherapy

Hypnotherapy is the use of hypnosis as an adjunctive therapy in the treatment of physical and mental disorders. A professional who is schooled in the art of hypnosis and who uses hypnosis as a healing method is a hypnotherapist.

Ever since Franz Mesmer told his first patient "You are getting very sleepy," there has been skepticism about the effectiveness of hypnosis. Most of the skeptics have been practitioners of orthodox medicine whose rigid adherence to scientific dogma precluded the belief in anything as theatrical as hypnosis.

Some evidence suggests that hypnosis, or the induction of a trancelike state, was known in ancient times, when the Druids were said to be able to induce a "magic sleep." Certain Egyptian writings also referred to hypnosis.

However, today the use of hypnosis is gaining additional respectability as both psychiatrists and psychologists employ a form of it in their practices.

Although not exactly asleep, a person in a hypnotic state is not fully awake either. The state is, if nothing else, an altered one wherein the subject is more responsive to the power of suggestion. A person who is hypnotized may have incredible powers of concentration and be able to accomplish things not necessarily possible in a more conscious state.

Contrary to popular myth, you cannot be hypnotized against your will or forced to do something you do not want to do. If you can be hypnotized, you may be able to use the power of your subconscious to focus all your mind's energy on one problem. The ability to focus on one problem is a result of being insulated from the distractions of the outside world.

Among orthodox medical practitioners, hypnotherapy has gained some respectability based on the results of trials conducted on burn victims. It seems that when hypnotized they were better able to deal with the pain associated with deep burn wounds. Other practitioners have used hypnotherapy to help patients deal with pain from migraine headaches, chronic pain, stress, stomach problems, arthritis, colitis, and hemophilia, to name just a few. Hypnosis may also be self-administered.

Learning to break an old habit or establish a new healthy habit can be accomplished through hypnosis. People wishing to quit smoking often use hypnosis, and there have also been reports of success in helping people to lose weight and adhere to a new diet. Some therapists, especially those in pediatric hospitals, use hypnosis to help patients overcome their fears of hospitalization.

For more information, contact:

American Society of Clinical Hypnosis
2200 East Devon, Suite 291
Des Plaines, IL 60018
708-297-3317

Psychotherapy

Psychotherapy is a healing art that approaches the treatment of disorders with mental rather than physical methods. Forms of psychotherapy include suggestion, dialogue, reeducation, confidence-building, and moral support. A person who uses any of the various forms of psychotherapy to treat mental disorders and behavioral disturbances is a psychotherapist. Practitioners include psychiatrists, psychologists, psychiatric social workers, psychiatric nurses, psychoanalysts, and pastoral counselors.

Psychotherapy seeks to help people overcome life's problems, which may or may not be rooted in deep emotional conflicts. Often the pressures of daily life create situations in which a person feels as though he or she can no longer cope. The emphasis in psychotherapy is in the cognitive arena, where dialogue is more important than drug therapy. Building a relationship with a therapist is one of the keys to making psychotherapy work. Another factor is the commitment the person has to making the therapy work.

The list of psychotherapies available is rather extensive and includes the following: Freudian, Jungian, Gestalt, Adlerian, Rogerian, group, reality, cognitive, integrity, shock, primal scream, hypnotherapy, behavior modification, biofeedback, Erhard Seminar Training (EST), orthomolecular psychiatry, rebirthing, and Rolfing.

However, most types of psychotherapy can be grouped into a few broad categories: traditional psychotherapies (Freudian, Jungian, and Adlerian), human potential therapies (client-centered, Gestalt, and bioenergetics), group therapies (psychodrama, family therapy, and transactional analysis), and cognitive-behavior therapies (behavior therapy and biofeedback).

Psychotherapy is intended to help people deal with reality, take charge of situations, and regain control of their lives. Those suffering from phobias may be helped by various therapies designed to free them from their fears, or at least to recognize what is frightening them. Group therapy is sometimes used to help people overcome feelings of loneliness and become more involved in society. Behavior modification can be utilized to correct behavior that is self-destructive by teaching adaptive skills.

The two most popular psychotherapists are the psychiatrist (an M.D. specializing in psychiatry) and the psychologist (a Ph.D. in psychology). Both have certifying organizations to help ensure that only qualified professionals are permitted to practice. Some of the other types of practitioners, such as counselors and social workers, have their own certifying organization, the American Board of Professional Psychology, which issues diplomas to candidates who have met both education and experience criteria. And there's a movement in many states toward the licensing of social workers and family counselors.

For more information, contact:

American Psychological Association
1200 17th Street, N.W.
Washington, DC 20036
202-955-7600

American Board of Professional Psychology
2100 East Broadway, Suite 313
Columbia, MO 65201
314-875-1267

American Board of Psychiatry and Neurology
500 Lake Cook Road, Suite 335
Deerfield, IL 60015
708-945-7900

YOGA

Yoga is a philosophy of life that originated in India and which espouses the uniting of body, mind, and spirit in order to achieve a higher self-realization; it has been practiced for some six thousand years. A person who practices yoga, follows its philosophy, or teaches yoga is a yogi.

As with all mystical philosophies, yoga requires the acceptance of a world in which disharmonies and interferences restrict an individual's spiritual growth. Some people see yoga as a religion, while others view it as a philosophy intended to help them achieve their goals.

According to legend, yoga exercises were designed by Lord Shiva at the beginning of time and have remained the same since then. The first codified yoga system is believed to have been written in the second century B.C. by the Indian sage Pantanjali. To this day yoga utilizes eighty-four of the postures handed down by Pantanjali.

Yoga is deeply rooted in Eastern mysticism and the belief in some formless god who creates and arranges all matter. The yogi attempts to unite with this force and reach a state of consciousness and awareness in which harmony exists. But before reaching this state, the yogi must perform a series of exercises involving breathing and posture. This is *hatha yoga.*

Other forms of yoga include:

Mantra yoga. A mantra is a word or phrase that is repeated thousands of times. The mind focuses on the vibrations of the mantra and thus increases concentration.

Bhakti yoga. This is the yoga of faith, devotion, and worship. Yogis chant to help increase their spiritual bliss.

Jnana yoga. This is the yoga of knowledge or intellect. It requires the yogi to focus on those things that have occurred and to learn from them.

Karma yoga. This is cause and effect, with good deeds producing good karma and bad deeds producing bad karma.

Raja yoga. This is the ultimate state of superconsciousness, or deep meditation, that yogis strive to attain. This form of perfect mind control permits the yogi to control all thought processes and keep them free from distractions.

Laya yoga. This yoga explores the seven energy centers of the body known as the *chakras.* It requires a person to still the mind and awaken the inner force called *kundalini.*

The practice of yoga in the West has been increasing as more people seek alternative methods for achieving a feeling of well-being and seek to improve their self-discipline, concentration, and positive thinking.

For further information, contact:

Integral Yoga Institute
227 West 13th Street
New York, NY 10011
212-929-0585

Himalayan International Institute of Yoga
Science and Philosophy
R.R. 1, P.O. Box 400
Honesdale, PA 18431
717-253-5551

THE RIGHT SETTING FOR YOUR NEEDS

2

Where you get your medical care is as important as who provides it. The backdrop not only makes a *big* difference in how much you pay, but also dictates what treatment you get or do not get.

You don't have to be a cost accountant to realize that certain settings are more expensive than others, with hospital-based care the steepest. One night in a hospital costs an average of $293 or a total of $2,080 for an average stay (January 1990 figures). And that only covers the room and meals; when drugs, medical tests, and other charges are factored in, the daily cost climbs sharply to $890.

Dollar figures like those are enough to convince most people to reduce the time spent in the hospital, if not completely eliminate hospitalization in favor of another setting. But first you've got to know what your choices are. If not the hospital, where else can you get that uncomfortable hernia repaired or that painful bunion removed?

The matter of your particular medical condition and the diagnostic procedures and treatment it requires is an important consideration. Not every setting is appropriate for every medical need. Your community hospital is not the place for the kidney transplant you so desperately need, but if all you require is a routine X ray, you have a wide range of settings from which to choose.

But beware! There is more to the strategy of finding the right setting for your needs than merely consumer choice. You will also want to look at your health insurance plan: *what it will pay for and where.*

For certain procedures to be covered, the plan may push you into a particular setting or mandate that you use a particular hospital with which the insurance company has signed an agreement. For instance, unless your doctor can prove medical necessity, you may be forced to have your cataract surgery done in an outpatient setting—in and out the same day—even though your wish, for whatever reason, is to be hospitalized overnight.

Before you do anything—talk to your doctor, call around to compare what is available in your community, or check with your insurance company—you need to know all the various settings where care is delivered. The medical delivery system is chockablock with options, but finding the right one will require some investigation.

Oh yes, one important introductory point. Many people are under the false impression that they cannot choose the hospital where they want to be treated. They think they have to go where the doctor sends them. Not so! Since most doctors have privileges at more than one hospital, there are a range of facilities to pick from. Furthermore, a recent survey reported, in just the last ten years the percentage of people who chose their own hospital for treatment went from 5 percent to 35 percent. So in actuality the choice is yours.

A SPECIALTY
HOSPITAL OR A
GENERAL HOSPITAL?

The two major categories of hospitals in the United States are specialty hospitals and general medical-surgical hospitals.

A specialty hospital takes care of only one kind of medical condition or one type of patient. It might admit only those patients with cancer or orthopedic problems, or only children, for example. The selling point of specialty hospitals is that they concentrate on a single disease or condition or type of patient, day in and day out, and presumably the staff becomes expert in dealing with it. The argument goes something like this: there is no better place for someone in your condition than an institution that deals with that condition solely.

True, studies do show that hospitals get better at procedures they perform often, and the results are usually better too. No surprise here. But a high rate of successful cesarean births or hysterectomies does not mean that you should enter without concern. The number of successes may be meaningless if these procedures are being performed more often than necessary.

Study after study has documented the fact that some facilities perform far more of one procedure than a hospital only a few miles away with the same number of persons entering with the same conditions. We may not know exactly why, but greed, convenience, habit, or the hospital's policies and aims have been prominently mentioned. Check it out. Call all the hospitals in your area and ask how many times a year they perform the procedure you are scheduled to have. You might also want to call a hospital or two in a city nearby to compare their numbers. In some instances, the travel to another city for the procedure may make better medical sense.

General medical and surgical hospitals are not necessarily better in terms of efficiency or proficiency than specialty hospitals, but they are equipped to handle a larger variety of medical eventualities. These facilities are what most people envision when they hear the word "hospital." They are, in effect, a conglomeration of little specialty hospitals under one roof. Still, a general hospital occasionally sends a patient to a specialty hospital for better, more focused, and more knowledgeable care.

COMMUNITY HOSPITAL OR MEDICAL CENTER?

Community hospitals, as the name implies, commonly dot the landscape of residential areas. They become, they like to think, one of your neighbors. Through their administrators or community relations staff, they invite you to drop in and spend some time with them. Such hospitals may have as few as 50 beds or as many as several hundred. A good-size community hospital has around 250 beds, and has virtually every kind of expensive technology that might be required for the best of what hospitals have to offer. The selling point of such places is that they are large enough to give you big-time medicine, yet small enough to provide personal attention.

The selling point medical centers stress, on the other hand, is that they are big institutions, and because of this they see many different kinds of patients and are able to treat rare conditions that might stump most community hospitals. These medical centers are usually affiliated with universities, an affiliation the medical center considers a plus because it implies that all the newest ideas, machines, techniques, and drugs are available to the practitioners. Many experts, world-famous in their fields, roam the halls of these hospitals.

But that is only half the story. Certainly, a big hospital is good for providing doctors with lots of patients to see, work on, and learn from. But for a patient hoping for a relaxed and easy recuperation or personalized care, a medical center or other large hospital is probably not the place. And don't forget, all that elaborate equipment they have is there to be used, and the staff will surely find ways to use it—*and pay for it.* If not, the doctors must answer to the trustees who authorized the large expenditures for the super-machines.

While medical centers have just about everything that could possibly be called on to take care of your condition, your condition might just be too "commonplace," too "boring," to interest the "best" people. Experts and eager young doctors come to these hospitals to pioneer the new medical frontier, to be in the eye of the healing hurricane, which they see as modern medicine. The odds are that they will find your very typical gallbladder operation something less than exciting. You might find yourself feeling like a second-class citizen, relegated to the second-string medical-surgical team because you have the misfortune of suffering from too mundane an ailment. And you'll be paying through the nose all the while.

If you do decide on a medical center, don't go there simply because some world-famous authority is on the staff. You might never see her, or she you, while you are there. This physician-researcher-scientist-personality may be too busy with her work or her next grant proposal to see patients. You might enter thinking you will be getting the attention of the Great Person herself, but instead you see flocks of her disciples fluttering around your bed. The attention might not be bad (it might be very good), but it is not what you had in mind when you were admitted. They advertised steak, and they served you hamburger.

A hospital's size is not always a reliable clue to the kind of treatment you can expect there. You might have a warm and caring experience at a 750-bed leviathan of a medical center, and you might be treated like yesterday's oatmeal at a 100-bed community hospital. Obviously, you need more information than the hospital's size if you are to make a wise choice. You need it to protect yourself from costly mistakes, costly in terms of your pocketbook and your health.

TO PROFIT OR NOT TO PROFIT

Along with the family farm, the independent community hospital is fast becoming a lone ranger. As you know, all sorts of people and organizations own hospitals: religious orders, universities, governments, doctors. Sometimes an owner or ownership group might buy and run a few hospitals in a fairly defined, fairly small and limited region. Not uncommon, such privately owned, for-profit (proprietary) hospitals are growing in number.

But that's not all. What is also happening in the for-profit hospital business (and never forget it is a business) is the rise and monumental growth of corporate chain ownership. Whereas privately owned hospitals split the profits among the various owners, the corporately owned, national chain hospitals distribute the wealth to shareholders who expect solid returns on their investment. The corporations run their hospitals as they would any other business—for maximum profits and earnings. A bold change from the hospital's traditional image as a financially imperiled do-gooder, wouldn't you say? And a far cry from the independent community hospital to the commercial entity with one eye on the ledger and another on the healing.

Today the top three for-profit medical corporations alone—Hospital Corporation of America, Humana, and American Medical International, in that order—either own or manage nearly 87,000 beds in 530 hospitals nationwide. Their total revenues in 1988 exceeded $10.7 billion, with the three giants sharing more than $600 million in profits.

Critics of medical chains have accused them of promoting overutilization of technology, overtesting of patients, and overpricing of dispensed goods, all in an effort to improve the bottom line.

Of course, for-profit chains certainly aren't *all* bad. In many instances they have brought hospitals to places that never had them. They have also helped to keep hospital care in some communities by purchasing or contracting to manage a failing local institution, refurbishing it, and putting it back in profit-making operation.

But the fact is that corporate-owned hospitals actually end up costing the consumer more—23 percent more, according to one survey—than a not-for-profit establishment. Paul Starr, in his Pulitzer Prize-winning book *The Social Transformation of American Medicine,* states that "national data also indicate that, for every bed-size category, for-profit hospitals have higher costs than the overall average for community hospitals."

What it comes down to is this: Before your doctor arranges for you to attend a certain hospital, find out who owns it and how that ownership might affect your care and its cost. Call the hospital and ask for the hospital administrator's office. Ask the administrator who owns the hospital. Ask if it is nonprofit, owned by a religious order, part of a large conglomerate that owns fifty other facilities around the country. Know the setup before you become a patient.

TEACHING OR NONTEACHING HOSPITAL?

The arguments for going to a teaching hospital are just about the same as the ones for going to a medical center: expertise, the newest technology, up-to-the-minute knowledge. In fact, many of the best and best-known teaching hospitals are university medical centers. These hospitals exist as much for the education of the medical students at the university as they do for the care of the patients. Many patients are convinced that the only reason they have been admitted is because the students, interns, and residents need patients to work on and learn from. In this way, going to a teaching hospital is like getting a trim at a barber college, except that a bad haircut grows back for a second chance. So be prepared to be used as a teaching tool if you become a patient at a teaching hospital.

Like medical centers and university-related hospitals, some community hospitals and specialty facilities also have good teaching programs, attracting top students as well as excellent specialists from around the world. These community hospitals are considered the most sophisticated, best-equipped, most desirable places in that category. The fresh, young, eager students are more than happy to attend to you and show off what they know. One thing you'll never be in a teaching hospital is lonely.

However, this cub-pack form of medicine is just not for everybody. Sure, it's nice to get attention, but how much do you need? How much can you take? Eight different white-coated interns might visit you, one by one, all before lunch. Each will ask the same questions, ask to see the same incision, maybe draw the same amount of blood until you are almost anemic. It may be quantity care, but is it quality care?

There are teaching rounds too—those times during the day when the students, interns, and residents will converge around your bed and you will be on display for all to see and comment on. This is a school session, and you have become today's show-and-tell. It can be awkward, embarrassing, even demeaning.

Beyond annoying depersonalization, there is also the matter of cost. Teaching hospitals have greater expenses than nonteaching hospitals. They usually pay a decent salary to postgraduates-in-training and pay what it takes to attract top-flight experts. The research that doesn't earn any money directly for the institution must be underwritten. Enormous sums must be paid for new technological marvels. No wonder the average cost of care in a teaching hospital can be as much as twice that in a nonteaching hospital.

A further explanation for higher cost, in the opinion of some medical experts, is the tendency for the new, inexperienced doctors to order too many tests and unnecessary procedures. They are understandably anxious about what they need to do to pin down a diagnosis, stabilize a condition, or lay down a paper trail for good defensive medicine. So they tend to do a lot. They are, after all, just learning. But bear in mind that they are learning on *you*.

Let's not forget new high-powered technology. Every new doodad, each new bell and whistle, all the rays and beams that come along for doctors to use cost money. A lot of money. Most are useful—some of the time and for some people. The large teaching hospitals tend to have more of these exotic products of engineering ingenuity, but that does not necessarily mean you need to use them. Therefore, talk to your doctor about your particular ailment and the technology required to treat it. If what you have is relatively common and is most often treated by low-tech instead of high-tech treatments, the lower-tech hospital may be just the cure. On the other hand, if your condition is one that warrants or responds to a $3-million zapper, St. High Tech may be for you.

A teaching or nonteaching hospital? Your condition, your personality, the role high-powered technology can play in treating your ailment, the need for uncommon sophistication among the caregivers, your pocketbook—these are factors to consider in making the decision.

OSTEOPATHIC HOSPITALS

The osteopathic hospital (staffed with doctors of osteopathy, or D.O.'s) differs little these days from the allopathic hospital (staffed with medical doctors, or M.D.'s). Despite legal and public relations wars, both types of hospitals provide well-rounded doctors and primary care physicians, as well as surgeons and specialists. In fact, some hospitals offer privileges to both D.O.'s and M.D.'s.

There are far fewer osteopathic hospitals than allopathic ones. Osteopaths and their hospitals tend to serve smaller, more rural communities than do M.D.'s and their hospitals.

If the doctor you prefer is a D.O., and if he or she plans to send you to a hospital, the least of your worries is that it might be osteopathic. That it is a hospital is what ought to concern you. A hospital is a hospital; whether it is allopathic or osteopathic makes little difference. The same good things—and awful things—happen in both.

VETERANS
ADMINISTRATION
HOSPITALS

Veterans Administration (VA) hospitals and the entire military care system have been under fire for several years, the result of reports that question the quality of military medicine. The VA inspector general's office found cases, it said, in which doctors employed by the VA or performing treatments for the agency were practicing while their medical licenses in one or more states were revoked, suspended, or limited in some way (Associated Press, October 10, 1985). A few years after reform was supposed to be the watchword in military medicine, a General Accounting Office study identified another problem area: the failure to investigate patient injuries and unexpected deaths (*New York Times,* May 21, 1987).

The most recent General Accounting Office report, released in 1989, accused the Department of Veterans Affairs of failing to fulfill repeated promises to Congress to check the credentials of physicians and medical residents practicing in the nation's 172 veterans' hospitals. Further, according to the report, doctors arrested for drunk driving, drug offenses, burglary, and other crimes have been allowed to treat patients (*Washington Post,* July 7, 1989).

If all this sounds like a "just when you thought it was safe to go back into veterans' hospitals" scenario, you may be right. Don't misunderstand though. Something good can be said about VA hospitals—they provide medical care to many people who otherwise could not afford it—but unfortunately the public's confidence in them is not going to return until these quality issues are resolved.

And a final word about VA hospitals. Make sure you check out well in advance whether you qualify to use one—or whether your spouse or children can avail themselves of services. Call the VA to check your eligibility.

AMBULATORY CARE (OR WALK-IN/WALK-OUT MEDICINE)

The medical market is a free-for-all, with private practice doctors being hurt and the traditional role of hospitals challenged in every possible scenario. This phenomenon is never more evident than in the relatively new development on the health care scene in America: ambulatory medical care.

Borrowing an idea from the fast-food industry, entrepreneurs in the early 1980s began moving in droves to provide people with a more convenient and less costly medical setting. And the novel approach to medical care has met with speedy success. Just since 1984 the number of freestanding (that is, not in a doctor's office or hospital) ambulatory care centers has more than doubled, from nearly 1,800 to more than 4,000 in 1989, according to the SMG Marketing Group, as reported in *Medical Economics.*

Ambulatory care centers, offering essentially walk-in/walk-out care, first sprang up in order to attract business away from the hospital emergency room, where an estimated 80 percent of visits are not considered true emergencies. Today these facilities emphasize primary rather than emergency care and offer a broad range of services. Generally, ambulatory centers fall into two categories.

Primary/Emergency/Urgent Care

The mission here is to treat minor injuries or short-term illnesses and provide immediate treatment for routine problems: for example,

---

THE PROS AND CONS

Proponents of ambulatory care centers contend they are practical health care alternatives for consumers who demand convenience, speedy service, and moderate prices.

Opponents call them "medical McDonalds" and put them down as crass merchandisers of medicine.

cuts, sprains, dislocated or broken bones, sore throats, earaches, and so on. Because they are alternatives to the hospital emergency room or doctor's office, they have been labeled everything from emergicenter, urgicenter, and medicenter to the less flattering "doc-in-a-box." To the savvy consumer they offer many advantages, primarily convenience and, depending upon the individual case, less expensive care.

Typically, they are open ten to sixteen hours a day, but some are open around the clock. Even with the extended office hours many doctors have launched in response, the competition from ambulatory centers is still fierce because many are open six to seven days a week. Located where traffic is brisk—in shopping malls or along commercial avenues—they usually operate on a no-appointment, walk-in basis (although it is becoming more common for centers to see people by appointment as well), and you are promised only a short wait (approximately fifteen to twenty minutes), unless your injury requires even quicker attention. Most offer ancillary services such as X rays and simple laboratory tests (urine and blood tests and the like) on site, with some facilities even adding sophisticated diagnostic equipment and specialists' services ranging from physical therapy to psychological counseling.

The thorny side of this rosy picture? Generally, little attention is paid to comprehensive or follow-up care. That doesn't mean the nurse or another staff member will not phone you the next day to ask how that dog bite is healing, but it does mean that most of these centers downplay extensive medical history-taking. In short, they don't expect you to become a regular visitor. But perhaps you don't either.

The cost factor tends to be rather sticky too, but the general rule is this: treatment at an emergency or urgent care clinic is usually less expensive than a hospital visit. However, depending on how the clinic operates and how sick or hurt you are, it may cost more than a physician's office visit.

Surgery

Ambulatory surgery is a natural outgrowth of the shift, for cost-cutting purposes, to outpatient surgery (surgery that avoids an overnight hospital stay). Outpatient surgery is performed in three kinds of settings: doctors' offices; freestanding surgery centers; and

TAKING CARE OF BUSINESS

With business in same-day surgery booming, surgicenters continue to carve out a bigger niche than ever before. A Chicago-based marketing firm estimates that by the end of 1991 there will be 1,320 surgery centers in this country performing more than 3 million procedures annually (*Modern Healthcare*, June 2, 1989).

Not to be outdone in the race for business, doctor's office surgery was supposed to match the volume growth of these freestanding centers, and account for around 1.3 million procedures in 1990, said the same marketing firm quoted in the June 20, 1988 issue of *Medical Economics*.

With so much trade in outpatient surgery, is it any wonder that the number of freestanding ambulatory surgery centers is increasing? A senior manager for health care at Ernst & Young, one of the nation's leading accounting and health care consulting companies, tallied the number at 1,000 in 1988, up from 39 in 1982, adding that 91 percent are for-profit entities (*Hospitals*, January 20, 1989).

The for-profit facilities are clustered in twelve markets, primarily in California. The most common types of surgical procedures they perform are, in descending order of volume: ophthalmologic (31 percent of all free-standing centers offer only cataract surgery); plastic; general; orthopedic; otolaryngological; ob-gyn; podiatric; urologic; oral; neurologic; cardiovascular; and thoracic.

hospital outpatient facilities (which currently account for most of such surgery done in this country). As to cost differences, the question on everyone's lips, a January-February 1987 *Consumers Digest* article on the subject summarizes the state of affairs: costs are usually higher at hospitals' outpatient departments than at freestanding centers, which are somewhat higher than at doctors' offices.

According to the same *Consumers Digest* report, most freestanding surgery centers are independently owned, a few are owned by hospitals that operate satellite facilities, and many are owned by the physicians themselves. Texas and California have the most surgery centers, followed by Arizona, Florida, and Illinois (*MGM Journal*, March-April 1989).

More than anything else, advances in medical and surgical technology, especially the administration of anesthesia, have been responsible for the surge in popularity of freestanding centers, also called surgicenters. With today's sophisticated equipment and delicate instruments such as lasers, surgicenters can perform minor surgical procedures—cataract surgery, oral surgery, tubal ligation, arthroscopic procedures, and the like—and send patients home a few hours after the operation.

Choosing an Ambulatory Care Center

Ambulatory care may be convenient, accessible, and less costly, and have the bright future that predictions describe, but as the consumer you have to make sure your future after such care is bright (or, indeed, that you even have a future). When choosing any ambulatory care facility—for whatever service, be it routine medical care, urgent or emergency care, or surgery—you must face one essential question: *whether quicker and less expensive medical care means a lowering of the quality of that care and less concern for safety.*

When shopping around for the right setting for your needs, bear in mind that competition is fierce and multipronged: walk-in medical clinics, hospital emergency rooms, private practice physicians, group medical practices, hospital outpatient surgery departments, and freestanding surgical centers—all vying for your dollar. So you don't have to settle on less than the best, but you do have to snoop around first. Why waste your money and time on a clinic that's not for you? Here are some pointers:

▶ Schedule a get-acquainted visit.

▶ Find out whether the center is licensed and/or accredited, the only two means by which you can ascertain whether the facility has met certain objective standards for medical care. A possible roadblock here is that not every state licenses (and, in turn, regulates) ambulatory care facilities or has comprehensive standards, and the accreditation process is voluntary. But there's another avenue open to you. Insurance companies, Medicare, and Medicaid do certify facilities that participate in their programs. While their inspection teams may be checking for compliance with standards more along the lines of staffing, equipment, plant, and recordkeeping, this is better than no certification and no standards at all.

▶ Verify the above information in any of these ways: contact your state health department, which will tell you whether the facility is licensed; call the facility's business manager and ask whether the clinic is certified by Medicare and Medicaid and any private insurance companies; contact the two major accrediting organizations (but be prepared—only a handful of centers have gone through a voluntary review for accreditation):

Accreditation Association for Ambulatory Health Care
9933 Lawler Avenue, Suite 512
Skokie, IL 60077-5702
708-676-9610

Joint Commission on the Accreditation of Healthcare
    Organizations
875 North Michigan Avenue
Chicago, IL 60611
312-642-6061

▶ Find out how the center functions, including its hours of operation and holiday schedule, whether appointments are necessary or recommended, and what medical problems it is prepared to treat. What does it *not* treat? Ask how the center works with local hospitals and emergency ambulance services. Should the need arise, can the center arrange rapid transportation to a hospital?

▶ Ask how the center maintains its records and whether you will be given copies of your medical record. If not, what provisions does it make for follow-up care elsewhere? Will the center send a copy to your regular physician?

▶ Find out how the center handles follow-up care such as having a cast removed or having additional lab tests done. Is there a one-time charge or must you pay again for a follow-up visit?

▶ Ask about the ancillary services available: Does the center have X-ray equipment? When was it last inspected and calibrated? Is there a laboratory on the premises? If so, what are the credentials of the lab staff? Is there an orthopedic room for treating broken bones and dislocations? A suture room?

▶ Find out what life-support equipment is available on-site—a critical issue if the center offers emergency and/or surgical care. A cardiac defibrillator? A properly supplied crash cart? Are the medical personnel trained in life-support techniques, especially cardiopulmonary resuscitation? Does the facility have the necessary equipment to handle a heart attack?

▶ Find out who the staff are and determine their credentials. Call your state's medical licensing board (see appendixes A and B, pp. 396–405) and make sure all the doctors who work there are licensed. Determining that the doctors, especially in the ambulatory surgery centers, are board-certified in their specialities is extremely important too. For that information you must check the particular medical specialty board (see appendix D or E, pp. 411–15). At what hospitals do the doctors have admitting privileges? In the case of a surgery center, is there an anesthesiologist on staff? Will the anesthesiologist be present during the procedure?

▶ Ask what the typical charges are. Must you pay at the time of treatment? Credit card or cash only, or can a payment schedule be arranged? What health insurance coverage does the center accept? You will want to check your insurance policy to find out what constitutes "emergency care" and under what conditions outpatient care and surgery will be covered. There is a chance that, if you are treated at a less expensive facility than a hospital, your plan will pay full costs and waive the usual deductible and copayment or perhaps just adjust the copayment. It's worth asking.

▶ Find out what volume of surgeries the surgicenter performs a year. More and more studies are corroborating what many people already suspected regarding quality of surgical care: practice makes perfect. One report's estimate of the optimum number is 1,200 to 1,500 (*Consumers Digest,* January-February 1987). Also ask the surgeon how many times a year he or she performs the procedure you are about to undergo.

Walk-in care is not limited merely to medical care. For some time now dental care has been available on an ambulatory basis.

PUTTING YOUR MONEY
WHERE YOUR MOUTH IS:
WALK-IN DENTAL CLINICS

You may have noticed the last time you were in your local department store that right there between the garden rakes and the girdles was a dental clinic offering the usual dental services on a walk-in or, if you prefer, appointment basis. Even if your local store doesn't sport the latest trend in the marketing of dental services to the masses, your community shopping mall probably has one.

Dental clinics experienced phenomenal growth in the early 1980s, and although their growth has slowed appreciably since then, they're still proliferating. And they're competing against the traditional dental practice—that is, private office—for your business.

What Are They? And What Can They Do
for You?

The phenomenon goes by a variety of names: department store dentistry, retail store dentistry, commercial dentistry, franchise dentistry—and the tongue-in-cheek "McDentist." Whether these clinics are owned independently or by corporations, all have a few things in common: aggressive marketing of their unique features, services unlike those found in a traditional practice, such as lower costs and walk-in visits; heavy patient traffic (often more than a hundred patients a day, according to one source); and a drive for profits.

Let us say right here that of course everyone in business is looking for a profit—including your friendly family dentist. But the incentive may be even greater for dental clinics, especially those owned by publicly held corporations, as some are. So one of your first questions should be "Who owns and manages this dental clinic?" Bear in mind that in a majority of states the dental practice acts bar corporations from owning or controlling dental clinics, so the clinics in these states are independently owned. That's not to say the profit motive isn't there, and in fact it may be right at the top of the list for the investors backing the clinic. Check it out.

As you might imagine, organized dentistry tends to look askance at these clinics, in part because of quality issues (it says) and no doubt in large part because of the competitive factor. Dental traditionalists claim that the pace in these clinics is hurried and the dentist-patient relationship too brief and transitory to make for good care, and some people liken the scene to an assembly line. Other objections include little or no follow-up, no continuity of care, and no emergency services in most of these clinics.

For their part, proponents of these clinics say they have tapped into the estimated 50 percent of the population who don't go to dentists: people who have no family dentist and who, because of cost, time, and/or convenience, have not seen a dentist in five years, on the average. But it's also true that these clinics cannot help but attract patients away from traditional practices, people wooed away by lower advertised prices and/or greater convenience. So, given the current surplus of dentists and the more aggressive competition for business, look for these dental clinics to continue changing the dental marketplace.

Now what about you? How do you determine if such a clinic offers you more for your dental dollar? First and foremost, what you need to look for in these clinics, as in the traditional practice, is quality work. You never want to sacrifice quality for lower costs and convenience, because you will end up paying more in the long run. *Are the dentists in these clinics less qualified than dentists in private practice?* It's hard to say. There are a lot of reasons for a dentist to decide to forgo private practice in favor of a salaried position in a dental clinic. No money or financing for the high start-up costs of a practice may have a lot to do with the decision. Or maybe the dentist feels that his or her inadequacies and incompetence have less of a chance of being discovered in such a setting. That's why you must shop carefully.

But just how do you judge quality care? In the spring of 1989 accreditation guidelines for these clinics went into effect. The accreditation process works like this: if a clinic wishes to pay for an on-site review and meets certain standards specific to the types of care delivered at that clinic, then the Accreditation Association for Ambulatory Health Care gives the facility its stamp of approval. To check on the accreditation status of any clinic in which you're interested, call or write:

Accreditation Association for Ambulatory Health Care
9933 Lawler
Skokie, IL 60077-5702
708-676-9610

Accreditation should not be seen as an absolute guarantee of high quality, but it is a place to start.

Here are more shopping tips as you browse through these dental clinics in search of one that fits your dental health needs and your pocketbook:

▶ Call the Better Business Bureau in your community to see if previous complaints have been filed against the clinic. The bureau will not be able to give you details, but at least you will find out if other consumers have had problems there.

▶ Call your state's dental licensing board (see appendix C, pp. 406–10). Even though the dentists in the clinic are not practicing in a traditional setting, they still must hold valid dental licenses, and you can verify that this is indeed the case.

▶ Ask if there is continuity of care at the clinic. In other words, can you see the same dentist every time, if you wish, or must you be shuffled from one to another. (Keep in mind that you may have to give up the walk-in convenience of some clinics for the privilege of seeing the same dentist time and again.)

▶ Ask if the clinic accepts any dental insurance plans. If it does not, or if you are not on a plan, then be sure to determine what financial arrangements the clinic will work out.

OTHER SETTINGS: KEEP AN EYE ON THE CARE AND A HAND ON YOUR WALLET

The old-fashioned medicine show was quite an experience in marketing. Some huckster would stand at the back of a wagon in an area where people normally gathered—like a town square or main street. Many people were immediately attracted by the wagon itself, deco-

STEP RIGHT UP

Not long ago I was contacted by a People's Medical Society member who complained of her dissatisfaction with one of the world's best-known pain clinics. She told how she spent $12,000 for a three-week treatment program (about average for the place) and came away not only poorer but also without pain relief. And that's not all—after they took her money, the doctors at this university-sponsored facility told her that her pain was really in her head, that they never claimed they would cure her, and that they were interested only in helping her manage to live with the pain. For twelve grand I could think of a lot more enjoyable ways to live with pain!

This put-upon woman sent us a series of newspaper articles on this world-class pain clinic that revealed a high level of dissatisfaction among former patients. We also received testimony from a hearing held in the Washington state legislature (the clinic is in Seattle), where the manager of psychological services for the state Department of Labor and Industry, after conducting an investigation of its own, said: "We found that the injured workers had very high expectations that their pain problems would be cured as a result of the pain program. This is not surprising, but is likely to result in dissatisfaction if the expectation is not met."

He went on to testify that "the thrust of a pain clinic is not to treat or eliminate chronic pain.... Instead its purpose is to provide injured workers with an opportunity to learn how to cope more successfully with pain that may persist the rest of their lives and to become more active and productive."

Sounds like a "Step right up" routine to me. Here's a renowned institution with a renowned faculty asking a person or his insurer to fork over $12,000 so that the person can be taught to cope. Come off it!

Pain clinics are not the only examples of modern-day medicine shows. Fertility clinics are another example. The record shows that many have never successfully brought a baby into this world. Among those in the fertility "business," a 20 percent success rate is considered a great accomplishment. Yet these places—often with fancy or official-sounding names—are themselves multiplying by leaps and bounds.

On a recent trip to Florida I drove down U.S. Highway 19 and saw signs for a clinic specializing in the knee; I saw another clinic housed in a gorgeous building with a fancy title proclaiming its exclusive practice of lens implantation. And there is not a city in America where some enterprising gynecologist has not put a sign out in front of his office that says something like "The Women's Health Center," with the doctor's name in small print underneath.

The point is simple. The old-fashioned medicine show never really left us. Today, instead of wagons, the hucksters have buildings. Instead of painted signs on the side, they have official-sounding titles and place ads on television, on radio, and in newspapers.

Of course, not all doctors are involved. Many of these programs, practices, and clinics are legitimate. But the old "Buyer Beware" warning must be remembered over and over again. The difference between the 1890s and the 1990s is only the degree of sophistication. The bottom line is just the same: someone is trying to get your money into his pocket. So, step right up, but be careful.

Charles B. Inlander
From "2nd Opinion," *People's Medical Society Newsletter*

rated on the side with pictures of healthy-looking people, bottles of special "medicines," and claims of relief and even cure.

The huckster himself was a smooth talker, usually dressed in a slick suit implying professorship or other scholarly attributes. Sometimes he would even call himself "Doctor." He began his pitch with the words "Step right up," and from there he proceeded to sell his elixir, "guaranteed" to cure what ailed you. Despite the fact that most of these patent medicine products were little more than water and alcohol, plenty of people would swear by the stuff. Either the stupor brought on by the alcohol or the placebo effect of taking something called medicine worked for these folks. But the majority of people discovered that the only result of buying the concoction was that they were a buck or two poorer.

Today, about a hundred or so years beyond the medicine-show days, we are witnessing another example of hucksterism. It's "Step right up" again, but this time it is being perpetrated on an unsuspecting public by people with legitimate medical degrees who are often affiliated with renowned universities or medical schools.

A Setting Fertile for Misrepresentation

In vitro fertilization made big news for the first time in England in the 1970s with the birth of Louise Brown, the first baby to start life outside a mother's womb. You may know the phenomenon by its popular name—test-tube babies—and if you're like many people, you probably take the technology for granted. But the fact is that at up to $7,000 per fertilization attempt, the procedure is an expensive last resort for infertile couples. And if the procedure is unsuccessful—that is, does not result in a live birth, which is very often the case—that's a lot of money to pay to have your heartfelt hopes dashed.

How do you know whether the clinic you've chosen can deliver? For the last decade there has been a lack of clear, unbiased information about the performance of in vitro fertilization clinics, but consumers now have their best information so far on the track record of infertility clinics that use high-technology techniques to produce babies. The information comes from the first national survey of such clinics released in 1989 by the House Subcommittee on Regulation, Business Opportunities, and Energy. Its findings, in brief: clinics offering in vitro fertilization services to infertile couples vary widely in success rates. The congressional report also said that some of the clinics "overstate" in their advertisements their success rates of resultant births. According to a March 10, 1989 *New York Times* article, of the 165 surveyed clinics that said they perform in vitro fertilization, the average reported success rate—measured in live births—was 11 percent for 1987 and 1988 "when using a conservative way of calculating these figures." The article goes on to recount the testimony of fertility experts who call these figures realistic, "even if slightly too conservative. But some clinics advertise rates up to three times higher . . . or cite other figures that imply greater success, such as using resulting pregnancies instead of live births."

Success can be measured in a number of ways, say the experts. Some clinics count egg retrieval, and others point to fertilization of embryos. But the number of live births is considered one of the best measures of success.

Another area of concern raised by the survey is the lack of regulation. The Federal Trade Commission and other government and professional organizations provide little if any oversight of in vitro fertilization practices, practices being performed in a variety of settings, from giant university medical complexes to single-doctor offices.

Copies of the congressional survey are in depository libraries throughout the country. To get the name of the one nearest you, contact your local library. If you wish, you may purchase a copy of the survey for $31 from the Government Printing Office at the following address:

Superintendent of Documents
Congressional Sales Office
U.S. Government Printing Office
North Capitol and H Streets, N.W.
Washington, DC 20401
202-275-2170

If you are considering using the services of a fertility clinic, what can you do to get the best care for your investment of time, money, and emotion? An article in the March 28, 1989 *Washington Post Health* (a weekly tabloid supplement) summarized experts' recommendations:

▶ Find a clinic with a board-certified endocrinologist on staff.

▶ Ask about the doctor's training in in vitro fertilization: how many procedures performed and when and where trained.

▶ Don't be fooled by membership in professional societies. According to the article, "Membership in the American Fertility Society connotes an interest—not special expertise or training—in fertility problems." At this time there are no special credentials or standards required for a doctor to perform any infertility treatment.

▶ Find out the clinic's success rate for the particular infertility problem you have. And, because some women are misdiagnosed and undergo an unnecessary procedure, find a clinic that performs a complete physical examination first, before in vitro fertilization is attempted.

▶ Search for a clinic that has a counseling referral service or itself offers psychological counseling for infertile couples.

▶ Ask about the clinic's payment schedule and whether it accepts insurance payment. Sliding-scale fees—that is, based on ability to pay—are desirable. As to insurance coverage, a March 5, 1989 *New York Times* article reported that less than half of for-profit health insurance companies pay for in vitro fertilization, but seven states—Arkansas, Connecticut, Hawaii, Maryland, Massachusetts, Rhode Island, and Texas—do require insurance companies to cover infertility treatments, including in vitro fertilization.

The proliferation of in vitro fertilization clinics nationwide is a perfect case in point of what a cash cow reproductive medicine has become. But there are plenty of other settings that cater exclusively to women.

Woman Care:
Woman, Beware

Hospitals and doctors are wooing women. Women are the latest marketing targets, not only for themselves and the fact that they account for more than half of all physician visits—the two most commonly performed surgical procedures, cesarean section and hysterectomy, are of course performed only on women—but also for their purchasing power: women are the primary health care decision-makers for their families.

When hospital admissions and lengths of stay began to drop some years back, bottom-line–conscious hospital administrators combed the medical issues of the day for potential revenue enhancers. They found ambulatory surgery, cardiac rehabilitation, and substance abuse. Now, with the influx of women into the work force, the consequences of delayed childbearing, women's need for health care that extends beyond the reproductive system, and the unquestionable fact that women are a powerful consumer population, hospitals and doctors are looking to women's medicine to fill empty beds and replenish coffers.

What a hospital must do to survive. That's the pervasive attitude among medical magnates toward women's health programs. Just read the trade literature if you doubt it. Or take a look at these figures: in its annual poll of two thousand hospital administrators, the American Hospital Association found that women's medicine ranked fourth in 1988 among the so-called biggest winners—that is, those services generating a profit or breaking even for at least 75 percent of the surveyed hospitals (*Medical Economics,* March 6, 1989). A third of the nation's hospitals have women's centers, either freestanding or within the hospital (*Medical Economics,* May 1, 1989), and 12 percent more plan to add such services in the near future.

Clearly, women's medicine is a growing venture. The medical system has made womanhood a disease and has packaged services to diagnose and treat it.

All too often, the lure is educational programs. You know the scene: friendly lunchtime or evening seminars with medical professionals who hold Dale Carnegie Institute certificates and speak on the latest diagnosis, "working women's stress," mood disorders in women, sports gynecology, or some such topic.

What they call education is really marketing. And what they call education may be useful, but its ultimate purpose is to entice you to purchase the other services the hospital has to offer a person with your condition, womanhood. The question, however, is, are you getting better care, or just more?

Reproductive medicine is at the core of women's medicine. A 1988 American Hospital Association survey, reported in the July 5, 1989 issue of *Hospitals,* found that 85 percent of hospital-affiliated women's centers provide obstetrics, the largest single source of admissions to hospitals in this country. And for that reason the hype for most hospitals' women's centers is primarily aimed at women aged twenty-five to forty-nine, and secondarily women sixty years and older. To lure the older crowd, women's centers trumpet services such as mammography and osteoporosis screening.

Elective cosmetic surgery is another growth industry, with women once again the targets of most of the hype for services ranging from breast implantation and nose reconstruction to liposuction. The environment is highly competitive here, so advertisements are hard-hitting, aiming straight at the heart of the matter—vanity.

Doctors looking to boost their bank accounts have also begun courting women. The ob-gyn who yesterday was regular Dr. Schwartz now has a new sign on his office door—"Woman Care Clinic," or some similar wording—but does not necessarily provide any different services than he did before or provide any better care.

The bottom line here? Womanhood is now a product for sale. Women, beware.

Sports Medicine:
Off and Running

Once sports medicine consisted of standing on the sidelines and examining athletes after they were injured. From a small table in a malodorous locker room to a multimillion-dollar sports "complex"—such as Baylor University's $16-million Tom Landry Sports Medicine and Research Center—sports medicine has come a long, long way.

Essentially, however, whether it's practiced in a huge complex or in a clinic, the components remain the same. Sports medicine encompasses a variety of services aimed at the treatment and prevention of injuries resulting from participation in professional or recreational sports. These services may include any or all of the following: stress testing; supervised exercise programs; strength testing; podiatric evaluations; physical therapy; surgical treatment; and cardiac, pulmonary, or musculoskeletal rehabilitation.

The growth of sports medicine over the last decade has been phenomenal. According to figures compiled by the National Institutes of Health and reported in the February 3, 1989 *American Medical News,* the 17 million amateur athlete injuries that occur every year cost $4 billion to mend. And sports medicine practitioners are right there to pick up the pieces—and the bucks.

In explaining this runaway growth some observers say that sports medicine, similar to health clubs, answers the baby-boom generation's nearly fanatical obsession with fitness. Some say that advances in technology and equipment and increasing knowledge of such procedures as arthroscopy have created an optimum environment for the practice of sports medicine. And still others opine that as the medical marketplace has become more competitive, doctors have been forced to find new and innovative ways to remain in business. Whatever its raison d'être, sports medicine these days may be a doctor's hot ticket to early retirement, in part because it is being marketed to every age group: from the seven-year-old child with a soccer injury to the seventy-year-old woman who wants to join in a seniors' aerobic program.

The question *you* have to ask yourself is, can you get the same service, the same care, at a lower cost, by going to either an orthopedist, a neurologist, a neurosurgeon, a pediatrician, a family practitioner, a chiropractor, a massage therapist, or a physical therapist? What's the difference? Does the sports medicine practitioner have any more experience, skills, or training than any other doctor? Isn't a sprain a sprain, whether it's a result of jogging or falling off a curb?

You should know that as yet there is no board certification for sports medicine. That means that there is no such "recognized" specialty as sports medicine. All a doctor has to do is hang out a shingle that says "Sports Medicine," and he or she is in business. And you, the consumer, have no guarantee that you are getting a quality product.

Keep in mind, too, that doctors are not the only ones vying for a piece of the action. According to the American Hospital Association, 18 percent of hospitals surveyed had established sports medicine facilities and an additional 12 percent were planning to offer such services.

Just make sure that the "special care" sports medicine clinics tout is just that—special, worth every penny you're paying—and not merely an advertising slogan.

Diet Clinics and Weight-Loss Centers:
Making Sure They Take It Off Without
Ripping You Off

If losing weight is your goal, then you are not alone. Just scan the yellow pages under "Weight Control Services" or "Diet Programs," and you'll discover how much in demand such programs are and how competitive the environment has become. Diet clinics and weight-loss centers abound, and even hospitals are marketing their own outpatient diet programs. Clearly, everyone wants a piece of the action—in 1989 Americans spent around $33 billion on diets and diet-related products—so you've got a lot of choices, different approaches, and varying prices.

All well and good, except for one important point. To avoid the rip-offs that go with the territory—and these programs can cost you big bucks—you will have to shop carefully. Without a thorough scrutiny of *any* program, be it hospital-based, doctor-owned, or otherwise, you may end up throwing a lot of money down the garbage disposal.

With so many choices, why not save yourself some time (and avoid the face-to-face hard sell) and do the initial interviewing by phone? That way you can narrow the choices and save the closer look for a personal visit. Here are some shopping tips for getting the most for your money:

▶ Decide whether you want individual counseling or a group approach. The secret to successful dieting is a motivated dieter, and what works for one person may not work for another. Overeaters Anonymous, for instance, pairs a dieter with a nutrition counselor and/or another dieter so that each person can help the others with problems and temptations. Or maybe you'd be better motivated in a group setting. TOPS (Take Off Pounds Sensibly) and Weight Watchers International are two examples of this approach.

▶ Ask under what sort of business arrangement the clinic operates—whether a national franchise or a local one. If there is a chance you'll be moving out of town or out of the state, then perhaps the national name is for you, of course assuming your affiliation will transfer with you. While it's hard to predict the economic success of one over the other, the national franchise may at least be able to financially bolster one of its troubled sites. On the other hand, a locally owned clinic has the advantage of local investors, people with ties to your own community, rather than an absent, faceless corporation.

▶ Ask to speak to the owner, and find out his or her business qualifications for running such a clinic. Are these qualifications sound?

▶ Find out the costs of the program and whether there are hidden costs for books, supplements, etc. Some programs charge as much as $50 a week for food supplies, not including the enrollment fees and charges for counseling services, medical testing, and supervision that many programs tack on. Ask what sort of payment schedule the clinic demands. Up-front? Weekly? Payment based on weight to be lost? Success of weight loss? As a general rule, you would be wise to stay away from programs demanding payment in advance of treatment. Watch out for long-term contracts and lifetime memberships too. If the clinic folds, you're stuck, with probably no way to recoup your money.

▶ Read the fine print in the agreement contract. Determine the exact nature of any rebate or guarantee—for instance, you get a rebate if you lose a specific number of pounds within a certain period. Under what circumstances is this provision null and void? Check with the Office of Consumer Protection to find out if your state has a "cooling-off period" for diet center contracts. This means that you can cancel your contract within a set number of working days and receive a full refund of any deposit.

▶ Check with your health insurance carrier before signing up for any program, especially if your weight loss is directly related to another health problem. Coverage may also depend on where you go for counseling—for instance, it may be limited to a hospital outpatient setting.

▶ Avoid the diet programs that use hard-sell or scare tactics such as appeals to your worst fears or anxieties about your health.

▶ Be wary of grandiose promises such as "Our program will cure whatever ails you," "Burn off body fat as you sleep," or "You'll live longer if you follow our diet plan." These statements, and others that promise magic cures and shortcuts, are sensational and misleading.

▶ Ask whether the program sells its own pills, liquids, powders, or food, which you must buy. Because they suppress the appetite, diet pills do work for many people, but usually for only as long as the supply lasts. Furthermore, the side effects associated with diet pills—including insomnia, anxiety, and heart palpitations—range from the merely unpleasant to the severe. Also, you should be aware that some diets using liquid formulas have led to serious health problems and even death for some people, according to a report in Susan R. Holman's *Essentials of Nutrition for the Health Professions* (Philadelphia: Lippincott, 1987). Be on the lookout for a possible conflict of interest in any diet program that pushes its own products.

▶ Ask to see sample diet plans. Are they well balanced or too strict? Many experts contend that diets below 1,000 to 1,200 calories a day for women and 1,800 for men need close medical supervision. Also keep in mind that the stricter and more rigid the diet, the harder it is to follow consistently and, therefore, successfully. Ask yourself whether you can live with this plan for, say, six months or more. If not, then why waste the money?

▶ Scrutinize the staff of the clinic and their credentials. Some programs are under the full-time supervision of a physician; others use the services of a licensed physician on a part-time or consulting basis only. In either case, what are the doctor's credentials? Knowledge of nutrition? Is there a registered nurse there? Don't be fooled by an office with a clinical or quasi-medical look or by a white-uniformed staff. Go beyond the program's superficial trappings and ask pointed questions about education, licenses, and credentials. You are looking for hard evidence that these people are trained, educated, and experienced in nutrition and diet plans.

▶ If you can, talk to people who have been through the program. Go beyond the salesperson's testimonies and the pictures on the wall, and try to get the names of people so that you can get their stories firsthand.

▶ Call the Better Business Bureau to find out if the clinic has had any complaints filed against it.

Remember, there is no magic formula to weight loss. Don't allow yourself to be tricked into something that will do you more harm than good.

MANAGED HEALTH CARE: WHAT CAN IT DO FOR YOU?

Around the time that health care spending rose to double the consumer price index, and accounted for over 10 percent of the gross national product, employers desperately began seeking ways to cut their annual tabs for employee health care. The direction their respective gazes took was to a concept called managed health care. While the impetus came from a combination of business and government efforts to restrain the mounting costs of health care, the concept was fueled in part by the willingness of at least a portion of the public to exchange some freedom of choice in health care decisions for lower costs and increased benefits.

And that is a fairly apt description of what managed health care offers you, the consumer. Managed-care plans are sometimes referred to as alternative delivery systems, which simply means alternatives to the traditional fee-for-service system.

Unlike traditional health insurance in which you pay a deductible—a fixed amount of your health care costs before coverage kicks in—and also share in the cost of services through copayments, managed health care is a prepaid health plan that combines a medical insurance program with a medical service delivery system. In other words, managed-care plans insure you *and* provide the care.

If you are in the dark about all of this, the time to learn the rudiments of managed-care plans is *now*—as the popularity of these plans increases every year and more employers drop traditional insurance entirely and offer managed-care plans or nothing. Understanding the nuances takes time, but it's worth the effort, given the trend for employers to view health care as an employee benefit, not an employee right. Now, more than ever before, getting the most for your medical dollar is imperative.

The major players in the game are health maintenance organizations and preferred-provider organizations.

Health Maintenance Organizations (HMOs)

Health maintenance organizations (HMOs), no longer the obscure alternative to conventional group medical insurance plans they once were, now boast 32 million subscribers nationwide. Likely to be multistate operations owned by large businesses, HMOs come in a variety of forms, but with some elements in common:

HMO members (usually called subscribers) receive comprehensive medical care for a fixed (or prepaid, meaning paid before you receive the services) monthly premium. The plan generally covers physician fees and services, hospitalization and surgery, home health care, outpatient surgery, some nursing home services, and preventive care such as routine checkups and immunizations.

The services are provided by an organized group of medical professionals who receive a fixed monthly payment per subscriber, regardless of the services rendered (or not rendered, whatever the case may be). In essence, the HMO requires that physicians live within a budget, because the HMO receives the same payment per subscriber per month regardless of the medical and hospital services used. If the services provided to the subscriber group exceed the monthly budget, then the HMO loses money. As you can see, this runs counter to the traditional fee-for-service system, which in effect encourages overutilization: the more services a physician provides or orders, the bigger the payment.

Subscribers, for the most part, are limited to those physicians, hospitals, and other medical providers approved by the HMO. In the classic HMO plan, you agree to give up an unlimited choice of doctors in exchange for economical health care. The first thing you do is choose a primary care physician (either a family practitioner, general practitioner, pediatrician, internist, or obstetrician-gynecologist) from the HMO's selected list. You receive all medical care from that doctor, who also decides whether you get a test or procedure, see a specialist, or go into the hospital. In HMO jargon this physician is your "gatekeeper" to the rest of the medical system.

This idea of being locked into the approved list of providers has discouraged many people from joining HMOs, but, according to a July 9, 1989 *Chicago Tribune* article, as many as a quarter of the nation's 643 HMOs now offer subscribers the opportunity to go to non-HMO doctors under certain circumstances.

Be aware, however, that freedom may carry a price tag. It is quite possible that when you use doctors outside the HMO network you will be required to pay a part of your medical bill (similar to a copayment in a traditional plan) and perhaps even meet a set dollar amount (in other words, a deductible) before the HMO will begin cost-sharing.

On the other hand, if you find this lock-in provision daunting and downright discouraging, bear in mind one important fact: classic free-choice plans—you choose who to go to and your company pays—are vanishing. In 1988 the Health Insurance Association of America reported that only 28 percent of all insurance plans fit this description. So any squeamishness about joining an HMO solely because of a "lock-in" restriction may be unnecessary as fewer and fewer plans of any kind—traditional or managed care—offer free choice.

HMOs are organized in several ways:

Staff model. The HMO hires physicians to work on a salary-plus-bonus basis at the HMO's own multispecialty clinic or hospital. They see only HMO subscribers. The classic organizational model for an HMO, the staff model is the progenitor of all other plans.

Group model. The HMO contracts with separately incorporated physician groups whose practitioners see only HMO subscribers but who continue to practice in their own offices or clinics.

Individual practice association (IPA). The HMO contracts with private practice physicians who agree to see some HMO subscribers along with their regular fee-paying patients in their own offices or clinics. Now the most popular HMO model, the IPA has grown more rapidly than any other type in recent years. One explanation proffered for this unprecedented rise is the heated competition between private practitioners and HMOs, resulting in physicians forming their own HMOs or joining existing ones.

Network model. The HMO contracts with two or more independent group practices, generally unrelated and located in different geographical locations. Along with the HMO subscribers, the physicians continue to see their regular fee-paying patients.

Preferred-Provider Organizations (PPOs)

A preferred-provider organization is a group of physicians and hospitals that contract with insurance companies, unions, or employers to provide health care at negotiated fees. In return, the "preferred" group is guaranteed a volume of patients. While a subscriber can use "outside" physicians and hospitals, there are compelling economic incentives to stay within the preferred group: reduced copayments and deductibles, a broader range of services, and simplified claims processing.

Medicare HMOs

Only since 1985 have HMOs been interested in enrolling significant numbers of older Americans. That year the Health Care Financing Administration (HCFA) opened the door for Medicare beneficiaries to enroll in HMOs. It also became possible for retiring employees who already belong to HMOs through their employers to retire into Medicare HMO programs. If you are nearing or already at Medicare age, you need to know some facts unique to Medicare HMO programs:

HMO Medicare coverage is a supplement to, not a substitute for, your Medicare coverage. When you join the HMO, you do not give up your Medicare Part A hospital insurance or Part B medical insurance coverage. You continue to pay your Part B premium as you always did and continue to be covered. The HMO program is supplemental, or "wrap-around" insurance, which covers the costs of hospital and/or medical services not covered by Medicare. Think of an HMO plan as competing with other Medicare supplemental insurance plans for your business. You do not have to give up Medicare to join an HMO, nor do you give up any part of your monthly Social Security check to an HMO.

You may be required to pay the HMO a monthly premium for coverage of hospital and medical expenses over and above basic Medicare coverage. Depending on the costs of medical care in your area and the particular HMO and options you pick, the individual HMO premium may be as high as $100 a month, or in some cases there is no premium at all. Some company retirement plans contribute to the HMO monthly payments. An HMO premium may seem high, but you should remember that you are likely to spend 15 percent or more of your annual income on medical care. The premium, in contrast to traditional

Medicare supplemental insurance, picks up many out-of-pocket expenses that you would otherwise have to pay. The proper comparison of two insurance plans is always this: *Compare premiums plus out-of-pocket costs for one plan to premiums plus out-of-pocket costs for the other.*

The Medicare HMO plan will cover all basic Medicare services and some additional services, usually including:

▶ Deductible for hospital and skilled nursing services

▶ Deductible and copayment for physician services in hospital and office settings

▶ Diagnostic and rehabilitation services and prescription drugs (sometimes an extra fee)

You will receive all your medical and hospital care from the HMO delivery system. So be sure you understand the HMO and are comfortable with its benefits and limitations.

An HMO cannot deny you membership because of any medical condition, unless you have end-stage renal disease (chronic kidney failure) or are receiving hospice benefits. Furthermore, HMOs cannot require you to have a medical examination as a condition of enrollment.

If you join the HMO and don't like it, you may withdraw at any time for any reason and return to your previous Medicare benefits. To withdraw you simply fill out a withdrawal form, which can take up to sixty days to process. Until you receive a letter clearly indicating reinstatement in Medicare, you are still covered by the HMO for all medical care needs. An HMO can drop you only if you move out of its service area or if it documents that you are completely uncooperative with its administrative rules—for example, you don't pay your monthly premium, or you permit misuse of your membership card.

All your medical and hospital claims will be sent to the HMO to process and pay on your behalf. Although you will have to pay for a few services as specified in your HMO contract, most will be handled on your behalf. Periodically, you will receive a printout from the HMO of all claims paid during the period.

CONCERNING MEDICARE HMOS: A FEW CAUTIONS

▶ Carefully consider the benefits that will be provided by the HMO. Do
they equal or exceed what you presently receive through Medicare
Parts A and B and your Medicare supplemental insurance?

▶ Do you have a choice in the selection of your primary care
physician? Are you required to give up your present physician if you
join the HMO?

▶ Does the monthly fee or premium you would pay to the HMO equal
or exceed the cost of your Medicare supplemental insurance?

▶ Do you fully understand the procedures for enrolling in and
withdrawing from the HMO?

IS AN HMO THE BEST
SETTING FOR YOU?

The array of insurance plans available to the average American,
employed or not, may be bewildering at times. Do you go HMO?
PPO? Or IPA? Maybe traditional health insurance is for you? Fee-
for-service or prepaid? Rather than land mines with the potential
to blow your budget to smithereens, think of the myriad of options
as opportunities to get the most for your medical dollar. The good
news here is that doctors, hospitals, and insurance companies are
fiercely competing for your business. They need you. And you need
to find the highest-quality medical care at the most reasonable cost.

It is possible to make an informed choice—simply follow the
steps outlined here to consider *eligibility*, *coverage*, and *costs*. But first
keep in mind these guidelines:

▶ The only purpose of health insurance is to protect you and
your family against large out-of-pocket medical expenses.

▶ HMOs usually offer more comprehensive hospital and
medical benefits than traditional health insurance, without
the costly deductibles and copayments. HMOs can save
you money—up to 28 percent—compared with

conventional health insurance. Your premiums may be a little less or about the same. And HMO subscribers do not submit claims, so there is little or no paperwork to complete.

▶ The biggest drawbacks we have touched on already: the lock-in restriction whereby subscribers can use only designated providers, and the fact that a physician's authorization (the "gatekeeper" philosophy again) is needed before nonemergency services to have the HMO cover the cost of such services. As to problems with convenience and care, anecdotes abound: there's been talk of out-of-the-way, inconveniently located offices and clinics; long waits for appointments; superficial, even perfunctory examinations; and the tendency to undertreat problems by limiting access to expensive diagnostic tests.

Now to what you need to consider before you make an informed choice.

Eligibility

Nearly everyone joins an HMO through an employer, and HMOs market primarily to companies with at least ten employees. Check with your personnel office or supervisor if you're not sure whether an HMO is offered. While you probably have no control over which HMO your employer asks you to join, you usually do get to say yes or no. During the annual "open enrollment" period, you can choose whether to stay enrolled in your current health insurance plan or sign up with an HMO or PPO. If you become dissatisfied with your choice, you probably will not be able to change until the next year's enrollment period.

Coverage

The government requires federally qualified HMOs to cover a comprehensive range of benefits; HMOs that are not federally qualified have no such requirement. So first check to see if the HMO you are considering is federally qualified, and if it is, these benefits will be covered:

▶ All hospital inpatient services with no limits on costs or days

▶ Hospital outpatient diagnostic and treatment services, including rehabilitation services, with some limitations

▶ Skilled nursing home and home health services

▶ Short-term detoxification for substance abuse

▶ Medical treatment and referral for alcohol and drugs

▶ Preventive care

To get a list of federally qualified HMOs throughout the country, write:

Department of Health and Human Services
Office of Prepaid Health Care
HCFA Office of Compliance
Security Boulevard
Baltimore, MD 21207
410-966-7626

Other services are not required but may be covered if the HMO so chooses: prescription drugs; vision care; dental care; long-term rehabilitation; intermediate nursing care; durable medical equipment; prosthetics; and chiropractic care. HMOs often offer a prescription drug or vision care "rider" separate from the main policy and at additional cost. Only a few HMOs cover dental care.

If the plan is a PPO or nonqualified HMO, and therefore without benefit requirements, check the benefit package. Be aware that some HMOs are beginning to offer "low-option plans," with deductibles, copayments, and fewer benefits—in short, return to concepts similar to those in traditional health insurance.

Costs

You must consider two types of expenses when estimating the total cost of your health insurance: the monthly premium contribution you pay regardless of the amount of services you use and the out-of-pocket costs you pay based on services you use.

First, determine what your annual premium contribution will be if you join an HMO rather than a traditional plan. It may be zero if your employer chooses to pay the full premium. According to a Health Insurance Association of America survey, the average monthly premiums in 1988 for the various types of plans stacked up as follows:

SINGLE (OR INDIVIDUAL) COVERAGE

Traditional plan	$98
IPA/HMO	$88
Staff/Group HMO	$93
PPO	$103

FAMILY COVERAGE

Traditional plan	$209
IPA/HMO	$226
Staff/Group HMO	$203
PPO	$232

There's also the matter of copayments. According to a survey by a Minnesota-based research firm, InterStudy, the average 1989 required copayments for five benefits were: $7.22 for office visits; $4.88 for prescription drugs; $33.31 for emergency room services; $18.58 for urgent care services; and $21.91 for mental health benefits (*Modern Healthcare,* September 15, 1989).

Next, examine all the important medical and hospital services not covered or only partially covered by the HMO and traditional plans, and liberally estimate what your annual out-of-pocket costs will be. Your annual expense under each plan will be a combination of your premium contribution and your estimated out-of-pocket expenses.

CLAIMS PROCEDURE

Depending upon how enamored you are of paperwork and bookkeeping, the matter of how claims are filed may be an important consideration in choosing an HMO or PPO over a traditional plan. HMOs and PPOs do all the claims filing, with the providers themselves sending all their bills directly to the head office. You are freed from figuring out and filling out claim forms. On a periodic basis the HMO sends you an "estimation of benefits" report, which lists all the services the HMO paid on your behalf.

You may find that the HMO is a good buy, and the PPO only slightly better than traditional health insurance. Important to note is the fact that the amount an HMO saves you increases as you use more medical services. In other words, the cost advantage of HMOs becomes evident when you most need to depend on your medical insurance—when you or someone in your family suffers a serious accident or illness.

HMO MEDICAL CARE AND THE QUESTION OF QUALITY

After all the scribbling and calculating we have had you do regarding matters of eligibility and cost, now sharpen your pencil and get ready to tackle the question of quality. At this point you may have concluded that an HMO provides excellent benefits at an economical cost, but that you will join the HMO only if it provides medical care that is as good as or better than what you now receive.

Regarding the obvious question—HMO quality versus fee-for-service plan quality—let us say this. The results of various studies over the last twenty-five years can be summed up in one sentence: there is no evidence that you will end up healthier or sicker by being treated in an HMO system as opposed to the traditional system. Just as there are good *and* bad fee-for-service providers, the same holds true for HMO providers.

What is quality medical care? In our opinion it includes these elements:

▶ *Technically competent medical treatment* provided by properly trained and credentialed professionals in clean, modern, well-equipped facilities

▶ *Accessible and convenient services* provided without bureaucratic hassles or unreasonable delays

▶ *Personal care* respectful of the dignity and intelligence of you and your family

▶ *Coordinated care* in which your primary care physician links all specialty or hospital services you need into one sensible treatment plan

▶ *Measurement of the results of treatment* to evaluate whether the medical system achieves its goal of curing your illness, relieving your pain, or assisting in your rehabilitation

MORE QUESTIONS YOU SHOULD ASK

Believe it or not, you're not yet ready to decide whether an HMO is the best setting for your medical care until you have more information in hand:

Is the HMO the multispecialty-clinic type or office-based?   You may want the convenience of a large facility where you can visit your primary physician, consult a specialist, have your laboratory or radiology tests done, and go to the pharmacy—all under one roof. Or you may want the quieter, more personal confines of a physician's private office, especially if you have an established rapport with this physician.

How long has the HMO been in business?   A number of HMOs, particularly in oversupplied cities, are in failing financial health, so an HMO's experience is a critical point. Two or three years may be adequate, but less than that is probably not.

Is the HMO the entity you will want to treat you when you are sick?   Whether it's a clinic or a private office, visit the facility and observe closely. Do the physical environment and medical equipment look clean, modern, and cared for? Do the staff treat patients and visitors courteously and professionally? Does the HMO adhere to its appointment schedule, or are a lot of appointments backed up? Patient confidentiality prevents HMOs from releasing subscribers' names, but ask your friends if they belong to the HMOs in your area. Are they satisfied with the performance?

What is the travel time to the primary care facility and to the hospital? This needs to be considered in anticipation of the time when you or a family member is very sick, and others are having to make repeated trips to visit.

How are appointments for both routine and urgent care made? How long will it take to be seen? If you are sick, you should not have to wait more than a day or two to see your physician, although some HMOs ask people to wait up to a week or two if the medical problem does not require immediate attention.

What do you do when you need emergency care? Ideally, an HMO will want you to use its emergency center or an affiliated hospital's emergency room for immediate treatment. However, as you know (and you hope the HMO realizes) not every emergency situation is so strategically and conveniently orchestrated. Some HMOs (and even some traditional insurance plans) establish complicated rules for their subscribers who seek emergency care during night and weekend hours or away from home (in HMO jargon, "outside the service area"). While it is reasonable and proper to have you call your primary physician first, if that doctor or his or her backups do not respond quickly, you should be able to use the closest available emergency service with full confidence that the HMO will pay the bill. Routine or nonemergency care outside the HMO service area may not be covered.

CHOOSING AN HMO PLAN: SOME FINAL CONSIDERATIONS

Consider your primary care physician. A good relationship with your primary care physician is imperative in an HMO setting, since he or she is the person responsible for all your medical services and the gatekeeper to specialty and hospital care. Ask to interview prospective physicians before joining the HMO. (Most HMOs and PPOs will not allow this until after you have enrolled, but insist upon it.)

What formal qualifications should you look for in selecting the doctor? Even though no amount of analysis is foolproof, a good place to start is the doctor's education and credentials. We also recommend you interview the potential candidate(s) and, at the least, talk about such matters as type of practice, telephone accessibility, commitment to prevention and health promotion, and how the HMO monitors and controls quality of care, among other things. Fortunately, if you are not satisfied with your final choice, it does not have to be final. Any good HMO will allow you to select a different doctor, although some require a month's notice to process the switch.

Consider the backup system of hospital and specialty care. Which hospital(s) will your primary care physician use? Is the hospital a community hospital or a major medical center? What is its reputation for quality and service? Find out if your primary care physician will remain fully involved in your care throughout a hospital stay.

What about specialized hospital or rehabilitation programs? If you need a specialized service (for example, physical rehabilitation or mental health counseling), find out how and with whom the HMO contracts for such services.

What are the HMO's rules about specialty referrals? Look at the HMO physician list and see if all major specialties are represented. Make sure it is the physician's responsibility, not yours, to ensure that the paperwork on referrals from your primary care doctor to specialists is completed.

What formal programs does the HMO have to help assure high-quality care? A good HMO will cover the costs of a second opinion on elective surgery, monitor the necessity of every hospital admission, and track infection, complication, and mortality rates. The HMO will periodically audit their physicians' medical charts and have a rigorous protocol for the investigation of subscriber complaints.

NURSING HOMES: GETTING THE MOST AND BEST FOR YOUR MONEY

You've worked hard all your life to provide for your needs and the comfort and needs of your family. You've worked hard all your life to build up a nest egg and provide a comfortable income for your retirement years, those years of leisure, recreation, volunteer work, or whatever else you so justly earned. What could possibly go wrong in this picture?

For the answer to that question, ask any one of the more than 2.3 million older Americans who live in nursing homes. Ask any one of them how much of his or her nest egg is going toward the monthly nursing home bill. Ask any one of them how much is left over for frills, or even necessities, after paying $22,000 per year (or $1,800 a month), on the average, for nursing home care. (Double or even triple those figures for some homes in certain urban areas.)

Contrary to popular belief, Medicare pays only a tiny fraction of the cost of nursing home care. Most people, says a report in the May 1988 *Consumer Reports,* are not poor when they enter a nursing home but become poor soon after. The fact is that most people are dipping into, and unfortunately wiping out, their retirement incomes. But what else can you do when faced with debilitating ill health that requires long-term care?

Get the most and best for your money, that's what. As difficult as it may seem, you *can* evaluate and choose a nursing home. You *can* get the best medical care for the best price and in the most appropriate setting. And the way to do that is to arm yourself with information and use it to compare facilities.

The term "nursing home" is actually a very general name for several different types of medical care facilities. It has the connotation of being a "last stop" for the elderly, but it actually can be a place for people of all ages to convalesce following an accident or serious illness, or a temporary placement for an elderly person while the family shops around and lines up alternative modes of care.

Nursing homes are for people who have difficulty caring for themselves, and as such provide three basic types of services:

1. *Nursing and medical care*—for example, injections of medications, catheterizations, physical therapy, and other forms of rehabilitative services

2. *Personal care*—for example, assistance in eating, dressing, bathing, and getting in and out of bed

3. *Residential services*—for example, providing a clean room, good food, and a pleasant atmosphere with appropriate social activities

Nursing homes can be classified in many different ways, but two common classifications result from the level of care they provide and the type of ownership.

Levels of Care

Skilled nursing. In a skilled nursing facility, care is delivered by registered and licensed practical nurses on the orders of an attending physician. The person who requires skilled nursing is often bedridden and not able to help himself, and may be placed in the facility for a short or an extended period of time, depending on the prognosis. By the way, skilled nursing facilities are the only type of nursing homes Medicare will reimburse for, and then only a very limited amount of coverage is provided.

Intermediate care. The intermediate care facility provides less intensive care than the skilled facility and usually costs less. Normally not confined to a bed, the resident has a greater degree of mobility. Here too care is delivered by registered and licensed practical nurses and an array of therapists. Intermediate care stresses rehabilitation therapy to enable the resident to go home or at least to regain or retain as many functions of daily living as possible. For people with chronic conditions, the intermediate care facility offers a full range of medical, social, recreational, and support services.

Sheltered, or custodial, care. This level of care is nonmedical in that residents do not require constant attention from nurses or aides, but do need help with such routine activities as getting out of bed, walking, eating, and bathing. The custodial care facility is for people who are capable of independent living but who may require some assistance with personal care and homemaking services.

Ownership

Aside from the obvious matter of the level of care needed, another key point in selecting the right setting is the question of nursing home ownership. Opinions differ as to which type offers the best quality of care, so we do not suggest that you choose or rule out a home based on ownership. Just keep it in mind.

Nonprofit. Operated by various religious, fraternal, charitable, or community groups, nonprofit homes use any cash surpluses they may have to improve operations, purchase new equipment, and so forth. So, when well funded and well managed, these homes can be an excellent choice. Because they are subsidized by their parent organizations, care in these homes may sometimes be less expensive.

For-profit. Also called proprietary nursing homes, for-profit homes are operated specifically to earn a profit for their investors, who may be individuals or corporations. Because these homes are often better funded and more responsive to competitive pressures, some people argue that the care is of a higher quality than that in nonprofit homes. In actuality, the quality of care varies from facility to facility; therefore, we believe that nothing can substitute for your personal observations and judgment.

Public (government) nonprofit. Some local or state governments operate nursing homes offering various levels of care. These homes are classified as public nonprofit institutions because they are funded through the collection of taxes or the sale of municipal bonds. When they are operated by the city or county, they are generally referred to as the city or county home or hospital, and, as such, admissions are usually restricted to local residents.

Things to Consider When Shopping for a Nursing Home

Your first step is to verify any home's licensure status by calling your state's nursing home licensing office (see appendix G, pp. 417–23). But remember, there is absolutely no substitute for your own close, firsthand inspection. Call the homes under consideration for appointments. Make it clear that you not only wish to speak to the administrator but also plan to tour the home. Set aside several hours for each appointment.

Licensing and certification. Find out if the facility is properly licensed and certified. Issued by governmental authority, usually the state, a license means that the home has been inspected and has met certain standards established by law relating to matters such as fire protection, the physical plant, housekeeping, maintenance, and standards of care. Another related matter is certification, as it applies to Medicare and Medicaid payments. If a home applies for certification under either program, it agrees to certain conditions— for example, the home agrees to set aside a certain number of beds for Medicare and Medicaid residents and to accept the prevailing rate paid by these programs, even though it may be less than the normal daily rate.

Building and grounds. Inspect the building and grounds. The physical layout and beauty of the facility should be among the least important considerations, but safety and livability are two of the most important. Regarding safety, things to look for or ask about are: Does the building appear to be fireproof? Are the emergency exits well marked? Are there sufficient smoke detectors? Is fire-fighting equipment—fire extinguishers and a sprinkler system—prominent?

Whether or not a building is livable depends upon things such as convenience, appearance, and the quality of life. Is the outside of the building neat and well maintained? Are there wheelchair ramps? Is there an area where residents can sit outside? Are the corridors wide enough for two wheelchairs to pass easily? Is there enough room in general for the residents? These are just some of the questions to ask.

Rooms. Inspect some of the rooms and observe the comfort they provide, the atmosphere they permit, and their safety. Here you are noting such factors as the amount of light, closet space, and spaciousness in general; whether residents have a choice between single and jointly occupied rooms; the placement of bathrooms and thermostats; whether the beds have screens or curtains for privacy; and so on. Whether all rooms open to a hallway is an important safety consideration in case of fire or the need for prompt nursing or medical attention. Also, are there grab bars by the toilet and bathtub? Do the tubs have nonslip surfaces?

Personnel. Ask about the staff, their credentials, and the availability of key personnel. Does the home's administrator have a current license? Are all the head nurses R.N.'s? Is a physician on the premises for a fixed time each day? On call twenty-four hours a day? Is a registered nurse on duty during the day, seven days a week? Go around to as many sections of the home as possible and observe the staff's demeanor to the residents. Are the staff friendly? Do the residents seem at ease with the staff?

Social and recreational arrangements. Determine if the home has a well-run social and recreational program. Both formal programs—such as social events, religious services on premises, outings, an on-site library and canteen—and atmosphere-related issues along the lines of visiting hours and designated nonsmoking areas can add to the quality of the residents' lives.

Food. Assess the level of sanitation in which the food is prepared and the aesthetic appeal and nutritional value of the final product. Although it may seem like a minor consideration to you, an elderly person's meals are a crucial part of his or her life, and this is especially true of an institutionalized person. Surveys have identified food as the aspect of nursing homes complained about most frequently.

Financial Planning: Can You Afford Nursing Home Care?

Nursing home care is expensive—there is no question about it—and some homes are more expensive than others. So you must determine what you or your family is willing and able to pay. We suggest you screen facilities with this in mind.

How much you can afford to pay may put limits upon your ultimate choice, so your first task is to systematically assess the financial resources available to maintain a placement. Remember, not all these sources of income may be available to the person in question.

Social Security. If the person collects Social Security (or is eligible to as a result of the crisis that precipitated the need for nursing home care), find out the amount of his or her monthly checks.

Other retirement plans. Do the same for the person's company or other retirement plan.

Private insurance. Some insurance plans cover care in a nursing home under certain circumstances and for varying lengths of time. Read the policy carefully, call the insurance company representative, contact the state insurance commissioner's office, and/or consult an attorney to get all the answers.

In recent years a new type of insurance policy (often termed long-term-care insurance) has cropped up that is specifically designed to cover nursing home stays, and there are now hundreds of different policies offered by scores of insurance companies in every state. The premiums vary, based on your age, services offered, and the length of time covered. The important issues for the potential buyer to consider are whether the cost is worth the benefit, and ultimately, whether you can afford what is often a high premium without harming yourself in other ways.

Bank accounts, stocks, bonds, or other liquid assets. You will need a thorough inventory of all the person's assets, a task that may include an exhaustive search for all relevant documents. Also estimate the monthly income derived from these sources—for example, stock dividends and interest on bank accounts.

Old debts owed to the person. This is not a particularly reliable source of revenue.

Real estate. Usually, this means the house the person is living in, and the options amount to either selling it (sometimes a traumatic step for the person) or renting it. Tread carefully.

Antiques and other valuables. These by themselves generate no income until they are sold, but the hitch is that antiques often hold a special sentimental value to the owner. You must definitely approach this option with caution.

Pledges from other family members. If the person in question has several children or other very close relatives, you should find out how much they are willing to contribute.

Medicaid. Medicaid is an assistance program administered by the state and funded by the federal and state governments. Applications for a determination of Medicaid eligibility are submitted to the local welfare, or public assistance, office. It is not at all unusual for Medicare patients to apply for Medicaid coverage once their skilled nursing benefits have been exhausted. Most long-term skilled and intermediate care nursing home residents usually end up using Medicaid as their source of payments after their personal assets and other insurance have run out.

Medicare. Medicare is a federal health insurance program for people sixty-five years of age and older. Administered by the Social Security Administration through the Health Care Financing Administration, Medicare covers hospitalization, physician services, home health care, and outpatient care, and will pay for skilled nursing care *if certain conditions are met.* You should be aware that Medicare is *not* a long-term solution to paying for nursing home care, because it does not cover intermediate or custodial care, the two most common levels of care required. For further information on the intricacies of Medicare coverage and how to get everything to which you are legally entitled, read the People's Medical Society's book *Medicare Made Easy* (Reading, Mass.: Addison-Wesley, 1991).

Supplemental Security Income (SSI): This is a public assistance program that applies to certain people who are legally blind, are disqualified for work due to physical or mental disability for a twelve-month period, or have severely limited financial resources. Contact your local Social Security or welfare office for more details about the rather complicated eligibility requirements for this assistance.

Union, fraternal, or veteran's benefits. Search for documentation of eligibility for these miscellaneous sources of income and call the relevant organizations to find out if they offer such benefits. Some organizations such as the Odd Fellows, the Masons, and church groups run their own system of nursing homes.

How Medicaid Pays for Nursing Home Care

The Medicaid program covers nursing home care. A state-run program that receives federal funds, Medicaid is intended for the *very* poor who have nowhere else to turn. States make most of the rules, and the trend in recent years has been to make Medicaid requirements more stringent. The old law virtually guaranteed that the spouse who stayed at home would have to impoverish himself or herself to pay for the care of the spouse in the nursing home.

In accordance with changes in Medicare law, these rules went into effect in 1989:

▶ In any month in which a married person is in a nursing home, no income of the at-home spouse is to be considered available to the spouse in the nursing home.

▶ Income is considered the property of the person to whom it is paid. Income paid to both spouses is attributed 50 percent to each.

▶ The home, household goods, and personal effects of both spouses are not counted in considering Medicaid eligibility.

▶ All assets other than these will be counted and divided in two. If the at-home spouse has less than $12,000, the spouse in the nursing home may transfer assets to him or her to make up to $12,000 available to the at-home spouse. (States may, at their option, raise this figure to any amount less than $60,000. The $12,000 amount will be indexed to inflation.)

▶ The assets that remain in the name of the spouse in the nursing home are considered available to pay for his or her nursing home care. All assets in excess of $60,000 are attributed to the spouse in the nursing home and are considered available to pay for nursing home care.

▶ States must allow nursing home residents to retain certain sums for medical expenses not covered by Medicare or Medicaid before contributing to the expense of their nursing home care. The states may place "reasonable limits" on the amounts spent.

▶ The states must allow the at-home spouse sufficient income
from the other spouse to bring total household income of
the at-home spouse to at least 122 percent of the federal
poverty level for a two-person household. Until July 1,
1991, this will be $789 per month. At that time it will be
raised to 133 percent of the poverty level, and to 150
percent on July 1, 1992. States will not be required to allow
more than $1,500 per month, except by court order or a
change in regulations.

These requirements dramatically reduce the economic stress on
the spouse who remains at home, but they still require him or her
to part with large amounts of income and assets. Your spouse or
parents do not *actually* have to give anything toward the cost of your
care, but your *eligibility* is determined as though they do. Exact
requirements for eligibility vary from state to state, so check with
your state Medicaid office (see appendix K, pp. 441–47.)

You are automatically eligible for Medicaid if you are eligible for,
or are receiving, Supplemental Security Income payments for the
aged, blind, and disabled, but you must apply at a state welfare
office. If you meet the requirements for SSI, there is little chance that
you would have to give up additional income or assets to qualify
for Medicaid.

If your income, minus certain deductibles and medical bills, is
within certain (low) limits, you may be eligible for Medicaid as
medically needy. You must "spend down" to pay medical bills to
the point at which you are eligible; after that, Medicaid pays for all
of them as long as you are eligible.

Don't misunderstand! You do not have to pay off all your medical
bills in order to get Medicaid to pay for future ones. The requirement for the medically needy spend-down is that you have *incurred*
enough medical expenses so that your income, minus allowances
and the medical bills, is less than the income limit for eligibility.
Medicaid pays all the bills, both current and future, if you meet this
test, have assets under the asset limit, and meet other requirements,
such as age and residency, your state may impose.

How do you apply for Medicaid? Applications are taken at local
welfare offices, but many states also take them at senior centers,
agencies on aging, and other locations. Call the Medicaid office in
your state.

Generally, you should bring proof of age, financial status, and
any disability you may have. The proof of financial status should
include the last six months' bank statements for checking and sav-

ings accounts, rent or mortgage payment receipts, loan papers for your car or the title to do it, any documents relating to stock or bond ownership, and check stubs for any regular payments you receive. You should also have the amount of your Social Security check, if you are currently receiving such payments. You should always have your Social Security number. Bring your medical bills, or copies of them, for the last year.

Financial planning can become quite complicated. The estimates of resources available must be tailored to the individual terms of the nursing homes you are considering. Some homes require larger down payments than others, and some have relatively lower monthly fees. Once you deduct the amount of the down payment from the assets, then you can determine how much monthly income the remaining assets will produce. But don't forget that you must also deduct any debts owed.

You may find it helpful to consult an accountant or financial planner. If you do not know where to find such a person, consult your state's nursing home ombudsman office (see appendix H, pp. 424–28).

QUICK CHECKLIST OF QUESTIONS FOR NURSING HOME ADMINISTRATORS

Even before you spend your time going around to various nursing homes, touring them, and interviewing the administrators, you should conduct phone interviews to establish a base of information on which to build. Find out:

1. What level of care is offered?

2. Are there special restrictions on the types of patients accepted?

3. How many beds (for the type of care you need) does the home provide?

4. Is there a waiting list, and, if so, approximately how long is it?

5. What type of license or accreditation does the home have?

6. Does the home accept Medicare and Medicaid?

7. Is there an initial deposit required, and, if so, how much is it?

8. What are the monthly room charges?

9. Are additional monthly services provided? What are their charges?

A FEDERAL GUIDE TO NURSING HOMES CAN HELP
IN YOUR DECISION

In December of 1988 the Health Care Financing Administration released a seventy-five-volume, state-by-state guide to the nation's 15,000
nursing homes. This massive report tabulates the performance of nursing
homes in all aspects considered important to consumers who are trying to
choose a good home. Each home was "graded" on thirty-two key measures
of the quality of care—ranging from cleanliness and privacy to prompt
care of bedsores and proper administration of medication—and the home's
success in meeting federal standards in these areas. At the time this report
first appeared, the agency promised annual updates.

Officially called *Medicare/Medicaid Nursing Home Information,* the
guide is available for purchase, but a more practical solution is to check
with your public library, local Medicare or Medicaid office, state welfare
office, or any groups that serve the elderly. Even some nursing homes may
keep copies on hand, and if a home doesn't or its representatives refuse
to discuss the findings, maybe that should tell you something.

MONEY-SAVING TIPS

$ If you need nursing home care, arrange for the lowest level
necessary. There are three levels of nursing home
care—skilled, intermediate, and custodial. Skilled care is the
most expensive because care is provided primarily by
qualified nurses.

$ Check to see if the nursing home accepts Medicare. Just as
with any other medical provider, you must ask to make
sure that the nursing home accepts Medicare payments and
any other insurance coverage you may have. Or you may
find yourself facing costs way beyond your ability to pay.

ALTERNATIVES TO
NURSING HOMES

Long a concern among policymakers, the nation's overemphasis on nursing home–based care rather than home or other community-based care is a growing problem. The fact is, nursing home placement is not, and should not be, the sole solution to the plight of an elderly person who is debilitated by ill health and who has increasing difficulty taking care of himself or herself. Nothing mandates nursing home placement if there is someone available to administer the needed care in the home or to coordinate delivery of alternative services. Humane and relatively inexpensive alternatives are out there if you know what they are and where to look.

The first thing to do is to take stock of the person's needs and attempt to match those needs with the alternative forms of care available in your area. Good sources of information on what your community has to offer are the local telephone directory, the office on aging, the welfare office, the visiting nurse association, the United Way office, senior citizen organizations, veteran and fraternal organizations, home health agencies, and the Red Cross.

While there is no way to list all the creative solutions that families have discovered, the following alternatives to nursing home care are the most common and widely used. We have placed them under three broad categories.

Alternatives for People Requiring Constant
Care or Monitoring

Most of these services can be combined with each other as well as with those in the second category.

Adult day care. An adult day care center lets an elderly person enjoy a full range of activities—including arts and crafts, games, and just plain old conversation—on a daily basis in a supervised setting. Nursing care is not provided. Many centers are operated by church groups and senior citizen organizations, and often funded by the United Way.

Ambulatory services. With more and more medical procedures being performed on an outpatient basis, thus saving the costs—and hazards—of an in-hospital stay, outpatient clinics may be a viable option for the person who needs frequent medical care or monitoring that is difficult to provide in the home.

Home health care. This program provides nursing services—from the very basic, such as giving medication, to providing extensive physical or speech therapies—right in the person's home. Home health care, provided on the orders of a doctor or purchased on your own, may be covered under Medicare, as long as certain conditions are met and the agency administering the services is certified. Visiting nurse associations and home health agencies are noted for their work in home care.

Family education. Some agencies—for example, the visiting nurse associations and the Red Cross—and church groups give instruction to the family members who will be caring for the person in need. The skills taught include monitoring vital signs, providing nutritious meals, preventing bedsores, and changing bandages.

Respite care. More for the family or caregiver than the person needing care, respite care simply provides a break for the person who is providing the care and who needs to get out of the house once in a while. Under such a program, someone from the respite agency will come to the home and spend a fixed number of hours there. Some hospitals and nursing homes are getting into this business. They board the person needing care for a specific amount of time and provide round-the-clock care. Medicare coverage for respite care services is limited to a five-day inpatient stay.

Alternatives for More Independent People

A number of excellent programs for elderly people who do not require constant supervision or that much nursing care may actually delay their need for nursing homes for many years.

Homemaker services. The primary purpose of homemaker services is to provide nonmedical support to a homebound person, the ideal candidate being an ambulatory person who maintains a relatively independent life-style but who may require some assistance in the preparation of meals or with housework. Such services are often contracted for by a home health agency and are not covered under Medicare or Medicaid, so other sources of reimbursement must be explored.

Home sharing. Persons who can still get around and take care of themselves may consider home sharing if they are tired of living alone and no longer want to be totally responsible for home maintenance. A typical home-sharing experience finds five to six older people renting a house together and sharing the expenses. The arrangement usually includes a resident manager who attends to day-to-day matters, leaving the residents free for other pursuits. A relatively expensive setup, home sharing is not for everyone. Check your telephone directory for listings such as "Share-a-home."

Meals on Wheels. An excellent program designed to provide hot, nutritious meals to homebound people, Meals on Wheels is usually operated by a social service agency or community group. The service delivers one hot meal a day directly to the person's residence, and the price of such a service is nominal, often based on ability to pay.

Telephone reassurance. For an elderly person living alone, telephone reassurance can take some of the worry out of being alone and can help the person maintain an independent life-style without risking total isolation. If you are elderly, or if you know an elderly person, think about setting up a system of telephone reassurance.

Shopping services. Tailored to the homebound elderly or convalescing person, this program entails having groceries and other needed items delivered. Some senior citizen centers and church groups offer this service.

Special transportation. Special transportation services, with vehicles equipped to handle wheelchairs and other devices, are valuable to people with limited mobility. Check in your telephone directory under county government or under "transportation," or call the Red Cross or other local groups working with handicapped citizens.

Special health aids or devices. Special devices such as walkers, mechanical feeding devices, geriatric chairs, artificial limbs, and orthopedic shoes can facilitate personal independence or make it more feasible for a family member to assist.

Institutional Alternatives

Nursing homes are not the only institutional arrangements for people who cannot or do not wish to be cared for at home. Three of the most common alternatives are:

Adult foster care. This permits a person sixty years of age or older to be placed in a home setting with another person or family, and there receive all the care required. This can be a very useful program for people who do not require intensive nursing care. Contact your local, county, or state office on aging.

Hospice. Hospices are for people who are terminally ill, and the program's hallmarks are control of pain and relief from suffering, as well as preparation for death and support for survivors. The mission of hospices is to inspirit death with dignity and allow the family to maintain close contact with the patient, free from the intrusive high technology of the hospital. Hospice services can be delivered in the home or in a separate facility with a homelike atmosphere. Medicare covers hospice care. Call your local Social Security office for details.

Life care communities. A relatively new concept, these communities provide residential care in an apartment-like setting, along with skilled and intermediate nursing care. As residents require nursing care, they are transferred to the nursing home section of the community, and once they recover return to their apartments. The life care community covers all costs of hospitalization, so, as you can imagine, the services do not come cheap. This option often requires a substantial, nonrefundable down payment as well as monthly fees. An excellent source of information on life care communities is available from the

American Association of Homes for the Aging
1129 20th Street, N.W.
Washington, DC 20036
202-296-5960

Two other groups who may help are:

American Health Care Association
1200 15th Street, N.W.
Washington, DC 20005
202-833-2050

National Consumers League
1522 K Street, N.W., Suite 406
Washington, DC 20005
202-797-7600

MONEY-SAVING TIPS

$ Check the yellow pages for your local visiting nurse association. Visiting nurse associations are the oldest home health care agencies in most communities. They provide services as well as referrals to other community agencies suitable to your needs. Appropriate home services are usually cheaper than institutional services.

$ Use adult day care. More and more communities are establishing adult day care facilities. These facilities provide a degree of supervision for elderly persons with minor physical disabilities and also provide appropriate activities for the clients. It is well established that elderly people remain healthier if they are able to continue to live in their own homes, and adult day care can often make the difference between being able to remain at home and needing institutionalization. Remaining at home is usually cheaper too.

$ Use Meals on Wheels. To assure that the elderly receive one balanced meal each day, most communities provide the service called Meals on Wheels. Look in the yellow pages.

$ If you can't die at home, go to a hospice. A hospice provides basic medical care and counseling for the patient and family, and prescribes pain relievers. Most hospices will care only for patients for whom a doctor's prognosis indicates that they have fewer than six months to live. Hospices are less expensive than hospitals because they do not use costly life-sustaining technologies.

HOME IS WHERE THE HEALTH IS—BUT MEDICARE STILL ISN'T LISTENING

The need for viable alternatives to hospitals and nursing homes is becoming more and more critical. Hospitals, under pressure from

Medicare and private insurers to contain costs, are discharging people more quickly than ever before. Treating long-term and chronic illness and disability in institutional settings, combined with the growing numbers of people attaining ages at which the need for such care is commonplace, is battering government budgets and too often wiping out the financial reserves that these people have so lovingly and diligently set aside over a lifetime.

We must find a humane and less expensive option—and home health care seems to fit the bill. In fact, many call it the "quiet revolution" taking place in the delivery of medical care in this country today. But others will tell you that the revolution is too quiet, that it's lagging way behind the ever-advancing need.

Medicare is a ready illustration of inchmeal improvements in home care coverage. Even with a relatively new agenda of covered services, Medicare is still far away from a real commitment to home care and the coverage people need.

Not unlike Medicare supplemental insurance and private insurance policies, Medicare covers only part-time, intermittent, and relatively intensive home care, and only if the person is confined to the home. Here is a quick rundown of what Medicare covers.

Medicare covers medical services that are needed to allow you to live at home. The scope of benefits includes part-time or intermittent nursing care; physical, occupational, or speech therapy; medical social services; part-time or intermittent services of a home health aide; medical supplies; durable medical equipment (for example, wheelchairs, hospital beds, and oxygen tanks); and the services of interns and residents if the home health agency is affiliated with a teaching hospital.

Medicare limits coverage of home health care to twenty-one consecutive days and mandates that the need for continuing care must be reviewed periodically by a physician.

Another tricky aspect of Medicare coverage concerns occupational therapy. If the person needs occupational therapy alone—the teaching of skills necessary to independent daily living, such as dressing, washing, and bathing—it is not covered. But if occupational therapy is started as part of a program of rehabilitation that includes physical or speech therapy, continuing services are paid for even after the physical or speech therapy is over.

Home health care is covered under both Part A, hospital insurance, and Part B, medical insurance, of Medicare. To qualify for this coverage, *all* of these conditions must exist:

▶ You are confined to your home (or to an institution that is not a nursing home).

▶ You need part-time skilled nursing care or physical and speech therapy.

▶ A doctor prescribed home health care.

▶ The home health agency is approved by Medicare.

HOME HEALTH CARE IS NOT JUST FOR THE ELDERLY

Home health care is not only for the elderly on Medicare. Many people under sixty-five who are not yet legally disabled—and who therefore would not normally qualify for Medicare—but who require rehabilitative or chronic care, are eligible to use the program. Home health services offer an opportunity for early discharge from a hospital or a skilled nursing facility, and in fact such specialized or rehabilitation services often meet a person's long-term needs more efficiently than acute care hospital settings. And better yet, they are also substantially less expensive than inpatient care in virtually all circumstances.

Find out what your insurance plan pays and what eligibility requirements you must meet. Do you have long-term or short-term disability insurance? Generally, a doctor must arrange for such services as part-time home nursing care, occupational therapy, speech therapy, and special meals and other nutritional services to be furnished in your home.

MINIMIZING YOUR OUT-OF-POCKET EXPENSES

Cost sharing under home health care consists of the $100 Part B deductible and 20 percent of the Medicare-deemed reasonable charge for durable medical equipment. (This latter obligation underscores how important it is for you to *make sure the medical equipment provider is approved by Medicare.* Otherwise, you may end up paying the entire cost.)

When ordering medical equipment and having your home checked for suitability for home care, make sure there is a way for you to terminate the rental or return the item if it turns out that it is not Medicare-approved and you decide you cannot afford it. Otherwise, you may be stuck with large expenses.

You should ask the doctor and the home health agency if any services being provided are not covered under Medicare, and ask what the charges will be. Based on what you hear, you may want to discuss your plan of care and any changes that can be made to it in order to have services covered under Medicare.

Be sure to examine your Medicare supplemental insurance to see what it pays for that Medicare does not.

Finally, as with all services, complain if you are not satisfied. Home health agencies cannot make up for all the burdens of being old and ill, but they should, at the very minimum, provide the medical services that were prescribed and any services that you are paying for—and provide them well. The state health departments, the authorities regulating home health agencies, are listed in appendix I, pp. 429–34. Complain to your state office if your discussions with the home health agency get you nowhere.

MONEY-SAVING TIP

$ Use home health care. Home health agencies can provide services ranging from cooking and cleaning to full nursing care at home. For the elderly—or the non-elderly—person with minor disabilities, someone to cook or clean is often all the support needed to allow the person to remain in his or her own home. A home health agency can help you evaluate the help that you need, but don't purchase any more care than necessary.

One in every five people can expect to need extended nursing care at some time. And long-term nursing care outside of the hospital is one aspect of medical care that is barely, if at all, covered by most health insurance policies. So if you or a member of your family is one of those who need such care, you need to know how to get it without paying more than necessary. The key is in knowing all of your options. Be sure to review the money-saving tips throughout this chapter.

Health
Insurance—
Covering
Your
Assets

We hope you stay healthy—but since there's a good chance you or a member of your family will get sick at some point, you need to know how to shop for the best health insurance for your money.

Medical costs alone are enough to make anyone sick. Hospital rates and doctors' bills continue to rise far faster than the cost-of-living index. The tab for a single day in the hospital—just room and board, mind you—now averages $293. Add in the inevitable charges for drugs, medical tests, and other services, and the daily expenditure can easily reach $900, or more. And don't forget the doctors' bills; they're separate from the $900. Even during a relatively short stay in the hospital, you could accumulate a bill of $10,000, $20,000, or more. Innovative, high-tech medical treatments—organ transplants, for example—can run to hundreds of thousands of dollars. If your family were faced with these enormous expenses, the resulting economic loss could be catastrophic.

Perhaps your insurance plan will cover the majority of your expenses, and you will need to pay only a few dollars out of your own pocket. But a sudden loss of coverage or a drop in protection, and you and your family could be facing serious financial loss. Health insurance is designed to protect against such loss, against ruinous medical bills, but almost no policy will pay all your medical bills all the time. So the guiding principle in shopping for insurance is, the more comprehensive the coverage, the better.

Like most people's, your health insurance is probably tied to your job. But what if your company goes out of business or goes through some sort of restructuring, and you're laid off? What if your benefits are significantly curtailed? What if your family status changes? What if you decide to go into business for yourself or retire? Such events, changes in circumstance and fate, among others, are behind the growing numbers of Americans who have no health insurance—a whopping 31 to 37 million people, as of 1989.

A happier scenario is the one where your employer, as many larger companies are doing, offers a wide range of policies and options at varying costs. Many workers are offered a "cafeteria package" of benefits and must choose from an assortment of possibilities, all of which create a baffling problem—how to choose the right health insurance and the right amount. Unfortunately, the decision-making tactic too many people employ is the toss of a coin. But an uninformed choice may be a poor one that leaves *you* poorer.

What is the right choice? What policy gives you the most for your money? We cannot answer that because everyone's needs are different, but we can give you the necessary tools to evaluate and select the best health insurance coverage at the price you can afford.

THE VOCABULARY OF
HEALTH INSURANCE

You should understand certain important terms before you begin to read through and consider different insurance policies.

Ambulatory benefits. Benefits available to you for health care services received while not confined to a hospital bed as an inpatient—for example, outpatient care, emergency room care, home health care, preadmission testing.

Assignment. An agreement in which you instruct your insurance company to pay the hospital, doctor, or medical supplier directly for services you receive and at the payment rate established by the insurer.

Basic coverage. Hospital and medical-surgical coverage, exclusive of major medical, dental coverage, and rider coverage; Medicare Parts A and B, exclusive of supplemental coverage.

Benefit. The amount of money or services an insurance company will pay or provide under the provisions of the policy.

Carrier. Any commercial insurance company.

Claim. Your (or your hospital's, doctor's, or medical supplier's) notification to your insurance company that you have received a medical service and are requesting payment of benefits.

Coinsurance/copayment. A cost-sharing requirement in many health insurance policies in which you, the insured, assume a portion or percentage of the costs of covered services. The most common cost-sharing provision makes you responsible for 20 percent of covered expenses while the insurer pays the remaining 80 percent.

Conversion clause. The privilege granted by a group policy to convert to an individual policy upon termination of group coverage.

Coordination of benefits. A clause sometimes found in group health insurance contracts to avoid paying duplicate benefits to a person covered by more than one policy. The companies determine how much of a claim each one will pay.

Deductible. The amount of money you must pay before your insurance company will step in and reimburse you. Deductibles are common in major medical policies.

Effective date. The date on which coverage provided by an insurance policy begins; the first date on which you as a policyholder can file a claim and have it paid.

Eligibility. Determination of whether an applicant qualifies for coverage for health care rendered.

Exclusions. Specific conditions or circumstances under which a policy will not provide benefits. The specific services excluded from a policy may be found in the policy's schedule of benefits.

First-dollar coverage. Coverage under an insurance policy which has no deductibles; starts with the first dollar of your expenses.

Free look. A period of time—usually ten to thirty days—during which you may return the policy and receive a full refund of any premium paid.

Grace period. A period of time after the date a premium is due during which the policy remains in force and the premium may still be paid without penalty.

Indemnity benefits. A fixed-dollar payment for a specific health care service, such as $100 a day for hospitalization. Should the cost of care be more than your policy pays, you are responsible for the difference.

Inpatient. A patient who is officially admitted and occupies a hospital room while receiving hospital care, including room, board, and general nursing care.

Inside limit. A provision that limits the payment for any type of service regardless of the actual cost of it.

Level of care. The type and intensity of treatment necessary to adequately and efficiently treat your illness or condition.

Outpatient. A patient, not officially admitted as an inpatient to a hospital, who receives hospital care (for example, laboratory work and X rays) without occupying a hospital bed or receiving room, board, or general nursing care.

Preexisting condition. An injury, disease, or any other physical or mental condition that occurred or existed prior to issuance of a health insurance policy. Usually, benefits will not be paid for services related to preexisting conditions, although many insurance companies cover these conditions after a certain waiting period.

Premium. The amount you pay—monthly, quarterly, semiannually, or annually—to purchase the insurance and keep it in force.

Provider. A new term used to describe doctors, nurses, hospitals, pharmacists, and anyone else who provides health care.

Renewal clause. A clause that indicates the provisions under which the policy may or may not be renewed. Since many individual health insurance policies are written for a limited time, usually one year, they must be renewed at the end of each term. The provisions you are most likely to encounter are:

> **Guaranteed renewable.** The company guarantees your right to renew your policy to a specific age, commonly sixty-five. (Medicare supplemental insurance is usually not purchased until age sixty-five, with some policies renewable for life.) A guaranteed renewable policy may also have a guaranteed premium which will not be raised during the term of the policy.
>
> **Conditionally renewable.** You may renew your policy until you reach a certain age, usually sixty-five, provided you have complied with the other conditions of the policy.

Optionally renewable. The company may decline to renew your policy on the anniversary date.

Rider. A provision added to your contract whereby the scope of its coverage is increased or restricted.

Schedule of benefits. The list of medical services that a particular insurance policy will cover.

Third-party payer. Any organization, public or private, that pays or insures health or medical expenses on behalf of beneficiaries or recipients (for example, Blue Cross/Blue Shield, commercial insurance companies, Medicare, and Medicaid).

Usual, customary, and reasonable charges. The fee most often charged by the specific provider, the fee most commonly charged in that area, and the fee recognized as reasonable by most people. Insurers often base their allowable payments on the lowest of these three fees.

Waiting period. The period of time you are required to wait either to become eligible for insurance coverage or to become eligible for a given benefit after overall coverage has commenced. This may also be referred to as the probationary period.

TYPES OF HEALTH INSURANCE

Now that you can decipher many of the codes you will come across in insurance policies, you're ready to shop around among the different types of insurance. First, a rundown on each type:

Hospital insurance. This provides coverage for inpatient and outpatient hospital services. For inpatient services this insurance usually specifies the number of days of hospitalization the policy covers and specifies dollar limits on total benefits payable.

Medical-surgical insurance. This coverage is divided into two portions: The medical portion pays for doctor visits to the hospital and may pay for office visits. Other medical services covered include drugs, X rays, anesthesia, and laboratory tests performed outside the hospital. The surgical portion covers the surgeon's fees, whether the surgery was performed in the hospital, the doctor's office, or an ambulatory surgical center. (An ambulatory surgical center is a medical facility where surgical procedures are performed on an out-patient basis. It may be a freestanding center or a facility associated with a hospital but separate from it.)

Major medical insurance. Often referred to as catastrophic insurance, this coverage protects against the high cost of medical care associated with a serious illness or accident. Before benefits are paid, this type of insurance usually requires you to pay a yearly deductible, typically ranging from $100 to $500, although deductibles vary from one policy to another. After the deductible is met, major medical insurance pays up to a certain percentage of covered expenses while you pay the remaining percentage. A typical coinsurance arrangement is 80 percent paid by your insurance company and 20 percent by you.

Once your out-of-pocket expenses reach a certain amount, many major medical policies protect you from further outlays of cash. This is known as a stop-loss provision. Your insurance company pays the remaining covered expenses up to the maximum limit. Because of such a provision, and the protection major medical insurance offers, if you can afford *only* one type of health insurance, you should consider purchasing a major medical policy.

It is important to remember that major medical insurance is usually cheaper than hospital or medical-surgical insurance because of the sometimes large deductibles these policies carry.

OTHER TYPES OF INSURANCE

The confusion surrounding the purchase of health insurance too often results in the inefficient outlay of health dollars. And the best way to avoid that is to buy only what you need. The following types of insurance provide coverage for very limited services or conditions; therefore, we do not recommend them as *substitutes* for what you really need: basic hospital, medical-surgical, or major medical insurance.

Accident. Very limited in coverage—and for this reason not the best insurance for your money—accident insurance excludes illness but does cover medical expenses resulting from an accident.

Dental. Dental insurance usually covers routine dental care as well as crowns, bridges, and root canals. Some policies do cover orthodontic work, but not if it is for cosmetic purposes. Because the premium for dental insurance is very high, your best opportunity to acquire dental insurance is probably through an employer-provided group plan. We have more to say about this type of insurance later in this chapter.

Disability. While technically not health insurance, but nevertheless often included in health insurance benefit packages, this insurance provides you with income when you are unable to work because of illness or accident. (If your disability was the result of a job-related accident, you are probably covered by your state's worker's compensation insurance.)

You may purchase disability income insurance policies on a long- or short-term basis, but you should know that these policies usually have a waiting period, anywhere from seven to fourteen days or longer, before any benefits are paid. The longer the waiting period, the lower the premium.

Depending upon the provisions of the policy, the degree of your disability could have a significant impact on whether you receive benefits. The more common types of disability are:

▶ Occupational disability, defined as a person's inability to perform the duties of his or her occupation.

▶ General disability, defined as a person's inability to perform the duties of any occupation for which he or she may be suited as a result of education, training, or experience.

▶ Combination disability, defined in terms of a specified time during which a person is unable to perform the duties of his or her occupation.

Disease-specific. This insurance usually covers one disease—for example, cancer or heart disease. Disease-specific insurance not only pays limited benefits, but it may duplicate what you already have or are about to purchase. For these reasons your money is better spent on more comprehensive types of insurance.

Long-term-care. This insurance is also known as nursing home insurance since it covers the services provided in a skilled nursing facility—an institution that offers nursing services similar to those provided in a hospital. The most important point to remember is that benefits will be paid *only* if you receive *skilled* nursing care, the need for which must be certified by a physician as being medically necessary. If you should no longer require care at the skilled level, your benefits may cease. The vast majority of policies do not cover services provided by intermediate or custodial care facilities, although most people in nursing homes are receiving custodial care.

Travel. Usually sold at airports or through automobile clubs and some credit card companies, this insurance offers to pay a certain amount of money if you are injured or killed as a result of an accident while traveling. The benefits are for a limited time only and probably duplicate coverage that you already have or are about to purchase. Not really health insurance, travel insurance is more a form of life insurance, with the money paid out not necessarily intended to pay for the cost of medical services.

WHERE DO YOU GET INSURANCE?

Individual Insurance

Independent of any group, you can purchase individual insurance coverage for you or your dependents. Given the fact that replacing first-rate group coverage with an equally good individual one is not easy, why would you want to do that? You may want to consider purchasing an individual policy if you have no group coverage, if your group coverage is not complete or comprehensive, or if you cannot cover your dependents through a group policy. Just remember that group coverage is generally 15 to 40 percent cheaper than comparable individual coverage, so you may find yourself paying a rather steep premium for individual coverage. Add in the deductible and copayments, and your out-of-pocket expenses swell.

Another major disadvantage to individual insurance is the sometimes temporary nature of such policies. You may not be able to buy coverage for more than 90 to 180 days for basic hospital and medical-surgical insurance; however, major medical policies may be purchased on a year-to-year basis. To head off cancellation of an individual policy, buy one that is guaranteed renewable.

Our best advice for shopping for individual insurance? To get the best for your money, measure the coverage against what is offered in a comprehensive company group plan.

Group Insurance

Most private health insurance is now sold in the form of group insurance, coverage bought at lower cost through an employer or organization. Since large numbers of people are being covered by one overall policy, insurers discount the premiums.

If you are eligible to join a group and purchase group insurance, by all means do so. Group insurance provided by an employer is by far the best way to obtain health insurance coverage; however, there may be ways of joining groups other than through an employer. Many associations, such as fraternal organizations or the American Association of Retired Persons, make group insurance available to their members. There are tens of thousands of these types of organizations. You might even be a member of such an organization without knowing they provide insurance programs. Call or write the headquarters of the group to see if they offer insurance, and if they do, what kind. If you do not belong to such a group, seek one out. Find out whether you are eligible for membership in a group that offers insurance to their members.

If group insurance is provided by your employer, you can usually extend coverage to your family, but be prepared to pay for that coverage in the likely event that your employer is not willing to pay the additional premium. The good news is that this will cost you far less than the purchase of individual policies for your family.

What happens in the event of death or divorce? A little-known but significant provision of the Consolidated Omnibus Budget Reconciliation Act of 1986, known as COBRA, allows persons who currently have group health insurance through their spouses' employers to continue coverage after divorce, death, or retirement of the spouse—or even in the event of unemployment or reduced hours of work. By paying the premiums—the employer can charge up to 4 percent for administrative fees, however—spouses and dependent children can continue to be part of their group insurance plans for up to three years. Unemployed workers and their families can continue coverage for up to eighteen months. The law applies to health plans offered by most private employers and by state and local governments. After the three-year or eighteen-month period, the insured has the option of continuing coverage with the carrier, but not necessarily at the group rate or at the same level of coverage. The benefit of exercising such an option is that one need not go through the normal insurability requirements nor be subject to typical restrictions such as preexisting-condition clauses.

Note the effective date of coverage in your group insurance plan. Some policies cover you immediately upon employment, while others require a waiting period. It is not uncommon to find group policies that require a thirty-day wait before you are eligible to file a claim.

Should you find yourself soon to be unemployed, you may still be able to retain some health insurance coverage. Group policies usually contain a conversion clause, which permits you to convert to individual coverage when you are no longer part of the group, but you will be responsible for paying the premium. Bear in mind that coverage may not be as extensive as it was under the group policy, and you may pay a larger deductible and an increased copayment. But at least you will have health insurance.

Stop-loss protection is another important provision found in major medical insurance; it limits your maximum out-of-pocket medical expenses in any year, typically in some policies to $1,500 for a single person or $3,000 for a family. The policy pays for everything above that. If your group policy does not include major medical insurance, and this valuable stop-loss provision, then investigate what it would cost you to purchase a major medical policy under the group. Typical monthly premiums for individuals run $10 to $15, and $30 to $50 for a family.

Franchise Insurance

Another way to purchase insurance is through a group or association that offers franchise insurance. Some employers do not pay for their employees' health benefits and instead offer franchise insurance, which may have lower rates and better benefits than a similar individual policy. With franchise insurance, individual policies, rather than a group policy, are issued to the members of the group (and their families too, if appropriate), and the group or association agrees to collect the premiums for the insurance company.

HOW BENEFITS ARE PAID

You're almost ready to review different health insurance policies, but first be aware of how benefits are paid to policyholders.

Indemnity benefit plans pay a specific amount for each day of hospitalization, typically between $100 and $300 for most such policies, for the set period of time indicated in the policy. The payment is made directly to you, and not the doctor or hospital unless you instruct your insurance company to do so. However, you are not obligated to use the money for expenses related to your hospitalization.

Purchase indemnity benefit plans with great caution. Most pay only a fraction of the actual costs of a day in the hospital, and you are responsible for paying the difference. Know when the benefits become payable because indemnity plans do not always pay benefits for the first day in the hospital. It's also a good idea to find out the current hospital room rate in your area before considering such an insurance plan.

Service benefit plans pay the hospital or doctor directly for the services you receive. How much the insurance company reimburses the hospital or doctor is a result of negotiation among the three groups. Hospitals and doctors who agree to accept the insurance company's terms are called participating, or member, providers. Should you obtain medical services from a hospital or doctor who is not a participating member, you may find yourself paying more out of your own pocket than you would if the institution or physician were a participating provider. When you purchase an insurance policy that pays service benefits, the company will give you the names of the participating members.

Blue Cross and Blue Shield are examples of service benefit plans because they sign contracts with hospitals and doctors to pay what's called the "usual, customary, and reasonable" fees of the providers in your area.

Service benefit plans are more comprehensive than indemnity plans, and for this reason we recommend that you purchase a health insurance policy that pays service benefits.

COMPARING POLICIES

Now that you have a handle on the vocabulary of health insurance, the types of insurance you need and some you can probably do without, and the ways benefits are paid, it's time we got down to helping you answer the question behind this chapter: what insurance policy gives you the most for your money?

We have designed Policy/Plan Comparison Worksheets (pp. 148–55) to help you compare the coverage offered by a number of different policies. Remember, you don't purchase the first new car you see without looking at several models, and the same logic should apply when buying health insurance. And don't be influenced by one particular aspect of a policy either, such as low premiums. While the price may be appealing, the coverage may not be the best your money can buy. *Cost* is certainly a major criterion, but *comprehensiveness* is fundamental in choosing a good health insurance plan. Whether the plan excludes or puts strict limits on certain illnesses, what services are offered, and how many days of hospitalization are allowed—all these, and more, are questions you should consider.

Each worksheet is arranged according to the particular type of insurance you're comparing—hospital, medical-surgical, and major medical.

First, collect the schedules of benefits for several policies. Each worksheet lists the services we believe should be covered by any policy you consider—the bare minimum, you might say—but ideally you're looking for policies that provide additional coverage. Some states require that all health insurance policies, whether group or individual, sold within their boundaries provide certain benefits called mandated benefits. Check with your state insurance department (see appendix J, pp. 435–40). to see if this is the case where you live and, if so, what the minimum benefits are.

Just as important as what's covered is what's *not* covered—the exclusions. Too many exclusions or even a few exclusions of important items can render a particular policy useless. If the policy's exclusions are not listed in its schedule of benefits, call the company to find out what they are. Also, injuries or illnesses that would ordinarily be covered may be excluded if they occur under the following circumstances: attempted suicide or self-inflicted injuries; injury or illness covered under worker's compensation; injury or illness resulting from war or military service; and treatment received in government hospitals.

If you already have health insurance, compare its coverage with other policies. Quite possibly your present policy's coverage has not kept up with the rising cost of medical services, and you may need to upgrade your coverage. Having partial benefits or limited coverage may be as dangerous as having no coverage at all. Do not under any circumstances cancel an existing policy before you have purchased a replacement policy. In fact, you really should not cancel until the effective date of the new policy.

Finally, bear in mind that a condition you have or had—called a preexisting condition—*may not* be eligible for coverage, and it's up to the insurance company to determine, based upon your medical history, if it will or will not be. Some consider a condition preexisting even if you did not know that you had the condition before you bought the policy. Find out how many years the company will go back in looking for preexisting conditions. As far back as birth? (Some do.) Furthermore, policies vary on how long they exclude benefits for preexisting conditions. Usually, they will not pay until one or two years after the effective date of the policy.

For many reasons, not the least of which is this matter of preexisting conditions, it's a good idea to give a complete and accurate medical history when you apply for health insurance coverage. If you *inadvertently* omit something, it may delay the start of your coverage. And if you *deliberately* omit something, it could be grounds for canceling your policy or denying you benefits should you file a claim.

QUESTIONS TO ASK BEFORE YOU SELECT ANY POLICY

These questions should help you evaluate the coverage provided by the policies you are comparing:

I. Hospital Insurance

1. Does the policy pay indemnity benefits or service benefits? (Service benefits tend to be more complete and are preferable.)

2. Does the policy cover the daily room-and-board rate of the hospitals in your area? (To get those rates, call your local hospitals or your state's hospital association.)

3. How many days of hospitalization does the policy cover? (If less than thirty days, this may not be the best policy you can buy.)

4. Does the policy have a waiting period before hospital benefits are provided? (We do not recommend hospital policies with waiting periods of seven days or longer.)

5. Does the policy cover preexisting conditions? (Some conditions may be excluded for a period of time, then covered later.)

6. Does the policy pay for prescription medicines and other services such as X rays, laboratory tests, etc.?

7. Does the policy cover the costs associated with surgery, such as charges for the operating, recovery, and other specialty rooms?

8. Does the policy cover specialty care, such as intensive care, coronary care, burn care, etc.? (Specialty care can cost as much as thousands of dollars a day. Avoid any policy that doesn't pay at least a portion of this cost.)

9. Does the policy cover inpatient and outpatient psychiatric care?

10. Does the policy cover outpatient services, either at a hospital or a freestanding ambulatory care center? (Coverage of such services is definitely a plus.)

11. Does the policy cover the expenses associated with an emergency room visit?

12. Does the policy require you to use one particular hospital, or do you have a choice?

13. Does the policy pay anything toward the services you receive in a hospital that does not have an agreement with your insurance company? (Sometimes an insurance company will pay a portion of expenses arising out of treatment in what are called noncontracting facilities.)

14. Does the policy require a deductible and copayments? (The less you pay out of pocket, the better.)

15. Can the policy be renewed? (We recommend a guaranteed-renewable policy and one that also guarantees that the premium will not change during the life of the contract.)

16. Can the benefits be changed at the discretion of the company? (If so, such a policy should be avoided.)

II. Medical-Surgical Insurance

1. Does the policy require a deductible and copayments? (We recommend policies for which you do not have to pay out of your own pocket for such basic services.)

2. How much does the policy pay toward doctor visits when you are in the hospital? (Check with your doctor to find out if this amount covers his or her usual fee.)

3. How many visits does the policy cover when you are in the hospital? (If you have an extended illness, your benefits could be used up quickly.)

4. Does the policy cover home visits by your doctor or office visits? If so, how many of each type?

5. Does the policy cover diagnostic tests performed in a doctor's office?

6. Does the policy cover outside laboratory services for the tests ordered by your doctor?

7. Does the policy cover second opinions?

8. Does the policy have a surgical schedule that pays one lump sum regardless of the surgeon's fee, or does it pay the "usual, customary, and reasonable" fee of the surgeons in your area? (Policies that pay benefits in line with surgeons' fees in your area are preferable.)

9. Does the policy pay for your surgeon to bring in a consultant on your case?

10. Does the policy cover the cost of an assistant surgeon? (Pay close attention to this because some policies pay only for the primary surgeon.)

11. Does the policy cover surgical procedures performed in the ambulatory care unit of a hospital or in a freestanding ambulatory care center? (Increasing numbers of insurance companies are recognizing the potential for cost containment in "same-day" surgery. Look for a policy that has this benefit.)

12. Can you pay the premium on an annual basis?

13. Can the policy be renewed? (Once again, a guaranteed-renewable policy is best.)

HOSPITAL INSURANCE: INPATIENT SERVICES

Insurance Company											
Policy/Plan Name											
Premium	$			$			$			$	
Maximum Days of Hospitalization											
Does it pay Indemnity Benefits?	Yes ☐ No ☐			Yes ☐ No ☐			Yes ☐ No ☐			Yes ☐ No ☐	
Does it pay Service Benefits?	Yes ☐ No ☐			Yes ☐ No ☐			Yes ☐ No ☐			Yes ☐ No ☐	
Is the policy renewable?	Yes ☐ No ☐			Yes ☐ No ☐			Yes ☐ No ☐			Yes ☐ No ☐	

The following INPATIENT services should be covered by any policy you consider.	Self	Spouse	Depndt	Self	Spouse	Depndt	Self	Spouse	Depndt	Self	Spouse	Depndt
Anesthesia and supplies												
Blood and blood components												
Casts and cast room												
Dental services (accident and injury)												
Detoxification services (alcohol and drugs)												
Diagnostic tests and procedures (example, laboratory services, blood tests, x-rays, ultrasound)												
Drugs and medications												
Electrocardiograms (EKG)												
Electroencephalograms (EEG)												
General nursing care												
Obstetrical services												
Labor and Delivery room												
Birthing center services												

Newborn care: isolette

intensive care

routine care

Oxygen and oxygen supplies

Pathology services

Physical therapy

Radiation therapy

Respiratory therapy

Room and board (semi-private)

Specialty hospital care: burn care

cardiac care

intensive care

psychiatric care

Surgical services (operating, recovery, other specialty rooms)

Surgical dressings and supplies

Transporation (ambulance)

Transplant procedures (approved procedures only)

List additional services covered.

EXCLUSIONS: List services *not* covered.

HOSPITAL INSURANCE: OUTPATIENT SERVICES

The following OUTPATIENT services should be covered by any policy you consider.	Self	Spouse	Depend	Self	Spouse	Depend	Self	Spouse	Depend	Self	Spouse	Depend
Accidental injury												
Detoxification services (alcohol and drugs)												
Diagnostic tests and procedures (example, laboratory services, blood tests, x-ray, ultrasound)												
Electrocardiogram (EKG)												
Electroencephalogram (EEG)												
Drugs and medications												
Emergency room (as deemed necessary by company)												
Home health care												
Hospice care												
Mental health and nervous disorders												
Newborn care												
Physical therapy												
Pre-admission testing												
Radiation therapy												
Respiratory therapy												

Surgery, short procedure (example, anesthesia, recovery room, supplies)		
Skilled nursing home care		
Speech therapy		
Transportation (ambulance)		
List additional services covered.		
EXCLUSIONS: List services *not* covered.		

MEDICAL-SURGICAL INSURANCE

Insurance Company												
Policy/Plan Name												
Premium	$				$				$			
Does it pay Indemnity Benefits?	Yes ☐ No ☐				Yes ☐ No ☐				Yes ☐ No ☐			
Does it pay Service Benefits?	Yes ☐ No ☐				Yes ☐ No ☐				Yes ☐ No ☐			
Is the policy renewable?	Yes ☐ No ☐				Yes ☐ No ☐				Yes ☐ No ☐			

The following services should be covered by any policy you consider.	Self	Spouse	Depend	Self	Spouse	Depend	Self	Spouse	Depend
Allergy testing									
Anesthesia: anesthesiologist/anesthetist fees, supplies									
Chemotherapy (including cost of drugs)									
Chiropractic care									
Consultation services									
Diagnostic services (in non-hospital settings)									
Doctor visits: office visits, hospital visits, emergency room visits, home visits									
Electrocardiogram (EKG)									
Electroencephalogram (EEG)									
Emergency accident care									
Immunizations									
Newborn care (routine)									
Obstetric services (pre and post natal care)									
Oral surgeon's fee									
Pathologist's fee (laboratory)									
Physical examinations									
Podiatry care									
Psychiatric care services									

Radiation therapy: radiologist's fees, supplies

Surgery: surgeon's fee/supplies, assistant surgeon's fees

Second surgical opinion

Therapist's services: occupational, physical, respiratory, speech

Transporation (ambulance)

List additional services covered.

EXCLUSIONS: List services *not* covered.

MAJOR MEDICAL INSURANCE

Insurance Company											
Policy/Plan Name											
Premium	$				$				$		
Deductible if any	$				$				$		
Co-Payment percent: Company _____ % You _____ %					_____ % _____ %				_____ % _____ %		
Maximum benefits payable	$				$				$		
Is the policy renewable?	Yes ☐ No ☐				Yes ☐ No ☐				Yes ☐ No ☐		
The following services should be covered by any policy you consider.	Self	Spouse	Depndt	Self	Spouse	Depndt	Self	Spouse	Depndt		
Blood and blood components (transfusions)											
Cosmetic surgery (as a result of accident/injury)											
Dental treatment (as a result of accident/injury)											
Diagnostic tests (example x-rays, laboratory)											
Durable medical equipment (rental of hospital bed, wheelchair, etc)											
Home health care											
Outpatient treatment services (example, chemotherapy, radiation therapy)											
Obstetric services											
Oxygen/oxygen supplies											
Physician/surgeon services											
Physical therapy											
Prescription drugs											
Private duty nursing											

Prosthetic appliances (limbs, eyes, orthopedic braces)	
Psychiatric care services	
Radiation therapy	
Rehabilitation services	
Respiratory therapy	
Room and board (semi-private)	
Skilled nursing facility care	
Special care beds: intensive care	
Surgery and supplies	
Transportation (ambulance)	
List additional services covered.	
EXCLUSIONS: List services *not* covered.	

III. Major Medical Insurance

1. What is the maximum dollar amount of coverage provided by the policy? (Ideally, you are trying to find a policy with unlimited benefits, but maximum benefits in the range of $1 million to $2 million are good.)

2. Does the policy have a deductible that you can afford? (Major medical policies usually have much higher deductibles than basic hospital and medical-surgical insurance.)

3. Does the deductible apply to a benefit period—for example, one year—or does it apply for each illness? (To avoid excessive out-of-pocket expenses, choose a policy with a yearly deductible rather than a per-usage deductible.)

4. Are the coinsurance/copayment provisions of the policy at least 80 percent/20 percent? (This arrangement is a common one among major medical policies.)

5. Does the policy restore any portion of the maximum benefits once you are well and can submit medical evidence to establish your improved health? (Some policies do this provided you have not made claims for a certain period of time.)

6. What is the stop-loss amount at which point you stop paying anything toward your medical expenses? (This amount is very important to know since it determines your maximum out-of-pocket expense.)

7. Does the policy cover all hospital and doctor expenses associated with your care, or are any services excluded?

8. Can the policy be renewed? (Find one that is guaranteed renewable.)

SELECTING HEALTH INSURANCE: A QUICK CHECKLIST OF TIPS

1. First decide how much you can afford to spend for health insurance. If you are unable to purchase a complete package of insurance, buy at least a major medical policy to protect yourself and your family from catastrophic financial loss. If you're counting pennies, look for a no-frills major medical policy that pays most doctors' and hospital bills but does not cover routine physicals or prescription drugs.

2. Look for a policy that will cover your expenses starting with your first day in the hospital, including room and board, any surgical procedures, and visits from your doctor.

3. Look for a policy that provides coverage for outpatient care, since more and more medical and surgical procedures are moving out of the hospital and into outpatient settings.

4. Keep in mind that the price you pay for the insurance—the premium— will vary and is determined by the extent of coverage and the presence of a deductible and any copayment. As a rule, the higher the deductible, the lower the premium. For this reason, take the highest deductible that you can afford.

5. Try to find policies in which coverage can be extended to a spouse or dependent without a large increase in the premium.

6. Keep in mind that you may save money if you pay the premium annually rather than monthly. If the premium rates are not listed in the policy, contact the company or agent.

7. Purchase a policy that pays service benefits if you can. Otherwise, be very careful when selecting an indemnity benefit plan; such a plan often does not cover the entire cost of your medical care, thus leaving you with a large out-of-pocket expense.

SIGNING ON THE DOTTED LINE

With careful consideration and comparison of different policies, you should be able to find a plan that gives you and your family the protection you need and at a price you can afford. But even these final decision-making stages call for some wariness.

▶ *Do not* be alarmed by claims of "last chance," "limited enrollment period," or other scare tactics. Reputable insurance companies and sales agents will not pressure.

▶ *Do not* be misled by celebrity endorsements. Examine all policies very carefully, whether or not your favorite TV star is paid to advertise them.

▶ *Do not* be fooled by the "government look" of some policies. The federal government does not sell health insurance.

▶ *Do* purchase insurance from a reputable company. How can you tell if it's reputable? Find out if any complaints have been filed against a particular company by checking with your state insurance department (see appendix J, pp. 435–40). Also check the rating given the company and its policies by *Best's Insurance Reports—Life/Health,* published by A. M. Best, and probably available at your local library.

▶ *Do* ask if the insurance plan offers discounts for nonsmokers (assuming you don't smoke). Looking for effective cost-containment strategies, some insurance companies have begun to offer nonsmoking discounts, and there's even talk of discounts being extended to other life-style factors, such as exercise habits, percentage of body fat, and seat-belt use.

▶ *Do* pay your premium by check, not cash, and make it payable to the insurance company, not the sales agent.

▶ *Do* take advantage of any "free look" mandated by your state insurance department. After you have signed the application and paid the premium, your state may permit you to review the policy for a certain number of days before you decide whether or not to keep it. If you have any questions in this interval, contact your sales agent immediately. Should you decide not to keep the policy, return it to the company within the time allotted and request a full refund of any premium. In the event you have a problem returning the policy within the specified time, contact your state insurance department.

CONSUMER PROTECTION: WHAT YOUR STATE INSURANCE DEPARTMENT CAN DO FOR YOU

Your state insurance department plays an important role in regulating insurance companies. Headed by a commissioner who is the chief administrative officer and responsible for enforcing the laws governing the insurance industry, the department licenses companies and agents to sell insurance, approves the policies that are sold, and mandates certain minimum benefits for each type of policy.

The department has the power to conduct investigations, take testimony, hold hearings, render verdicts, and impose punishment, usually fines, suspensions, and revocations of licenses. In some extreme cases an insurance company could be banned from selling its policies in your state.

Your state insurance department may also be able to help you if you have a problem with an insurance company or agent. Any formal complaint you file with the department will be investigated and, if possible, resolved. While the insurance department cannot act as your legal counsel, it can advise you of your rights under the insurance laws.

How to File a Complaint

Your complaint should be in writing and contain the following information:

▶ Your name, address, and telephone number

▶ The name, address, and telephone number of your insurance company

▶ The identification number of your policy

▶ The type of policy

▶ The nature of your complaint: the premium, the coverage, a claim, or the actions of your agent

Make sure you keep copies of everything you send to the department. You must be willing to follow through on your complaint and appear at any hearings if so directed. If the law and the facts are on your side, the insurance department can usually help resolve the problem.

WHAT TO DO IF YOUR HEALTH INSURER WON'T PAY

No matter what type of health insurance you've chosen, or even how good it is, some time or another you may have to defend a claim that your insurer has denied. The claim may be unjustly rejected because of a clerical or other error, and usually a phone call or letter will quickly resolve the matter in dispute. Then there are the times that insurers deny coverage for treatments that are not medically necessary or for treatments that are considered experimental. Be prepared to persist against what at times will seem an impenetrable insurance bureaucracy. Surveys have found that policyholders who contest denials of benefits have at least a 50 percent chance of gaining satisfaction.

Here's how to protect your rights:

▶ Keep copies of medical bills you submit with claims. Once you're notified that a claim has been denied, check over the paperwork for clerical errors, including mathematical miscalculations.

▶ Ask for your doctor's help. If the claim is denied because the doctor charged more than is customary, have the doctor write a letter explaining why. If special circumstance were involved, there's always a chance the insurance company will accept this explanation and pay the claim. If the denial involves medical interpretation, ask your doctor to write to the insurance company.

▶ If your claim is denied because "medical necessity" is in question, find out your plan's definition of this. Authorities differ on what medical necessity is and what it's not. Your best defense against this denial is a second opinion or some other evidence.

▶ If the insurer labels the treatment experimental and denies your claim, enlist your doctor's help in explaining why the treatment is no longer, or never was, experimental. You also may want to ask the maker of any breakthrough drug or device used in your treatment to help you prove that the drug or device is not experimental.

▶ If the insurer refuses your claim on the grounds that the condition existed before the policy was issued, determine whether there's proof that the affliction developed after you took out the policy. Again, your doctor's help may be invaluable.

▶ Take and keep all notes from phone calls or meetings.

▶ Put your policy and claim numbers on all your correspondence.

▶ Keep copies of all your correspondence.

MONEY-SAVING TIPS

$ Don't duplicate coverage. Most health insurance policies will not allow you to collect from two companies (policies) for the same medical claim, so the premium for the second policy is essentially money down the drain.

$ Don't buy disease-specific insurance. The main reason for not purchasing a policy that covers you for only one disease is that the coverage most likely duplicates your existing coverage.

$ Don't buy accident insurance. Accident insurance frequently duplicates coverage you already have. Further, most insurers will not allow you to collect from more than one policy for a single injury.

UNDERSTANDING
MEDICARE

When the Medicare Act was signed in the summer of 1965, promises rang out: No longer would the elderly be denied medical care because of inability to pay. No longer would illness and accompanying medical costs destroy the savings that the elderly had spent their lives accumulating.

You see, at the time the law was passed, the elderly were spending about 15 percent of their incomes on health care—a figure that was thought to be intolerable. Yet today the elderly spend as much as 18 to 20 percent of their incomes on health care, *even with Medicare.*

In 1988 it was a toss-up between the Medicare program and the elderly themselves as to who paid the larger share of the elderly's health care. And the latest word on the fifty-fifty split is that it is changing, with the elderly finding themselves increasingly responsible for a greater share of the burden. Why doesn't the federal government, overseers of this mammoth entitlement program, do something? Congress is reluctant to increase benefits as long as beneficiaries will tolerate the situation—a point proven by the backlash senior citizens exhibited after Congress passed the ill-fated Catastrophic Coverage Act of 1988.

Medicare is not a charity program. All beneficiaries have paid a premium, before being eligible, through Social Security taxes withheld while employed. If you are sixty-five or older, Medicare is *your* health insurance plan. *You* pay for it; *you* elect the people who oversee it. And only by knowing how it works, what it covers (and doesn't), and how to pick the best supplemental insurance can you make Medicare work for you. Only then can you get your sizable investment's worth.

Who Is Eligible for Medicare

For many reasons it is important to know your Medicare and Social Security status before you retire, and equally important to know what Medicare covers before retiring—and possibly losing any coverage you might have through your employer—or before dropping any personal medical coverage you might have.

Medicare was originally intended for the elderly, defined as people sixty-five or older, and those people are still covered. But it also covers those who are permanently and totally disabled and those who have end-stage renal disease, the medical term for kidney disease that is severe enough to require dialysis or a transplant.

If you think you are eligible for Medicare, apply at your local Social Security office.

What Medicare Covers and What It Doesn't

Many people are unaware of how relatively little of their necessary medical care Medicare covers. A common misconception about Medicare is that it has a wide scope of coverage, comparable with the best private insurance plans. It doesn't, and, in fact, if Medicare were sold as private insurance at the current buy-in premium, it is doubtful that there would be many takers. Without a doubt, coverage under Medicare is limited. By "covered" we mean that Medicare is willing to pay something for the service—not necessarily the full amount the provider wants, not necessarily enough to relieve you of the burden of payment, not necessarily enough to attract enough providers to make the service routinely available, but something.

Medicare is divided into Part A, hospital insurance, and Part B, medical insurance. The chart on pages 164–65 shows the specific benefits under each, and the current edition of *Your Medicare Handbook* will have the latest information. But here's a brief summary just to acquaint you with some terms we'll be using: Part A, under which you are automatically covered when you enroll in Medicare, provides coverage for hospital and related services, posthospital skilled-nursing care, home health care, and hospice services. Except for the deductible, which rises every year and which you pay either out of your own wallet or through any supplemental insurance you may have, virtually all of your hospital expenses are paid by Medicare. Part B, medical insurance, is optional and provides coverage for doctors' fees, various outpatient services, medical laboratory fees, outpatient hospital treatment, home health care, durable medical equipment, and the services of various therapists.

How to Maximize Your Medicare Benefits

No matter what the United States Congress does, short of passing a national health insurance law, there will always be gaps in Medi-

THE MEDICARE PROGRAM
WHAT IT PAYS...WHAT YOU PAY
1993

MEDICARE SERVICES	BENEFIT PERIOD	MEDICARE PAYS	YOU PAY
PART A: HOSPITAL INSURANCE			
Hospital services Semiprivate room rate Miscellaneous hospital services & supplies Dietary & meal services Special care units Diagnostic procedures, X rays, etc. Laboratory services Operating & recovery rooms Anesthesia & supplies Rehabilitation services	First 60 days	All but deductible	Deductible of $676
	61 to 90 days	All but $169 / day	$169 / day
	91 to 150 days	All but $338 / day	$338 / day
	Beyond 150 days	Nothing	All costs
Skilled nursing facility care In approved facility after a three-day hospital stay and admitted to the facility within 30 days of discharge	First 20 days	All costs	Nothing
	21 to 100 days	All but $84.50 / day	$84.50 / day
	Beyond 100 days	Nothing	All costs
Home health care	Unlimited as medically necessary	All costs	Nothing

Hospice care	Two 90-day periods One 30-day period	All costs but outpatient drugs and respite care	Limited drug costs and respite care
Blood service	As needed	All but first three pints	First three pints
PART B: MEDICAL INSURANCE			
Physician & surgeon fees Therapists (physical/speech) Diagnostic tests Medical supplies Ambulatory services Ambulance service	As medically necessary	80 percent of approved amount after $100 deductible	$100 deductible and 20 percent of the Medicare-approved charge (plus any cost above approved charge)
Outpatient hospital services	As medically necessary	80 percent of approved amount after $100 deductible	20 percent of approved charge after deductible
Home health care	As medically necessary	All costs	Nothing
Immunosuppressive drugs	As medically necessary	One year of drugs used in immuno-suppressive therapy after transplant	20 percent of the cost
Blood service	As needed	80 percent of the cost after first three pints[1]	First three pints and 20 percent of the cost

[1] Unless blood deductible met under Part A.

care coverage. Big gaps. Remember, Medicare was never intended to pay for everything—and, as you can see from the chart, where there is a benefit, in some cases it is only partial. This means that, if you can afford it, you should obtain supplemental insurance— often called medigap insurance—one of the most effective ways to maximize the value of your Medicare dollar. Without it you're going to have to pay for the gaps out of your own pocket.

In 1990 Congress made it easier to shop for medigap insurance when it mandated that the states and the insurance industry design a series of standardized Medicare supplemental policies. The first order of business was to reduce the confusion created by the hundreds of different policies on the market. The solution was the design of ten standard Medicare supplemental policies.

Each plan contains a core of basic services, and the nine optional plans offer expanded coverage. All policies must be in clear, concise language that makes it easy for consumers to compare the different plans. A benefit of the new standards is the protection they offer the consumer against purchasing more insurance than necessary.

In earlier days buying supplemental insurance could be downright hazardous to your financial health. The Health Insurance Association of America (HIAA) estimates that more than 5 million older Americans are paying for unnecessary, duplicative health insurance in the mistaken belief that they are adding to private coverage that supplements Medicare (*New York Times,* February 26, 1989). Because federal and state laws set a minimum level of benefits that any Medicare supplemental policy must pay, one such policy is enough in virtually every case. Yet the 1987 HIAA study found that 25 percent of supplemental policyholders had more than one policy, and many did not even know how many policies they had. Another problem, this one recounted in a 1989 General Accounting Office report, is that many companies offering medigap insurance "continue to bilk elderly citizens by offering unlawful and unconscionable low returns on premium payments" (*Washington Post,* April 4, 1989). According to the report, many such policies pay benefits equal to only 38 to 40 percent of all premiums collected.

First things first—what it is: medigap, or Medicare supplemental, policies are specially designed policies coordinated with Medicare and are not intended as your primary health insurance. They pay the traditional hospital and major medical benefits, less what Medicare pays. There may be several options: The lowest of the low will work almost like a limited indemnity policy. The highest of the high may cover so much that it will seem like a health maintenance organization, or HMO. The big difference will not be in what is covered but in how much of the charge for it is covered.

The Health Care Financing Administration, the federal agency that oversees Medicare, in cooperation with state insurance departments, certifies insurance policies as meeting the new federal medigap requirements. Only policies that meet the new federal standards may be advertised and sold as Medicare supplemental policies.

By law, all supplemental insurance plans must provide the following basic coverage:

▶ Hospital Part A copayment of $169 per day for days 61-90

▶ Hospital Part A copayment of $338 per day for days 91-150

▶ 100 percent coverage for an additional 365 days of hospital care after Medicare benefits end

▶ Medicare Part B 20 percent copayment on Medicare-approved charges (it pays nothing on charges not allowed by Medicare)

▶ The cost of the first three pints of blood or packed red cells whether received under Part A or B

The biggest gaps in the Medicare program for supplemental insurance to cover are found in Part B, medical insurance—in short, doctors' fees. As a June 1989 report in *Consumer Reports* put it, "Part B coverages separate the sheep from the goats in the field of supplemental policies." By law the basic plan must cover the 20 percent copayment; however, only four of the plans cover both the $100 Part B deductible and excess doctors' fees. This means that you may still be faced with out-of-pocket expenses up to the balance billing limits on doctors' fees.

It is under Part B that you can incur enormous out-of-pocket expenses. How? It all comes down to doctors and their proven adeptness at increasing their fees, for both Medicare and non-Medicare patients. Medicare gives doctors the option of accepting Medicare's allowable charge (what Medicare has decided is appropriate for the service) as payment in full, *or* requiring the patient to pay the difference between the allowable charge and the balance billing limit. As we have said before, when the doctor chooses the former course of action, in Medicare parlance she is said to *accept Medicare assignment*. This does not mean that the doctor has agreed to accept it as payment *in full*. She is supposed to charge you 20 percent of the Medicare price (your copayment); Medicare pays the other 80 percent. The Medicare check goes to the doctor, and you have to deal only with your copayment portion of the bill and with your insurance company. If you have supplemental insurance that covers the 20 percent that Medicare doesn't pay, you pay nothing. Four of the new standardized Medicare supplemental policies provide coverage for excess physician fees, including three that pay up to 100 percent of the balance billing limit.

Until recently, doctors could pick and choose whether or not to accept assignment on a service-by-service basis. Now they are either participating doctors—which means that they accept assignment on *all services they render to all Medicare patients*—or non-participating doctors, which means they can still pick and choose among patients and services, taking assignment on some but not on others. Coverage for excess charges from physicians is a *major reason to buy supplemental insurance*. Our earlier examples in chapter 1 illustrated the effects of assignment, or lack of it, on your wallet.

About half of all physicians are participating physicians, accepting assignment regularly. The rest accept assignment willy-nilly. While you can make sure that any new physician you choose is participating or will accept assignment for all *your* Medicare claims—and be sure to do so—it is more difficult to know about a physician's participation status when you are referred for specialized services, either in or outside the hospital.

SHOPPING FOR THE BEST SUPPLEMENTAL POLICY FOR YOUR MONEY

Now to the question of what supplemental insurance to buy so that you are not bankrupted in your senior years by health care costs. Before we go into this, just remember that almost no form of supplemental insurance will cover everything you need or close every gap in Medicare coverage. You will end up paying out of your own pocket for some expenses, but the supplemental policy you buy, if

TYPES OF SUPPLEMENTAL POLICIES

There are four ways to supplement Medicare coverage: medigap insurance, employer-paid retiree health insurance, health maintenance organizations, and Medicaid.

Medigap insurance is available in a basic plan as well as nine expanded coverage plans. Only those policies that meet the new federal standards may be advertised and sold as Medicare supplemental insurance.

Employer-paid retiree health insurance is something that you may receive as a retirement benefit. If you have employer-provided insurance, make sure that the plan provides the same coverage as a basic medigap policy.

Health maintenance organizations for Medicare beneficiaries are relatively new and may not be available in all areas. However, HMOs offer some distinct advantages over medigap insurance plans, especially in the area of preventive health care, reduced paperwork, and no 20 percent copayment.

Medicaid coverage is designed for Medicare beneficiaries whose income is at or below the poverty level. These so-called Qualified Medicare Beneficiaries are eligible to have Medicaid pay the Part B premium, deductible, and copayment.

it's any good, should minimize this. As you shop around among different supplemental policies, keep in mind that a good policy should cover charges of doctors in excess of the Medicare-approved amounts.

Before we start with our recommendations, here are our criteria for supplemental insurance: First, we assume that you will not have a large amount of personal resources and that your earning potential is limited. This means that the most important thing an insurance policy can do for you is to *protect the assets you have and keep you out of debt.* Second, we assume that you want to devote as small a portion of your income, beyond your health insurance premiums, to health care as you possibly can, and therefore want to *reduce your out-of-pocket expenses as much as possible.* And third, we assume that like most people—older or younger than you—you are a little bit frightened of the cost of health care and *want to buy some peace of mind* as well as some insurance.

Therefore, buy yourself some peace of mind and select a medigap plan that also covers the Part A and Part B deductibles in addition to the basic coverage. Under the new standard medigap plans, this is Plan C. Your other choices are employer-provided retiree health insurance, health maintenance organizations, and Medicaid. However, Medicaid may not be a viable option if your income is above the poverty level.

Of the three, we believe you should keep any employer plan that you have. Employer-provided retiree health insurance—health insurance for Medicare beneficiaries who work after aged sixty-five—usually pays for all or most of a defined set of services, so it looks like a service benefit plan with low out-of-pocket costs to those enrolled. Since Medicare has become the *secondary payer* for plans covering employees over sixty-five, they have gotten somewhat less generous.

Be aware that there are problems associated with rejecting your employer's health plan if you are over sixty-five and continue working. If you reject the plan, legally your employer cannot offer you a plan that is the equivalent of a medigap policy. Since Medicare, in this case, becomes the primary payer, any employer plan can pay only for the services that Medicare does not cover at all. In other words, Medicare puts the burden on *you* of buying your own supplemental insurance if you want the extra protection.

Keeping any employer plan that you have may require a small contribution on your part. These plans were modeled after benefit plans in more generous days, and many companies haven't gotten around to cutting them yet. With rare exceptions they are as good as high-option medigap policies, and possibly better. Further, several court cases have severely limited the right of companies to reduce the benefits of retirees.

Here's an important note that affects many people. What if your spouse turns sixty-five before you do and that spouse is covered under your employer group plan? Who pays the medical bills? Under the federal law that went into effect at the beginning of 1989, persons sixty-five or older who are covered by a working spouse's group health insurance plan continue to be covered by that plan until the working spouse reaches age sixty-five and retires. At that time, if the younger spouse is still covered by the former employer's health insurance program, the older spouse will be required to use Medicare as their primary payer. Be sure to contact the working spouse's insurance carrier before either of the above situations arises to guarantee that you are adequately covered.

Of course, even with an employer plan you should make sure that you are enrolled in Part A of Medicare when you turn sixty-five.

You should also purchase Part B, or doctor insurance. Why? First, if you don't purchase it during your individual enrollment period (the time from three months before your sixty-fifth birthday to three months after), you will have to wait until the next general enrollment period (the time from January 1 to March 31 of each year when anyone eligible for Part B of Medicare can enroll in it). You will pay an additional 10 percent premium for every year you wait. Second, enrolling keeps the cost to your employer down and helps to preserve the benefits of your plan. Third, because premiums for Part B cover only 50 percent of the cost, enrolling gives your employer's plan a de facto injection of federal money.

If you don't have employer-provided retiree health insurance or it is a wholly unsatisfactory plan, we recommend that you purchase one of the new standard medigap plans. Here is where we have to tell you what *not* to do:

▶ *Do not* purchase limited-purpose insurance, such as cancer insurance, accident insurance, and so on.

▶ *Do not* buy a policy that excludes preexisting conditions, if at all possible. If you do, make sure that the exclusion is limited to six months at most. (Federal law prevents any company from calling any policy that excludes preexisting conditions for more than six months a "Medicare supplement." The fact that this is against the law, however, doesn't mean that it won't be done.)

▶ *Do not* buy policies that duplicate ones you already have.

▶ *Do not* buy a policy just because it is endorsed by a celebrity.

▶ *Do not* buy a policy whose advertising claim is that you'll face bankruptcy if you don't buy it.

▶ *Do not* buy a policy by mail, if at all possible. If you believe you must, before you buy, call or write the company and ask if there is an office or agent near you. If so, deal directly with that office.

▶ *Do not* buy a policy that has a dollar limit on the total annual payment or payments over your lifetime, unless that limit is reasonably high. The ideal medigap policy has no annual maximum expenditure limit and a lifetime limit of between $1 million and $2 million.

▶ *Do not* purchase nonrenewable policies or ones that have unduly restrictive renewal clauses.

▶ *Do not* cancel an existing policy until the effective date of your new policy.

▶ *Do not* replace existing coverage without careful consideration of the advantages and disadvantages of both policies.

▶ *Do not* buy a policy just because it claims to pay for reductions in Medicare payments due to the Gramm-Rudman-Hollings balanced budget law. You'll be paying for something Medicare already provides if you fall for this one.

Some dos:

▶ *Do* make sure the company that sells the policy is licensed in your state.

▶ *Do* check the rating of the company in *Best's Insurance Reports—Life/Health,* published by A. M. Best and available in most public libraries.

▶ *Do* make sure that you know *exactly* what your premium will be and *exactly* what it covers. Many features that companies quite honestly say they offer are available only as riders, or amendments to the basic policy, and cost extra. Get a complete schedule of benefits and ask the salesperson to mark the benefits the premium covers.

▶ *Do* look carefully at the coverage offered for doctors' fees over and above the Medicare-approved price. A policy that covers only your 20 percent copayment is better than nothing but leaves you unprotected against excess charges up to the balance billing limit.

▶ *Do* ask the salesperson for information on the average out-of-pocket expenses for holders of the policy. This will tell you how much protection you really are buying.

▶ *Do* choose a policy that has a stop-loss provision, if you can get it. Even if there isn't one in the policy you're considering, the agent may be able to add it in the form of a rider, for which there will be an additional (usually small) fee.

▶ *Do* call your state insurance department and make sure that it approves the policy before you buy. Just remember that approval to sell a policy in a state does not mean that it is a good buy, simply that it does not violate any of the laws and conditions regarding insurance in your state.

▶ *Do* make sure that the policy you select is automatically adjusted to cover increases in Medicare's copayments and deductibles.

▶ *Do* pay by check, made out to the company, not the salesperson. Your canceled check is proof that you paid and keeps the salesperson from pocketing your payment.

▶ *Do* take advantage of any "free look" provisions mandated by the laws of your state. These allow you to buy a policy and cancel it with no obligation within a certain period if you decide that it is not what you want.

MONEY-SAVING TIPS

$ Pay premiums annually if you can afford to. You may be able to receive a discount on your premium if you can pay yearly in one lump sum.

$ Pay premiums on time. An insurance company can cancel your policy if you fail to pay the premiums or continually pay the premiums late. Be sure to keep on top of any necessary employee deductions if yours is an employer-sponsored policy.

THE MERITS OF HEALTH
MAINTENANCE
ORGANIZATIONS

We discussed health maintenance organizations (HMOs) a good deal in chapter 2, which explained what they are and how they work. The big advantage of an HMO, given our assumptions about what you want, is that all but a trivial portion of care is prepaid. There are no worries about having cash to go to the hospital. There are no service-specific charges, so there is no need to negotiate with the doctor about accepting Medicare assignment. There are far fewer, or no, forms to fill out. One payment covers everything.

Depending on the costs of medical care in your area and the particular HMO and options you pick, the individual HMO premium may be as high as $100 a month. An HMO premium may seem high, but remember that you are likely to spend 15 percent or more of your income on medical care. In contrast to traditional medigap coverage, the HMO premium picks up many out-of-pocket expenses that you would otherwise have to pay. More important is the peace of mind knowing that this is the *only* cost, except for nominal copayments. As we've said before, the proper comparison of two insurance plans is always this: *compare premiums plus out-of-pocket costs for one plan to premiums plus out-of-pocket costs for the other.*

Get exact figures from the HMOs that you are considering—including the average out-of-pocket costs for their Medicare members—but bear in mind that HMO benefit packages differ to some degree. Medicare requires the low-option plan in Medicare-approved HMOs to be at least equal to Medicare benefits, *without* the Medicare copayments and deductibles. Compare these to 15 percent of your annual income. Depending on your income, the HMO may save you anywhere from nothing (a break-even situation, but with added peace of mind) to a lot.

A big issue with HMOs is freedom of choice of doctors and hospitals. A number of alternatives that look like HMOs in some respects have emerged in recent years. *Preferred-provider organizations* (PPOs) have closed panels of doctors like HMOs, but not quite: for an extra fee you can go to the doctor or hospital of your choice; the PPO just covers less of the cost to you if you stray from the preferred providers. Generally, a PPO's benefits are not as generous as those of an HMO but a little better than a traditional fee-for-service plan—Blue Cross and Blue Shield, for example.

PPOs are just one variety of *competitive medical plans* (CMPs) with which the Health Care Financing Administration has been experimenting. Basically, CMPs are prepaid plans that do not have to meet the very stringent (and costly) federal requirements for Medicare HMOs. They receive a set amount, based on the average cost of treating a Medicare beneficiary in the counties they serve, adjusted for local wage and price differences. For this they are supposed to offer medical care. Depending on the cost of the care in the area and the options available within an individual CMP, they can be as generous as an HMO but should not offer less than the standard Medicare benefits.

For people who travel a good deal, a major disadvantage of HMOs is their reluctance to cover health care other than severe emergencies outside of their service area. If your HMO is in North Dakota and you are vacationing in Florida, you can expect that an emergency room visit for something serious will be covered but not a visit to a local doctor for a cold. On the other hand, many HMOs offer a toll-free number to call for preapproval of treatment. And because of consumer demand, many HMOs have loosened their requirements.

Joining an HMO is not a lifetime commitment. You may decide that, no matter how great the savings and the peace-of-mind factor, HMOs are just not for you. Don't worry. You have the right to drop out, and you will be covered by Medicare just as before. You can give one a try without any fear—assuming, of course, that your area has an HMO that accepts Medicare patients.

MEDICARE HMOS

Health maintenance organization membership was not available for Medicare beneficiaries until 1985. Now it is almost routine, although there are some eligibility requirements you must meet to be an HMO member as a Medicare beneficiary:

▶ You must be enrolled in both Parts A and B of Medicare.

▶ You can join only an HMO that has a contract with Medicare.

▶ You must live in the service area of the HMO—that is, the geographical area from which the HMO is licensed to enroll members. (Though HMOs are growing rapidly, only about half of the Medicare beneficiaries in the nation live in the service areas of HMOs with Medicare contracts.)

▶ You must enroll during the open-enrollment period designated by the HMO. This may be all year or limited to a few months.

▶ You cannot join a Medicare HMO if you are entitled to Medicare coverage because of kidney failure requiring dialysis or kidney transplant.

▶ You can drop out at any time by notifying the HMO in writing, on a form it prescribes for this purpose. A letter will not do unless the HMO specifically allows this. You must submit the withdrawal request by the tenth day of the month in order to be returned to the regular Medicare program on the first of the next month.

You do have certain protections as an HMO member. Medicare requirements for HMO beneficiaries may go beyond what the state requires to license an HMO.

▶ You cannot be denied enrollment because of your state of health—although the HMO is allowed to deny high-option coverage (services not normally covered by Medicare) to persons with some medical conditions.

▶ All Medicare-covered services must be available with reasonable promptness when needed, and emergency facilities available around the clock.

▶ The HMO cannot revoke your membership because of poor health or because of the cost of treating you.

▶ If the HMO ends its contract with Medicare—thereby dropping all Medicare beneficiaries—you must be given at least sixty days' notice.

MONEY-SAVING TIPS

$ Take advantage of any "free look" period. Most states allow you up to thirty days to review a policy and return it for a full refund if not satisfied. Call your state insurance department to learn the specific provisions.

$ Ask if your employer pays bounty for erroneous hospital bills. Many companies will pay rewards to employees who find inaccuracies in hospital bills that result in savings to the companies.

$ Be prepared to fight with your insurer over an error in any medical bill. Don't be surprised if your insurer is not overly enthusiastic if you call to report a hospital's or doctor's overcharge. Insurance companies often find it easier to pay erroneous claims rather than go to the trouble of auditing the bill and possibly demanding a refund. But you and everyone else pay for overcharges, so be persistent.

$ Get preapproval to make sure services are covered. Many insurance companies encourage this practice, which entails submitting a request for preapproval that consists of your doctor's recommendations and the reasons behind them. The insurance company will then either approve or disapprove coverage for the recommended procedure.

WHEN YOU TURN TO NONTRADITIONAL TREATMENT, IS THERE INSURANCE TO COVER IT?

If you are someone who searches out, whenever possible, an alternative path to healing—chiropractic, acupuncture, massage, biofeedback, or whatever—rest assured that you are not alone. Plenty of other people boldly venture outside the medical mainstream in search of nontraditional treatment, and experts say the numbers of people like you are increasing.

So wouldn't you think that insurance companies would get the message and seriously consider reimbursement for viable diagnostic and treatment choices? You would, if you were not aware that the medical monopoly (and that means the organized insurance system as well as organized medicine), through incessant accusations of quackery and fraud, attempts to steer everyone away from alterna-

tive practitioners. As a result, the consumer who seeks the nontraditional steps smack into the middle of a maze of insurance problems:
namely, while the practitioner may charge less for an office visit or
procedure than his or her traditional counterpart, you won't receive
insurance reimbursement. Consequently, what may be at least a
partial motivation for seeking such care—to minimize out-of-
pocket costs—backfires, and you end up spending more of your
own money.

That's not to say that no alternative treatment is covered. The
alternative treatment most likely to be covered is chiropractic treatment of back pain. As a report in the October 1988 *Sylvia Porter's
Personal Finance* pointed out, "Medicare, union health plans, most
group insurance plans, some Medicaid, some Blue Cross and Blue
Shield policies, some HMOs, and some individual insurance contracts cover this because chiropractors, unlike other alternative
health care providers, are now licensed in every state, which makes
them by law 'eligible renderers of medical care.' "

What about the procedures that more and more of the so-called
traditionalists are incorporating into their practices—the most
popular being acupuncture, biofeedback, and hypnosis? Some
plans (but not the "Blues") will reimburse for these in certain
situations, especially when physicians supervise or actually do
the procedures. But you can forget about reimbursement for
those times you seek alternative practitioners in the interest of
disease prevention.

So how do you cope with all the intricacies and inconsistencies?
As always, our best advice is: When in doubt, check with your
insurance company or benefits supervisor *before* you visit the alternative practitioner.

On a more optimistic note, here is a lead for where you might get
insurance coverage specifically for alternative care. Alternative
Health Insurance Services, Inc., is an independent insurance agency
that provides health insurance plans for both individuals and
groups. Located in California, the eight-year-old company deals
with some thirty health insurance companies that offer more than
twelve hundred different policies. Alternative Health Insurance
Services targets coverage for both alternative treatments and conventional medical and dental care, but the company's founder and
president, Steve Gorman, says it specializes in the alternative side
of the business. The company's goal, according to its advertising
literature, is the "most reasonable rates" for the "best coverage."
Contact:

Alternative Health Insurance Services, Inc.
P.O. Box 91178
Calabasas, CA 91372
818-509-5742 or 800-331-2713

Just remember: Before you buy any policy, follow the evaluation and selection process we outlined earlier in this chapter, especially the dos and don'ts.

DENTAL INSURANCE: YOU CAN'T ALWAYS GET WHAT YOU WANT, BUT DO YOU GET WHAT YOU NEED?

Although not yet as prevalent as medical insurance, dental insurance is fast making the rounds, with approximately one out of every three people in this country having dental coverage. A survey of 227 major U.S. employers found 98 percent offering dental plans in 1988 (*Hospitals,* September 1989). Virtually all dental insurance plans are group policies rather than individual ones. As to coverage, just remember the simple philosophy of insurance: You can have anything insured if you are willing to pay the premium—which is why the buyers of contracts, employers already stunned by through-the-roof health care costs, often buy limited benefits based on low monthly premiums.

The Council on Dental Care Programs of the American Dental Association (ADA) has designed the following chart on suggested dental procedures for coverage under a dental benefit plan. These suggestions should take a lot of the guesswork out of deciding whether the plan your employer offers or one you may be purchasing on your own meets a minimum level of acceptable benefits. And for your information, the ADA believes that rather than excluding services, the best way to contain costs in a dental benefits program is through copayments and annual limitations or maximums.

Dental insurance does not cover everything, and because it sometimes covers the least expensive treatment, it's important that you

Dental Benefit Plan Designs

For those seeking either a *limited cost* or *expanded cost dental benefit plan design*, the Association suggests the following:

I. Preventive, Diagnostic and Emergency Services

1. Initial oral examination — once per dentist
2. Complete radiographic survey — once in five years
3. Examination — twice per contract year
4. Annual bite-wing radiographs
5. Prophylaxis — twice per contract year
6. Topical fluoride treatment — under age 18 — twice per contract year
7. Sealants
8. Emergency treatment

II. Routine Dental Care

1. Restorative — amalgam and composite resin restorations; stainless steel crowns on primary teeth
2. Endodontics — pulpotomy; treatment and filling of root canals
3. Oral Surgery — simple tooth removal (not requiring cutting of tissue or bone); simple surgical procedures
4. Periodontics — treatment of uncomplicated periodontal disease with scaling, curettage and/or root planing; management of acute infections and lesions of the mouth
5. Prosthetics — repair and/or rebase of existing full or partial dentures and bridges
6. Orthodontics — space maintainers

III. Complex Dental Care

1. Restorative — gold restorations; individual crowns
2. Oral Surgery — surgical tooth removal; removal of impacted teeth; complex oral surgical procedures
3. Periodontics — treatment of complicated periodontal disease with osseous surgery, mucogingival surgery, gingival flaps, gingivectomy, tissue and bone grafts
4. Prosthetics — removable full and partial dentures; bridges
5. Orthodontics — orthodontic treatment, including diagnostic materials; retainers

find a good match between your particular insurance plan, assuming you have one, and your dentist. In short, find out if he or she will cooperate with the restrictions imposed by your insurance plan. There's no question about it—dentists are confused about dental insurance; all their practice management and other professional journals bemoan the "paper chase" that dentists have with insurance and decry the scant labor pool of savvy office personnel willing to keep up with the forms and ever-changing insurance company rules. While dentists clearly have profited from dental insurance—most experts agree that it is a primary factor in the increased number of people seeking dental care—dentists think it's a nuisance.

So, if you are to maximize your dental insurance benefits, you may have to take the lead in a number of areas:

▶ Get a copy of the brochure that details your plan and find out what your benefits are, what the deductible is, and if there are any exclusions and limitations.

▶ Ask your dentist a few questions: Will the dentist file your claim for you? Will the dentist agree to accept as 100 percent payment the amount that your insurance company "allows" for specific procedures? This latter issue is especially critical, since the practice of balance billing—billing you for the difference between the actual charge and the amount received by your dentist from your insurance program—can rapidly run up your out-of-pocket expenses: the very thing you're trying to avoid with dental insurance. You will probably find that many dentists will accept whatever your insurance company pays for the basics—cleaning and polishing, X rays, and simple extractions—but that crowns, bridges, orthodontic and periodontic work, and oral surgery are another matter. It's

Reprinted with permission:
American Dental Association
Council on Dental Care Programs

not as easy to find a dentist who will accept as 100 percent payment what your insurance company "allows" for these more complicated (and more expensive) dental services.

▶ Make sure your dentist itemizes fees on the claims form rather than lumps them together under one service. For instance, if you go into the office on an emergency basis but have an X ray taken and a filling put in, then the dentist should itemize for the filling, the X ray, *and* the emergency visit.

▶ Know your plan's requirements concerning predetermination (sometimes called pretreatment review or precertification). This is a procedure whereby your dentist submits his treatment plan to the insurance company *before* treatment is begun; the insurer usually returns the treatment plan indicating what benefits are available. If the predetermination is not approved, your dentist can request a review, but make sure he clearly details the reasons that the particular recommended treatment is the only way to go. Suggest that the dentist send any models, X rays, or photographs that clarify his treatment plan.

▶ Remind your dentist to request a special review (often called a special consideration) when certain procedures require more time—in other words, an extra long appointment—or more work than usual. The dentist should detail the circumstances for the higher-than-usual fees.

▶ Find out if your plan has an alternate benefit clause, which allows the insurance company to substitute payment for a less expensive treatment plan than the one the dentist proposed. Clearly aimed at minimizing your insurer's financial liability, this clause may maximize *your* financial liability and therefore is something you will wish to discuss with your dentist ahead of the treatment.

▶ Find out if your plan has an exclusion for preexisting conditions, and if so be sure to emphasize to your dentist the compelling need for predetermination in such cases.

▶ Have your dentist call your insurance carrier's toll-free number (many companies offer such numbers) or even call collect if he has specific questions concerning your coverage.

CAN YOU AFFORD NURSING HOME INSURANCE? CAN YOU AFFORD *NOT* TO HAVE NURSING HOME INSURANCE?

The nursing home business is a $40-billion-a-year industry. Of the nation's 31.3 million citizens aged sixty-five and above, 2.3 million (7.4 percent) live in nursing homes. The average cost of a year's stay is $22,000. The average stay, 465 days, costs $28,000. The average charge is around $60 a day. The Brookings Institution, a Washington think tank, estimates that by the year 2018, almost 8 percent of the elderly will live in nursing homes, at an annual cost of $55,000 per person.

Now these are statistics to make your blood run cold, and maybe even make you run to your Medicare booklet to see what the program covers. Save yourself a trip. Contrary to popular belief (and wishful thinking), Medicare pays only a small fraction of the cost of nursing home care in a skilled nursing facility (care prescribed by a doctor, given by a nurse, and available twenty-four hours a day), and none of the costs associated with the two most common levels of care required by the elderly: intermediate care (less intensive care than in a skilled facility) and custodial care (nonmedical care, assistance with daily activities). The federal government's position is that unless you're poor you should seek private insurance to protect yourself against the potentially devastating financial effects of a prolonged stay in a nursing home.

In early 1987 only two companies were offering nursing home, or long-term care, insurance. Today there are more than a hundred. That's the good news, but the bad news is that many of them exclude so much that you may pay more than $100 a month for essentially useless coverage.

In May 1988, *Consumer Reports,* a highly respected magazine that rates various products and accepts no advertising, cut through a great deal of confusion by offering a set of features that should be found in a good policy.

▶ The policy should provide a daily nursing home benefit of at least $80.

▶ The waiting period before benefits begin should be no more than twenty days.

▶ The maximum benefit period should be at least four years for one stay. If no time period is given, the dollar ceiling per benefit period should be at least 1,460 (365 days times four) times the daily benefit.

▶ The maximum benefit period for all stays should be unlimited.

▶ The policy should pay full benefits for skilled nursing facilities, intermediate care facilities, and custodial care.

▶ If there is a rule requiring that you be in a hospital before entering the nursing home, coverage should begin within thirty days after a hospital stay of three days or more.

▶ The policy should pay home care benefits, and pay them without requiring a prior nursing home or hospital stay.

▶ The policy should have a waiver of premium, which means that you need not pay premiums while you are in a hospital or nursing home. (You may have to pay extra for a waiver of premium, but it should be available at least as an option.)

▶ The policy should be guaranteed renewable for life.

▶ The policy should specifically state that Alzheimer's disease is covered.

▶ The premium should stay "level" for life—that is, not increase after you buy the policy. (A caveat here: a company *can* increase even a level premium when it also increases the premiums of all the people in your state who bought the same policy.)

▶ The Best's rating of the company should be A or A+. (Your local public library should have the directory *Best's Insurance Reports—Life/Health.*)

The *Consumer Reports* article did not recommend a premium because, as with life insurance, the older you are when you buy the policy, the higher the premium. Some other points to watch out for:

▶ Ask for a specimen policy if the insurance salesperson does not give you adequate answers to your questions. If the agent or company does not send one, shop around for another company.

▶ Find out if the company decides whether or not you qualify for payments (such decisions usually are made on the basis of medical necessity, an issue quite open to interpretation). If so, what are your appeal rights?

▶ Find out how many nursing homes in your state the policy will pay for. (Some policies pay only for selected homes.)

▶ Find out if the company limits coverage for preexisting conditions (those illnesses or diseases you have had before you bought the policy or have at the time the policy is issued). Most do. The question is, how bad are the restrictions? A waiting period during which Medicare will pay for the nursing home (skilled-nursing facility only), after which the policy picks up coverage, is not bad. Since most nursing home stays last an average of 1.3 years (465 days), a two-year exclusion is too much, however.

No policy *Consumer Reports* reviewed had an unlimited daily benefit, so resign yourself to the fact that no policy currently offered has adequate inflation coverage. The Brookings Institution has estimated that private insurance will cover only 7 to 12 percent of nursing home expenses in the year 2018 and that, at best, no more than half of the elderly will buy nursing home coverage.

Consumer Reports advises that no one under sixty buy a nursing home policy unless it offers some definite way to cover cost increases due to inflation. For people over sixty, policies should be bought only by those who have more than modest assets. The rest of us should rely on Medicaid for nursing home coverage.

COMPANIES SELLING LONG-TERM CARE INSURANCE
(As of July 1989)

Company names that are italicized are affiliates or subsidiaries of the company above them. Unless otherwise noted, all companies listed provide individual plans.

Acceleration Life Insurance Company
Acceleration Life Insurance Company of Pennsylvania
Aetna Life & Casualty[1]
AIG Life Insurance Company
Aid Association for Lutherans
Allstate Life Insurance Company
American Independent Insurance Company
American Integrity Insurance Company
American Progressive Life & Health Insurance Company of New York
Life Insurance Company of Connecticut
American Republic Insurance Company
American Sun Life Insurance Company
American Travellers Life Insurance Company[6]
AMEX Life Assurance Company
Associated Doctors Health & Life Insurance Company
Atlantic American Life Insurance Company
Bankers Fidelity Life Insurance Company
Atlantic & Pacific Life Insurance Company of America
Bankers Life & Casualty Company
Bankers Multiple Line Insurance Company
Certified Life Insurance Company of California
Union Bankers Insurance Company
Blue Cross & Blue Shield of Arizona
Blue Cross & Blue Shield of Connecticut
Blue Cross & Blue Shield of Indiana
Blue Cross & Blue Shield of Iowa
Blue Cross & Blue Shield of Kentucky[1]
Blue Cross & Blue Shield of Minnesota
Blue Cross & Blue Shield of North Dakota
Blue Cross & Blue Shield of Northern Ohio
Blue Cross & Blue Shield of the Rochester Area[1]
Blue Cross & Blue Shield of Wisconsin
Blue Cross & Blue Shield of Wyoming
Blue Cross of Washington & Alaska
Blue Cross of Western Pennsylvania
Blue Shield of California
Central Security Life Insurance Company
Central States Health & Life Company of Omaha
Colonial Penn Life Insurance Company
Colonial Penn Franklin Insurance Company
Combined Insurance Company of America
Commonwealth Life Insurance Company[2]

Continental Casualty Company (CNA)[1]
Valley Forge Life Insurance Company[2]
Continental Western Life Insurance Company[2]
Country Life Insurance Company
Equitable Life & Casualty Insurance Company
Federal Home Life Insurance Company
Harvest Life Insurance Company
First Penn Pacific Life Insurance Company[2]
Gerber Life Insurance Company
Golden Rule Insurance Company[2]
Great Fidelity Life Insurance Company
Great Republic Insurance Company
Hartford Life Insurance Company
Independent Nursing Insurance Company
ITT Life Insurance Company[2]
Integrity National Life Insurance Company
John Hancock Mutual Life Insurance Company[1]
Life & Health Insurance Company of America
Life Insurance Company of Georgia[2]
Life Investors Insurance Company of America
NN Investors Life Insurance Company
Lutheran Brotherhood
Medical Life Insurance Company
Medico Life Insurance Company
Mutual Protective Insurance Company
Metropolitan Life Insurance Company[4]
Mid-America Mutual Life Insurance Company
Midland Mutual Life Insurance Company
MONY Financial Services
Mutual of Omaha[1]
National Fidelity Life Insurance Company[2]
National Foundation Life Insurance Company
National States Insurance Company
National Travelers Life Insurance Company[2]
New York Life Insurance Company
North American Life & Casualty Company
Old Southern Life Insurance Company
Pekin Life Insurance Company
Penn Treaty Life Insurance Company
People's Security Life Insurance Company[2]
Physicians Mutual Insurance Company
Pilgrim Life Insurance Company
Pioneer Life Insurance Company of Illinois
Union Benefit Life Insurance Company
The Principal Financial Group[3]
Provident Life & Accident Insurance Company
Washington Square Life Insurance Company
Providers Fidelity Life Insurance Company
Prudential Insurance Company of America
Pyramid Life Insurance Company

Reserve Life Insurance Company
Security Connecticut Life Insurance Company[2]
Sentry Life Insurance Company[1]
Standard Life & Accident Insurance Company
State Life Insurance Company[2]
Time Insurance Company
Transport Life Insurance Company
Travelers Insurance Company[1]
Union Fidelity Life Insurance Company
Union Labor Life Insurance Company
United American Insurance Company
United Farm Bureau Family Life Insurance Company[2]
United General Life Insurance Company
United Security Assurance Company of Pennsylvania
UNUM Life Insurance Company[5]
Washington Health Services
World Life & Health Insurance Company of Pennsylvania

[1]Provides an individual plan and an employer-sponsored plan.
[2]Provides coverage as part of a life insurance policy.
[3]Provides an employer-sponsored plan.
[4]Provides an employer-sponsored plan and coverage to members of a continuing-care retirement community.
[5]Provides coverage to employer groups and specifically defined senior-age groups, including residents of retirement housing.
[6]Provides an individual plan and coverage as part of a life insurance policy.

SOURCES: Department of Health and Human Services, Health Insurance Association of America, American Council of Life Insurance, Blue Cross and Blue Shield Association, and Consumers Union.

MONEY-SAVING TIPS

$ Check all employer-sponsored health policy options carefully. Each health insurance policy offered by your employer may cover different kinds of care and services. To get the best value for your money, carefully compare all the policies with your needs in mind. Do not settle for less coverage than you need. Your premium for more coverage will probably not be much higher.

10 FEATURES OF A GOOD LONG-TERM CARE POLICY

According to an article in the September 11, 1989 *National Underwriter,* a group of experts, consumers, and retirees agreed that the best long-term care policy will:

1. Cover care in skilled, intermediate, and custodial facilities.

2. Offer a choice in benefit levels.

3. Allow the insured to enter at any level of care without prior hospitalization.

4. Be guaranteed renewable for life.

5. Specify that organically based mental or nervous disorders (including Alzheimer's disease) are covered.

6. Contain an inflation adjustment feature.

7. Waive the premium during benefit periods (or after confinement begins).

8. Offer the option to start benefit payments as soon as twenty days after eligibility begins.

9. Set the minimum benefit period per stay at three years (or offer benefit period options of, for example, three, five, and seven years).

10. Offer a home health care option, preferably without requiring prior hospitalization or skilled nursing care).

$ Donate blood—join a blood bank. By committing yourself to the donation of a specified amount of blood per year, you can receive insurance coverage for blood supplies for yourself and possibly for your family as well.

$ Subscribe to an ambulance service. Similar to the arrangement with a blood bank—private, voluntary ambulance services often offer a specified amount of service for a yearly donation.

4

Saving on Drugs and Medications

Pharmacy is a profession in transition. Once upon a time, the community pharmacy was the home and work site of the owner-employer pharmacist, the sole proprietor responsible for ordering and dispensing medications and perhaps even dusting and stocking the shelves. He stood behind the counter ready with price and advice for every prescription you brought in.

Nowadays corporate ownership of chain pharmacies is becoming more and more common. The hometown pharmacist is giving way to the employee or manager pharmacist, and you may not see the same face on Tuesdays that you see on Thursdays—and you may not even care.

What's the big deal about choosing a pharmacist? And what does it have to do with your health and pocketbook anyway, you ask. Just find a pharmacy that's close and cheap, and there you are, right? Sure, those are two valid considerations, but others are probably more important to your health and ultimately your mission, to get the most for your medical dollar. Most important are details such as how willing and able the pharmacist is to help you with generic drugs and over-the-counter medications, and what the pharmacy's policies are regarding generic substitutions, refills, and emergency prescriptions.

You see, more than just a pill counter, your pharmacist is *the most readily accessible health care professional most of us have.* And no appointment is needed. The pharmacist is a highly trained drug expert who probably knows more than your own physician about the relative benefits and risks of various drugs. Of the pharmacists surveyed by the journal *Drug Topics* and reported in its June 15, 1987 issue, around half said they found as many as two physician prescribing errors a week, and nearly a quarter of the pharmacists caught ten or more mistakes in the same interval.

190

With today's medications more expensive, more complex, and in some cases more potent, and with drug prescribing on the increase (61 percent of office visits result in a prescription), you need to find a competent and communicative pharmacist—now more than ever.

You're looking for a pharmacist willing to talk to you, to tell you when and how to take your medications, how frequently and for how long. You should expect straight answers when you ask about side effects, potential drug-food interactions, drug allergies, and nutrition and drug therapy, and more, because, after all, it's a matter of health—and economics: about $2 billion a year is spent on drugs that treat the adverse effects of other drugs, according to Health Information Designs, Inc., of Arlington, Virginia. Clearly, appropriate drug use can save you money, not to mention your life in some cases.

Finally, remember that as convenient as it may be to skip around from pharmacy to pharmacy, it's a good idea to limit yourself to one. That way you are more likely to find someone you can trust, someone who keeps an ongoing record of your medications and any problems, and someone who is more than a faceless person behind a counter.

FIND A PHARMACIST WHO...

▶ *Does* more than merely read a doctor's prescription, fill it, label it, and charge for it.

▶ *Keeps* important family medication records called patient medication profiles, and uses them to help prevent allergic reactions to drugs, dangerous interactions, duplicate medications, and drug abuse.

▶ *Advises* how to use prescription and nonprescription medications: how and when to take the medication; what the possible side effects are; what the shelf life is; how to store the medication; and whether there is potential for dangerous interactions with foods and/or other medications.

▶ *Answers* your questions about the staggering variety of medicines, remedies, tonics, pills, elixirs, lotions, salves, capsules, and powders on the market.

▶ *Advises* you, when necessary, to seek a medical practitioner's help.

THE PATIENT MEDICATION PROFILE: WHAT IT IS, WHY YOU NEED IT

No doubt about it—someone should be keeping a medication profile on you, indeed on everyone in your household. It's a system that monitors all the drugs you are taking, in hopes of avoiding medication errors. And while this may sound like exactly the sort of thing your doctor is already doing, think again. Many doctors don't know the drugs their patients are taking, even when the doctors themselves are prescribing the medications!

A study reported in the January 11, 1986 *British Medical Journal* uncovered poor and careless recordkeeping—mishandling of pertinent details such as what drugs are being prescribed—in 70 percent of hospital *and* general practitioners' medical records. For more than one patient out of ten, the inaccuracies were considered major, such as asthmatic patients taking heart medications expressly prohibited for people in their condition. Unfortunately, the same study found that the patients themselves could not accurately describe their drug treatments without their medications at hand.

A better testimony for the value and usefulness of a patient medication profile cannot be found. While this is a record you may want to keep for yourself (and we urge you to do so), your pharmacy is the logical site for the information. A patient medication profile (sometimes simply called a patient profile) ranges from the simple (a card file) to the high tech (a computerized system that will retrieve new and old information and even type labels). The American Pharmaceutical Association recommends that such a profile contain the following information:

▶ Your name, address, and phone number

▶ Your and your family's birthdays, so that the pharmacist can check whether the dosage is appropriate to the age of the user

▶ Any allergies, reactions, or adverse effects you've demonstrated

▶ Any drugs that have proved ineffective for you

▶ A concise health history, including any conditions or diseases (for instance, diabetes, high blood pressure, or an ulcer) that would preclude the use of certain drugs

▶ The over-the-counter, or nonprescription, medicines you take.

▶ The date and number of each prescription filled for you, the name of the drug, its dosage and strength, quantity, directions for use, and price

▶ **The prescriber and dispenser of every medication you take**

Keep in mind that this service will be useful only if you buy all your medicine from the same pharmacy.

MONEY-SAVING TIPS

$ Shop around for prescription prices. Telephone calls to your local pharmacies will reveal a surprising difference in prices. Since the medication is the same wherever you buy it, always purchase where it is the least expensive.

$ Watch for sales. Occasionally, pharmacies will put commonly prescribed drugs and popular over-the-counter medications on sale.

$ Know your pharmacist. A pharmacist can be an invaluable resource of information regarding drugs—interactions to watch out for, alternative forms of the same drug (i.e., liquid or pills), and less expensive alternatives. Talk with your pharmacist. The better she knows you, the more she will be able to help.

PHARMACIES: CHAINS VERSUS INDEPENDENTS— WHO OFFERS THE BEST BARGAIN FOR YOU?

While the independently owned community pharmacy is still a visible, and certainly a viable, part of the American scene—two out of every three prescription drugs are dispensed there—chain stores owned by large national corporations such as Eckerd, Thrift, Revco, and the Walgreen Company are steadily making inroads into the market. Another part of the changing scene is the inclusion of pharmacies in supermarkets and discount stores.

What are the advantages to your health and wallet of one over the other? Frankly, that's a question for which there's no pat answer—it depends upon the individual pharmacy and its policies, as well as the pharmacist and her knowledge and competence. However, there are questions you can ask concerning how business is run at a particular pharmacy, whatever the setting:

1. What personalized services are offered? Free home delivery? Convenient hours, especially during evenings and weekends? Arrangements for you to receive emergency medications when the pharmacy is closed or the pharmacist away? Patient medication profiles? Patient counseling on drug interactions, side effects, etc.? Help with orthopedic and prosthetic devices or other medical aids? Compliance with your preferences, such as nonchildproof caps, capsules instead of tablets, etc.?

2. Is there an area set aside for you to speak privately, if you wish, with the pharmacist?

3. Are consumer health education materials available?

4. Does the pharmacy have the refill policies that you want? Phone-in refills? Refills available at other locations? Is the pharmacist willing to contact your physician for you, if necessary?

5. Can a rare drug be easily and quickly obtained should your doctor prescribe it for you? Will the pharmacist compound special prescriptions?

6. Are the pharmacy's prices competitive with others in your community? (You won't know until you ask and can compare the prices.)

7. Does the pharmacy allow purchases to be charged or offer charge accounts to its customers?

8. Does the pharmacy accept your prescription drug insurance plan?

9. Does the pharmacy provide end-of-the-year prescription cost statements for income tax and insurance purposes?

10. Does the pharmacy offer a senior citizen discount?

11. Is the physical layout convenient? Accessible to the handicapped?

GENERICS: WHAT ROLE
DO THEY PLAY IN
SAVING YOU MONEY?

Shopping for generic forms of life's daily necessities is relatively easy. In many grocery stores you can wheel your cart down the aisle and select from shelves stocked full of tissues, adhesive strips, raisins, and the like, all bearing the unmistakable packaging and labeling of the generic: black and white—it's hard to miss.

But the issue of generic drugs is a much more complicated proposition, a much more difficult shopping expedition. Unlike coffee filters, prescription medicines are locked away, out of your sight and reach, and only two people hold the key to that medicine cabinet: your doctor and your pharmacist. But *you* can help unlock the door by knowing who and what to ask about generics.

First, what it is: a generic drug (the name of which is usually a condensed version of the drug's original chemical name) is one whose active ingredients duplicate those of the brand-name product. Acetaminophen, for example, is the generic name of a nonprescription painkiller; Tylenol, Anacin 3, and Panadol are the brand names. While a generic does not have to be the same size, shape, or color of the brand name, by law it does have to be bioequivalent, determined by measuring how much of the drug is absorbed into the bloodstream and how quickly absorption takes place. A generic cannot differ from the pioneer drug by more than 20 percent in either the speed or amount of absorption.

Unlike shopping for generic items in the grocery store, however, the issue of generic drugs does not come down to black and white. And the last few years have been especially troublesome for the generic drug industry, which some say is in the middle of a credibility crisis with critics all around. You see, generic drugs usually are sold at substantially lower prices, and therein lies the rub—to the brand-name manufacturers, that is. On the average, generic drugs are 30 percent cheaper than brand-name drugs—even 50 to 70 percent cheaper than the more expensive medicines—because their manufacturers do not go to the expense of advertising them, nor do they sink money into inventing new products. Instead, they copy older, well-known drugs once these drugs' patents expire.

Of late, many brand-name "bestsellers," such as Valium, have come off patent and, therefore, are being marketed—and sold less expensively—in generic forms. As a result, the manufacturers of brand-name drugs and even some medical groups have been questioning the safety and effectiveness of lower-priced generic drugs and urging action against their proliferation and use.

In 1989 the American Academy of Family Physicians, having just completed its own two-year study, asked the nation's sixty thousand family doctors to stop prescribing generic drugs for patients seventy-five years of age and older, older women with multiple diseases who are taking multiple drugs, and anyone with depression, asthma, congestive heart failure or other heart problems, diabetes, or any type of psychosis. The academy's own study found that some generic drugs have different inactive ingredients than their brand-name counterparts and that these differences can affect how the drugs treat the symptoms.

While critics of generics are hard at work trying to persuade consumers, doctors, and pharmacists that generic drugs don't do the job as well as the brand-name drugs they replace and claiming that they do not have the same therapeutic effects, the Food and Drug Administration says this is not true. The FDA says a generic can be safely substituted if it is bioequivalent to the brand-name product—that is, has the same active ingredient(s), dosage form, strength, and route of administration, and if the rate and extent of absorption of the drug is no greater or less than 20 percent of the rate and extent of absorption of the original product. (See box on p. 198.)

While the behemoths in the drug industry argue that generics are not always safe and effective because the inactive ingredients in some differ from those in brand-name drugs, consumer groups have labeled these tactics a "campaign of fear." Meanwhile, the few existing clinical studies on generic drugs indicate that *generic products are likely to be as beneficial as brand-name ones.*

However, even though thousands of generics are available, doctors prescribe generic drugs only 15 percent of the time—in part, according to a survey in the October 1987 *New York State Journal of Medicine,* because few patients request them. So, if you wish to save money by using generics, you'll have to make your desires clear to your doctor *and* your pharmacist. Start by asking your doctor, "Is there a generic drug available for this medication?" If your doctor doesn't know—and the chances are good she won't because doctors don't put a high value on learning the names of generic drugs— make sure she leaves the option open to the pharmacist to substitute a generic if one's available.

What if the physician insists the brand-name drug is necessary? Take the prescription to your pharmacist, and ask her to call your doctor. If the pharmacist doesn't want to call, find another pharmacy. And if the physician still insists on the brand name, and fails to convince you of the necessity, then consider switching doctors.

Physicians learn most about the medications they prescribe from so-called detail men, the drug manufacturers' representatives who visit each doctor on a regular basis, telling her what their drugs do and doling out free samples. As for the potential adverse reactions or contraindications relevant to each medication, the average physician gets that information from package inserts that are provided by the manufacturer. While obviously helpful, reading such information on a little sheet of paper, or even from the famed *Physicians' Desk Reference (PDR)* (which is merely a reprint of the package insert), is not what one would call a medical school course in the proper use of what is potentially a very powerful drug. The point here is that there may very well be a generic that does the job just as well but has not been hyped to the practitioner like the name brand.

Finally, comparison-shop for lower generic drug prices. If you are like most people, who have three or four pharmacies in their neighborhood, this should not be too difficult to do, but you may want to save your major time and effort for expensive drugs that must be taken regularly for long periods.

Although you generally will pay less for generic drugs than name brands, unfortunately this is not always the rule at every pharmacy. Surveys have found astonishing price-per-pill fluctuations at different pharmacies. Forty-six states require that when a generic is substituted for a prescribed brand-name drug, the wholesale savings must be passed on to the consumer, but only fourteen mandate that the *full* savings be passed along. So the bargains (or rip-offs) may vary from pharmacy to pharmacy. Shop around.

A Matter of Substitution or Safety?

Actually, the battle over generic drugs may have as much to do with substitution as with safety, and the fact that doctors aren't happy with what they see as a loss of autonomy and control when pharmacists substitute generics for brand-name drugs.

You see, most states have repealed their antisubstitution laws, under which if a doctor prescribed a certain brand of a drug, the pharmacist could not substitute the generic version, even if it cost less and was the chemical twin of the prescribed brand. Now pharmacists nearly everywhere can fill a prescription with a generic, but

GENERICS: ANOTHER LOOK AT THEIR SAFETY

A curious and unsettling story about generic drugs began unfolding in 1989. In August of that year the Food and Drug Administration (FDA) was roundly chastised by the Department of Health and Human Services' Office of the Inspector General for failing to keep close rein on its generic review process. Three former employees of the FDA's generic drug division pleaded guilty to accepting illegal payments from drug manufacturers in exchange for handling drug applications more quickly, three generic drug company officers were indicted on bribery charges, and the FDA began investigating eleven generic drug firms implicated in faulty or fraudulent practices. By September 1989, 26 drugs had been recalled and suspensions issued for 141 others.

Fortunately, no consumers have been known to be injured by using an approved generic substitute. But the congressional subcommittee on oversight and investigations, worried about widespread manufacturing irregularities in the generic industry, called for changes to be made in the FDA's drug approval system. What's going on here? "Shakeout time," according to an FDA official quoted in the September 11, 1989 issue of *Medical World News,* who predicted that "companies that are weak or have bad records will probably get swallowed up or go out of business."

How has the FDA responded to the strong criticism? Its first step was to create a new division for approving generics. Meanwhile, another section of the agency launched an expanded investigation of the generic drug industry, collecting more than a thousand samples of the thirty most popular forms of generics for chemical analysis at federal laboratories. The object, according to an August 17, 1989 *New York Times* article, "is to determine whether the pharmaceuticals being sold match the formulations that received federal approval. The brand-name drugs that the generics copy will also be examined as a safeguard."

While it would be unfortunate if this situation crippled consumers' ability to get less expensive drugs, a clean sweep of the drug industry to pinpoint *any* unscrupulous company—whether it manufactures generic or brand-name drugs—will be beneficial to all. Consumer safety is paramount. But we can't forget that people have been using generics to rein in rising medical costs for years—and with good results.

the process varies depending on whether the state's substitution law is permissive or mandatory. Half require the doctor to write "Dispense as written," or similar words to that effect, and in most of the other states the doctor must sign on either one of two signature lines—one line allows the pharmacist to substitute, the other to dispense only as written.

Currently, there is a move afoot in many states to make generic

THE 10 MOST COMMONLY PRESCRIBED DRUGS AND THEIR GENERIC VERSIONS (1988)

Brand Name/Generic Name	Prescribed For
Amoxil/amoxicillin	antibiotic
Lanoxin/digoxin	heart
Xanax/alprazolam	anxiety
Zantac/ranitidine hydrochloride	ulcer
Premarin/conjugated estrogens	estrogen
Dyazide/hydrochlorothiazide, triamterene	high blood pressure
Tagamet/cimetidine	ulcer
Tenormin/atenolol	heart
Naprosyn/naproxen	arthritis
Cardizem/diltiazem hydrochloride	heart

SOURCES: *U.S. News & World Report,* May 1, 1989, and Pharmaceutical Data Services, Inc.

substitution even easier, according to a March 4, 1989 *New York Times* article. Several state legislatures are considering bills that would change prescription forms and procedures to actually encourage substitution. Doctors would have to write out the words "brand medically necessary" or some such phrase. In the twelve states that currently require the handwritten phrase, surveys have found that doctors just do not bother to do that.

Find out what your state's law is concerning the substitution of a generic drug. These laws strengthen the role (and responsibility) of the consumer *and* the pharmacist in decision-making.

MONEY-SAVING TIPS

$ Ask for an initial one-to-two day supply of any new prescription to check for side effects. Since there is a possibility of an adverse reaction to any medication, you will save money if you initially request only a limited supply of any new prescription. You can pick up the remainder of the prescription (and pay for it) the next day if no adverse reaction occurs.

$ Store drugs properly. Most drug items need to be kept "fresh" just as many food products do. A cool, dry climate is best for preserving most drugs. Never keep your medications in the glove compartment of your car, where temperatures can rise and fall beyond the range recommended to maintain most drugs' efficacy.

$ Purchase a prescription plan. Most group health insurance policies offer prescription coverage for a small additional premium. Ask if your plan offers this additional coverage as an option.

$ Purchase drugs from your HMO pharmacy. If you are a member of a health maintenance organization, find out if yours has an in-house pharmacy. HMO pharmacies often sell drugs to HMO members at wholesale cost or slightly above.

THERAPEUTIC SUBSTITUTION

Depending on who you are and how you look at the issue, therapeutic substitution is either a way that pharmacists, with their superior knowledge of medicines, can fine-tune your doctor's orders to ensure that you get the best drug for your problem at the best price—or a dangerous encroachment on physicians' prescribing privileges and a threat to your health.

A big step beyond generic substitution, therapeutic substitution (pharmacists prefer to call it therapeutic *interchange*) allows a pharmacist to switch to an entirely different drug believed by the pharmacist to be therapeutically similar to the drug prescribed by the physician. This practice differs from generic substitution in that the drug dispensed is not a generic version of the prescribed drug, but is one with an entirely different chemical composition.

As you can imagine, organized medicine is on the warpath against therapeutic substitution. True, it is standard practice in many hospitals, but doctors fear its spread to the corner drugstore and health care settings beyond the hospital, specifically health maintenance organizations (HMOs) and nursing homes. The worst-case scenario here, say the doctors, is that cost-slashing budgeteers will try to save money without regard for patient well-being and substitute cheaper drugs in the pharmacy without telling the doctors who care for HMO patients through independent practice models or staff models.

The director of the American Medical Association's division of drugs and toxicology, interviewed in the April 10, 1989 issue of *Medical World News*, summed up organized medicine's position on extending therapeutic substitution to large HMOs: an "acceptable and sensible" arrangement only if practiced with physicians' knowledge and consent.

Only three states have statutes addressing therapeutic substitution: Illinois and Wisconsin prohibit it except in hospitals, and Washington State permits it only with the physician's prior consent. But by 1988 nearly a third of HMOs nationwide allowed therapeutic interchange, although questions remain as to whether it violates state laws that prohibit prescribing by pharmacists (*Medical Economics*, March 6, 1989).

Does therapeutic substitution threaten the health of consumers? Does it undermine the system of checks and balances that conscribes the traditional roles of physician and pharmacist? Or does therapeutic substitution benefit consumers by involving pharmacists in determining the most effective drug with the least possible side effects at the most economical cost? No doubt the debate will rage on as more and more HMOs adopt the practice of therapeutic substitution to help contain ever-rising pharmaceutical costs. But the question really comes down to how much of a factor cost should be in drug selection. That's a question you should take up with your physician and your pharmacist anytime a drug is prescribed for you.

The medical profession, staunchly opposed to therapeutic substitution, maintains that therapeutic decisions reached by physicians are based on a complex body of medical information relevant to a specific patient—make sure this is indeed the case with you.

OVER-THE-COUNTER DRUGS: THEY HAVE A PLACE IN YOUR MEDICINE CABINET, BUT ARE THEY WORTH THE INVESTMENT?

Few consumers realize the cost-squandering that goes along with nonprescription, or over-the-counter (OTC), drugs. They don't worry about OTCs because, as the argument goes, the fact that they're available without a prescription is evidence enough of their efficacy and safety. After all, the Food and Drug Administration, which oversees the effectiveness of over-the-counter remedies as well as of prescription drugs, wouldn't approve anything that wasn't good, right? That didn't do what ads claim, right?

Well, the truth is that no drug is harmless and completely safe. Each one is a chemical, designed to alter the body's function in some way—for the better, it is hoped. Compared to prescription drugs, yes, OTCs are relatively safe. Nonetheless, they must be used with caution, not only to get your money's worth but also for the sake of health.

The point is that some nonprescription drugs are as strong as the medications your doctor prescribes. And as for the FDA's stamp of approval or the agency's ability to remove a suspect drug from the market, let's just say that ineffective and marginally effective drugs do exist.

And unsuspecting consumers are buying them. F. James Grogan, a leading pharmacist-writer, estimates that more than $1 billion is squandered on what he calls "second-rate OTC drugs" (*The Pharmacist's Prescription: Your Complete Guide to Over-the-Counter Remedies*, [Riverside, N.J.: Rawson Associates, 1987]).

With more than 300,000 OTC products on the market, the choices can be confusing, and as wary a consumer as you may be, in your confusion you may turn to the most visible source of "information" on OTCs—advertising. But no doubt you're painfully aware that television and magazine ads do not always point you in the most cost-effective direction, nor do their claims ensure that you find the safest, most effective drug for your problem or condition. That's where a good pharmacist can make all the difference.

Another reason to turn to the pharmacist is that doctors tend to underplay—if not actually dispute—the therapeutic role OTCs can play in your health care. The health care professional right there on the scene, where the OTCs are being sold, is the pharmacist. Use that resource. Whatever your questions may be, about whatever type of OTC you're interested in, ask right on the spot.

Ask your pharmacist what previously prescription-only medicines are now available over-the-counter. Benadryl, topical hydrocortisone, Tinactin, and Actifed are examples of this.

Here are a few other cost-saving strategies for getting the most for your money with OTCs:

▶ Find out the risks or side effects of any OTC you're considering buying and taking, or you'll end up paying for a doctor visit or emergency room trip *on top of* the cost of the medicine.

▶ Ask about potentially dangerous interactions between over-the-counter medications and any prescription drugs you may be taking.

▶ Go over with your pharmacist the label instructions of any medication so that you can be sure you're taking it wisely and appropriately. If you are taking drug preparations in forms you do not normally use or fully understand—for instance, suppositories or prolonged-release tablets—find a pharmacist willing to provide detailed, perhaps even written, instructions. A lot of pharmacists assume that people can choose the best OTC remedy merely by reading labels, and that they will automatically comply with the manufacturers' recommendations. This is simply not true.

The entire process of getting the best for your money goes something like this:

▶ First, determine what your symptoms are.

▶ Ask the pharmacist what ingredients are needed to treat your diagnosed condition.

▶ Work together to find the products containing the needed ingredient(s) so that you don't pay for ingredients you don't need.

BUSINESS IS BOOMING

OTC drug sales are big business—really big. In 1988 sales were $17 billion, according to Nielsen Marketing Research (*Drug Topics*, April 17, 1989). And if the calculations of the Proprietary Association (the trade organization of manufacturers of nonprescription drugs) are on target, business will get even better.

A WORD OF WARNING REGARDING OTCS

In the interest of health and economy, be sure to consult a pharmacist and possibly a physician before buying any OTC preparation for babies, young children, elderly or debilitated persons, or pregnant or breast-feeding women.

A good resource to find out more about nonprescription drugs and their value in economical, responsible health care is *Over-the-Counter Pills That Don't Work* (Washington, D.C.: Public Citizen Health Research Group, 1983).

▶ Choose a safe, effective, and economical product from that list.

MONEY-SAVING TIPS

$ Buy generic prescription drugs when possible. The generic form of the drug is usually cheaper than the brand-name drug, but always check with your doctor or pharmacist to determine whether a generic form of the drug you need is available and safe, and is indeed less expensive.

$ Buy store-brand over-the-counter drugs when possible. Many pharmacies and some grocery store chains purchase bulk over-the-counter drugs and package them under their own store-brand names or labels. By reading labels, you can compare prices on brand-name items to the less expensive, but identical, store-brand item.

$ Buy single-ingredient over-the-counter drugs. Many over-the-counter drugs are preparations of several drugs, such as an antihistamine combined with a decongestant as a "cold" medication. It is less expensive to purchase a decongestant and an antihistamine separately, because you often will need only one of these to treat your symptoms and because mixtures are often more expensive.

$ Check to see if an effective over-the-counter drug is available before buying a prescription drug. For many categories of prescription drugs, over-the-counter medications are available to treat the same symptoms. Talk with your doctor or pharmacist about similar over-the-counter drugs before purchasing the possibly more expensive prescription medication.

PRESCRIPTION DRUGS POSTHASTE?

Getting prescription drugs by mail is one of the hottest ideas around right now in health care. Not really a new phenomenon—mail-order pharmacies have existed for more than twenty-five years—the concept has gained quite a following over the last few years amid growing pressure on businesses to reduce their employee medical costs. A report in the Spring 1988 issue of *Money* reckoned that mail-order sales of prescription drugs since the early 1980s have climbed 30 to 50 percent annually, with total sales in the $900-million range.

The workings of a typical system are simple. Most mail-order pharmacy services supply "maintenance" drugs—used to treat conditions such as high blood pressure, diabetes, ulcers, and asthma. Whereas normally you would take the prescription to a local pharmacy and receive a thirty-day supply, with a mail-order plan you send the prescription to a pharmaceutical distribution house, which provides a three-month or sometimes a six-month supply. The drugs are mailed to your home, usually a week or two after you send the order.

Without a doubt, the scheme is an attractive one for consumers and employers alike. The cost savings, according to the industry's trade organization, the American Managed Care Pharmacy Association, range anywhere from 5 to 40 percent off prices at your local pharmacy, and it's easy to see why:

▶ First, the drugs usually cost less through the distribution houses because the drugs are bought in bulk (at about 10 percent less than the average wholesale price), so drug prices to the consumer usually exclude the retail markup.

▶ And since the drugs are sold to consumers in volume (that is, quantities that last several months) there are fewer dispensing and administrative fees.

▶ Plus, whenever possible the distribution houses substitute generic drugs, which are traditionally less costly than brand-name drugs.

Mail-order plans are convenient, especially for the elderly who are on maintenance drugs and can save repeated trips to the pharmacy for refills.

The National Association of Retail Druggists, among others, has launched a campaign against prescription drugs by mail—understandably, since the independent pharmacist is in direct competition with such a service. The group asks questions any consumer would want to know: What do you do until the medicine arrives in the mail? What do you do if the medicine is stolen? What do you do when the medicine you take runs out? How long will it be before you can be resupplied? Do you really want to receive larger than normal quantities of a medicine, which can lead to abuse and waste?

It is true there may be serious "design flaws" in the mail-order pharmacy business. A study commissioned by PCS, an Arizona-based prescription claims processor and a subsidiary of a wholesale drug distributor, found that the time lag inherent in many mail-order programs is an incentive for consumers to buy more monthly refills in advance and perhaps more than they need. This waste of unused purchased drugs, among other things, results in higher costs for employers to cover, according to the researchers—as much as 5.2 percent more than traditional drug-dispensing systems (*Modern Healthcare,* October 28, 1988).

Then there's the question of the lack of personalized service when you're dealing with a form rather than a face. And, the system's detractors ask, what if you need counseling on potential drug interactions and side effects? What do you do—correspond by mail for this as well?

True, it is a matter of caveat emptor. Before you sign on with a mail-order service, make sure it has what you need. The better plans have safeguards—in the form of computerized medication profiles of all participants—against prescription drug abuse and potentially serious drug interactions. Some even have toll-free numbers and offer phone-in advisory services for any questions you may have about the drugs you're taking.

As to a frequently heard criticism that mail-order services indiscriminately substitute generics—whether or not equivalent to the prescribed brand-name drug—quite a few of the plans, especially some of the newer ones, use generic drugs only when doctors authorize a generic substitution.

Of course, as economical and convenient as mail-order prescription drugs can be, especially for people with certain chronic conditions, you still need a good pharmacist: someone who knows you, your health problems, why you're taking the drug you are—and someone you can turn to in an emergency. Saving money but losing a valued drug expert and counselor is no bargain.

Where do you sign up for mail-order prescription drugs? More and more companies have begun to offer such programs as part of their employee benefit packages. So if you're employed, first check with your employer. If this tactic isn't feasible—you're not employed, you're retired, your company doesn't offer such a plan, or whatever—there are other avenues to explore:

▶ The Veterans Administration, which dispenses two-thirds of all mail-service prescription orders, is the giant in the business. However, besides being a U.S. veteran, you must meet certain eligibility requirements. Check with the VA facility nearest you for details.

▶ The American Association of Retired Persons (AARP), through its affiliated organization Retired Persons Services, Inc., offers a mail-order pharmacy service to dues-paying members and their families. Call 703-684-0244 for further information.

PHYSICIANS ARE DISPENSING DRUGS, BUT ARE THEY DISPENSING BETTER CARE WITH THEM?

A big hue and cry in the prescription drug industry these days involves physician dispensing, an issue which—as the name implies—has overturned the so-called natural order of business wherein doctors prescribe and pharmacists dispense. The pharmacists call it an encroachment on their territory and a source of potential harm to consumers. Meanwhile, the doctors call it good for their patients and bottom-line smart for their incomes. But is it good for you? First, what it is.

Before it became the latest rendition of the classic Hatfields-and-McCoys feud, physician dispensing was hardly unheard of. For years doctors practicing in small rural towns without easy access to pharmacies have dispensed drugs, especially in the days before the proliferation of chain drugstores. But it's just recently been touted as an income booster (some estimate an added $20,000 to $40,000 a year) for urban and suburban doctors, practitioners far from rural areas or emergency situations. "Today the practice is growing in population centers where consumers have enjoyed choice among alternative dispensers," says a 1988 report commissioned by the American Pharmaceutical Association (*American Pharmacy*, May 1988).

What has made this a growth industry is a relatively new business called "repackaging": companies (called repackagers) buy drugs in bulk at wholesale costs from drug manufacturers, then resell to doctors in convenient, safety-sealed containers, ready for on-the-spot dispensing to their patients.

A neat scheme, to be sure, but its critics complain that it circumvents the pharmacist, an important link between the prescriber and the patient, and that without checks and balances the patient is at greater risk of medication errors, overprescribing, and unnecessary prescribing—expensive *and* potentially dangerous propositions. Aside from the obvious conflict of interest, the doctor may be tempted to prescribe a drug he or she sells when another the doctor doesn't sell may be preferable. Or the doctor may be tempted to sell brand-name drugs with higher markups when cheaper generics are available.

Critics who question the practice of physician dispensing do so generally because doctors are profiting from it, not because of the practice itself. According to an article in *Medical Self-Care,* an Oregon insurance company found that some doctors who dispense prescription drugs are marking up drug prices by 200 percent or more. Actual figures are hard to come by and depend on many factors, but according to a report in the July 28, 1989 issue of *American Medical News,* repackagers say that "prescriptions typically are priced at $2 to $5 higher than wholesale cost."

Furthermore, many if not most physicians who dispense do not list or advertise their drug prices or even write prescription orders. So the person who does not ask the physician the price of the drug, call into question whether it may be available elsewhere at a lower price, or ask for a written prescription order to gain the option of having it filled at a pharmacy stands a good chance of being ripped off by a practice that *should* be done for the patient's convenience.

Is physician dispensing a patient convenience or exploitation? While undoubtedly the question will be debated for some time to come, the answer has more to do with the individual physician than with the practice as a whole. Clearly, opportunities for abuse do exist—not the least of which may be the tendency for a physician with a financial interest in prescribing drugs to overprescribe. If physician dispensing means less price information to consumers, less competitive pricing, and less monitoring, then consumers are getting the wrong end of the pestle.

Physician dispensing is permitted in some degree nationwide, but out of concern for possible anticompetitive and anticonsumer abuses, various states have enacted physician-dispensing laws, which require physicians to follow the same recordkeeping, labeling, and dispensing protocols as pharmacists. Strictly regulated in some states, drug dispensing by physicians also may be allowed only in emergencies or special circumstances in other states. In some cases these laws also mandate that dispensing physicians register with the appropriate state licensing boards. There's even talk of federal legislation to limit doctors' ability to sell drugs to patients.

In the meantime, another question remains: *Is it in the best interest of your own health to buy prescription medications from your physician?* That's something you'll have to decide for yourself, based upon the trust you place in your own physician and the relationship the two of you have. As you determine what's right for you, here are some things to keep in mind:

▶ Ask your physician if the repackaging firm she does business with supplies a storage cabinet with a lock and key. The reputable firm typically does this to ensure drug security and, we might add, to discourage tampering.

▶ Repackaging companies that promote professional standards also provide computer systems, not merely for the physician's recordkeeping but also for monitoring what drugs are dispensed to what patients. In this way potential negative drug interactions—and the accompanying dangers and expense—can be prevented. Remember, multiple doctors mean multiple prescriptions, so it's smart to ask your primary physician to keep track of all the medications you take. Ask your physician how she keeps track of what drugs you're taking. That way you'll get some idea of the caliber of the repackaging firm with which your physician is dealing—and an idea of how interested your doctor is in dispensing for your health and convenience.

▶ Before you buy your prescriptions from your doctor, compare her prices with those of drugstores in your area. A 1987 Pennsylvania Department of Aging report based on 2.7 million insurance claims found that the average price of a prescription at independent and chain pharmacies was around $13.24, versus $15.11 for dispensing physicians. But other reports confirm the opposite—that there is an economic advantage to buying medications from some doctors. Find out for yourself.

▶ Ask your physician if anyone in the office verifies that the drugs dispensed are the right ones, the dosages correct, and the directions clear, complete, and accurate. And find out what the procedure is for doing so. A busy doctor's office can be full of distractions—and potential disasters if a system is not in place to prevent them.

▶ Get all the facts before you take, or for that matter buy, any prescription drug. Ask your dispensing physician all the questions the National Council on Patient Information and Education recommends you ask whenever you get a prescription filled.

QUESTIONS TO ASK

1. What is the name of the drug, and what is it supposed to do?

2. How and when do I take it, and for how long?

3. What foods, drinks, other medicines, or activities should I avoid while taking this drug?

4. Are there any side effects, and what do I do if they occur?

5. Is there any written information available about the drug?

DOCTORS PRESCRIBE SOME DRUGS JUST TO PACIFY PATIENTS

Many doctors prescribe useless or unnecessarily expensive drugs simply to satisfy their patients' demands or to make patients feel they are getting good care. That is the finding, reported in the October 4, 1989 *Wall Street Journal,* of three Harvard Medical School researchers who randomly selected 141 doctors, all moderate or heavy prescribers of three particular drugs. The researchers mailed the doctors information indicating these drugs were ineffective or far more expensive than equally effective alternatives, then had specially trained pharmacists *twice* follow up with these physicians to discuss the clinical evidence with them. Almost half the doctors said they were merely satisfying patients' demands for these drugs, and that failure to do so would mean losing patients to more obliging physicians. Another quarter of the doctors cited a "placebo" effect as justification, and the remaining quarter insisted the scientific evidence was simply all wet!

This finding is all the more reason to question the need for every prescription and not to give your doctor the impression that you're begging for a particular drug.

MONEY-SAVING TIPS

$ Ask your doctor for free samples. Physicians regularly receive free samples of prescription and over-the-counter medications from pharmaceutical company representatives. Don't hesitate to ask if the doctor has any such samples of the medication he or she is prescribing for you.

$ Purchase in bulk. Although individuals cannot purchase drugs directly from wholesalers, some pharmacies will sell large quantities of drugs at substantially discounted prices. If you need medication on a long-term basis, ask your pharmacy if you can save by purchasing in bulk.

$ Ask the pharmacist about any available discounts. Many, if not most, pharmacies offer senior citizen discounts, and discounts even on infants' and children's medications are available in some pharmacies.

MEDICATION ERRORS: AVOIDING THEM MAY SAVE YOU A BUNDLE— NOT TO MENTION YOUR LIFE

A big reason for taking the time to shop around for that special pharmacy or that special pharmacist to suit your needs and pocketbook is to help ensure that you do not become a deplorable statistic: death or injury due to medication error—unfortunately a legitimate and realistic possibility.

According to Neil M. Davis in his book *Medication Errors: Causes and Prevention* (Philadelphia: George F. Stickley, 1981), four important studies have documented an average error rate in hospitals close to 12 percent. And according to Kenneth Barker, a pharmacist at Auburn University, hospitals with the *best* drug-problem records make mistakes 2 to 3 percent of the time. In some small hospitals, medication errors run as high as 11 percent. If the problem is that prevalent in the supervised and controlled environment that a hospital is supposed to be, then what's going on "out there"—in physicians' offices, in drugstores nationwide, in your own home? A 1989 report prepared by the Office of the Inspector General of the Department of Health and Human Services had more bad news: adverse drug reactions due to medication errors hospitalize nearly 250,000 older Americans every year (*Modern Healthcare,* September 8, 1989).

The fault in large part lies with physicians whose orders are often illegible, inaudible, ambiguous, or incomplete. And let's not forget the physicians' mental blunders: miscalculation of dosage or out-and-out wrong selection of dosage. All of these factors and more—such as the too many times when people take the wrong dosage of their medicines, prematurely stop taking them, or do not take them at all—contribute to the serious problem of medication errors. Medication errors are costly in suffering, not to mention the expense of hospital or doctor visits to investigate and treat the problem.

To get the most, and best, for your money, communicating about medicines must be a *routine* part of every encounter when medicines are prescribed or dispensed. An FDA survey some years back found that consumers are not getting the information they need about their drugs: 70 percent of the consumers surveyed who had received prescriptions within the last two weeks reported that their physicians and pharmacists did not tell them about precautions and possible side effects (Joe Graedon and Teresa Graedon, *Fifty Plus: The Graedons' People's Pharmacy for Older Adults* [New York: Bantam Books, 1988]).

For your part, ask questions. Get as much information as you can about what drug is being prescribed. Learn the names of the drugs you need to take, their doses, sizes, and even their colors, so that you will be able to spot a mistake or question a change. Take nothing for granted.

Don't let the Latin directions to the pharmacist keep you from figuring out what you're supposed to do with the medicine. Here's a list of some Latin phrases that turn up frequently on prescription sheets:

Original Phrase (Latin)	Abbreviation (on prescription)	English Meaning
ad libitum	ad lib.	as needed
ante cibum	a.c.	before meals
bis in die	b.i.d.	twice a day
ter in die	t.i.d.	three times a day
quater in die	q.i.d.	four times a day
hora somni	h.s.	at bedtime
per os	p.o.	orally (by mouth)
quaque 4 hora	q.4h.	every 4 hours
quaque 8 hora	q.8h.	every 8 hours
ut dictum	ut dict.	as directed by doctor

OD Spells...

Most of us are unfamiliar with Egyptian hieroglyphics, but then most of us are not in the business of deciphering enigmatic scribblings. Pharmacists are, in large part because too many doctors expect them to decode the too often illegible handwriting on prescription orders, and because, as we all know, so much of what the doctor writes is in abbreviated form and/or in Latin. An ambiguous order, a misinterpretation—and you're in trouble. Big trouble, given the potency of many modern drugs.

A case in point is the story, recounted in a letter to the editor in the *Journal of the American Medical Association,* of an unfortunate woman just discharged from a hospital—a woman who, through her doctor's inept communication of a mere two-letter message, wound up in the hospital emergency room. Here's how it happened.

"OD." Doctors often write this on prescriptions to indicate that a drug is to be taken "once daily." Unfortunately, as the letter writer says, "this particular abbreviation is used in several branches of medicine and means different things to different people"—"one dose," or from the Latin *omni die* "every day," or "on demand," or "one drop at a time." In this woman's case her doctor intended the abbreviation to mean "on departure," to assure that she would get the pills he set aside for her when she was leaving the hospital. The problem is obvious: amidst all the ambiguity, the doctor did not guarantee that the participants in this little tragicomedy would get the correct message.

When the curtain rose on the next act, the discharge nurse was insisting the doctor meant for the woman to take ten tablets as "one dose," meaning all at once. After initially objecting, the woman agreed.

The final scene took place four hours later when the unconscious woman was brought to the emergency room with a diagnosis of "drug OD." (It's not clear from the letter whether the woman recovered.)

What can you do so that you don't "OD"? Take a few extra minutes before leaving the doctor's office to discuss the prescription, then double-check your doctor's verbal instructions against your pharmacist's final interpretation. You might even write down what your doctor tells you and make certain you understand everything you need to know about taking the drug. Prescription drugs can speed healing and even save lives, but if they're administered in the wrong doses and with incorrect frequency, they spell disaster.

OVERMEDICATION OF THE ELDERLY: A WEIGHTY PROBLEM

It's a fact that drug overdosing occurs in many hospitals' pediatric wards and nurseries. The dosages—some as much as ten times greater than prescribed—are the result of misplaced decimal points and sloppy computational skills of nurses and doctors who do not understand the appropriate doses for different age groups. But that's not the whole story: an important study a few years back in the May 1987 issue of *Archives of Internal Medicine* found new evidence of drug overdosing, but this time the victims were the low-weight elderly who, although not as helpless as hospitalized children, are nonetheless at the mercy of a medical system that overmedicates and then turns around and labels "senile" the behaviors resulting from the overdosages.

The elderly are paying the price—in more ways than one.

The study further found that not only are doctors failing to adjust doses for body weight, but they also do not take into account the ages of the patients—an omission that flies in the face of the well-established physiologic fact that with age comes changes in drug metabolism. In short, the older you get, the longer it takes for drugs to clear out of your system, so dosages must be adjusted accordingly.

If we know this, shouldn't doctors know it too? Yes, but according to the study's researchers, the immediate problem is that doctors prescribe "by habit, with little adjustment for individual patients." They just scribble the standard dose regimens, show you the door, then repeat the pattern for the next person.

So the next time your doctor writes a prescription for you, first ask if the drug is absolutely necessary. If so—and you're convinced—then ask the doctor to double-check your weight against the recommended standard dosage for that medication. If you are elderly and of small stature or of low weight relative to your height, remind your doctor to take this into account and find the lowest effective drug dose. You'll save money and increase your margin of safety for dose-related side effects.

MONEY-SAVING TIPS

$ Consult the *Physician's Desk Reference.* This book—available at most public libraries or perhaps at your local pharmacy— describes such essential information as types of adverse reactions to watch for and reasons not to take certain drugs (contraindications). You may discover that the drug is not an appropriate one for you, and of course the best time to find this out is before you have gone to the expense of having the prescription filled.

$ Consult consumer buying guides to drugs. Consumer guides to drugs are available in most libraries, and in addition to giving you information about specific medications, they also point out which drugs are the most effective and which drugs are not effective. Using the most effective drug for a given condition is ultimately cheaper.

SAVING MONEY IN THE DOCTOR'S OFFICE AND THE HOSPITAL

5

Up to this point we've looked at the larger issues of what's involved in getting the most for your medical dollar: the matter of finding the right practitioner, including the question of whether you need a doctor at all, and how to avoid wasting time and money on inappropriate medical specialists; the different settings where health care is delivered, and the question of where you will spend less for more; and the issue of health insurance, what you need to know to find the best plan or arrangement for your money and health.

But now the battle begins. Big-time expenditures start at the doctor's office and the hospital. These sometimes benign, sometimes momentous encounters with the medical system have the potential to catapult you into the poorhouse, all in the wink of an eye. However, just as the big costs start here, so does the potential for cost savings. Whether in his or her own office or in the hospital, your doctor is the broker for all tests and all procedures—these both necessary and, too often, unnecessary. The key is for you to know when to give the "no buy" signal to your broker—to know when the investment is too costly and/or too risky.

THE DOCTOR'S OFFICE

Let's start with the office visit. Our best advice here? Don't go alone. Whenever possible, take along a spouse, relative, or friend to act as your advocate, and if necessary to help you exercise your veto power.

What follows is a column written by Lowell S. Levin, Ed. D., M.P.H., a professor at the Yale University School of Medicine and Public Health and chairman of the People's Medical Society, for the People's Medical Society *Newsletter.*

DON'T GO ALONE

When a person becomes a patient, it's not easy to be coldly objective about illness and remain in full charge when visiting a doctor. Pain and fear of the unknown cloud our sense of self-ownership. We often revert to a childlike role of listening and obeying, often becoming uncustomarily silent and passive.

This can happen to the strongest, most independent of us. We want to be taken care of, to have our problem diagnosed for us, the treatment decided for us, and action taken on our behalf. In some respects we shut down our usual instincts to question and evaluate the answers before we "buy." And even when we resolve to enter the health care process with a mature and self-possessed attitude—even with a written list of questions we want to ask—somehow the situation is too intimidating, too overwhelming. We assume a supplicant's role. We forget (or don't dare) to ask our questions. Or if we succeed in that, we don't hear or remember the answers.

In such circumstances the stage is set for trouble. A one-way interview results, with the doctor getting answers to an often routine set of questions that from his or her experience contribute most efficiently to certain diagnostic possibilities. It is not that these are unimportant questions. It is simply that they may not be the *most* important. Insights or explanations *you* may have may not be brought out.

And a similar problem affects the doctor's explanations, advice, and instructions. Being under stress is not the best time to hear accurately or comprehend fully what is being said to you. Often there is "selected listening" or interpreting words out of proportion to what was intended. And even more serious is the possibility that you may fail to evaluate recommendations from the standpoint of their safety, relative benefits, costs, and effects on your future functioning.

This becomes a perfect environment for becoming a victim of yet another health problem—iatrogenic disease. ("Iatrogenic" literally means doctor-caused.) Tragically, it is a very common disease. While most iatrogenic illnesses have short-term effects, a substantial proportion can have serious long-term effects, and some actually result in death. But any iatrogenic illness is serious when it prolongs recovery or sets in motion another round of medical interventions. The social cost of iatrogenic disease is also high—billions of dollars a year.

There is no magic formula for eliminating iatrogenic disease, but certainly the most effective approach is to prevent the need for medical care in the first place. A second level of control is for you to have a knowledge of your right to informed choice and the ability to get and use information relative to your problem and treatment options.

Another idea seems worthy of trying. That is simply to *never* undertake a professional visit to your doctor alone. Take along a spouse, other relative, or a friend. A "third-party presence" can work wonders in several ways:

▶ The doctor senses the presence of an observer in the room and may feel more inclined to be more communicative and supportive. And a friend helps you stay relaxed and focused so you get the most out of the consultation.

▶ Your companion also can help both you and the doctor by bringing up questions, concerns, and considerations that neither you nor your doctor thought of.

▶ Facts important to your doctor's diagnosis and treatment plan also can be raised by the advocate—for example, your life-style, work environment, or the way a current family problem may be affecting your health: all escaping your own notice simply because they are so commonplace in your life.

▶ It is really helpful to have someone who can remind the doctor about practical things he or she should consider in deciding about care after surgery, such as who will feed the children or the fact that you may live in a fourth-floor walk-up and won't be able to negotiate stairs.

▶ Your chances of remembering what was said by your doctor are at least doubled by having a friend who was there. In fact, you are generally in a better position to objectively evaluate the whole experience and to make further decisions about your care. You are not alone.

Having a friend or relative accompany you on your visits to the doctor may not always be a comfortable choice if you feel shy about sharing personal health information with others. Some doctors may even frown on the practice, saying that it interferes with their efficiency in caring for you, or even claiming that it isn't ethical.

But the fact is that you *do* have the choice, and it is *your* choice. Everything considered, it is probably one of the best ways to reduce a stressful situation, get more information to and from the doctor, gain more control over your care, and start on the road to a safer and more beneficial result.

How to Get the Most Out of the Office Visit

Calculated on a minute-by-minute basis, the time you spend with your doctor (*not* counting the minutes you may spend cooling your heels in the waiting room—that, unfortunately, is *your* time) is expensive. So it behooves you to maximize what you get in return. Aside from the help someone else with you has to offer, here are some things you can do:

▶ Ahead of the visit, define your goals. What do you want from the doctor? A complete checkup? A consultation on a specific problem you're having? A follow-up to a previous visit? An answer to one simple question? Once you decide this, determine whether a phone consultation might accomplish the same thing—at a lower cost in time and money. (If you followed our advice in chapter 1, you have chosen a doctor who sets aside time for phone consultations, perhaps at a nominal charge.)

▶ Be prepared. Organize your symptoms, your chief complaint, and everything that makes you seek medical attention. Jot down these questions and concerns and bring them with you to the doctor's office. Make the most of every minute you're paying for. (See "Making a List, Checking It Twice," below.)

▶ Obtain your medical records. Write your former physician to request copies and/or transfer of your records, including all laboratory and X-ray reports. (We have more to say about this process in chapter 7.) If you encounter trouble getting a copy of your records, jot down what you remember about your past medical history: surgeries, major illnesses, hospitalizations, previous drug regimens, and drug allergies. Try to organize this chronologically, working back from the most recent. Know your family history as well.

▶ Know what drugs you are currently taking. If you are unsure of the names and dosages, check with your pharmacist and by all means bring along the medications to the doctor's office.

▶ Know your rights as a patient, including the right to give informed consent. "Informed consent" means that your doctor must fully explain *in simple terms* the advantages and disadvantages of any proposed procedure, including surgery, that poses a threat to your life or continuing good health. The doctor must also tell you why he or she feels the procedure or treatment is necessary and any risks that accompany it. Before you sign a written consent form, be sure that you fully understand what the doctor has said. If you do not understand, say no to the proposed treatment or procedure. Ask your doctor to explain the options until you do understand and can make a reasonable decision.

Making a List, Checking It Twice

Going to the doctor can be an overwhelming experience, and in the throes of even mild apprehension we're liable to forget everything we want to ask or bring to the doctor's attention. So we go prepared—clutching our written list of aches, twinges, symptoms, medication side effects, or whatever. We want answers, but too often what we get instead from our doctor is an unvoiced diagnosis of mental illness.

That's right. Traditional medical "wisdom" holds that patients who produce a written list of complaints when visiting their doctors should be written off as emotionally ill. There's even a widely accepted term for this stigma, *la maladie du petit papier,* or "the illness of the little piece of paper."

All these years doctors have thought such people were crazy, but finally there is a doctor who has spoken out (publicly) in favor of the practice. Rather than condemning and ridiculing this (as at least one major medical textbook, DeGowin and DeGowin's *Bedside Diagnostic Examination,* does), Alabama physician John F. Burnum defends the patient-scribbler in an article in the September 12, 1985 *New England Journal of Medicine.*

Why is he so positive in the face of rampant bias in his own profession? Because he conducted a survey in his own practice and found that patients on the "write" track were emotionally sound people who had some sound reasons and good use for lists. Mostly, they wanted "to get things straight." They were looking for "clarity, order, information, and control" when they were feeling anxious or distraught. Others didn't want to waste the doctor's time, so they organized their thoughts to get quickly to the point—hardly a crazy notion considering that many doctors seem to travel at twice the speed of sound in and out of examining rooms.

But the really telling revelation in Burnum's article gets to the crux of a doctor's irritation with note writers. Not only do these conscientious patients sometimes try the patience of their doctors, but Burnum says they try a doctor's intelligence too. The doctor is uncomfortable with and often downright hostile to patients who demand to know as much information about their own health as the doctor knows. This demand may converge with the doctor's worst fear—"What if he asks a question I can't answer?"

While ideally your doctor should know more than you do about medicine—presumably that's why you pay what you do to tap this knowledge—a good way to get the most for your medical dollar is to make a list. You have a right to write, and your doctor has a responsibility to listen, and respond professionally.

GUARDING AGAINST UNNECESSARY OR EXCESSIVE TESTING

Millions of medical tests are performed annually, and Americans and insurers spend billions of dollars for them. Yet many millions of these medical tests are not necessary, say some experts. And many of the tests aren't very accurate. Others have serious risks and iffy benefits. So, you may well wonder—should you have that test? Does your malady really require two or three tests to determine a diagnosis?

If you feel healthy and don't seem to have any problems, should you spend the money every year to have certain medical tests done? For instance, how effective or essential is the annual physical—starting at about $100 a visit?

In a manner of speaking, that was the question raised by a group of independent experts appointed by the Department of Health and Human Services to critique the value and cost-effectiveness of the routine tests and screenings that have long been part of the annual physical. From their analysis of several thousand medical studies dealing with the most popular screening tests and preventive services, the physicians—known as the U.S. Preventive Services Task Force—have compiled the country's first set of comprehensive guidelines for the annual physical (see chart on pp. 226–27). The bottom line? More talking and counseling, and less testing and screening.

As you can see from the chart, many popular screenings got the thumbs-down from the task force because medical statistics have not shown them to be worthwhile. Particularly problematic are screenings for glaucoma, several types of heart disease, lung cancer, liver disease, ovarian cancer in women, and prostate and testicular cancer in men—tests said to be so unreliable that the results are questionable, or tests that detect diseases that have no effective treatment. Either way, you are subjected to a great deal of additional testing and the accompanying emotional stress—*and expense*—for something of little or no value.

How do you get your money's worth from the periodic examination? Among the procedures the task force recommends for adults with symptoms are one skin exam in early adulthood, two lifetime cardiac exams, annual dental exams, blood pressure measurements every two years, weigh-ins every four years, and, for women, Pap tests every three years (after two negative tests obtained one year apart). Nonfasting total blood cholesterol tests are also recommended. More procedures are advised for the older person: Visual acuity and hearing should be checked annually from age sixty, the task force says. And women fifty years and older should have an annual breast exam and mammogram.

You should know that the new recommendations do not jibe with guidelines issued by other medical organizations. *So be ready to hear your doctor quote from other groups' recommendations that call for annual or routine exams that the task force singles out as unnecessary.* One large area of disagreement hinges on the value of routine cancer screenings. For instance, the American Cancer Society recommends annual rectal exams for men over forty to detect prostate cancer. The U.S. Preventive Services Task Force found no evidence that early identification of cancer by screening will save lives. That test, and others such as the fecal occult blood test for early detection of colorectal cancer, should be limited to high-risk people, the team said.

Not surprisingly, many in the medical field roundly attacked the task force for tampering with the sacrosanct annual physical, as cursory as it often is. But the intent of the task force was to see that doctors use every minute of an office visit wisely. (And who can argue with that?) The average family physician spends only about twelve minutes with a person, and the average internist about eighteen minutes, according to the task force chairperson (*Medical Tribune,* November 17, 1988). So the recommendations seek to maximize those few moments with tests and screenings of some value, not testing for the sake of testing.

The entire issue comes down to this: the specter of excessive and unnecessary testing lurks in every corner of the doctor's office. A notion that has insinuated itself into the core of medical-practice habits is, "If testing is good, a lot of it is even better." And as Edward R. Pinckney, M.D., former editor of the *Journal of the American Medical Association,* is quoted as saying in the *Wall Street Journal*: "Most medical tests—and by that I mean well over half—do not really contribute to a patient's diagnosis or therapy."

You *can* take charge, however, and minimize the risks *and* costs of overtesting in your doctor's office.

▶ Ask why you need the test. In their comprehensive guide to more than two hundred diagnostic and home medical tests, *The People's Book of Medical Tests* (New York: Summit Books, 1985), David S. Sobel, M.D., and Tom Ferguson, M.D., recommended that before you agree to any test you ask your doctor what will be done if the test results are abnormal *and* what will be done if the test results are normal. They advise that you may not need the test if the doctor's answers are the same for both questions. Also be sure to demand additional information or clarification if you don't understand something.

▶ Ask how reliable the test is, what the chance is of a false-positive or false-negative indication, and how risks of either can be minimized. (A *false-positive* result means that the test shows up positive, or abnormal, but no disease is actually present. A *false-negative* result means that the test shows up negative, or normal, but you actually have the disease.) No test is 100 percent accurate, but you should be told the usefulness *and* the limits of tests if you are to make an informed decision—and get your money's worth. False—or even misread results, for that matter—can direct your doctor to perform inappropriate actions.

▶ Ask where the test will be processed, whether in the office or an outside commercial lab. If the test is scheduled to go outside, ask if the commercial lab is accredited by the College of American Pathologists. As for tests processed in the doctor's in-office lab, you should know that evidence points to some inaccuracy problems. We will talk more about that later in this chapter.

▶ Find out what alternatives you have if you refuse the test.

▶ Ask how much the test will cost. And check with your insurance company prior to undergoing an expensive test to see if it will cover the total cost.

▶ Talk to your doctor. While this advice sounds facetious, it really isn't. Admittedly, doctors don't always listen to their patients' explanations and questions or even ask the right questions themselves. And certainly there's an economic incentive for doctors to order many tests—too many tests, to be sure. But consumers do share in the responsibility of communicating well, and too often they don't mention all symptoms, or they downplay them. Keep notes of everything you feel, every disturbance, every symptom, and bring in the notes to your appointment—this is also where an advocate can help. Give your doctor as much information as you can, and demand the same in return.

▶ Use the U.S. Preventive Services Task Force recommendations covering the annual physical as a guide to assist you in discussions with your doctor. But don't be surprised if your doctor is slow to comply with the recommendations. Weaning doctors from testing is not going to be easy, nor is it going to happen anytime soon. Face it—they don't make as much money talking to patients as they do testing.

TAKING THE MEASURE OF MEDICAL PROCEDURES

The new *Guide to Clinical Preventive Services* issued by the U.S. Preventive Services Task Force questions the need for many procedures frequently performed in a doctor's office. The table below divides these commonplace procedures into three groups. "Most important" indicates clear value in preventing serious diseases and disabilities. "Moderately important" suggests procedures whose effectiveness or ability to prevent less serious diseases is not so well established. "Occasionally needed" identifies procedures to be done case by case for higher-risk patients. Some counseling measures listed for younger age groups refer to advice given to a parent rather than to a child.

Age group	Most Important	Moderately important	Occasionally needed
Ages 2 through 6	**Tests:** Height and weight; dimness of vision and "lazy eye." **Counseling:** Diet; car safety belts; falls, burns, poisoning; dental care. **Immunizations:** Diphtheria-tetanus-pertussis; oral polio.	**Tests:** Blood pressure, urinary infection. **Counseling:** Exercise; effects of passive smoking.	**Tests:** Lead poisoning; tuberculosis; hearing. **Counseling:** Sun exposure. **Supplements:** Fluoride.
Ages 7 through 12	**Tests:** Blood pressure. **Counseling:** Diet; exercise; car safety belts; dental care.	**Tests:** Height and weight. **Counseling:** Preventing burns, falls, firearms accidents, etc.; bicycle safety helmets.	**Tests:** Tuberculosis. **Counseling:** Sun exposure. **Supplements:** Fluoride.
Ages 13 through 18	**Tests:** Complete medical history; blood pressure. **Counseling:** Diet; exercise; tobacco, alcohol and other drugs; drinking and driving; sexual behavior; car safety belts; firearms. **Immunizations:** Tetanus-diphtheria booster.	**Tests:** Height and weight. **Counseling:** Motorcycle and bicycle safety helmets; fire prevention; regular dental care, including brushing, flossing and checkups.	**Tests:** Skin; testicles; rubella antibodies; sexually transmitted diseases (STD's); tuberculosis; hearing; Pap smear. **Counseling:** Shared or unsterilized needles; sickle-cell disease; thalassemia; sun exposure. **Supplements:** Fluoride.

Ages 19 through 39	**Tests:** Complete medical history; blood pressure; nonfasting total blood cholesterol; Pap smear. **Counseling:** Diet; exercise; tobacco, alcohol and other drugs; sexual behavior; use of car safety belts; drinking and driving; violent behavior; firearms. **Immunizations:** Tetanus-diphtheria booster.	**Tests:** Height and weight. **Counseling:** Motorcycle and bicycle safety helmets; smoke detectors; smoking near bedding or upholstery; regular dental care, including brushing, flossing and checkups.	**Tests:** Skin; mouth; hearing; thyroid nodules; breasts; testicles; diabetes; rubella antibodies; STD's; urinary infection; tuberculosis; electrocardiogram; mammogram, colonoscopy. **Counseling:** Shared or unsterilized needles; lower-back exercises; sickle-cell disease; thalassemia; sun exposure. **Immunizations:** Hepatitis B; pneumococcus; influenza; measles-mumps-rubella.
Ages 40 through 64	**Tests:** Complete medical history; blood pressure, breast exam; nonfasting blood cholesterol; Pap smear, mammogram. **Counseling:** Diet; exercise; tobacco, alcohol, other drugs; sexual behavior; use of car safety belts. **Immunizations:** Tetanus-diphtheria booster.	**Tests:** Height and weight. **Counseling:** Motorcycle and bicycle safety helmets; smoke detectors; smoking near bedding or upholstery; regular dental care, including brushing, flossing and checkups.	**Tests:** Skin; mouth; thyroid nodules; carotid artery; diabetes; STD's; urinary infection; hearing; tuberculosis; EKG; fecal occult blood; sigmoidoscopy; colonoscopy; bone mineral content. **Counseling:** Shared or unsterilized needles; lower-back exercises; sun exposure; aspirin for heart; estrogen replacement. **Immunizations:** Hepatitis B; pneumococcus; influenza.
Age 65 and over	**Tests:** Complete medical history; blood pressure; breast exam; mammogram. **Counseling:** Diet; exercise; tobacco, alcohol and other drugs; preventing falls; car safety belts. **Immunizations:** Tetanus-diphtheria booster; influenza; pneumococcus.	**Tests:** Height and weight; visual acuity; hearing and hearing aids; nonfasting total blood cholesterol; dipstick urinalysis; thyroid function. **Counseling:** Fire prevention; hot-water temperature; dental care; glaucoma test by eye specialist.	**Tests:** Skin; mouth; carotid artery; thyroid nodules; diabetes; tuberculosis; EKG; Pap smear; fecal occult blood; sigmoidoscopy; colonoscopy. **Counseling:** Estrogen replacement; aspirin for heart; sun exposure. **Immunizations:** Hepatitis B.

Ripe for money-saving strategies is the area of testing for high blood pressure. Certainly one of the most common tests, blood pressure measurements form the basis of expensive, often interminable treatment, usually in the form of prescription drugs. For many people the medications themselves are far from perfect, and fraught with undesirable side effects that in and of themselves may necessitate treatment—and more bills. If you are currently being treated for high blood pressure, talk to your doctor about these two issues:

White-Coat Hypertension. Do your palms get clammy or your stomach fluttery during a visit to the doctor? Well, you're not alone. Most of us experience these reactions, but you also may have an above-normal, transient rise in blood pressure provoked by the anxiety. Not uncommon, this phenomenon is called white-coat hypertension. The potential problem here is that your high blood pressure, the result of a measurement taken in your doctor's office, may not be truly representative of your average daily blood pressure.

For many years the casual blood pressure reading taken in a doctor's office has been used as the standard for diagnosing hypertension. However, more and more studies are discovering that blood pressure is a constantly changing variable, influenced by psychological and physiological factors as well as stimuli, such as a visit to the doctor. A study by the Hypertension Center of the New York Hospital–Cornell University Medical College some years back found that home blood pressure readings fall somewhere between the extremes of those recorded at work and those at sleep. Doctor's office readings are closer to the blood pressures recorded at work.

Talk with your doctor about this issue. If you both agree that your diagnosis deserves a second look, look into continuous, or twenty-four-hour, ambulatory blood pressure monitoring.

Once Is Not Enough. There's also the issue of how many measurements over how long a period of time constitute a diagnosis of hypertension—a diagnosis usually followed by a cavalcade of medications and follow-up office visits. A 1987 *Canadian Medical Association Journal* report pointed out that a single reading has limited benefit when it comes to blood pressure. Only over a period of time and

Previous pages: Reprinted, by permission, from *U.S. News & World Report,* May 15, 1989.
BASIC DATA: *Guide to Clinical Preventive Services*; Dr. Steven H. Woolf, scientific adviser, U.S. Preventive Services Task Force.

after a number of readings is it possible to tell for sure whether you have high, low, or acceptable blood pressure levels. Once is not enough.

The Canadian study showed the pitfalls and damage that can occur. Looking at nearly three thousand people who had had their blood pressure taken, the researchers found that if the attending medical professionals relied on a single reading, hypertension was overestimated by 30 percent—resulting in a large number of people who got started on medications and protocols that were totally unnecessary and perhaps harmful. Single-visit determinations of high blood pressure also lead to high levels of undetected hypertension, which then lead to untreated hypertension.

You shouldn't allow yourself to be started on a medication regimen based on one reading.

Five Health-Screening Tests You Don't Need

Finding a disease at its earliest stage often has no beneficial effect, according to the Center for Medical Consumers, a New York City-based nonprofit public interest organization that offers a free medical library for the lay public. Screening healthy people for early disease brings thousands to their physicians yearly in the belief that this is good preventive medicine. While this may be true for certain screening measures, the center says in its April 1989 newsletter *HealthFacts,* it clearly does not apply to all, and moreover, indiscriminate health screening adds considerably to health care costs. The screening tests you don't need are for five common diseases: colorectal cancer, endometrial cancer, glaucoma, osteoporosis, and prostate cancer.

"The purpose of testing healthy people for early-stage disease is to initiate treatment before symptoms develop," explains editor Maryann Napoli. "Unfortunately, studies show no advantage either in terms of reduced complications or survival for the five diseases in [the *HealthFacts*] report."

Here are excerpts from that report:

Colorectal Cancer
Although recommended by the American Cancer Society and widely publicized in the lay media, the fecal occult blood test for early colorectal cancer has hardly proven its worth. The chief advantage is the fact that it can be self-administered in the privacy of your own home. The value of screening for hidden blood in the stool has been debated by

gastroenterologists for nearly two decades. So far, there are no winners, primarily due to the lack of any controlled study to show that
colon cancer survival is improved by discovery prior to symptom development. The stool test shows a very high rate of false-positive,
which means that most people with this result will be needlessly
subjected to invasive diagnostic tests, such as sigmoidoscopy and barium enema, to rule out the presence of colorectal cancer. While true
early-stage colorectal cancer is often detected by all these tests, the
fallacy of equating the earlier stage with better prognosis was observed
by gastroenterologist Jerome B. Simon, M.D., Queen's University,
Kingston, Ontario, in his review of all relevant studies. "Screening
may merely advance the time of diagnosis, without delaying the time
of death" (*Cancer and Metastasis Reviews* 6:397–411, 1987).

Endometrial Cancer
Since the Pap test is inadequate for the early detection of endometrial
cancer, the recommended screening procedure is endometrial tissue
sampling, which removes cells from the uterine lining. While this may
be the best available screening test for endometrial cancer, it was
excluded from the Canadian Task Force's recommendations because
the evidence to justify its use is so poor. In the sole large-scale study
to assess the value of endometrial biopsy for symptomless women, the
procedure produced an excessively high number (more than 80 percent) of false-positive results—that is, erroneous indication of cancer.
Thus, women with this result are subjected to an unnecessary dilation
and curettage, usually performed in the hospital and under general
anesthesia, in order to rule out cancer.

Even if the screening were confined only to high-risk women, the
Canadian Task Force estimated that only 50 percent of all cases of
endometrial cancer would be detected. Most importantly, no well-
designed study has determined whether early detection improves the
survival of women with endometrial cancer. The Task Force's decision
not to recommend endometrial screening runs counter to the advice of
the American Cancer Society as well as the Canadian Cancer Society.

Glaucoma
All people over the age of 35 are advised to have their eyes tested every
two years for glaucoma. . . . The screening advice is based on the
premise that early detection and prompt treatment will prevent blindness. Unfortunately, the advice represents more wishful thinking than
solid research. None of the currently available screening tests—
tonometry, cup-disc ratio, and visual fields—are either practical or
accurate, according to the American College of Physicians (ACP) report. And more importantly, the ACP did not recommend these tests
because there is no convincing evidence that the treatment of a symptomless person will prevent the development of glaucoma or prevent
blindness. Earlier diagnosis does not appear to make a substantial
difference in outcome. Furthermore, the tests produce unnecessary
anxiety for a significant number of people with positive results. Of all
whose testing shows elevated intraocular pressure, the vast majority
(90 percent) will never develop glaucoma.

Osteoporosis

The measurement of bone density to predict osteoporosis has been advocated in the last few years as an essential screening procedure for women over the age of 40. The exact role of these tests—single- or dual-photon absorptiometry, and CT scanning—has yet to be determined. . . . The Canadian Task Force did not recommend bone density measurement because "There are no studies on the effectiveness of early detection in achieving decreased incidence of fracture or of bone demineralization." Although a correlation clearly exists between loss of bone density and risk of fracture, the tests' ability to *predict* who is likely to experience bone fracture in old age remains uncertain.

Prostate Cancer

The American Cancer Society recommends an annual rectal examination to men over age 40 for the early detection of prostate cancer. The Canadian Task Force and the American College of Physicians do not recommend this screening examination because "no study has yet showed that identification by screening alters mortality." A study that followed members of a prepaid medical plan found no significant difference in prostate cancer survival between men whose disease was detected during periodic screening and those who sought treatment only after symptoms appeared.

Excerpted with permission: Center for Medical Consumers, Inc.,
237 Thompson Street, New York, NY 10012. Subscriptions to *HealthFacts*
are $18 for one year.

DOCTOR'S OFFICE LABS

Once you have determined that a test is useful, you still face another area of concern: where and by whom the test is to be processed.

In a growing number of doctors' offices around the country, beeping sounds and flashing lights herald a new source of physician income: automated in-office laboratories, made possible by a new breed of compact diagnostic equipment. Diagnostic testing is moving out of the medical laboratory and into the doctor's office, where, according to an American Public Health Association study, about half of the lab tests in this country now are performed. Doctors in great numbers have jumped on the bandwagon of this new technology—especially since the bandwagon is making frequent stops at the bank.

We've come a long way—some would say too far—from the time when a doctor's two most valuable tools were a stethoscope and a tongue depressor, devices that encouraged close, hands-on encounters between patient and caregiver. Now you're just as liable to see electronic gadgets and digitalized equipment: machines that are compact enough to fit into any office and deliver almost instantaneous readings on blood chemistries, hemoglobins, electrolytes, therapeutic drug levels, and more. For an investment as low as $1,000, a physician can buy an analyzer, and with little training a person can operate this scaled-down version of its commercial counterpart. Of course, doctors' offices have long been the site of a variety of routine tests, including routine blood testing and dipstick urinalysis, but more sophisticated equipment makes more sophisticated tests possible these days.

Doctors have snapped up the new diagnostic equipment for a variety of reasons—they cite convenience for patients, quicker results, more control over results, and savings for patients—but one particular inducement cannot be ignored: the in-office lab is a way for physicians to generate additional revenue without seeing more patients and without doing more work. Practice management consultants say office tests can yield a profit of 50 percent or more—"an exceptional return on an average investment of $20,000" (*Medical Economics,* April 28, 1986). Noted health care economist at Princeton University, Uwe Reinhardt calls the profit margins "outrageous," in a *U.S. News & World Report* article of November 23, 1987.

True, the arrangement offers ease and speed of in-office handling of tests versus sending work out to commercial laboratories. And true, the new equipment assures results in five to ten minutes, in most cases, and the doctor is able to make diagnostic decisions while you are still in the office. But is your doctor taking advantage of this and giving you more for your money in the way of spending more time with you, explaining the results and therapeutic choices? In fact, is your doctor even giving you the results? After the physician's initial investment for the equipment and set-up costs have been recouped, will the subsequent savings be passed on to you? Or will the in-office laboratory remain merely an additional source of physician income? What's in it for you, the consumer? Is this arrangement health-promoting or wallet-emptying?

Obviously, the answers to many of these questions will depend upon the individual practitioner, but red flags have been raised over this issue. Critics of office-based testing point to problems with accuracy, quality and quality control, the lack of adequately trained laboratory staff and staff turnover—and the incentive to profit through overtesting. Study after study shows small in-office laboratories tend to have a greater variability in test results than do large, regulated labs. Any one of these can take a toll on your health and finances.

Until the passage of the Clinical Laboratory Improvement Act of 1988, office-based testing had slipped through the regulatory net. Office labs had been exempt from the Medicare standards imposed on independent laboratories and exempt from inspection in most states, but nonregulation of the 100,000 (some estimates go as high as 200,000) doctors' office labs is scheduled to come to an end July 1, 1991. By that date the legislation requires the Department of Health and Human Services to establish uniform certification, inspection, and licensure for all labs, including those in doctors' offices.

Under the law the only labs waived from regulation are ones performing so-called low-risk tests. Not surprisingly, no one has been able to agree on the definition of a low-risk test because there is always some possibility that a miscalculation of a lab test will harm a patient, so as it stands now the only tests that can be waived from regulation under the law are "simple" ones. But again, there has been little consensus about what constitutes a simple test. What all this means is that probably all office labs will be regulated, assuming the mammoth undertaking of 100,000 to 200,000 inspections can be choreographed.

No doubt the experts will wrestle with the details and syntax of regulation for years to come. Meanwhile, you're the one who's paying to be poked, prodded, and punctured—all at some profit to your practitioner. Just because the testing is being done by your doctor, in the perhaps familiar setting of his or her office, doesn't mean that you should accept with blind faith that every test is necessary. The practice of repeating routine, simple tests has been a common one for some time now, and is especially enticing to a doctor who has an in-office lab. Beware of this, and keep your chances as low as possible that you'll be the victim of an inaccurate test and subsequent unnecessary surgery or treatment.

As we emphasize throughout this book, to get the most for your medical dollar, you have to question the worth and cost-effectiveness of every test, every procedure your doctor recommends. Find out why the doctor is recommending the test. What does he or she hope to learn? How will the outcome change the doctor's diagnosis, prognosis, or treatment plan? What are the risks? Is there an equally good alternative to the test? How much will the test cost?

In this particular scenario—the office-based lab—find out the qualifications of the people working in the lab. What are their credentials? Is anyone a medical technologist, trained in the proper collection and preparation of specimens, and the operation of the equipment? How often is the equipment inspected and calibrated, and when was the last time this was done?

If your doctor continues to send lab work outside to commercial entities, another potential problem crops up, one that demands sleuthing on your part to determine whether you are getting the most for your money.

REFERRAL FOR PROFIT: RICHER DOCTOR, POORER (BUT MORE EXPENSIVE) CARE?

No judge should preside over a case in which he or she has a personal, vested interest. Ethics panels and the public just wouldn't stand for it. No government official should give contracts to friends, or hire relatives, or purchase supplies from a company the official owns or has stock in.

So then why have we let physicians refer patients to X-ray labs, pharmacies, specialty clinics, private hospitals, kidney dialysis units, and physical therapy practices that these same physicians either own or have a financial interest in? Why do we permit this conflict of interest, ripe for the exploitation of the consumer?

In medicine it's called referral for profit—more hard-nosed critics have labeled it a kickback scheme—and in this age of physician glut the opportunity for abuse in the name of greater physician profits is clear.

"The scenario goes like this," writes Bonnie Teschendorf, assistant professor in the physical therapy program at Columbia University's College of Physicians and Surgeons, in a letter to the *New York Times*.

Doctor A hears from a colleague, Doctor B, that he is making an extra $100,000 above his income from his own medical practice. The augmented income is derived from his investment and ownership in a physical therapy unit.

Doctor A begins a similar practice in his town by renting more space, buying some equipment, and hiring a recent graduate to treat the patients. He pays the therapist a salary above the going rate at the local hospital (draining off manpower from that facility, to which he previously referred his patients).

Now the revenue of the practice of physical therapy shifts from the hospital outpatient department to Doctor A's practice. You would think that the hospitals would be outraged and seek to end this relationship, but they do not. They need Doctor A to produce inpatients, and so they remain neutral.

Doctor A has his own patients to examine as a follow-up to surgery. Instead of giving the patient a referral to a therapist at the hospital or a therapist in private practice, he walks the patient next door to see "his" therapist.

Now, granted, you may find one-stop shopping convenient. No running around, perhaps a shorter waiting time to get an appointment. What may not be so good for you is the quality of care, the cost, and the length of the course of treatment. For one thing, some studies hint that physician-owned physical therapy practices are less well equipped than outside physical therapy practices, and the practitioners are less extensively trained.

While this may pose a threat, an even greater one is the possibility that a physician who stands to profit by owning an outside referral business may refer you too frequently to these places, and may overtest. A 1989 General Accounting Office study preliminarily found that physician-owners of Maryland labs or imaging centers ordered, on the average, *14 percent more expensive lab tests and 82 percent more expensive imaging tests than nonowner doctors.* Doctors with ownership interests also ordered *more* lab tests—one test for every two patients—compared with one test for every four ordered by nonowner doctors. And doctor-owners tended to order slightly fewer *but more costly* imaging services than nonowners: $96.51 versus $52.92, according to a June 12, 1989 *HealthWeek* article.

In its own national survey yet another government agency, the Department of Health and Human Services, found that when doctors own shares in laboratories outside their offices, their Medicare patients get as much as 45 percent more tests than the patients of other doctors (*Washington Post,* April 29, 1989). The cost to the Medicare program of this increased utilization of laboratory services by doctor-owners? Twenty-eight million dollars in 1987 is the study's calculation. Clearly, referral for profit is running up the cost of medical care, which is an inflationary runaway train as it is.

Diagnostic laboratories, radiology or imaging centers, and physical rehabilitation centers are not the only services doctors these days invest in or own. Not surprisingly, the list of services runs the gamut of every medical enterprise to which doctors can send patients: cardiac rehabilitation centers; sports medicine clinics; women's health centers; home-health-care and visiting nurse services; medical equipment leasing and sale businesses; radiation therapy centers; and same-day surgery centers—this according to a March 1989 *Wall Street Journal* series entitled "Patients for Sale." The series reported that some doctors are realizing annual returns of 100 percent and more on investments of between $5,000 and $20,000.

Where is the consumer in all of this? Out of the loop, say the critics, because a major problem is that patients usually are unaware of their doctor's holdings or investments, so they are easy prey to unnecessary and excessive tests and treatment.

Until the controversy over whether physicians should refer people to laboratories and other services they own is resolved, all you can do is closely question your doctor. Question the need for every referral. Find out whether your doctor has any financial interest whatsoever in the lab, service, clinic, or outside allied practice to which he or she is referring you. *Ask your doctor outright.* And if the answer is yes, ask your doctor to offer alternatives.

Above all, be aware that the business of referral for profit is becoming a common practice, that it can lead to overutilization and duplication of services, that it can seriously jeopardize the physician's ability to exercise independent judgement—*and that it can cost you a bundle.* Be on guard against the doctor who is more interested in protecting his or her investment than in healing the sick.

MONEY-SAVING TIPS:
AT THE DOCTOR'S OFFICE

Doctors are the so-called gatekeepers of the medical world. Through them you enter the worlds of the hospital, the laboratory, and the pharmacy. By working carefully and assertively with your doctor, you can greatly lower your health costs.

$ Make it clear to your doctor that all tests must be specifically approved by you before ordering. Diagnostic tests are big money-eaters, both in hospitals and in the doctor's office. Make sure you know what each test is for and that you feel it is necessary before agreeing to it. Say no to a test if you are not clear about its purposes.

$ Make it clear to your doctor that all consultations must be specifically approved by you. Especially during periods of hospitalization, you may find yourself being billed for consultations by specialists that you were unaware of. Making it clear to your physician that you must specifically approve any such consultations will assure that you pay only for necessary consultations.

$ Buy a medical guide to aid you in deciding whether or not to see a doctor. Books authored by major university medical schools, and even the American Medical Association, are useful and easily available at bookstores throughout the country. They are a good first line of very basic information.

$ Always go to a nonspecialist first—specialists are rarely necessary. General practitioners and family practitioners are able to diagnose and treat the vast majority of illnesses. They will readily refer you to a specialist if necessary, but in the meantime you will have paid less for the care you received.

$ Do not use a specialist as a primary care physician. A primary care physician is one who cares for the whole patient, and does not specialize in any one area or condition. If you require the care of a specialist for a specific problem (such as a cardiologist for a heart problem), do not ask that person to treat any problems not related to that particular specialty. Not only are a specialist's time and care more expensive, but she is not qualified to deal with problems outside of her specific area of expertise.

$ Don't offhandedly substitute an emergency room for your doctor. Except in absolute emergencies, never go to an emergency room unless you try to contact your doctor first. If your doctor does not make provisions for seeing people at relatively short notice during office hours, find another doctor.

$ Use an urgicenter, or emergicenter, rather than a hospital emergency room if your doctor is not available. Anytime you feel you need a doctor's care, you should call your doctor first. But if your doctor is not available, an urgicenter is usually less expensive than a hospital emergency room—and your wait there probably will be shorter. Urgicenters are independent clinics that offer basic medical care on a walk-in basis for twelve or even twenty-four hours a day, rather than only during traditional office hours.

$ Get a second opinion. It is always a good idea, for your health as well as your pocketbook, to get a second opinion on any invasive procedure your doctor recommends.

$ Don't get a second-opinion referral from your doctor. You are less likely to get an impartial, objective second opinion from a doctor who's your doctor's friend or close colleague.

$ Get more than two opinions when the first two disagree.

$ Explore non-M.D. providers whenever possible or appropriate. Basic health care can often be provided safely and less expensively by non-M.D.'s such as optometrists, podiatrists, chiropractors, and audiologists. Always compare fees first.

$ Ask for a get-acquainted visit. You may save money in the long run by making an appointment for a short, get-acquainted visit with a new doctor. You can establish quickly whether he or she is a doctor with whom you will be able to work.

$ Check fees in advance. There is a surprising amount of variation among doctors' fees, even for basic care such as office visits and tests.

$ Negotiate charges and fees. Most doctors are willing to lower their standard fees for patients with limited incomes or special economic circumstances. You should also bargain with the doctor if you think a particular fee is too high.

$ Demand that your doctor accept Medicare payments on assignment. Most doctors are willing to accept Medicare on assignment—which means that you will be responsible only for your 20 percent copayment under Medicare—on a case-by-case basis.

$ Seek telephone advice from your doctor whenever possible. Most doctors are happy to answer simple questions and provide advice over the phone about medication, reactions, or recurring health problems. You can save a considerable amount of money on office visits, even if the doctor charges a nominal fee for the phone consultation.

$ Call ahead to see if the doctor's appointments are on schedule. This can save a lot of your time, a valuable commodity.

$ Send the doctor a bill if he or she keeps you waiting more than thirty minutes. Although this tip is somewhat tongue-in-cheek, still you should value your time and remember that you have lost not only the time in the waiting room but also the time it took you to get there and back. And, if you are forced to leave without seeing the doctor because of your other commitments, you will be forced to reschedule and take time out of another day.

$ Use a doctor with separate waiting rooms for sick and well visits. More and more doctors are offering this convenience, particularly for children, since doctors' offices are prime places to pick up illnesses.

$ Make sure the doctor accepts your insurance coverage. Always confirm, at the time you make the appointment, that the doctor accepts the health insurance that you carry. You can't take this for granted.

$ Read about your condition. You will be able to make more informed decisions about your treatment and avoid unnecessary tests and procedures if you know a lot about your condition.

$ Say "No" if you do not understand, and ask questions until you do. Never submit to a test, treatment, or procedure that you do not fully understand.

$ Demand a full justification of any tests or procedures.

HOSPITALIZATION—TOO OFTEN THE WRONG TREATMENT

Doctors and hospitals are made for each other. Literally. It's a relationship at the basis of which is mutual need: A physician needs a place to send sick patients, and a hospital needs sick patients to fill beds. Voilà! A deal is struck, and the partnership continues along its usually beneficial course—lucrative for the hospital, lucrative for the doctor. But what about the consumer? Far from a financially gainful proposition, hospitalization has the potential to push the consumer to the brink of bankruptcy, and even beyond.

Most of the money spent on health care in the United States is spent in hospitals—some $200-plus billion a year. So it stands to reason that a close scrutiny of the entire process, from preadmission talks with your doctor, to admission, and on to discharge, has the potential to save your money, and probably large amounts of it. The rule of thumb here is *don't go unless absolutely necessary.* Start the critical process with your doctor, and question, question, question.

What you need to consider before you and your doctor agree to schedule a hospital stay is whether hospitalization is really required for your situation. Some of the questions you asked before going to the specialist—what do you hope to find? Do the advantages outweigh the risks?—can be asked in deciding whether your ailment needs to be treated in a hospital. But at the very least, be sure to ask your doctor five basic questions before you consent to enter the hospital: *Why am I going? What will be done? How long will I stay? What will it produce? What will happen if I don't go?*

Remember, just because your doctor says you belong in the hospital doesn't mean you positively do. Many hospitalized patients should not be in the hospital at all. In a survey of the records of more than seven thousand Medicare patients, the Office of the Inspector General of the Department of Health and Human Services found that *more than one out of every ten Medicare hospital admissions is unnecessary.*

Another significant study—this one an eight-year project reported in the November 13, 1986 issue of the *New England Journal of Medicine*—pinpointed the numbers of inappropriate, avoidable, and unnecessary hospitalizations of nonelderly adults: an astounding 40 percent. Of that percentage some 23 percent were totally avoidable, and another 17 percent could have been avoided by the use of ambulatory, or outpatient, surgery.

An article in the *Medical Tribune* of June 15, 1989, related more evidence of overadmission, the setting in this case being the cardiac care unit, or CCU. According to the article, approximately half of the 1.5 million people admitted to CCUs annually in this country do not have "acute cardiac ischemia" (sudden onset of blockage or cutoff of blood flow, and thus oxygen, to the heart—a condition that necessitates the kind of intensive cardiac care found in CCUs). "For each such 'lucky' patient," the article said, "who does not have a myocardial infarction [heart attack], the CCU tab amounts to nearly $4,000. This adds up to $3 billion spent annually to rule out [heart attacks]."

NOSOCOMIAL INFECTIONS —COSTLY SOUVENIRS OF HOSPITALIZATION

An unnecessary stay in the hospital threatens far more than your wallet, as if that weren't reason enough to quibble over the necessity of hospitalization. While in the hospital you are at risk of piling up mounds of charges for procedures and tests, but you are also at risk of acquiring a condition you did not have when you went in—called iatrogenic disease ("iatrogenic" from the Greek meaning "doctor-caused" or "doctor-produced"). Iatrogenesis, especially one of its manifestations—nosocomial infection—is why we say a hospital is no place for a sick person. Acquired during hospitalization, nosocomial infections are produced by microorganisms that dwell with relative impunity in hospitals. Nosocomial infections aren't present in patients on admission. In other words, you didn't have it when you came in, but you got it while you were there. Most develop at least seventy-two hours after admission, which means that some may not become manifest until after discharge (R. P.

Wenzel, ed., *CRC Handbook of Hospital-Acquired Infections* [Boca Raton, Fla.: CRC Press, 1981]).

You could say nosocomial infections are expensive souvenirs of your hospital stay. It is estimated that the recovery time necessary to combat a nosocomial infection is about four extra days of stay at an average additional cost of $800 per day (factoring in both room and ancillary charges). That's $3,200 per infection! Nosocomial infections account for 15 percent of all hospital charges and end up adding, at a minimum, $2.5 billion to America's medical bill. Some say the true figure is double that, especially since about a fourth of all infections acquired in the hospital don't show up until after the patient is discharged. Then work-related expenses and costly readmission to the hospital have to be factored in.

Robert Haley, M.D., director of the Division of Epidemiology and Preventive Medicine at the University of Texas Southwestern Medical School, states flatly that nosocomial infections are adding "an unnecessary $4 billion a year to our national medical bill." Another group of experts says the figure is much higher. They explain, in the November 1986 issue of the *American Journal of Surgery,* that surgical wound infections alone (of which there are more than a million each year in the United States) "add an average of seven days to the usual hospital stay of surgical patients and cost more than $10 billion in direct and indirect expenses."

Expensive as it is, a nosocomial infection can also be a most deadly souvenir: some estimates of infection-related deaths run as high as 100,000 (some even higher, 300,000 or so) a year. Annually, 5 to 10 percent of hospitalized patients (or about 2 million people) acquire hospital infections, and in approximately 3 percent of those cases, the infection is the cause of death.

Nosocomial infection rates are highest in large teaching hospitals and lowest in nonteaching hospitals. Obviously, the large teaching facilities attract the sickest patients, but this fact also points out the difficulties large facilities have in maintaining necessary sanitary discipline.

Here are some more disturbing infection-related facts:

▶ Annually, more than 100,000 hospital patients in the United States acquire nosocomial bacteremia—the presence of bacteria in the blood. Richard E. Dixon, M.D., says the mortality rates "range from 20 percent for patients who do not develop shock, to greater than 80 percent for those who do."

▶ Infection is the most frequent cause of death in cancer patients.

▶ Pneumonia, now reported as the most common hospital-acquired infection leading to death, occurs in 0.5 to 5 percent of all in-hospital patients and in 12 to 15 percent of patients ill enough to require intensive care, and may be responsible for 15 percent of all hospital-associated deaths. It may be introduced into the lungs by way of contaminated respiratory therapy equipment or simply by breathing the air filled with droplets of infection from other patients or coughing medical personnel, especially in the close quarters of intensive care units.

Why is nosocomial infection so widespread, so lethal a problem in modern hospitals? For one thing hospitals are where sick people are. Those who are weak when hospitalized and those weakened in the hospital are highly susceptible to infection. These infections come from the microorganisms and pathogens that thrive in the hospital setting or arrive with new patients from the community at large.

Add to that the increase in invasive procedures and major surgeries. Consider the increased use of drugs that reduce the body's rejection of implants but at the same time suppress the body's immune system, leaving the door wide open for infections that can kill—for example, nosocomial pneumonia. Nosocomial infections frequently attack the urinary tract—most commonly because of urinary catheters, the cause of approximately 40 percent of all nosocomial infections—surgical wounds (about 25 percent), and the lower respiratory tract (approximately 15 percent).

Another cause of patient susceptibility to hospital infections is, ironically, antibiotics. Typically, when there is a rash of infections, hospitals haul out the antibiotics to do away with the monsters that the antibiotics themselves have nurtured. And it may work for a while—until the aftereffects set in. Not only do patients have bad reactions to the drugs, but there is a rapid development of strains of bacteria resistant to the antibiotics that were once effective against these organisms. The amount of penicillin required to treat an infection today is fifty times greater than it was thirty years ago.

"As many as two-thirds of the hospital patients given antibiotics are receiving them inappropriately," stated an editorial in the May 1, 1983 issue of the *Canadian Medical Association Journal.* Research from the University of California at San Francisco bears this out: 62 percent of patients receiving antibiotics in community hospitals "failed to have definite evidence of infection" before the drug regimen was begun. About the same figure applies to university hospitals.

The ways nosocomial infections are spread are numerous. Organisms can be transmitted in food and water, in transfused blood and intravenous fluids, in pharmaceuticals, through the air, by direct human contact, on towels and sheets, and via the housekeeping crew, to name but a few.

Certain places in the hospital must be diligently monitored, for they can be especially hazardous for patients and hospital personnel as well. These include the hemodialysis unit (the equipment can be a source of hepatitis B, a virulent organism that is difficult to destroy), intensive care units (occupied by patients who are extremely weak and thus susceptible to infection and operated under emergency measures that often have to forsake pristine sanitary procedures in order to save a life), the infant nursery, and the operating room.

To these potential sources of infection add plain old carelessness, if not callousness. The Institute for Child Health Policy reports that many hospital workers who come in direct contact with patients don't take the time, or are not concerned enough, to perform the simplest and best known of precautionary actions: *washing their hands properly*. And doctors are among the worst offenders. No wonder: "Most medical schools don't teach practical prevention, stressing things like washing," explains Timothy R. Franson, M.D., hospital epidemiologist at the Medical College of Wisconsin. Case in point: in two intensive care units studied, hands were washed after patient contact less than half the time. Unwashed hands are prime culprits in the spread of many nosocomial infections.

Nosocomial infections can also pass to patients via the procedural chain of the food services department, due to any one or more of the following—nearly all of them with their roots in human error, and any one of them preventable: lack of hand washing; poor personal hygiene; faulty patient care technique; inadequate refrigeration (the culprit in nearly half of all nosocomial salmonellosis outbreaks); inadequate cooking; inadequate reheating; holding food in warming devices at bacteria-incubating temperatures; using contaminated raw ingredients in uncooked foods; and improper cleaning of equipment (John V. Bennett and Philip S. Brachman, eds., *Hospital Infections* [Boston: Little, Brown, 1979]).

A myriad of studies also point to other work areas in the hospital that, because of persistently poor and unprofessional hygiene practices, are breeding grounds for nosocomial infections: central service department, the unit responsible for processing, storing, and dispensing hospital supplies; the pharmacy; the laundry; the laboratory (where, more than one story goes, workers have to be admonished not to keep their lunches in the same refrigerators as the ones that contain serum or other specimens)—and the list goes on.

How Do You Protect Yourself?

What can be done to protect yourself from nosocomial infections? There is no surefire defense for you if the rest of the hospital is a vast and bubbling breeding ground. So the first step in infection protection is to try to gain admission to a hospital that has a good nosocomial record. Ask your doctor about it. Contact your local department of health. Ask the hospital directly, but be on your guard if the hospital paints too rosy a picture. That may mean that the staff is not properly surveying the facility's infection rate, or not surveying at all.

An active infection control committee is a good sign that the hospital is concerned about infections and is trying to monitor and control them. Ask if that is the case. Another good sign is if someone on the staff is a member of the infection watchdog organization, the Association for Practitioners in Infection Control. Hospitals with a greater than average concern for the nosocomial infection danger will have at least one nurse-epidemiologist on staff to maintain surveillance. Find out if there's one in your hospital.

Little has changed in the more than two decades since two prominent researchers, H. N. Beaty and R. G. Petersdorf, wrote in the October 1966 issue of the *Annals of Internal Medicine* about the most important preventive of iatrogenic disease: "Administer drugs only when they are needed, and . . . perform diagnostic procedures only when they are likely to yield meaningful information."

What Else Can You Do?

While it is true that one-third of all infections treated in hospitals are nosocomial infections, it is also estimated that as many as half of all such infections are preventable. With luck, information, and diligence you might be able to prevent your own. Some things you can do personally and actively while in the hospital are:

▶ Try to make sure that all hospital personnel who come in contact with you have washed their hands. If you so desire, ask them to do so, in your room, in your presence. You can greatly lower your chances of catching an infection—and paying for its treatment.

▶ If your roommate becomes infected, or if you are concerned that what he or she has could possibly be transmitted to you via the air or through the use of a common bathroom, ask your doctor or the staff nurse-epidemiologist about your risks. Change your room at once if there is any chance you might become infected, because once you are infected, it is too late. You may have to be put in isolation along with your roommate.

▶ If you are undergoing surgery or a procedure that requires the removal of hair, refuse to be shaven the night before surgery. One study indicates that among people shaved the day prior to their operations, the nosocomial infection rate was 5.6 percent. Chemical depilatories reduce the rate to just 0.6 percent. Using barber clippers to remove hair the morning of surgery yields a low infection rate too.

    Of course, there is a good question you might ask: Is shaving or clipping or any other form of hair removal necessary at all? Maybe not—and especially when it comes to ob-gyn situations. Removing hair before vaginal delivery or surgery in that area is probably uncalled for, because the old idea that hair creates a climate for infection is unsubstantiated by clinical studies.

▶ Have nurses regularly check the drainage of urinary catheters to help you maintain cleanliness.

IATROGENIC DISEASE

Iatrogenic disease may be considered a nosocomial problem in a general sense because it takes place most often in a hospital. Its origin, though, is with the doctor.

Iatrogenic disease is no small problem. In one major study conducted at a teaching hospital, researchers from Boston University Medical Center found that of 815 consecutive admissions, 36 percent were there because of an iatrogenic problem, and in 2 percent of the patients, iatrogenesis was a contributing factor in the patients' deaths. If one were able to generalize from this study, one would arrive at the conclusion that iatrogenic mishaps kill nearly half a million people a year and add at least a billion dollars to America's medical bill.

Iatrogenesis comes in all sizes and types. There is the iatrogenesis that occurs when a doctor performs a procedure that has greater risks than benefits, and the gamble is lost. There is the iatrogenesis that occurs when the doctor hasn't prepared for the unexpected complication, although it was always a possibility. There is the iatrogenesis that occurs when a doctor makes a mistake, in judgment or handiwork. He or she might go ahead and do something without having adequate knowledge of, or skills for, the procedure.

High-Risk Areas for Iatrogenesis

There are several areas of medical practice in which iatrogenesis is most prevalent. To avoid becoming a victim of iatrogenesis and paying large sums of money for treatment of it, you need to know the dangers that could lie in these areas.

Diagnosis. Diagnosing disease is the keystone of medicine, its very foundation. Without an accurate diagnosis, medical practice has no purpose, and patients are treated in ways that are ineffective and expensive or worse—a lot worse. What's the problem? The studies point the finger at too great a reliance on technology and statistics and lab results, and not enough use of human skills, common sense, and brain work. You could say the medical profession has come a long way from the words of Sir William Osler: "Learn to see, learn to hear, learn to feel, learn to smell, and know that by practice alone can you become expert. Medicine is learned by the bedside, and not in the classroom."

Doctors may be believing the machines and mistrusting their own eyes. And the fact of the matter is that, aside from the astronomical costs of high-tech testing, *a person can become ill because of those very tests.* Some very good studies in important journals have made it clear that faulty diagnosis is a major iatrogenic problem. For example, a study by researchers from Baptist Memorial Hospital and the University of Tennessee College of Medicine in Memphis revealed that heart attacks were misdiagnosed 47 percent of the time. From the Baylor College of Medicine in Houston came the report that medical residents made diagnostic errors—incorrect findings and oversights—13.1 percent of the time, interns 15.6 percent of the time, and that at least one error occurred during the examination of two-thirds of all patients seen. Both studies appeared in the *Journal of the American Medical Association.*

The *New England Journal of Medicine* reported a Harvard hospital study showing that 10 percent of all patients who had died *might have lived* if they had received the correct diagnosis. In some categories of disease the misdiagnosis figures were as high as 24 percent.

Surgery. Unnecessary surgery is an iatrogenic nightmare. How prevalent is it? Some claim unnecessary surgery comprises somewhere between 10 and 20 percent of all surgery. Heart specialist Robert G. Schneider, M.D., in *When to Say No to Surgery* (Englewood Cliffs, N.J.: Prentice-Hall, 1982) puts the unnecessary-surgery figure at 15 to 25 percent as an average, multiples it by the number of operations performed each year, and comes up with a total of somewhere between 3 million and 6.25 million annual unnecessary operations, leading to a ballpark figure of 40,000 to 80,000 unnecessary surgery deaths in America every year.

In fact, one of the most common vascular operations in this country, carotid endarterectomy—the removal of blockages from arteries carrying blood to the brain—is often done unnecessarily, according to many reports. A Canadian study published in the *New England Journal of Medicine* of October 2, 1986, said that half of the more than 100,000 such operations done in this country every year are performed on patients without symptoms of carotid disease. And there is a 10 percent risk of suffering a stroke or dying from the surgery—a risk roughly five times greater than that from the condition it's supposed to correct. A five-year Rand Corporation study of 5,000 Medicare patients found carotid endarterectomy to be a common unnecessary surgery, with 65 percent of the surgeries done for inappropriate or questionable reasons. Of the people studied, 10 percent died or had a stroke as a direct result of the surgery (*Parade Magazine,* May 21, 1989).

The same Rand study also found that death occurs in roughly 5 percent of coronary bypass surgeries (to help or replace constricted or blocked arteries), and even the successful ones can have problems: the new vessel may close within eight years and thus require more surgery.

Other operations most often mentioned as probably unnecessary are many that are elective, many that are female-oriented (mastectomies, hysterectomies, cesarean sections), tonsillectomies, knee operations, and back operations. Because enough evidence exists to charge ample numbers of physicians with performing inappropriate or unnecessary surgery on Medicare patients, the Office of Management and Budget has suggested a reduction in payments to physicians for these procedures:

▶ Arthroscopic, or fiberoptic tube, examinations of knee joints, lungs, esophagus, stomach, and duodenum

▶ Carpal tunnel surgery for hand pain

▶ Lens implant after cataract removal, or lens implant without cataract removal

▶ Coronary bypass surgery

▶ Dilation and curettage of the uterus to diagnose disease

▶ Hip or knee replacement

▶ Heart pacemaker implant

▶ Prostate surgery

Both critics and surgeons agree on one fact: statistics show that the number of operations each year increases, not in proportion to the rise in population but rather in proportion to the rise in the number of surgeons. The more surgeons looking to make a living, the more operations there are. And various Rand Corporation studies point to unnecessary, inappropriate, and overpriced surgeries as substantial causes behind the ever-mounting costs of health care.

Drugs. As an area of iatrogenic abuse, drugs are probably in the lead. As we discussed in some detail in chapter 4, doctors just aren't as well educated in dosages and side effects as they might be. That is why they are so easily influenced, duped, or co-opted by pharmaceutical salespersons who have commissions and promotions on their minds. Also, there is the matter of sloppy prescribing—a great deal of overprescribing, mostly, and also unwise, uncertain, and sometimes unethical prescribing.

How can you protect yourself against doctor-produced problems, against iatrogenic mishaps? So long as medical care is provided by humans, there will be error and greed and iatrogenesis. That is why you must maintain an attitude of wariness. As we said at the beginning of this chapter, if you are not yet in a hospital, be wary of going into one. A hospital ought to be the place your doctor sends you when all else fails, when there is no other choice and no better place to continue your care. If you find yourself in a hospital, be wary of everything scheduled to be done to you. Get as much information as you can about what is to be done to you, what drug is being prescribed for you. Learn the names of the drugs you need to take, their doses and sizes, and even their colors, so that you will be able to spot a mistake or question a change. Before you give the green light to anything, be sure the benefits outweigh the risks. Don't be talked into "fad" operations. Get second opinions and third opinions. When in doubt—and especially if that doubt has to do with elective surgery—don't. Take nothing for granted. And, we'll say it again—question, question, question.

Ask certain specific questions of each surgeon you visit: At what hospital do you operate? What is the nosocomial infection rate there? How often is the operation performed at that hospital? How often do you perform this operation? What's been the result? What are the risks? What will or may the consequences be if you do not perform this surgery?

Numerous studies have demonstrated that the more times a hospital performs certain operations, the lower the death and/or complication rates for people undergoing the procedures. The most recent research on the subject, published in the July 28, 1989 issue of the *Journal of the American Medical Association,* found that death rates for four common operations are higher when done by surgeons with less experience. The four procedures studied were: removal of part of the stomach for ulcers; removal of all or part of the colon for cancer; coronary artery bypass grafts for arteriosclerotic heart disease; and repair of the main abdominal artery weakened or torn by an aneurysm. Death rates for these four, plus a fifth operation—

gallbladder removal—also were found to be higher at hospitals that performed them less often.

So the dictum to question everything is much more than a challenge to nitpick. It's in the interest of survival.

Of course, once you are in the hospital, the questions follow logically. Just be sure to ask them: What's happening tomorrow? What will the tests determine? What will each drug accomplish?

THE SURGEONS' HIT PARADE

Some operations are more necessary than others just as some are more trendy than others, and to help you decide what's what we have listed the top twenty-five most frequently performed surgeries in 1988. While a procedure is not necessarily faddish just because it is popular or frequently performed, you should know if the one being recommended for you is on the surgeons' hit parade. By the same token, we have also included average lengths of stay for certain surgical procedures since it is *your* body and you alone are at risk of iatrogenesis and any other nasty souvenir of a hospital stay.

FIRST ISN'T ALWAYS BEST

It's odd. People are willing, even eager, to ask for seconds on just about everything—except medical diagnoses. Too many people blithely accept the opinion of their friendly family doctor or surgeon and undergo a lot of pain, financial hardship, and perhaps complications and iatrogenic mishaps because of procedures that might not have been necessary in the first place if they'd only asked for another view on the matter.

A second opinion is vitally important, especially if a trip to the hospital looms in your near future. Even a good doctor, convinced that the benefits of surgery outweigh more conservative and less

TOP 25 MOST FREQUENTLY
PERFORMED SURGERIES IN U.S. SHORT-TERM,
GENERAL, NONFEDERAL HOSPITALS, 1988

Rank

1   Cervical cesarean section

2   Total cholecystectomy (gallbladder removal)

3   Abdominal hysterectomy

4   Left cardiac catheterization

5   Transurethral prostatectomy

6   Repair of obstetric laceration

7   Appendectomy

8   Intervertebral disc excision

9   Forceps delivery with episiotomy

10   Wound debridement (removal of foreign material)

11   Contrast myelogram

12   Open reduction of fracture with internal fixation (femur)

13   Balloon angioplasty

14   Combined right/left heart catheterization

15   Vaginal hysterectomy

16   Cystoscopy (examination of bladder with cystoscope)

17   Venous catheter

18   Unilateral simple mastectomy

19   Knee replacement

20   Vacuum extraction with episiotomy

21   Dilation and curettage, postdelivery

22   Open reduction of fracture with internal fixation (tibia/fibula)

23   Repair of inguinal hernia

24   Bone marrow biopsy

25   Tonsillectomy/adenoidectomy

SOURCE: Healthcare Knowledge Systems (Commission on Professional and Hospital Activities).

AVERAGE LENGTH OF STAY FOR SELECTED OPERATIVE PROCEDURES FOR PATIENTS DISCHARGED FROM SHORT-STAY HOSPITALS, 1987

Operation	Average length of stay (in days)
Procedures to assist delivery	2.5
Cesarean section	4.8
Hysterectomy	5.6
Cardiac catheterization	4.4
Cholecystectomy	8.0
Biopsy	8.7
Repair of current obstetric laceration	2.5
Arthroplasty of joints	10.1
Open reduction of fracture	9.4
Operations on spinal cord and spinal canal structures except biopsies	7.5
Prostatectomy	6.4
Excision or destruction of lesion or tissue of skin or subcutaneous tissue	11.1
Repair of inguinal hernia	2.9
Dilation and curettage of uterus	2.3
Excision or destruction of intervertebral disc and spinal fusion	8.4
Appendectomy, excluding incidental	4.6
Tonsillectomy with and without adenoidectomy	1.3
Partial gastrectomy and resection of intestine	15.3
Direct heart revascularization	13.9
Bilateral destruction or occlusion of fallopian tubes	2.8

NOTE: Average length of stay may reflect days in the hospital for operations in addition to the first-listed operation. For example, average length of stay for biopsy may also include days in the hospital for subsequent operative procedures. Excludes newborn infants and federal hospitals.
SOURCE: Division of Health Care Statistics, National Center for Health Statistics. Unpublished data from the National Hospital Discharge Survey for 1987, Department of Health and Human Services.

costly treatment, can be overly eager to rush you into the operating room. True, a second opinion might confirm the original diagnosis (and perhaps the need for hospitalization), but it could also contradict the first doctor's conclusions and thus precipitate some doubt about the need for hospitalization. You might require a third, tie-breaking opinion.

But don't limit the search for a second opinion merely to procedures that involve surgery. Many types of therapy performed in a hospital are risky or invasive even though not surgical. Ask another doctor for assurance about the need for any procedure that concerns you.

Who do you ask? A lot of second-opinion doctors recommended by first-opinion doctors turn out to be professional ditto marks and not all that valuable in terms of independent judgments. This is true in part because surgeons are the doctors most often asked for second opinions, and they're hardly predisposed to recommend sheathing the knife. The other, more prevalent problem is that second-opinion doctors may be reluctant to disagree with the friend who recommended them. Let's face it—doctors depend on each other for referrals. Referrals mean bucks in the bank, and a doctor who bucks such a system may find his or her main source of patients drying up. So you should consider finding yourself a doctor for a fair and original second opinion.

How do you do that? Check the *Directory of Medical Specialists* in your local library's reference section. In addition, check with your company's benefits department or ask your insurance company to provide you with a list of physicians it uses for its second opinion program. New York Hospital-Cornell Medical Center's Health Benefits Research Center also sponsors a toll-free referral service called the National Second Opinion Program. The number there is 800-522-0036.

Making these opinion rounds may mean extra time, trouble, and expense, with the costs varying according to the type of surgery and the going rates in your region. For instance, for a simple procedure, such as a tonsillectomy, you may pay $50 or so for a second opinion; on the other hand, second opinions for more complicated surgeries, such as heart bypass or carotid endarterectomy, may run as high as $400 or $500. Be sure to first check your insurance plan's guidelines on second opinions.

However, prepare yourself for some surprises there. The fact is that some employers are having second thoughts about second opinions, primarily because they almost always confirm the first, says a May 24, 1989 *Wall Street Journal* article. When that happens, the employer ends up paying for the second opinion *and* the surgery. As a result, many companies are changing their second-opinion programs to make them more flexible—such as making second opinions voluntary or increasing the numbers of nonsurgeons among the practitioners they recommend to give second opinions. There are, however, companies still committed to the spirit of the second opinion and its ability to save the costs of unnecessary surgery. And in fact, some believe that for second-opinion programs to *really* save money they must include other treatments besides surgery.

A Problem of Excess

Where second opinions are especially valuable is in minimizing excessive testing, a major problem in hospitals. Just as surely as a faulty diagnosis jeopardizes your health and puts you at immediate risk of an iatrogenic condition, so does overtesting. And, at the very least, you will pay for tests you need not have had in the first place. Add to that the costs of an extra day or more in the hospital, should the tests be done on a strictly inpatient basis (and many are).

A study, published in the June 28, 1985 issue of the *Journal of the American Medical Association,* of 2,000 people entering a hospital for nonemergency, or elective, surgery found that 60 percent of the approximately 20,000 "routine," presurgery blood tests were medically unjustified. Only four tests (a minuscule 0.22 percent) revealed any abnormalities that might have a bearing on what doctors call the surgical or anesthetic management of a patient. But in none of these four cases did the doctors do anything differently as a result of the tests—in other words, the results did not change the surgeons' plans.

A definitive study by the Rand Corporation in 1981 found that one in every six Medicare patients who were given an angiography—a diagnostic X-ray technique in which radioactive dye is injected into the coronary arteries to check for blockages—underwent the procedure needlessly. Additionally, one in every six Medicare patients who had endoscopies—a diagnostic procedure in which a camera-tipped tube examines the stomach and intestinal tract—underwent the procedure needlessly. Robert Brook, M.D., a study coauthor quoted in *U.S. News & World Report,* November 23, 1987, says that although the cases go back some years ago a "much higher percentage [of these two procedures] would be deemed inappropriate by today's standards." We're talking big numbers here, and big bucks: millions of these procedures are performed in this country every year.

There are a couple of different ways to look at the problem of excessive testing in hospitals. Some say it all boils down to dollars. Economics is the name of the game in hospital administration, and these routine preoperative tests have been a veritable gold mine for hospitals. Today, more than ever, hospitals are looking to replenish their coffers. With declines in admissions and shortened lengths of stay, hospitals are trying to maximize their profits on a smaller pool of patients, and some say that one way they go about this is by heaping extra charges for tests and supplies.

Still others place the problem squarely at the (clay) feet of doctors. After all, tests are not performed in hospitals *unless* doctors order them. And frankly, say the critics, a large part of the problem is the built-in incentive for doctors to overtest—the system tends to reward doctors (and hospitals) financially for excessive testing.

The hospital's side of the story is that all but the most severely ill patients have been screened out of inpatient hospital stays; consequently, the typical patient requires more intensive, and thus more expensive, treatment. They argue that this justifies the large number of tests performed.

So what *is* going on? Whether too great a reliance on technology and statistics and lab results, and not enough use of human skills, common sense, and brain work, or a profit-making strategy that stresses the bottom line rather than the patient's health—or a combination of all these things—the fact remains that, with enough testing, sooner or later a person will have a real disease caused by the process of diagnosing and treating. So here we are—back to iatrogenesis and the costs associated with it.

And here you are—back to questioning—and we cannot overstress its importance. The line of questioning is the same as we outlined in chapter 1:

"Why does this test or retest need to be done?"   In the case of a retest, ask if it wasn't done before and why it's necessary again. Was the first flawed, inconclusive, or is there something new and important to be done? If tests need to be done over and over—and especially if the tests are hazardous (for example, invasive tests or those involving repeated exposure to radiation)— call a halt.

"What will you be looking for in the results of these tests?"
This is a key question because it requires your doctor to let you in on the process, diagnosis, and prognosis, and to justify the need for further testing.

"Will the procedure be painful, and is it dangerous?"   Don't hesitate to ask this question, because if the test might cause more pain (or might lead to complications more dangerous) than the condition itself, you should think twice about having the test.

"How much will it cost?"   This is an important question, because you will want to shop around for the best doctor at the best price.

"How much time will it take?"   This is not as selfish and trivial a question as it may seem at first glance. Certainly, to decide against having essential medical care simply because you don't want to juggle your schedule would be foolish. However, if an examination or testing procedure is of questionable diagnostic value and to have it performed means losing work time, some much-needed pay, and maybe even your job itself, then the matter of time—how long, what time of day, and whether multiple visits are involved—is a consideration. When you have the information, discussions with your family doctor and employer will help you to determine if you can afford to—or not afford to—pursue a certain medical course.

"Must I remain in the hospital for this test, or can it be done on an outpatient basis?"   We've added this question here because of the additional problems, hazards, and costs that overnight hospitalization (or longer) holds for anyone.

"Do the potential advantages of the tests outweigh their risks?"   The tests themselves might be dangerous or cause serious problems as a side effect. Have your doctor give you a rundown on the possibilities.

"Is this the most appropriate test?"   Tests mean big money for doctors and facilities. Today any number of tests are used to diagnose or rule out a condition. Because of this, many doctors have fallen victim to "testitis"—they use all the tests available instead of the most comprehensive one. Watch out for the doctor who wants to move you up the test ladder. Ask why he or she is not recommending the most comprehensive one *in the first place.* Remember, one comprehensive test may be a lot cheaper than three lesser ones.

"What will happen if I don't have this procedure done?"   This is a question you must ask. It may be the single most important query anyone could pose at any and every level of dealings with the medical system, and it should be asked every time a procedure is recommended. What could you possibly lose by asking? And you could gain a great deal.

NEW STUDY: DOCTORS FUEL COST INCREASES BY USING OUTMODED DIAGNOSTIC TESTS

A *big* problem today is the lure of newfangled technology. Doctors are antsy to try out the new baubles and toys constantly being added to the inventory of high-tech diagnostic equipment: imaging devices that create detailed pictures of vital body parts; fiberoptic tubes that snake through your arteries; and scans that noninvasively

---

FOUR FREQUENTLY ORDERED TESTS THAT ARE LABOR-INTENSIVE AND COSTLY

Without a doubt, cutting out unnecessary or inappropriate tests can save a lot of money—both yours and the amount spent in the system as a whole. According to an article in the March 28, 1989 *Washington Post Health,* charges for laboratory services have risen drastically over the past two decades, accounting for as much as 25 percent of total hospital costs. That means you stand to save up to one-fourth of your hospital bill if you and your doctor work together to eliminate the tests *you don't need.*

Where can you start? A study at the University of California at Los Angeles Medical Center singled out four frequently ordered medical tests that are labor-intensive and costly: routine urinalysis; chest X rays; and two blood tests—a white blood cell count and a measurement of how fast the blood clots.

---

pinpoint problems. But as you quickly find out, *you* pay for *their* play.

While you may understand the fascination these toys hold for physicians—they're brand-spanking new, usually improved and more accurate, and perhaps even glamorous—how do you explain this: even with their shiny, state-of-the-art contrivances, *doctors continue to use older, outmoded diagnostic tests even after new, improved techniques are adopted.* In fact, new technologies are augmenting, rather than replacing, older tests and may be performing the same function.

These are the findings of an important study begun in 1981 by a team of researchers from the University of Pennsylvania and published in the *Journal of the American Medical Association,* September 1, 1989. No small undertaking, the study analyzed sixty-three hospitals in five regions, comparing the use of five older diagnostic tests with five newer tests that, in the words of the researchers, "could largely substitute for the older [ones]." The tests compared were (older technology listed first):

1. Cholecystogram (gallbladder X ray) with gallbladder ultrasound

2. Brain scan (involving injection of radioactive dye) with a computerized tomographic (CT, or CAT) scan of the head

3. Skull X ray with brain scan

4. Bone survey with bone scan

5. Blood type and cross with blood type and screen

The two gallbladder tests are a prime example of what the researchers describe as a "gradual accretion of technology, rather than a dynamic process of appropriate adoption and abandonment." And in fact, the cholecystogram was the only one of the five older technologies studied to actually decrease in use. While the average annual use of the newer gallbladder ultrasound rose from 0.1 per 100 admissions in 1978 to 0.7 per 100 in 1980, the use of the older gallbladder X ray decreased *only slightly,* from 7.5 to 7 per 100, during the same period.

So back to our earlier question—what do you make of that? Fact is, *you* don't make much of it (in fact, you lose), but the doctors and the hospitals are making plenty—of money, that is. The financial rewards to be reaped from such a formula are plentiful. True, as the study's authors speculated, doctors may be unwilling to stop using older tests if they are uncertain about the accuracy of new ones or if they want to compare the results of two different kinds of tests. But in the meantime, it's you who are being exposed to excessive radiation, you who are stuck in the hospital another day or two or three for more tests, and you who are footing the bill for all this.

Whether or not this is an outright scam in every instance is immaterial. What *is* important is that you be aware of the practice of using new diagnostic tests *in addition to* older, outmoded alternatives, and call a halt to it when the practice is not in your best interest. As always, questioning the whys and wherefores of all procedures your doctor recommends is a good place to start—before you start the expensive climb up the ladder of tests.

We could not end this section without raising the issue of "defensive medicine." If the term is new to you, it is doctor talk meaning "I gotta do the test because if I don't the litigious patient might later sue me if something goes wrong."

There is no doubt that defensive medicine is a reality (if not an excuse). Physicians are worried that each consumer who crosses their medical threshold is high-risk—that is, a high risk to zing his medical eminence with a malpractice suit.

But there is another school of thought on the subject. Some medical critics and consumer advocates have suggested that "defensive medicine" is merely a cover-up for medical laziness. It's easier to push a single button and get a dozen tests than use the gray cells nature implanted to arrive at medical conclusions. Why think when a piece of ringing, buzzing, and flashing equipment can send a printout by fax machine to any one of the doctor's satellite offices, (not to mention the tenth tee) with a patient's chemical profile?

As a result, physicians are subjecting unsuspecting (and usually litigiously low-risk) customers to a battery of worthless pokes and probes that would send Hippocrates, if he were alive today, back to his famed Oath to add a new canon (after "First, do no harm"), which would state "Second, do no unnecessary test."

Unfortunately, Hippocrates is now drifting in medical heaven and we are left to cope. So what can you do?

First, do not agree to a test merely because the doctor recommends it. Follow the advice we have given throughout this section and earlier sections of the book and ask questions. Remember, the choice is yours.

If you say no to a test, be prepared for more than just scowls and grumblings. The doctor may ask you to sign a form releasing him from any liability if something later goes wrong that would have been discovered if you had submitted to his recommendation. Sign it if the form clearly spells out what the test was designed to do, what the doctor was looking for, and if it represents what the doctor explained to you as you understood it. *Do not sign* if it merely states that the doctor wanted to give you the test and you said no.

Don't be bullied. If the doctor says that if you don't take the test he will not continue to treat you, be prepared to find another doctor. It may be in your best medical interest to do so. On the other hand, if the doctor is actively treating you for a serious condition, the law says you cannot be abandoned by the practitioner.

Remember, you are the one who is in control and the only one who can defend yourself from "defensive medicine."

KEEPING TRACK OF YOUR HOSPITAL BILL AND SERVICES

Did you hear the one about the eighty-year-old woman who was billed for a pregnancy test when she entered the hospital for gallbladder surgery?

Since most of the money spent on health care in this country is spent in hospitals, it makes obvious sense that the greatest potential for savings is in hospitals. Unless you're one of the lucky few with a spectacular health insurance plan that pays down to the last penny of your hospital costs, chances are you'll be responsible for 10 to 20 percent of the bill when you check out. What specifically can you do to save money in the hospital? Charges for hospital services are very high, so if you are able to manage without some routine services (such as routine admission tests or unnecessary repetition of other tests), you can save considerable sums of money. But aside from that, probably the most important advice we have is this: *Demand an itemized bill and scrutinize it carefully for errors.* If an itemized bill is not ready when you leave the hospital, make certain the hospital mails it to you. Don't accept a summary bill that doesn't list charges. If the itemized bill comes in full of undecipherable computer codes, ask for a bill you can understand.

And by all means, do not pay a hospital bill as you're leaving. There is hardly a worst time to examine a complicated and baffling financial issue. Tell the billing office you'll pay the bill after you have looked at it.

How good are your chances of finding errors? Equifax Services, an Atlanta firm that audits around forty thousand hospital bills annually for insurers, found in one audit of selected bills that more than 97 percent of hospital bills contain errors! And, according to the firm's calculations, hospital overcharges exceed undercharges by three to one. You can spot these errors only if you receive an itemized bill, and nine times out of ten a hospital will not give you an itemized bill unless you ask for it.

Check the bill carefully and *do not pay for any goods or services you did not receive.* Just as you review your bill in a restaurant to make sure the waiter's record jibes with your order, just as you routinely check your telephone and hotel bills before paying them, just as you do in conducting everyday business affairs, pay the same attention to a hospital bill, because health care is far more expensive than probably anything else you purchase today.

When the *Philadelphia Daily News* took a look at hospital billing in that city, it printed stories about errors that occurred in teaching hospitals and which were uncovered during audits. In one case a man had his $25,185.85 bill for a two-week hospital stay reduced by more than $2,000 after an auditor discovered overcharges. His bill included charges of $5 an hour for oxygen therapy—not an outlandish sum, except that his total charge was based on *thirty-two-hour days!* Time flies when you're having fun, but this is ridiculous.

In another weird error—and they happen more than you'd suspect—a man who underwent open-heart surgery was overcharged a whopping $186,120. It seems the guy, who received two replacement heart valves, was billed for two hundred of them, at $940 a pop. Somebody hit the wrong data-processing key.

The way most hospital billing systems operate is to charge patients for treatments, services, and supplies *before* they actually are received—in fact, usually when they are ordered by the physician. If the treatments or services are never rendered or the supplies not received, because of a change in the doctor's orders or an early discharge from the hospital, the charges still may remain on the bill. Many errors also occur when the surgery is involved, because surgery is a high-dollar item with a myriad of accompanying services and charges. An error here can be significant. Then there's the problem of clerical or simple typographical errors: a charge of $30 for an aspirin tablet instead of $.30, or a bill for twelve blood tests instead of one umbrella test that analyzes twelve components.

If your bill is going to be paid by your insurer, be sure to inform your insurer directly, and in writing, of any inaccuracies in the bill. Everyone saves money by making sure that insurers do not overpay hospitals, and gone are the days when nobody cared enough to scrutinize a hospital bill—including the insurance company paying it. In fact, some employers and insurance companies now offer rewards to people who spot overcharges and other errors on their hospital bills. But even if yours doesn't, you can save money by giving any bill a checkup.

Hospital Billing Errors: What to Look For

American Claims Evaluation, Inc., another firm in the business of auditing hospital bills, recommends that you ask yourself the following questions to help identify possible errors on a bill:

1. Was I billed for the right kind of room (semiprivate, private, etc.)?

2. Was I billed for the correct number of days I occupied the hospital room?

3. Was I billed correctly for any time spent in specialized units (intensive care unit, coronary care unit, etc.)?

4. If I left before "checkout time," was I billed for an extra day even though I'd already gone?

5. Was I billed only for those X rays and tests that I actually received?

6. If I had preadmission testing, did the hospital bill me for the "standard admission test battery" even though I never had it?

7. Was I charged only for supplies, medications, therapy, dressings, injections, etc., that I received? Were the quantities correct?

8. Were medications that my doctor prescribed billed over the entire stay even though I took them only once or twice?

9. Were drugs prescribed for me to take home actually received?

NO SALE

I stood and watched with great interest in a supermarket checkout line not too long ago while the person in front of me went over the cash register tape, item by item. After about a minute this person pointed out to the clerk that there was a charge of 50 cents for an item not purchased. The clerk went through the bag and found that the patron was correct, and the 50 cents were returned. Everyone lived happily ever after.

It's amazing. The same people who will take the time and trouble to look for a 50-cent error at the supermarket checkout counter won't even review the bill they get from a hospital. And yet all too often a careful review of the hospital bill will disclose charges for services never received.

In January 1982 my wife gave birth to our daughter. Prior to entering the hospital, we arranged with the doctor for a number of things *not* to be done while we were in the facility. For example, my wife asked that she not be given an IV unless it was an emergency. We asked that the child not be delivered in the delivery room, but rather in the birthing room, if it was available, or in the labor room. She asked that no medication be given during the labor, unless at the time both of us agreed it might be necessary. In addition, we brought our own vitamins to the hospital, ones the doctor had recommended.

Everything about the delivery went without a hitch. Everything we asked for was done as agreed.

About a week after my wife was discharged, I received a copy of the bill sent to my insurer. On it were charges for vitamins we had never ordered or received. There was a charge for the delivery room, which was not used. There were charges for predelivery and postdelivery IVs, none of which was ever administered. There were charges for medications that we did not use. There were even pediatrician charges for "well-baby" care that never took place, in that the pediatrician to whom this charge was credited was not even at the hospital those three days.

I called the hospital to tell them they had made a mistake. They said not to worry, it had already been paid. I called the insurance company, and after being referred to three or four different persons, was gently told they would look into it. But they gave me the feeling that I was bothering them more than helping them.

I persisted between the hospital and the insurer for a few weeks and eventually was told by the insurer that they had received the money back from the hospital. The hospital told me (or at least a candid representative said) that this billing for services *not* rendered is quite common practice. Charges such as those I objected to are automatically put on the bill regardless of whether the services are provided or not, because normally these services are used in a delivery. Unless the doctor specifically notes services not used, you get charged for them. In my case they almost got about $1,000 for things they never did.

Charles B. Inlander
From "2nd Opinion,"
People's Medical Society Newsletter

10. Was I billed for bedpans, humidifiers, admission kits, thermometers, etc., that I never received and/or was not allowed to take home?

11. If I received a blood transfusion, was I charged for blood that a donor, blood bank, Red Cross family, or community assurance program replaced?

12. If admitted to a maternity unit, was I billed for a labor room that may not have been used because of a swift delivery?

13. If I was able to keep my newborn in my room, was I charged for excess nursery care?

14. Was I charged for personal items not received or that I was not allowed to take home?

15. Was I billed for daily hospital visits by my doctor or surgeon that did not occur?

16. Was I billed for consultations with specialists to whom I was referred but that did not take place?

17. Was I charged for the correct type of treatment and number of hours of treatment by physical, radiation, inhalation, speech, or occupational therapists?

Clarify vague or unclear charges. If any are summarized or listed as "miscellaneous" or "routine medication," have the hospital's business office explain them to your satisfaction. You may want to ask your doctor to assist you in your review of the bills.

Keep a Daily Log

No one knows better than *you* whether or not you received the services and medications listed on the bill. But given the length of time between discharge from the hospital and the arrival of the bill, who can remember? And if you can't remember, how can you check for clerical errors and charges that seem out of line? Simple. Keep a diary of daily events as they occur in the hospital. (Not a bad idea either to help alleviate the boredom that sets in with any hospital stay, protracted or not.) As you read over the bill, this diary or log will help you to remember what happened to you. In it note such information as:

▶ Your date of admission and release

▶ Dates of confinement in a specialized unit (intensive care, coronary care, etc.)

▶ X rays, laboratory tests, and any other goings-on in ancillary departments, where there often is a high volume of services

▶ Medications received

▶ Doctors' visits

▶ Physical (or other) therapy

▶ Personal items received (admission kits, thermometers, plastic cups, etc.)

If there's something happening that you don't understand, write it down. The more details, the better chance you have of spotting overcharges and other errors that you (or your insurance company) should not have to pay for. If it's not possible for you to keep the diary, perhaps a friend or family member can help. It's worth the trouble.

YOUR HOSPITAL BILL: UNDERSTANDING THE HIEROGLYPHICS

You have to review your bill with some care to pick out any over-charges and dispute them. Easier said than done, you say? True, translating the cuneiform carvings on the Rosetta stone was proba-bly a lot easier than deciphering a hospital bill. And true, some hospital bills are yards long and usually hard to read and difficult to understand; most hospital bills are full of abbreviations and shorthand entries, and lots of charges for items and services are crammed into that catchall category "Miscellaneous."

However, there's no getting around it—if you want to get the most for your medical dollar, and avoid paying for what you did not get, you have to go over the hospital bill item by item, no matter how long it takes. The daily log and other records, the forms for which we have included in this book, can serve as guides and evidence. Review the pointers on the sample bill that follows on pages 278–79.

Put a check mark next to the items that seem unclear or odd, and refuse to pay those portions of the bill. If the bill is riddled with inaccuracies, errors, and overcharges, to the point where you question the entire bill, *don't pay it.* To clarify and rectify any errors, first approach the hospital: talk to the head of the billing office, even the hospital administrator if you must. If there are major problems that nobody at the hospital seems able or willing to resolve, or if they refuse to clear an error or explain a muddled entry, you have other avenues open to you.

How to Request a Review

Call your attorney if you need help or guidance. But by all means contact your insurance company to instruct them not to pay your bill when the hospital submits it. The insurance company may (and should) hop right on your side when the situation is explained. Your employer, or any other group or association who may be paying a good chunk of your insurance, should be informed about what you are doing, why you are refusing to accept or pay the bill. Your employer may even go to bat for you.

When you contact your insurance company, you are requesting an audit of your account. This audit is called a utilization review. And of course any documentation (the daily log, record of tests and medications administered, and so on) you have will be valuable in pleading your case. If you suspect fraud, contact your state attorney general's office.

In any event, assert your rights, including your right to refuse to pay a bill that is questionable. Bear in mind, though, that the hospital has a right to send collection agencies after you or sue you for your actions if you and the hospital don't come to an agreement. Even here you have recourse: if the hospital threatens you with legal action or has a collection agency pursue you, contact your state's consumer protection office.

DAILY LOG—WHO DID WHAT

People don't always do what they say they are going to do, or they might even do something and then say they didn't. It happens all the time in the real world, and it happens in hospitals, too. In hospitals, the gulf between what is reportedly done and what is actually done is sometimes a wide one. Frequently the discrepancy is grounds for complaint and action, sometimes escalating to a malpractice suit or other litigation.

Documentation is what you need in such situations. Using this form you can keep a daily record of visits to your room by your medical professionals and the vast array of hospital personnel. With this log you will be able to see—and to demonstrate at the cashier's office or in the courtroom—whether the anesthesiologist really did drop by to chat about your complaints, or how often your doctor stopped in to see how you were doing. You will also be able to determine who really provided care and concern and rank that all on a "Satisfaction Scale" of 1 to 10, with 10 a perfect experience.

Make sure this log is accurate. It may come in very handy somewhere up the road.

Name/ Job Title	Date	What Was Done/Said	Comments	Satisfaction Scale (1–10)

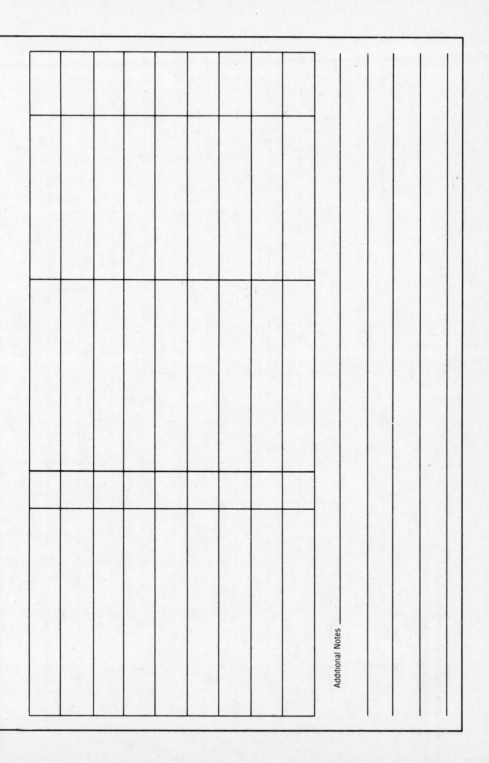

Additional Notes

DAILY LOG—WHO DID WHAT WHEN

This is the flip side of the previous form. In this one, time is of the essence. In the "Daily Log—Who Did What," you were recording who in fact showed up. In this log, the major concern is how much time they spent with you, at what time of day, and what they did.

This form is important for keeping track of quantity (and, perhaps, quality) of care. How much time does it take for the new nurse to take blood from you? Is it a painful eternity or a quick stick? When your doctor comes to check on your progress, does he just pop his head in the door for 10 mechanically cheery seconds or does he spend a reasonable amount of time with you? And is he charging you the same visitation fee for 10 worthless seconds as for 10 valuable minutes?

Personnel	Date	Time	Length of Visit	What Did/Said	How You Felt Afterward	Satisfaction Scale (1–10)

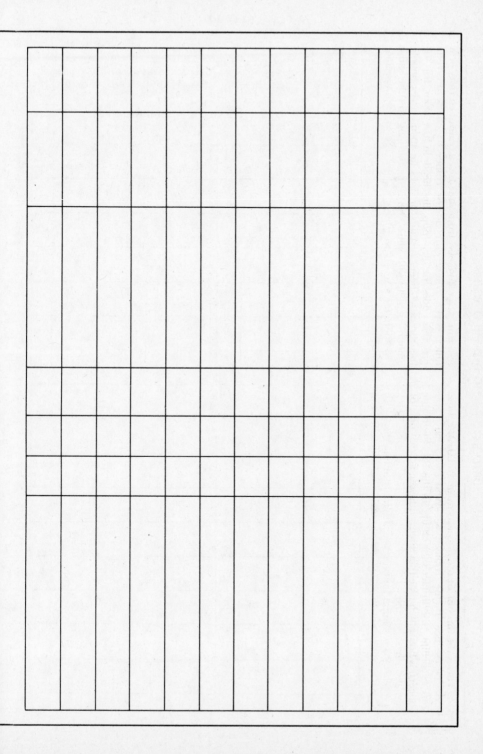

TESTS RECORD

This form records the types of tests you are getting and what you are getting out of them. Hospital lab tests—blood, urine, and other specimens—as well as X rays, ought to be listed here. Keep good notes. This is a prime overuse/overcharge area, and a few tests that you never actually suffered through could show up on your bill.

Date	Time	Name of Test/ Procedure	Who Gave It/ Where

Additional Notes _____

_____

_____

Reason Given for Having Test	Cost	Results (Doctor's Interpretation)	Side Effects (If Any)

DISPENSED ITEMS LOG

For everything from the oxygen tank next to your bed, to the cotton swabs dispensed for a nonemergency ear waxectomy, you will be getting the bill. "Free," in the hospital lexicon, only describes the sensation experienced by patients upon leaving. Everything costs—plenty and often.

Frequently, lots of little items are lumped together in so-called itemized bills under large categories labeled "Misc." Missed "misc.'s" are probably *the* major overcharge and false charge culprits.

Why pay for stuff you don't need or never saw? Keep track of it all on this form.

Date	Item/ Product Given	Who Gave It

Additional Notes _____

_____

_____

_____

_____

Reason for Giving	Cost of Item	If Item Refused, Check Here and Get Nurse's Signature

MEDICATION RECORD

In the hospital world nothing is certain. Except medication.

Drugs can be miraculous lifesavers. But if these powerful drugs are given in the wrong dose or given too often or mistakenly given to a patient, the effects can be devastating. Be on guard.

This chart will help you double-check your medications. Mistakes happen; charts and prescription orders may not be accurate. One good way to avoid becoming a victim is to keep your own complete record of what you are taking. Who will be more concerned about you than you?

If what you are being given doesn't jibe with what was prescribed, point it out in no uncertain terms. And *don't take the medication* until you have personally double-checked with your doctor, your nurse, or the hospital pharmacist. And mark it all down on this record form.

Date/Time	Drug	Dosage

Additional Notes _____

_____

_____

_____

_____

Dispensed by	Form (Pill, Liquid, Injection)	Side Effects (If Any)	Reason Given for Taking Drug

1. This line contains some very important information such as your name, account number, dates of admission and discharge. Make sure the information on this line is the same as on line 4.

2. This line contains the name of your insurance company as well as the identification numbers of your plan. Make sure these numbers correspond to the identification numbers on your insurance card.

3. This line contains the name of the person to whom the bill is sent. This may be referred to as the "guarantor" on some bills.

4. See note 1.

5. This line tells you what to do if you have a question about your bill.

6. This column lists the days on which services were provided; make sure the entries correspond to the dates between your admission and discharge.

7. This column lists the internal codes used by the hospital to record the services provided. These codes will vary from hospital to hospital, depending upon the information system in use. The billing department can give you complete information on the codes.

8. This column lists the summary of charges for the services you received. You need to carefully examine these entries to verify that you actually received the service or treatment.

9. This column lists the actual charges for the services provided. Don't be awed by the large figures and don't let the smaller charges go by unchecked. Just because they may not amount to much individually doesn't mean they don't add up to real money.

10. This line explains how much of your bill is covered by your insurance company. If you suspect that something wasn't covered contact your company.

11. This line indicates how much of the bill is your responsibility, or the responsibility of the person listed at line 3. Examine this closely to make sure that your insurance company paid its correct amount of the bill.

12. This line indicates the final discharge diagnosis and is the basis for all charges incurred in connection with your admission. Some hospitals also list an admitting diagnosis; however, all charges are based upon the final diagnosis.

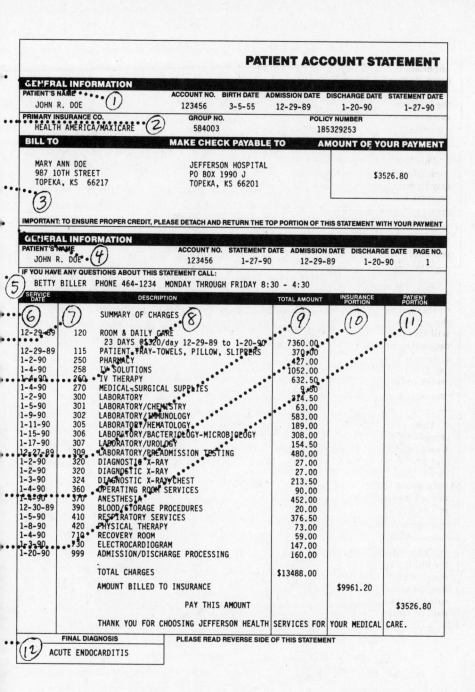

PATIENT ACCOUNT STATEMENT

GENERAL INFORMATION

PATIENT'S NAME		ACCOUNT NO.	BIRTH DATE	ADMISSION DATE	DISCHARGE DATE	STATEMENT DATE
JOHN R. DOE ①		123456	3-5-55	12-29-89	1-20-90	1-27-90

PRIMARY INSURANCE CO.	GROUP NO.	POLICY NUMBER
HEALTH AMERICA/MAXICARE ②	584003	185329253

BILL TO	MAKE CHECK PAYABLE TO	AMOUNT OF YOUR PAYMENT
MARY ANN DOE 987 10TH STREET TOPEKA, KS 66217 ③	JEFFERSON HOSPITAL PO BOX 1990 J TOPEKA, KS 66201	$3526.80

IMPORTANT: TO ENSURE PROPER CREDIT, PLEASE DETACH AND RETURN THE TOP PORTION OF THIS STATEMENT WITH YOUR PAYMENT

GENERAL INFORMATION

PATIENT'S NAME		ACCOUNT NO.	STATEMENT DATE	ADMISSION DATE	DISCHARGE DATE	PAGE NO.
JOHN R. DOE ④		123456	1-27-90	12-29-89	1-20-90	1

IF YOU HAVE ANY QUESTIONS ABOUT THIS STATEMENT CALL:

⑤ BETTY BILLER   PHONE 464-1234   MONDAY THROUGH FRIDAY 8:30 - 4:30

SERVICE DATE		DESCRIPTION		TOTAL AMOUNT	INSURANCE PORTION	PATIENT PORTION
⑥	⑦	SUMMARY OF CHARGES ⑧		⑨	⑩	⑪
12-29-89	120	ROOM & DAILY CARE				
		23 DAYS @$320/day 12-29-89 to 1-20-90		7360.00		
12-29-89	115	PATIENT TRAY-TOWELS, PILLOW, SLIPPERS		370.00		
1-2-90	250	PHARMACY		427.00		
1-4-90	258	IV SOLUTIONS		1052.00		
1-4-90	260	IV THERAPY		632.50		
1-4-90	270	MEDICAL-SURGICAL SUPPLIES		9.50		
1-2-90	300	LABORATORY		214.50		
1-5-90	301	LABORATORY/CHEMISTRY		63.00		
1-9-90	302	LABORATORY/IMMUNOLOGY		583.00		
1-11-90	305	LABORATORY/HEMATOLOGY		189.00		
1-15-90	306	LABORATORY/BACTERIOLOGY-MICROBIOLOGY		308.00		
1-17-90	307	LABORATORY/UROLOGY		154.50		
12-27-89	309	LABORATORY/PREADMISSION TESTING		480.00		
1-2-90	320	DIAGNOSTIC X-RAY		27.00		
1-2-90	320	DIAGNOSTIC X-RAY		27.00		
1-3-90	324	DIAGNOSTIC X-RAY/CHEST		213.50		
1-4-90	360	OPERATING ROOM SERVICES		90.00		
1-4-90	370	ANESTHESIA		452.00		
12-30-89	390	BLOOD/STORAGE PROCEDURES		20.00		
1-5-90	410	RESPIRATORY SERVICES		376.50		
1-8-90	420	PHYSICAL THERAPY		73.00		
1-4-90	710	RECOVERY ROOM		59.00		
1-3-90	730	ELECTROCARDIOGRAM		147.00		
1-20-90	999	ADMISSION/DISCHARGE PROCESSING		160.00		
		TOTAL CHARGES		$13488.00		
		AMOUNT BILLED TO INSURANCE			$9961.20	
		PAY THIS AMOUNT				$3526.80

THANK YOU FOR CHOOSING JEFFERSON HEALTH SERVICES FOR YOUR MEDICAL CARE.

FINAL DIAGNOSIS	PLEASE READ REVERSE SIDE OF THIS STATEMENT
⑫ ACUTE ENDOCARDITIS	

MEDICARE BILLS: THE
BEST WAYS TO TACKLE
A MAMMOTH
BUREAUCRACY

How do you handle an erroneous hospital bill if you are enrolled in the Medicare program? Differently. You see, the process is somewhat more complicated than it is for the person under sixty-five who is filing claims only with a private insurance company. The process is also complicated by the fact that Medicare, aside from the one-time deductible, pays *all* inpatient hospital expenses (minus miscellaneous charges for telephone and television). And, as a result of all the complexities of the program, when you compare your daily log with the itemized hospital bill, the two probably won't tally.

That's because Medicare reimburses hospitals on a prospective payment system, with payments based on the diagnosis-related group (DRG) to which you are assigned during your hospitalization. Here's how it works: You are admitted to the hospital as a Medicare patient. Your particular DRG—out of the 467 distilled from the billions of possible combinations of primary and secondary diagnoses, procedures performed, and resulting costs—cannot be assigned when you come in because your diagnosis may be unknown or wrong. Also, the operation(s) that you will have cannot be predicted in advance, especially if you are admitted for a diagnostic workup, a process of testing and checking to determine the condition you have. Once everything has been done, and you are ready to be discharged (dead or alive), the hospital prepares a cover sheet for your hospital chart. This sheet indicates your DRG, which will probably have been assigned by a computer program that was purchased by the hospital and designed to pick the highest-paying DRG possible, based on a combination of your age, diagnoses, operations, and other factors. Medicare pays the hospital that DRG's rate, a set amount determined ahead of time by Medicare, after a computer review of the hospital's coding.

Now what about that itemized hospital bill you're holding in your hands? It looks like a bill, it has all the charges for room and board, any medications you received, the tests and procedures performed in the ancillary departments, and it has a total of all the expenses for your hospitalization. And what about those charges that do not jibe with your daily log? Your first inclination is to believe that you have been overcharged or charged for services you did not receive, and that may be true. *However,* Medicare is not directly concerned with the itemized bill—reimbursement is made according to the DRG, that preset rate that Medicare will pay the hospital, *whether your hospital charges go under or over that amount.* The result is that on some admissions the hospital will lose money, and on some will make money.

On the average, hospitals that are generally as "good"—measured by their use of resources on patients, not by the results they produce—as the average hospital will break even. Those that are better, in this sense, will make money, and they are allowed to keep their profits. Those that are worse will lose money, and they will have to swallow their losses.

Does that mean that you should not question a suspected erroneous bill? Of course not, you should lodge a complaint with the hospital and with Medicare, which has a phone number to handle such complaints. If you believe that a doctor, hospital, or other provider of health care services is performing unnecessary or inappropriate services *or* is billing Medicare for services you did not receive, you may call a toll-free hot line, installed by the Department of Health and Human Services' inspector general. The number is 800-368-5779. In Maryland call 800-638-3986.

Where you *really* need to be eagle-eyed in making sure that you get your money's worth, and pay *only* for what you get, are the expenses you incur under Medicare Part B, medical insurance: physicians' services, outpatient hospital care, outpatient therapy, home health care, and the other services not covered by Part A, hospital insurance. Under Part B is where you, and all other Medicare enrollees, run up your largest out-of-pocket expenses. No party involved—the hospital, your doctor, the insurance company that handles Medicare payments in your state—sees it as their job to determine exactly what has and hasn't been approved and to bill you only for your share of the approved charges. No one but you has, as a main concern, making sure that you get billed for only what you really have to pay for. You have to look after yourself.

Because the payment system under Medicare is so complicated, it is virtually certain that at least one of your encounters with a health care provider will result in a bill for something you don't really owe. Because of this same complexity, and because there can be a considerable time lag before your case is reviewed (if it needs it) or the hospital is audited, a long time can pass before who gets what and who has to pay for what are finally decided. That's as good a reason as any to keep a daily log and records of tests, medications, and so on.

Or even better yet, keep a Medicare claims log (see sample on pp. 283–84) to keep track of services you received, what you had to pay, and when you paid it. The "Explanation of Medicare Benefits" (EOMB) (see sample on pp. 285–86), which is sent to you by the Medicare carrier every time a medical service is rendered under Medicare Part B, in conjunction with the information you receive from your insurance company when you file a claim with your supplemental insurance, should enable you to complete the claims log.

How to Request a Review

Now back to the business at hand—how do you request a review of overcharges, billing inaccuracies, or outright denials of coverage? After all, you are responsible for the 20 percent that Medicare doesn't pay, and 20 percent of anything is something—that's how your out-of-pocket expenses add up: overcharges for lab work and supplies; a bill for a cardiology consultation that you never had; nine visits to an ancillary department for respiratory therapy when you went three times; and pharmacy overcharges for an IV that was removed the second day you were in the hospital. What do you do? You have to file what's called a *request for reconsideration,* and (remember, you're dealing here with a mammoth bureaucracy) you should use Form HCFA-2649, shown on page 287. You never *have to* use the form, but using it will help you record all the information you need. And you can always supplement the form with a letter if you wish. Be sure to include all the documentation you can.

MONEY-SAVING TIPS: AT THE HOSPITAL

$ Check room rates in advance. Room rates do differ from hospital to hospital, even in the same community. And some hospitals offer three- or four-bed rooms, which are cheaper than semiprivate rooms.

Medicare Claims Log

(1) DATE OF SERVICE	(2) NAME OF PROVIDER OR FACILITY	(3) MEDICARE CLAIM NUMBER	(4) CLAIM UNDER		(5) AMOUNT OF CLAIM		(6) DEDUCTIBLE MET	
			PART A	PART B	BILLED	APPROVED	PART A	PART B

Medicare Claims Log, Parts A and B

(7) DATE CLAIM SUBMITTED TO CARRIER	(8) BALANCE OR COPAYMENT DUE	(9) AMOUNT CLAIMED	(10) AMOUNT RECEIVED	(11) OUT-OF-POCKET PAYMENT	(12) COMMENTS

Explanation of Your Medicare Part B Benefits

Name of Beneficiary
Iphigenia Smith
4321 Edgar Allen Poe Drive
San Diego, CA 99110

Your Medicare number: 120-99-6789

A summary about this notice dated
September 30, 1992

Total charges:	$1,755.00
Total Medicare approved:	$1,339.00
Medicare paid your provider:	$1,071.20
You are responsible for:	$ 367.80

Details about this claim (See the back of this notice for more information.)

You received these services from your provider;
Dr. Sherman T. Potter, claim #9876-1234-2468

Midway Medical Clinic
2552 Baskerville Rd,
San Diego, Ca 99110

THIS INDICATES AMOUNT BILLED AND APPROVED

Services and Service Codes	Date	Charges	Medicare approved	Notes
65850 surgery, incision of eye	Aug. 15, 1992	$975.00	$780.00	a
90040 brief office visit	Aug. 19, 1992	$100.00	$ 0	b
90070 extended office visits	Aug. 17-29, 1992	$600.00	$516.00	a
90040 brief office visit	Aug. 30, 1992	$ 40.00	$ 21.50	a
90040 brief office visit	Aug. 31, 1992	$ 40.00	$ 21.50	a
	Total	$1,755.00	$1,339.00	

THIS INDICATES THE SERVICE AND DATE PROVIDED.

Notes:

a   We based the approved amount on the fee schedule for this service.

b   Medicare did not pay for this test. Medicare pays for this only when the laboratory is certified for this type of test.

THIS TELLS YOU IF ASSIGNMENT WAS TAKEN AND THE DOLLAR AMOUNT BILLED.

Here's an example of this claim:

Of the total charges, Medicare approved $1,339.00   The provider accepted this amount. See #4 on the back of this notice.

The deductible you still owe $ 0   You have met the $100 deductible for 1992.

$1,339.00   Medicare pays 80 percent of this total.
x .80

We are paying the provider $1,071.20   Your copayment is 20 percent or $267.80

THIS INDICATES WHETHER OR NOT YOU HAVE MET THE $100 DEDUCTIBLE THIS YEAR.

Of the amount approved $1,339.00
Subtract what we pay the provider $1,071.20

You are responsible for $ 267.80
plus charges not covered by Medicare $ 100.00

The total you are responsible for: $ 367.80   The provider may bill you for this amount. If you have other insurance, the other insurance may pay this amount.

THIS EXPLAINS WHAT YOU PAY.

If you have questions about this notice, call Blue Cross Blue Shield of Maryland at (301) 861-2273 or toll free at 1-800-662-5170 or visit us at 1946 Greenspring Drive, Timonium, MD. You'll need this notice when you call or visit us about this claim. If you want to appeal this claim, see #5 on the other side. You must write us by March 30, 1993

THIS IS YOUR PART B CARRIER. IF YOU SUSPECT A MISTAKE, CONTACT THIS OFFICE.

THIS GIVES YOU THE TIME FRAME TO FILE ANY APPEAL.

Important Information You Should Know About Your Medicare Part B Benefits

This part of the notice answers some common questions that people ask about collecting Medicare benefits. If you have other questions, see your copy of *The Medicare Handbook* or call us for more information.

1. What should I do if I have questions about this notice?
If you have questions about this notice, call, write, or visit us and we will tell you the facts that we used to decide what and how much to pay. Turn to the front of this notice: our address and phone number are on the bottom of the page.

2.

Can I appeal how much Medicare paid for these services?
If you do not agree with what Medicare approved for these services, you may appeal our decision. To make sure that we are fair to you, we will not allow the same people who originally processed these services to conduct this review.

However, in order to be eligible for a review, you **must** write to us within **6 months** of the date of this notice, unless you have a good reason for being late (for example, if you had an extended illness which kept you from being able to file on time).

Turn to the front of this notice: the deadline date and our address are on the bottom of the page. It may help your case if you include a note from your doctor or supplier (provider) that tells us what was done and why.

If you want help with your appeal, you can have a friend, lawyer, or someone else help you. Some lawyers do not charge unless you win your appeal. There are groups, such as lawyer referral services, that can help you find a lawyer. There are also groups, such as legal aid services, who will give you free legal services if you qualify.

3.

How much does Medicare Pay?
The details on the front of this notice explain how much Medicare paid for these services. See your copy of *The Medicare Handbook* for more information about the benefits you are entitled to as a beneficiary in the Medicare Part B program. If you need another copy of the handbook, call or visit your local Social Security office.

Medicare may make adjustments to your payment. We may reduce the amount we pay for services by a certain percentage (Balanced Budget Law). If your provider accepted assignment, you are not liable to pay the amount of this reduction. We pay interest on some claims not paid within the required time.

All Medicare payments are made on the condition that you will pay Medicare back if benefits are also paid under insurance that is primary to Medicare. Examples of other insurance are employer group health plans, automobile medical liability, no fault, or workers' compensation. Notify us immediately if you have filed or could file a claim with insurance that is primary to Medicare.

4. How can I reduce my medical costs?
Many providers have agreed to be part of **Medicare's participation program.** That means that they will always accept the amount the Medicare approves as their full payment. Write or call us for the name of a participating provider or for a toll free list of participating providers.

A provider who accepts assignment can charge you only for the part of the annual deductible you have not met and the copayment which is the remaining 20 percent of the approved amount.

If you are treated by one of these doctors you can save money. See *The Medicare Handbook* for more information about how you can reduce your medical costs.

5. How can I use this notice?
You can use this notice to:
- Contact us immediately if you think Medicare paid for a service you did not receive

- Show your provider how much of your deductible you have met

- Claim benefits with another insurance company. If you send this notice to them, make a copy of it for your records.

DEPARTMENT OF HEALTH, EDUCATION, AND WELFARE
HEALTH CARE FINANCING ADMINISTRATION

Form Approved.
OMB No. 088-R-0087

REQUEST FOR RECONSIDERATION OF PART A HEALTH INSURANCE BENEFITS

INSTRUCTIONS: *Please type or print firmly.* Leave the block empty if you cannot answer it. Take or mail the WHOLE form to your Social Security office which will be glad to help you. Please read the statement on the reverse side of page 2.

1. BENEFICIARY'S NAME	2. HEALTH INSURANCE CLAIM NUMBER

3. REPRESENTATIVE'S NAME, IF APPLICABLE

☐ RELATIVE   ☐ ATTORNEY   ☐ OTHER PERSON   ☐ PROVIDER FILING

4. PLEASE ATTACH A COPY OF THE NOTICE(S) YOU RECEIVED ABOUT YOUR CLAIM TO THIS FORM.

5. THIS CLAIM IS FOR

☐ INPATIENT HOSPITAL   ☐ SKILLED NURSING FACILITY (SNF)   ☐ HEALTH MAINTENANCE
☐ EMERGENCY HOSPITAL   ☐ HOME HEALTH AGENCY (HHA)   ORGANIZATION (HMO)

6. NAME AND ADDRESS OF PROVIDER *(Hospital, SNF, HHA, HMO)*	CITY AND STATE	PROVIDER NUMBER

7. NAME OF INTERMEDIARY	CITY AND STATE	INTERMEDIARY NUMBER

8. DATE OF ADMISSION OR START OF SERVICES	9. DATE(S) OF THE NOTICE(S) YOU RECEIVED

10. I DO NOT AGREE WITH THE DETERMINATION ON MY CLAIM. PLEASE RECONSIDER MY CLAIM BECAUSE

11. YOU MUST OBTAIN ANY EVIDENCE *(For example, a letter from a doctor)* YOU WISH TO SUBMIT.

☐ I HAVE ATTACHED THE FOLLOWING EVIDENCE:

☐ I WILL SEND THIS EVIDENCE WITHIN 10 DAYS:

☐ I HAVE NO ADDITIONAL EVIDENCE OR OTHER INFORMATION TO SUBMIT WITH MY CLAIM.

13. ONLY ONE SIGNATURE IS NEEDED. THIS FORM IS SIGNED BY:

☐ BENEFICIARY   ☐ REPRESENTATIVE   ☐ PROVIDER REP.

SIGN HERE ▶

14. STREET ADDRESS

12. IS THIS REQUEST FILED WITHIN 60 DAYS OF THE DATE OF YOUR NOTICE?

☐ YES   ☐ NO

IF YOU CHECKED "NO" ATTACH AN EXPLANATION OF THE REASON FOR THE DELAY TO THIS FORM.

CITY, STATE, ZIP CODE

TELEPHONE	DATE

15. If this request is signed by mark (X), TWO WITNESSES who know the person requesting reconsideration must sign in the space provided on the reverse side of this page of the form.

DO NOT FILL IN BELOW THIS LINE — FOR SOCIAL SECURITY USE — THANK YOU

16. ROUTING

☐ INTERMEDIARY

☐ HCFA, RO-MEDICARE

☐ BSS, ODR

18. SSA OR INTERMEDIARY DATE STAMP

17. ADDITIONAL INFORMATION

FORM **HCFA-2649** (8-79 FORMERLY SSA-2649)
DESTROY PRIOR EDITIONS

INTERMEDIARY

Page 1 of 4

$ Avoid for-profit hospitals. These hospitals tend to be more expensive—as much as 23 percent more expensive, according to some reports.

$ Go to the hospital that does the largest number of the procedure you need. Studies have shown that you are less likely to suffer complications or die if you have your surgery done at a hospital that performs a large number (more than two hundred) of such procedures. You can save yourself a lot of money and suffering if you do what you can to assure the best outcome from the start. After all, you pay the price in more than dollars for their mistakes or inadequacies.

$ Use outpatient services. Many diagnostic tests—including invasive ones—and simple surgeries can be done on an outpatient basis, thereby saving you the costs and aggravations associated with a hospital stay. Remember, the less time you spend in the hospital, the cheaper it will be.

$ Refuse preadmission tests that are not pertinent to your illness or the reason for your hospitalization. Most hospitals routinely require a variety of blood and urine tests and an X ray upon admission, whatever your age and physical health, and whether or not you need them—even though the American College of Radiology has urged that chest X rays be eliminated as a routine procedure for hospital admissions, tuberculosis screening, and preemployment physicals.

$ Refuse to pay a hospital admitting fee or release fee to your doctor. These fees are common but unjustifiable on the basis of services rendered to *you,* the patient. Find out whether your doctor customarily charges such fees and discuss your objections prior to your admission to the hospital.

$ Avoid weekend admission. Weekend admission equals an extra one or two days in the hospital, *at your expense.* In most cases you will receive no medical care, but instead be paying the tab—at up to $500 a day—merely for basic care. It's bound to be cheaper and just as healthy to stay home and enter the hospital on Monday.

$ Avoid admissions during Thanksgiving or Christmas holidays. Staffing is low and you may sit around waiting for lab work, tests, and treatment.

$ Bring your own food. Hospital meals are very expensive, in part because of the cost of hiring clinical dietitians who order menus (supposedly) based upon patients' nutritional needs. But if you are permitted to eat a normal diet and require no special meals, you will save a lot of money by providing your own food. (Skeptics of hospital food—and there are many, including probably most people who have ever eaten such food—maintain that you won't miss much either.) If you are on a restricted diet anyway, such as vegetarian or kosher, providing your own food may be a necessity. Remember, the hospital machinery automatically turns out three meals a day. Be sure to make your wishes clear so that no meals—and the accompanying charges—come your way.

$ Bring your own vitamins. Hospitals do not ordinarily supply vitamin or mineral supplements—and if they did, you can be sure the price would be exorbitant. So, if you customarily follow such a regimen, take them with you (and tell your doctor to note that in your chart).

$ Bring your own drugs. This is an easy money-saving technique because the hospital will charge you far more for the same dosage than you paid. The same holds true for basic analgesics, such as aspirin or acetaminophen. If you are unable to administer the medications yourself, ask a family member to help, and in any case notify your doctor and nurses.

$ Refuse to be seen by any doctor you don't know. If any doctor you don't know enters your room to see you, even if the visit entails only a grin and a handshake, you can be sure you will receive a bill for the "service"—unless you immediately make it clear that you do not want the service. Find out who the doctor is and why he or she is there, then follow through later to make sure your insurer does not pay for the service.

$ Refuse to pay for bad service. Refusing to pay for deficient service or lack of service, such as poor meals or a lack of response to a call for a nurse, will draw attention to the fact that you are a customer. You can be sure you will receive better service in the future.

$ Complain if you are being disturbed. Hospital staff are accustomed to dealing with uncomplaining, often drugged patients. If your room is noisy at night and your sleep is disturbed, complain. You will get better faster with fewer disturbances—it's a fact.

$ Become acquainted with the hospital's birthing policies before choosing to deliver there. To save money you should be looking for hospital policies that encourage "rooming in" (keeping the baby in the room with you) and early discharge (discharge generally after twenty-four hours rather than three days).

$ Use a nurse-midwife or family practitioner as your birth attendant. There are two reasons you save money by choosing a practitioner other than an obstetrician: a nurse-midwife or family practitioner usually charges less in basic delivery fees *and* generally will not recommend a costly cesarean section or other expensive, high-technology interventions unless they are absolutely necessary.

$ Avoid cesarean-section deliveries. Studies have shown that more cesarean sections are performed at night and on weekends—partly because doctors want to get the delivery over with quickly and, therefore, are less willing to wait through a long labor. Cesarean-section deliveries are major surgery. They expose the mother and baby to additional risks, and are much more expensive than vaginal deliveries. The best way to avoid a cesarean-section delivery is to be as knowledgeable as you can about the birth process; then you will be better able to evaluate your doctor's recommendations. If you have had a cesarean section before, remind your doctor that the dictum "Once a C-section, always a C-section" is not true any longer, according to the American College of Obstetricians and Gynecologists, which has issued new guidelines. Not all cesareans are avoidable, but a good many are.

$ Do not routinely circumcise your male babies. Circumcision is an operative procedure and, as such, is costly and risky. It is recognized to be unnecesary for health reasons; consequently, increasing numbers of health insurance companies are refusing to pay for the procedure. That means you pick up the charge, which typically is around $75.

$ If you deliver your baby in the hospital, get him or her out of there as soon as possible. Although this is somewhat tongue-in-cheek advice, there is a valid reason for concern. Birthing in hospitals exposes infants to the full range of hospital-acquired infections. Upper-respiratory and staph infections are common in hospital nurseries. And you will just end up paying for the care required to combat these infections.

$ Have a friend or relative act as an advocate. As a patient, you will have some trouble being an assertive consumer. Always bring along a friend or family member to be your advocate—his or her most important task being to make sure you do not agree to anything without fully understanding it.

$ Make sure you get what you pay for. Most hospitals are teaching hospitals in the sense that they have staffs of interns and residents who work with "attending" physicians (such as your doctor) as they care for their patients. Unfortunately, this means that although you are paying full fees to your doctor he or she may be doing very little of the work. You should specify, in writing, that any surgery or invasive procedure *be done by the person you are paying* for the service. If you are paying for a fully trained physician, that is who you should get.

$ Make a living will. A living will is a legal document that is used to inform family and medical personnel of your wishes concerning medical care, should you be unable to personally make those wishes known. Most often used to limit the types of medical care you wish to receive if you are known to be in a terminal stage of illness, the living will, for instance, may proscribe the use of artificial life-sustaining treatment, such as an automatic ventilator.

$ Die at home. More than 50 percent of medical costs are incurred in the last five days of life. The decision about where to die, of course, is very personal—and one that you may never get the opportunity to make. But it is a valid consideration for many reasons, including cost, and should be considered seriously.

GETTING WHAT YOU'RE ENTITLED TO

6

One of the best ways to save money is to take advantage of any entitlement programs—programs that already exist thanks to tax dollars or the contributions in other ways of people eligible for such programs. Medicare, Medicaid, public clinics run by your county or municipal government, and veterans' services are common and popular sources of medical and health services, but you've got to know where to look for them, how to sign up, and what's available.

THREE OF MEDICARE'S BEST-KEPT SECRETS— AND HOW THEY CAN SAVE YOU MONEY

Medicare is probably the largest and the most expensive single program the federal government runs—and also one of the most complex. If at times Medicare seems not to make sense to you, keep in mind that it was never supposed to. The current law is the result of a long series of political deals that had to satisfy diverse interests in order for there to be any law at all.

You probably won't think too much about Medicare until you have occasion to file a claim. That's when the enormity—some would say monstrosity—of the program and its complexities will hit home. Unfortunately, "home" may well be your pocketbook! Aside from the $100 billion or so paid out each year by Medicare to doctors and hospitals, over $100 billion *more* is paid out from either the pockets of Medicare beneficiaries or their private supplemental insurers.

With that kind of national *and* personal investment at stake, *how can you maximize your benefits under Medicare?* You need to know three of Medicare's best-kept secrets, that's how, and they are:

1. You never have to pay more for a Medicare Part B service than the balance billing limit.

2. You are not responsible for any medical bill you could not reasonably have been expected to know was not covered.

3. You cannot be "dumped" from the hospital—that is, discharged from the hospital before you are medically able to go.

Medicare's Balance Billing Limit

Medicare has set a maximum billing limit for each service provided by a nonparticipating physician. Beginning in 1993 and continuing through 1994 and 1995, nonparticipating physicians may charge no more than 115 percent of the Medicare-approved charge. The balance billing limit applies only to doctors who do not take assignment, since the Medicare-approved charge is all that the doctor may charge for assigned claims. If your doctor's charges to you exceed the 115 percent limit, neither you nor your insurance company has to pay the difference between the balance billing limit and what the doctor charged. For example, if the Medicare-approved charge for a procedure is $100, the most a nonparticipating physician could charge you is $115, even though the actual fee is $175. You would be responsible for the $20 copayment ($100 x 20 percent) and the additional $15, but not the remaining $60, thus you are protected from an additional out-of-pocket expense.

This example should make the concept clearer: Let's say the Medicare-approved charge for a cardiac catheterization is $2,000, and the nonparticipating doctor's actual charge is $3,000. In this case, the balance billing limit is $2,300 ($2,000 x 115 percent). Medicare will pay $1,600—that is, 80 percent of the reasonable (according to Medicare) cost. You (or your insurance company) will pay the difference between the balance billing limit of $2,300 and the $1,600 payment from Medicare, or $700. The doctor does not collect the remaining $700 (that is, the difference between his actual charge, which is $3,000, and the billing limit). The table below compares the effect on your pocketbook, with and without the balance billing limit.

THE EFFECTS OF THE BALANCE BILLING LIMIT ON UNASSIGNED CLAIMS IN 1993

Actual charge:	$3,000
Medicare-approved charge:	$2,000
Balance billing limit:	$2,300
Medicare pays:	$1,600
With limit you pay:	$ 700
Without limit you pay:	$1,400
With limit you save:	$ 700

As we have said before—and as the chart makes clear—persuading your doctor to take assignment on all *your* bills or going to a participating doctor who accepts assignment can save you large sums of money. That's because, by definition, the doctor agrees to take what Medicare decides is a fair payment for the services, and you are responsible only for your 20 percent copayment. Since most people over sixty-five are not particularly wealthy, the potential savings really count. Above all, don't feel you're cheating your doctor by asking her to accept assignment. The charge that Medicare has determined as "reasonable," in most cases, takes into account what other doctors charge. Your doctor may *feel* that the Medicare payment is too low, but unless she presents you with hard evidence that Medicare is not covering her real costs, don't worry. Point out that other doctors who accept assignment seem to do well.

"Reasonably Have Been Expected to Know"

"Reasonably have been expected to know" is a legal phrase. What it means, basically, is this: if you have not been informed *in writing* by an appropriate review authority, the provider, a Medicare intermediary or carrier, or Medicare itself that a service is not covered or is not medically reasonable and necessary, and you could not be expected to know it from official sources (such as Medicare pamphlets or prior notices), *then you are protected from having to pay for the service, even if Medicare doesn't.* As stated in the program regulations, there are two key factors here: you have to receive a written notice, and you have to receive it from an appropriate source.

For the sake of example, let's say you go into the hospital for surgery. The operation, or procedure, is one that Medicare normally requires to be done in an outpatient facility, because it has been proven that this can be done safely and at a lower cost than in the hospital. Your doctor believes that she can show that your case required inpatient surgery, but the peer review organization that deals with such cases disagrees. The hospital gets paid nothing. *But you do not have to pay anything either.* Why? Because you cannot reasonably have been expected to know which operations are required to be done as outpatient operations, or to know the steps your doctor should have followed to check.

Even if this example is not specifically appropriate to your case, what you need to understand is the general principle: when Medicare makes a payment, all sorts of wheels turn that you cannot reasonably be expected to know about. You are protected from the consequences of behind-the-scenes decisions if you are not informed of them. The fact that Medicare has refused payment doesn't mean that you have to pay.

Medicare Patients' Hospital Discharge Rights

Ironic as it may seem given the fact that a hospital is hardly a place in which most people want to spend any more time than they need to, a legitimate fear of many older Americans is that they will be "dumped" from the hospital before they are well enough to leave. You know, the proverbial official note—*"We're sorry, but federal regulations require that you be discharged from the hospital in two days or accept financial responsibility for any expenses and charges thereafter"*—and the swift, official kick out the door. Well, the truth is, you do have rights of appeal under the diagnosis-related group system. Know them, and use them!

You *cannot* be discharged for any of the following reasons:

▶ Because your care has cost more than the money amount of
  · your particular DRG

▶ Because you have been in the hospital more days than the
  number of days assigned to your DRG

▶ Because your hospital has not requested so-called outlier
  payments (for cases that fall outside statistical norms of the
  DRG system)

▶ Because your hospital has not received outlier payments

Only medical necessity should govern the length of your hospital
stay. If you're a Medicare patient, make sure you're being discharged because you're no longer in need of medical attention—not
because your "DRGs" or Medicare payments have been used up. By
federal law, the hospital must issue you a form when you're admitted. (See form below.) If you have doubts about whether you're
really ready to be discharged, you have the right to have your case
reviewed by your state's peer review organization (PRO), which
will determine if a longer stay can be covered by Medicare. PROs
are groups of doctors that contract with Medicare to make judgments about the medical necessity of everything Medicare pays for.

How does the PRO's decision affect Medicare's payment for your
hospital stay, and, just as important, what you must pay? You can
stay in the hospital until the third day following the date the PRO
informs you that your continued stay is indeed no longer necessary.
If you do not request a reconsideration of the PRO's decision, Medicare will cease payment on the third day following the notice. If you
do request reconsideration and get a favorable ruling at any stage of
the process, Medicare will pay for time spent in the hospital up until
you are discharged or die. If you lose the appeal, you or your insurer
must pay for these days.

WHAT YOU NEED TO
KNOW ABOUT MEDICAID

Established through Title XIX of the Social Security Act Amendments of 1965, Medicaid is another federal government entitlement

AN IMPORTANT MESSAGE FROM MEDICARE

YOUR RIGHTS WHILE YOU ARE A MEDICARE HOSPITAL PATIENT

• You have the right to receive all the hospital care that is necessary for the proper diagnosis and treatment of your illness or injury. According to Federal law, **your discharge date must be determined solely by your medical needs,** not by "DRGs" or Medicare payments.

• You have the right to be fully informed about decisions affecting your Medicare coverage and payment for your hospital stay and for any post-hospital services.

• You have the right to request a review by a Peer Review Organization of any written Notice of Noncoverage that you receive from the hospital stating that Medicare will no longer pay for your hospital care. Peer Review Organizations (PROs) are groups of doctors who are paid by the Federal Government to review medical necessity, appropriateness and quality of hospital treatment furnished to Medicare patients. The phone number and address of the PRO for your area are:

_____

_____

TALK TO YOUR DOCTOR ABOUT YOUR STAY IN THE HOSPITAL

You and your doctor know more about your condition and your health needs than anyone else. Decisions about your medical treatment should be made between you and your doctor. **If you have any questions about your medical treatment, your need for continued hospital care, your discharge, or your need for possible post-hospital care, don't hesitate to ask your doctor.** The hospital's patient representative or social worker will also help you with your questions and concerns about hospital services.

IF YOU THINK YOU ARE BEING ASKED TO LEAVE THE HOSPITAL TOO SOON

- Ask a hospital representative for a written notice of explanation immediately, if you have not already received one. This notice is called a "Notice of Noncoverage." You must have this Notice of Noncoverage if you wish to exercise your right to request a review by the PRO.

- The Notice of Noncoverage will state either that your doctor or the PRO agrees with the hospital's decision that Medicare will no longer pay for your hospital care.

  + If the hospital and your doctor agree, the PRO does not review your case before a Notice of Noncoverage is issued. But the PRO will respond to your request for a review of your Notice of Noncoverage and seek your opinion. You cannot be made to pay for your hospital care until the PRO makes its decision, if you request the review by noon of the first work day after you receive the Notice of Noncoverage.

+ If the hospital and your doctor disagree, the hospital may request the PRO to review your case. If it does make such a request, the hospital is required to send you a notice to that effect. In this situation the PRO must agree with the hospital or the hospital cannot issue a Notice of Noncoverage. You may request that the PRO reconsider your case after you receive a Notice of Noncoverage but since the PRO has already reviewed your case once, you may have to pay for **at least one day of hospital care** before the PRO completes this reconsideration.

IF YOU **DO NOT** REQUEST A REVIEW, **THE HOSPITAL MAY BILL YOU** FOR ALL THE COSTS OF YOUR STAY BEGINNING WITH THE THIRD DAY AFTER YOU RECEIVE THE NO-TICE OF NONCOVERAGE. THE HOSPITAL, HOWEVER, CANNOT CHARGE YOU FOR CARE UNLESS IT PROVIDES YOU WITH A NOTICE OF NONCOVERAGE.

HOW TO REQUEST A REVIEW OF THE NOTICE OF NONCOVERAGE

• If the Notice of Noncoverage states that your **physician agrees** with the hospital's decision:

+ You must make your request for review to the PRO by **noon of the first work day** after you receive the Notice of Noncoverage by contacting the PRO by phone or in writing.

+ The PRO must ask for your views about your case before making its decision. The PRO will inform you by phone and in writing of its decision on the review.

+ If the PRO agrees with the Notice of Noncoverage, you may be billed for all costs of your stay beginning at noon of the day **after** you receive the PRO's decision.

- If the Notice of Noncoverage states that the PRO agrees with the hospital's decision:

  + You should make your request for reconsideration to the PRO **immediately** upon receipt of the Notice of Noncoverage by contacting the PRO by phone or in writing.

  + The PRO can take up to three working days from receipt of your request to complete the review. The PRO will inform you in writing of its decision on the review.

  + Since the PRO has already reviewed your case once, prior to the issuance of the Notice of Noncoverage, the hospital is permitted to begin billing you for the cost of your stay beginning with the third calendar day after you receive your Notice of Noncoverage **even if the PRO has not completed its review.**

  + Thus, if the PRO continues to agree with the Notice of Noncoverage, **you may have to pay for at least one day of hospital care.**

NOTE: The process described above is called "immediate review." If you miss the deadline for this immediate review while you are in the hospital, you may still request a review of Medicare's decision to no longer pay for your care at any point during your hospital stay or after you have left the hospital. The Notice of Noncoverage will tell you how to request this review.

POST-HOSPITAL CARE

When your doctor determines that you no longer need all the specialized services provided in a hospital, but you still require medical care, he or she may discharge you to a skilled nursing facility or home care. The discharge planner at the hospital will help arrange for the services you may need after your discharge. Medicare and supplemental insurance policies have limited coverage for skilled nursing facility care and home health care. Therefore, you should find out which services will or will not be covered and how payment will be made. Consult with your doctor, hospital discharge planner, patient representative and your family in making preparations for care after you leave the hospital. **Don't hesitate to ask questions.**

ACKNOWLEDGEMENT OF RECEIPT — My signature only acknowledges my receipt of this Message from (name of hospital) on (date) and does not waive any of my rights to request a review or make me liable for any payment.

_____

Signature of beneficiary or
person acting on behalf of beneficiary.

program, but unlike Medicare it is means-tested, with income and asset limitations for eligibility. Administered by your state through the local welfare departments, Medicaid is an assistance program primarily for people with low incomes who require health care services. If you believe that your medical expenses are so overwhelming and your financial status such that you require outside assistance in paying these bills, Medicaid *may* be a program that can help you. But you should be aware of two important points:

1. Since Medicaid is a federal-state program, states have considerable flexibility in setting service and eligibility requirements, so each state's definitions and limitations are different from another's.

2. While the requirements for eligibility vary from state to state, the federal government has defined three *general* categorical groups that may be eligible for Medicaid within a specific state:

   a. The *mandated* categorically needy are those people and families that receive cash benefits from two programs: Aid to Families with Dependent Children (AFDC) and Supplemental Security Income (SSI). SSI is for people who are aged, blind, or disabled. All states choosing to participate in Medicaid must include these groups in their programs.

   b. The *medically needy* are families with incomes above the AFDC income and asset criteria but who become eligible for Medicaid if they incur significant medical expenses resulting in the reduction of their net incomes to the Medicaid eligibility limits. As of 1988, thirty-five states, the District of Columbia, Puerto Rico, and the Virgin Islands had established medically needy programs. (An important point to remember: many states also have medical assistance programs to serve people who do not meet Medicaid's eligibility requirements but who do lack health care coverage; however, these are state-only programs and do not receive the matching federal funds that Medicaid does. You should call your local welfare office for details.)

   c. The *optional* categorically needy (which a state may elect to include in its program) are selected groups of people who are financially eligible for cash assistance but are ineligible because they do not meet certain family status requirements or because they choose not to receive cash assistance.

What Health Care Costs Does Medicaid Cover?

By law, Medicaid recipients receiving federally supported financial assistance *must* receive these core services:

▶ Inpatient hospital care

▶ Outpatient hospital care

▶ Rural health clinic services

▶ Laboratory and X-ray services

▶ Skilled-nursing facility care for people twenty-one and older

▶ Home health services for people twenty-one and older

▶ Early and periodic screening, diagnosis, and treatment services for people under twenty-one

▶ Family-planning services and supplies

▶ Physician services

▶ Nurse-midwife services

Some states offer up to thirty-two additional medical services, such as chiropractic and podiatric care, dental care, occupational therapy, and prescription drugs and medical supplies.

Medicaid Program: Income and Resources Eligibility Limits

States have a great amount of flexibility in deciding who is eligible for any of the categories, so it is mandatory that you check with your local welfare office for program particulars in your state. This is especially important for people who do not meet the requirements of any of the Medicaid categories, but who need some form of medical assistance.

MEDICAID AND NURSING HOME COVERAGE

In chapter 2 we explained that it is not unusual for Medicare patients to apply for Medicaid coverage once Medicare's payments for skilled-nursing-home care have been exhausted or if you have spent all your savings and assets on intermediate care. Medicaid, it is true, may be your chief option when Medicare runs out, but since the states have a wide range of latitude in whom they cover, what services they cover, and the income and resource limits they use, you must call your local welfare or public assistance office for details.

The incomes shown on the chart are annual figures. And the resources refer to total assets and *may* include personal property—for example, real estate, trusts, stocks and bonds, and cars.

How to Apply for Medicaid

Medicaid applications are taken at your local welfare office, but many states also take them at senior citizen centers, agencies on aging, and other locations. Call the Medicaid office in your state to find out where you can apply in your area. And when you make the call, find out what you need to bring with you for the application process.

Generally, you should bring proof of age, financial status, and any disability you have. The proof of financial status should include the last six months' bank statements for checking and savings accounts, rent or mortgage payment receipts, loan papers for your car or the title to it, any documents relating to stock or bond ownership, and check stubs for any regular payments you receive. You should also have the amount of your Social Security check, if you are currently receiving Social Security payments. You should always have your Social Security number. Bring your medical bills, or copies of them, for the last year.

MEDICAID PROGRAM: Income and Resources Eligibility Limits

State	Income/ Resources	Family Size 1	Family Size 2	Family Size 3	Family Size 4	Notes
Alabama		No medically needy program./Only mandated categorically needy program.				
Alaska		No medically needy program./Only mandated categorically needy program.				
Arizona		No medically needy program./Only mandated categorically needy program.				
Arkansas	I	$3900	7800	9900	12000	
	R	$2000	3000	3100	3200	

State					
California	I	$7200	9000* 10800**	11208	13200
	R	$2000	3000	3150	3300
				*Adult & child **2 adults	
Colorado	No medically needy program./Only mandated categorically needy program.				
Connecticut	I:Urban	$6304	8027	9943	11602
	I:Rural	$5202	6926	8522	10006
	R:Aged/Blind	$1600	2400	2500	2600
	R:AFDC	$2000	3000	3100	3200
Delaware	No medically needy program./Only mandated categorically needy program.				
District of Columbia	I	$4692	4944	6288	7680
	R	$2600	3000	3100	3200

MEDICAID PROGRAM: Income and Resources Eligibility Limits

State	Income/Resources	Family Size				Notes
		1	2	3	4	
Florida	I	$3600	3600	4800	5592	
	R	$5000	6000	6000	6500	
Georgia	I	$2496	3696	4404	5196	Program presently limited to pregnant women & children under 18. New programs will expand eligible category in April 1990.
	R	$1000	1000	1000	1000	
Hawaii	I	$4284	5760	7224	8748	
	R	$2000	3000	3250	3500	
Idaho	No medically needy program./Only mandated categorically needy program.					

State					
Illinois	I	$3204	3996	5496	6204
	R	$2000	3000	3050	3100
Indiana	No medically needy program./Only mandated categorically needy program.				
Iowa	I	$5400	5400	6300	7392
	R	$5000	7500	7500	7500
Kansas	I	$4416	5700	5760	6072
	R	$2000	3000	3000	3000
Kentucky	I	$2604	3204	3696	4596
	R	$2000	4000	4050	4100

MEDICAID PROGRAM: Income and Resources Eligibility Limits

State	Income/Resources	Family Size				Notes
		1	2	3	4	
Louisiana	I	$1200	2304	3096	3804	
	R	$2000	3000	3025	3050	
Maine	I	$4800	5300	7100	8900	
	R	$2000	3000	3100	3200	
Maryland	I	$4308	4800	5304	5808	
	R	$2500	2850	2950	3050	
Massachusetts	I	$5628	7800	9300	10692	
	R	$2000	3000	3100	3200	

State						Notes
Michigan	I	*	*	*	*	*Income levels vary across the state. Check with your local welfare office.
	R	$2000	3000	3200	3400	
Minnesota	I	$4824	6984	8508	9936	*General Assistance Medical Card **Medical Assistance
	R*	$1000	1000	1000	1000	
	R**	$3000	6000	6200	6400	
Mississippi	No medically needy program./Only mandated categorically needy program.					
Missouri	No medically needy program./Only mandated categorically needy program.					

MEDICAID PROGRAM: Income and Resources Eligibility Limits

State	Income/Resources	Family Size				Notes
		1	2	3	4	
Montana	I	$4416	4596	4896	3996	
	R	$2000	3000	3100	3200	
Nebraska	I	$4704	4704	5904	7008	
	R	$2000	3000	3025	3050	
Nevada						No medically needy program./Only mandated categorically needy program.
New Hampshire	I	$4416	6396	6636	6888	
	R	$2500	4000	4100	4200	

New Jersey	I	$4200	5196	6792	7896
	R*	$3800	5700	5800	5900
					*plus $1500 burial fund
New Mexico	No medically needy program./Only mandated categorically needy program.				
New York	I	$5508	7908	8508	10200
	R	$3250	4950	5750	7100
North Carolina	I	$2904	3804	4404	4800
	R	$1500	2250	2350	2450
North Dakota	I	$4140	4800	5220	6360
	R	$3000	6000	6025	6050

MEDICAID PROGRAM: Income and Resources Eligibility Limits

State	Income/ Resources	Family Size				Notes
		1	2	3	4	
Ohio		No medically needy program./Only mandated categorically needy program.				
Oklahoma	I	$3300	4092	5196	6492	
	R	$2000	3000	3100	3200	
Oregon		Limited program available.				
Pennsylvania	I	$4900	5100	5400	6500	
	R	$2400	3200	3500	3800	

State					
Puerto Rico	I	$3750	4800	5700	6600
	R	$6000	7000	7500	8400
Rhode Island	I	$6600	7100	8780	10000
	R	$4000	6000	6100	6200
South Carolina	No medically needy program./Only mandated categorically needy program.				
South Dakota	No medically needy program./Only mandated categorically needy program.				
Tennessee	I	$2100	2304	3000	3600
	R	$2000	3000	3000	3000

MEDICAID PROGRAM: Income and Resources Eligibility Limits

State	Income/Resources	Family Size 1	2	3	4	Notes
Texas	I	$1200	2532	3204	3612	
	R	$1000	1000	1000	1000	
Utah	I	$4044	4956	6192	7224	
	R	$2000	3000	3025	3050	
Vermont	I:Urban	$8496	8496	10092	11292	
	I:Rural	$7692	7692	9300	10500	
	R	$2000	3000	3150	3300	
Virgin Islands	I	$4000	4800	5600	6400	
	R	$1500		1700	1800	

State						
Virginia	I:Group* 1	$2600	3400	3900	4400	*Based upon economic areas within the state.
	2	3000	3700	4300	4800	
	3	3900	4800	5300	5800	
	R	$2000	3000	3100	3200	
Washington	I	$4752	6834	7188	8004	
	R	$2000	3000	3050	3100	
West Virginia	I	$2400	3300	3480	3744	
	R	$2000	3000	3050	3100	
Wisconsin	Limited program for SSI eligible. All inquiries should be directed to local Social Security Administration Office.					
Wyoming	No medically needy program./Only mandated categorically needy program.					

PUBLIC CLINICS: WHO RUNS THEM AND WHERE TO FIND THEM

Your county health department—and in some cases your city or municipal health department—operates public clinics, often free of charge. The services at these clinics usually take the form of screenings: general health screenings—such as blood pressure and cholesterol testing—dental health screenings, screenings for sexually transmitted diseases, children's health and development screenings, and so on. Other services may include immunizations, both for children and adults, and seasonal flu shots for the elderly.

The services at these public clinics, if not free, usually are provided on a sliding-fee scale—that is, based on the ability to pay—and often provided in conjunction with local hospitals. And any resident of the county or municipality operating the clinic can use the services. Check with your county health department, county government, or municipal government for what's available. Or check your newspaper, where these services usually are advertised.

VETERANS' BENEFITS

If you are a veteran and cannot afford a lot of out-of-pocket expenses for medical care, then by all means take advantage of what the Veterans Administration offers. As you probably know already, the VA operates diverse programs to benefit veterans and their families, including a medical care program incorporating nursing homes, clinics, and 172 medical centers. At last count, the VA had 228 clinics in the United States, Puerto Rico, and the Philippines. If you live in an area with no specially designated VA hospitals or clinics, there's a good chance you can use certain local facilities that have contracted with the VA. In either case, call 202-872-1151 for information and referrals.

AND **THAT AIN'T ALL, FOLKS**

7

Now that we've gotten you this far—comfortable with choosing the practitioners, medical settings, and insurance plans that fit the bill given your health needs and financial situation; familiar with hospital dangers, routines, and billing practices that spell trouble for your physical and/or financial well-being; knowledgeable in the ways you can save money on drugs and medications; and ready to get what you're entitled to in federal, state, county, and municipal programs—it's time to dot the *i*'s and cross the *t*'s. There are a few more areas in which smart thinking and knowing what to do can save you a lot of money.

THE IMPORTANCE OF YOUR MEDICAL RECORD: HOW TO GET IT, HOW TO READ IT, AND HOW TO KEEP YOUR OWN

The medical chart is a mystery to most of us. Just the way the doctor handles it—cradling it as he or she strides into the room, scribbling on it, rustling its pages, snapping it shut at the end of the session—is enough to pique the curiosity of even the least inquisitive among us. What's in it and why are its secrets so closely guarded?

The medical chart is one of the most important aspects of good care. Aside from a history of your ailments, the chart is a repository for all the information regarding where you've been medically and where you're going. In it are housed your complaints, your questions, your doctor's notes on your visits and your health, laboratory results, X-ray reports, medications you take or have taken, descriptions of procedures, other doctors' findings, and any communications among doctors about you. A thorough, well-organized, and accurate chart is the best documentation around for ascertaining where your medical dollars are going.

Unfortunately, many doctors are reluctant to share your medical record with you, claiming that you might not understand their notes or that you might be frightened away from a "needed" procedure. Hospitals also hedge at releasing records even though the American Hospital Association Patient's Bill of Rights gives you the right to see information on your record. (Hospitals, however, are not required to observe the bill, so many do not.) Unfortunately, too, few consumers work up the courage to ask to read their chart or get a copy.

The irony of all this is that more people than you think see your record—and not just those who need to see it, the doctors and nurses involved in your health care, but other prying eyes as well: health and life insurance carriers, employers, company medical examiners, and others with legitimate access. Aside from the matter of privacy, another problem with this arrangement—other people know what's in your record, but you don't—is that too often the record is inaccurate, in fact, largely flawed. "At the very time information machines are improving and records are becoming more important, the information transferred is getting worse," writes John F. Burnum, M.D., in "The Misinformation Age: The Fall of the Medical Record" (*Annals of Internal Medicine,* March 15, 1989). Consequently, inaccuracies and problems "follow you around" for life and become the basis for denial of coverage or benefits or even outright harassment.

Protect yourself *and* your investment in your health by knowing what's in your record so that you can correct any misinformation when necessary. As a better-informed consumer, you stand a much better chance of getting the most for your medical dollar.

Do you have the legal right to see your medical record? Yes and no. You see, the answer depends upon where you live and your state's law governing access to medical records. The reality is that for the most part, you cannot see the records directly related to your health and well-being unless state laws give you the thumbs up. What can you do?

▶ Find out where your state stands on the issue of access to medical records. (See chart on p. 322.) Some states allow people to get a copy or a summary (an edited version) of some records but not all. Other states give consumers access to physician, hospital, *and* mental health records.

▶ Go directly to your doctor. Even if access laws aren't on the books in your state, your doctor can certainly share your records with you. In fact, just because a state does not have laws assuring you access to your medical record does not mean there is a law against it. And of course a good doctor should be eager to keep you informed.

▶ Maintain your own medical record. Keep a record of your doctor visits, any medications taken, time spent in the hospital, and so on. This way you know that the information you give to doctors is accurate and complete.

▶ You may have a fourth option, according to a May 2, 1989 *Baltimore Sun* article. It may be possible to check medical data that your insurance companies have on record in their computers. Approximately 750 life, health, and disability insurance companies share information about clients (consumers) through the Medical Information Bureau, Inc., a Boston-based association of insurance companies that maintains computerized files. It's similar to a credit bureau, and, like a credit bureau, it can make its records available to you if your insurer is a member. You can find out what information is in your computerized file with the Medical Information Bureau and how to correct any errors by writing:

MIB Information Office
P.O. Box 105
Essex Station
Boston, MA 02112

A STATE-BY-STATE GUIDE TO YOUR MEDICAL RECORD RIGHTS

Records:	AL	AK	AZ	AR	CA	CO	CT	DE	DC	FL	GA	HI	ID	IL	IN
Doctor	no	yes	no	no	yes	yes	yes	no	no	yes	yes	yes	no	yes	no
Hospital	no	yes	no	no	yes	yes	yes	no	no	yes	yes	yes	no	yes	yes
Mental health	no*	yes	yes	no	yes	yes	yes	no*	yes	yes	yes	yes	no*	yes	yes

Records:	IA	KS	KY	LA	ME	MD	MA	MI	MN	MS	MO	MT	NB	NV	NH
Doctor	no	no	no	no*	no	no*	no	yes	yes	no	no	no	no	yes	no
Hospital	no	no	no	yes	yes	yes	yes	yes	yes	no*	no	no	yes	yes	no
Mental health	no	yes	yes	no*	no*	yes	no*	yes	yes	no*	no*	no*	no	no*	no

Records:	NJ	NM	NY	NC	ND	OH	OK	OR	PA	RI	SC	SD	TN	TX
Doctor	yes	no	yes	no	no	no	yes	no*	no	no	no	no	no	no
Hospital	no	no	yes	no	no	yes	yes	no*	yes	no	no	yes	no*	yes
Mental health	no	yes	yes	no*	no*	yes	no	yes	no	no	no*	yes	no	no

Records:	UT	VT	VA	WA	WV	WI	WY
Doctor	no*	no	yes	no	yes	yes	no
Hospital	no*	no	yes	no	yes	yes	no
Mental health	no	no	yes	no*	yes	yes	no

*Records may be available under special conditions. Contact your state health department for clarification.

Adapted from *Medical Records: Getting Yours* by the Public Citizen Health Research Group, 1986, available for $5 from Public Citizen, 2000 P Street, N.W., Washington, DC 20036.

HOW TO READ YOUR MEDICAL RECORD: DON'T LET YOUR EQUAL PARTNERSHIP WITH YOUR PHYSICIAN BE ABBREVIATED BY INDECIPHERABLE CODES

One thing the medical profession loves to do is abbreviate, especially on your chart and medical records. They all know the code. But you don't. And when you look at your chart or record, you are shut out from what your doctor is thinking about you, about your condition, about your prognosis, and about what you're paying for. Coded language is an obstacle blocking your participation in your own care, and certainly not a just situation when you consider that you are the primary investor. Here are abbreviations you might encounter in records, on forms or prescriptions, or in hospital chatter:

a = before

aa = of each

a.c. = before meals

ad = to, up to

ADL = activities of daily living

ad lib = as needed, as desired

AF = auricular fibrillation

agit = shake, stir

AMA = against medical advice

Ap. = appendicities

Aq. = water

ASHD = arteriosclerotic heart disease

B.E. = barium enema

b. i. d. = twice a day

Bl. time = bleeding time

BM = bowel movement

BMR = basal metabolic rate

BP = blood pressure

BRP = bathroom privileges

Bx = biopsy

C. = centigrade

$\bar{c}$ = with

CA = cancer

CAD = coronary artery disease

cap(s) = capsule(s)

CBC = complete blood count

CBD = common bile duct

CC = chief complaint

cc = cubic centimeter

CCU = coronary care unit

CHD = coronary heart disease; or congenital heart disease

CHF = congestive heart failure

Chol = cholesterol

Cl. time = clotting time

CNS = central nervous system

comp = compound

cont rem = continue the medicine

COPD = chronic obstructive pulmonary disease

CSF = cerebrospinal fluid

CV = cardiovascular

CVA = cerebrovascular accident

CVP = central venous pressure

CXR = chest X ray

d = give

D&C = dilation and curettage

dd in d = from day to day

dec = pour off

dexter = the right

dil = dilute

disp. = dispense

div = divide

DM = diabetes mellitus

dos = dose

dur dolor = while pain lasts

D/W = dextrose in water

Dx = diagnosis

ECG or EKG = electrocardiogram

EEG = electroencephalogram

emp = as directed

ER = emergency room

F. = Fahrenheit

FBS = fasting blood sugar

febris = fever

FH = family history

Fx = fracture

GA = general anesthesia

garg = gargle

GB = gallbladder

GC = gonorrhea

GI = gastrointestinal

GL = glaucoma

gm = grams

gr = grains

grad = by degrees

gravida = pregnancies

gtt = drops

GTT = glucose tolerance test

GU = genitourinary

GYN = gynecology

h = hour

HASHD = hypertensive arteriosclerotic heart disease

Hb or Hgb = hemoglobin

HCT = hematocrit

HHD = hypertensive heart disease

HOB = head of bed

HPI = history of present illness

h.s. = at bedtime, before retiring

Hx = history

ICU = intensive care unit

I&D = incision and drainage

IM = intramuscular

I.M. = infectious mononucleosis

I&O = intake and output (measure fluids going into and out of body)

IPPB = intermittent positive pressure breathing

ind = daily

IV = intravenous

IVP = intravenous pyelogram

L = left

liq = liquid

LLE = left lower extremity

LLQ = left lower quadrant

LMP = last menstrual period

LP = lumbar puncture

LUE = left upper extremity

LUQ = left upper quadrant

(m) = murmur

M = mix

m et n = morning and night

mg = milligrams

MI = heart attack (myocardial infarction)

mor. dict. = in the manner directed

M.S. = morphine sulfate

neg = negative

NG = nasogastric

no. = number

non rep; nr = do not repeat

n.p.o. = non per os (nothing by mouth)

NS = normal saline

NSR = normal heart rate

N&V = nausea and vomiting

O_2 = oxygen

o = none

O.D. = right eye

o.d. = once a day

O.L. = left eye

OOB = out of bed

OPD = outpatient department

OR = operating room

O.S. = left eye

OT = occupational therapy

OU = both eyes

P; $\overline{P}$ = after

Para = number of births

Path. = pathology

p.c. = after meals

PE = physical examination; or pulmonary embolus

PI = present illness

pil = pill

p.o. = by mouth

Post. = posterior

post-op = postoperative, after the operation

PR = pulse rate; or, rectally

p.r.n. = as needed, as often as necessary

Prog. = prognosis

pt = patient

PT = physical therapy

PTA = prior to admission

Px = prognosis

q. = every

q.h. = every hour (q.4h. = every four hours; q.8h. = every eight hours, and so on)

q.i.d. = four times a day

q.n. = every night

q.o.d. = every other day

q.s. = proper amount, quantity sufficient

q.v. = as much as desired

R = right

rbc = red blood cell

RBC = red blood cell count

rep = repeat

RHD = rheumatic heart disease

RLQ = right lower quadrant

R.N. = registered nurse

ROM = range of motion

RR = respiratory rate; or recovery room

RT = radiation therapy

rub = red

RUQ = right upper quadrant

Rx = prescription; or therapy

$\overline{s}$ = without

S&A = sugar and acetone (a urine test for diabetics)

SC = subcutaneous

Scop. = scopolamine

SH = social history

SICU = surgical intensive care unit

sig = write, let it be imprinted

sing = of each

SOB = shortness of breath

sol = solution

solv = dissolve

SOP = standard operating procedure

SOS = can repeat in emergency

ss = half

S&S = signs and symptoms

SSE = soapsuds enema

stat = right away, immediately

sub Q = subcutaneous

suppos = suppository

Sx = symptoms

T&A = tonsillectomy and adenoidectomy

tab = tablet

TAT = tetanus antitoxin

tere = rub

TIA = transient ischemic attack

t.i.d. = three times a day

tinc or tinct = tincture

TPR = temperature, pulse, and respiration

Tx = treatment

ung = ointment

URI = upper respiratory infection

ut dict = as directed

UTI = urinary tract infection

VD = venereal disease

VS = vital signs

WBC = white blood cell count

WC = wheelchair

YO = year old

ABBREVIATIONS AND ACRONYMS

During a rather heavy episode of editing just before writing this editor's page, I became particularly exasperated by an abbreviation, IUGR, which an author had used without explanation in his manuscript. After a fair amount of sleuthing I concluded that IUGR stood for intrauterine growth retardation and was able to confirm my conclusion through the fourth edition of Neil M. Davis's *Medical Abbreviations: 5500 Conveniences at the Expense of Communications and Safety* (Huntingdon Valley, Pa.: Neil M. Davis Associates, 1988). But the title of Davis's book also confirmed my long-standing feeling that writers use abbreviations and acronyms more for their own convenience and status than for readers' comprehension.

Some authors seem obsessed with producing an abbreviation or acronym for almost every medical term in their manuscript, no matter how often the term is subsequently used, and editors are compelled to convert all but the most essential back to the original full term to protect readers from becoming lost in a morass of cryptic combinations of capital letters.

No one would deny the usefulness of abbreviations. Indeed, some, such as e.g. and i.e., are so universally understood and have been around so long that few can remember—if indeed they ever knew—the terms from which they were derived *(exempli gratia* and *id est)*. Others (e.g., ECG, AIDS, and DNA) are so common in the biomedical literature that they no longer need be defined. But editors and, more important, readers rapidly lose interest in an article made incomprehensible by a plethora of strange abbreviations. In addition, some abbreviations are downright confusing. Davis's 5500 abbreviations have 7480 possible meanings. For example, BS may mean "blood sugar" to the endocrinologist, "breath sounds" to the respirologist, "bowel sounds" to the gastroenterologist, and something else entirely to the veterinarian (and the rest of the world).

Acronyms are a special case. Although some are fortuitous—AIDS, for example—others have been carefully manipulated to form a catchy symbolic word or phrase: MADD, Mothers Against Drunk Driving, for instance. The game of creating catchy acronyms can lead to some odd full names or terms; note in James Hale's report of the Montreal AIDS congress . . . that one group of particularly feisty activists have taken ACT UP (AIDS Coalition to Unleash Power) as their title. Occasionally the fortuitous acronym is unrelated to the term for which it stands, misleading, silly, and even unfortunate—CAD, GUT, MANOVA, and HONDA, for example.

It all boils down to a very simple rule: Don't use an abbreviation or acronym unless you are certain the intended readers will understand it immediately or accept and learn it quickly.

Bruce P. Squires, M.D., Ph.D.
Editor-in-Chief
Canadian Medical Association Journal

Reprinted, by permission, from the *Canadian Medical Association Journal,* July 15, 1989.

HOW TO KEEP YOUR
OWN MEDICAL RECORD

Keeping an accurate record of your medical history can be a valuable endeavor, yet very few of us keep any more than billing statements as evidence of our encounters with doctors. We usually assume that the doctor is paid to keep our medical record and, should we require a copy, we merely request it. However, this is not always true. Not only do some states' laws severely restrict a person's access to his or her own medical record, but some doctors withhold the information as a sort of power play.

That's why we strongly advocate that you keep you own personal medical history; the forms on pages 330–35 will enable you to get started on this. Here are some hints to help you:

▶ Start with the "Quick Reference Guide" and complete all the information it calls for. Keep this record in a convenient place, since you never know when a medical emergency may arise.

▶ Now complete the form "Your Medical History," including the "Condition Profile Checklist." It's also a good idea to record some of the more pertinent information regarding your family's medical history, so we've provided space for this.

▶ Keep track of doctor visits with the form "Record of Your Individual Visits." The form has three columns where you will record the date of the visit—to the doctor's office, the urgent care center, or the emergency room—your symptoms or complaints, and the diagnosis and treatment. Make sure you also note any lab tests or other diagnostic procedures. This section is the heart of your medical record, so be sure to make detailed and accurate entries.

▶ Maintain a record of all prescription and nonprescription medications, and any vitamins and minerals you are taking.

▶ Keep track of your major hospitalizations, laboratory tests, and dental and eye examinations.

Quick Reference Guide

List all of Your Medical Providers and Emergency Telephone Numbers

NAME	SPECIALTY	ADDRESS	TELEPHONE

POLICE / FIRE / AMBULANCE	TELEPHONE	HOSPITAL	TELEPHONE

CRISIS HOT LINES	TELEPHONE	PHARMACIES	TELEPHONE

PEOPLE'S MEDICAL SOCIETY®

Your Medical Record

Michael Rooney *EDITOR*
Director of Projects

Charles B. Inlander *President*
Bill Bauman *Director of Membership Services*
Karla Morales *Director of Communications*
Ed Weiner *Senior Editor*

Paper & Pencil Design Group *Art Direction*

≡People's Medical Society®

BOARD OF DIRECTORS

Chairperson —**Lowell Levin** *Yale University*
Vice Chairperson —**Lori Andrews** *American Bar Foundation*
Secretary —**W. Harrison Wellford** *Wellford, Wegman, Krulwich, Gold and Hoff*
Treasurer —**Tom Belford** *Better World Society*
Belita Cowan *Co-Founder, National Women's Health Network*

Ron Draper *Director General, Health Promotion Directorate, Health & Welfare, Canada*
John L. McKnight *Northwestern University Center for Urban Affairs and Policy Research*
Jackie Richmond *Prospect Associates*
Robert Rodale *Rodale Press and People's Medical Society Founder*
Alma Rose *Coordinator, South Florida People's Medical Society Local Action Group*

PEOPLE'S MEDICAL SOCIETY HEALTH BULLETIN © by the PEOPLE'S MEDICAL SOCIETY, INC., a nonprofit, tax-exempt organization. 14 East Minor Street, Emmaus, PA 18049: (215) 967-2136. Membership dues: $15 annually. Copies of this publication: $2 for members; $3 for nonmembers.

Your Medical History

This record belongs to: _____

Date of Birth _____ Place of Birth _____

Insurance Company _____ ID # _____ Telephone (___) _____

Medicare Number _____ Social Security Office Telephone (___) _____

CONDITION PROFILE CHECKLIST*
Indicate by check mark those conditions which you have/had.

Blood
- ____ Bleeding tendency
- ____ Bruise easily
- ____ Hemolytic anemia
- ____ Other anemia

Bones, Muscles & Joints
- ____ Arthritis
- ____ Backache
- ____ Bone tumors
- ____ Fractures
- ____ Muscle pain
- ____ Osteomyelitis

Digestive — Stomach & Intestine
- ____ Appetite changes
- ____ Blood-streaked stools
- ____ Diverticulitis
- ____ Gallbladder disease
- ____ Hemorrhoids
- ____ Tarry stools
- ____ Tumors — stomach, colon, rectum
- ____ Ulcers
- ____ Weight gain
- ____ Weight loss

Ears
- ____ Deafness
- ____ Dizziness
- ____ Drainage from ears
- ____ Hearing aid
- ____ Ringing in ears

Eye
- ____ Blurred vision
- ____ Cataracts
- ____ Double vision
- ____ Eye infection
- ____ Glaucoma
- ____ Sudden blindness

Genital and Urinary
- ____ Bloody urination
- ____ Excessive urination
- ____ Kidney stones
- ____ Losing urine when coughing, straining, laughing, etc.
- ____ Painful urination
- ____ Urinary tract infections
- ____ Urination at night

Glands and Hormones
- ____ Diabetes
- ____ Goiter (enlarged thyroid)
- ____ Persistent fever
- ____ Protruding eyeballs
- ____ Sugar in urine
- ____ Thyroid tumors
- ____ Unusual thirst
- ____ Weakness and general tiredness

Heart & Lungs
- ____ Abnormal electrocardiogram
- ____ Ankle and leg swelling
- ____ Asthma
- ____ Blueness of lips and fingers
- ____ Bronchitis
- ____ Chest pain
- ____ Chest x-ray abnormalities
- ____ Chronic cough
- ____ Coughing up blood
- ____ Fainting with coughing
- ____ Heart attack
- ____ Heart enlargement
- ____ Heart murmur
- ____ High blood pressure
- ____ Irregular heartbeats
- ____ Leg cramps
- ____ Low blood pressure
- ____ Lung tumors
- ____ Night sweats
- ____ Pneumonia
- ____ Shortness of breath at night
- ____ Shortness of breath lying down
- ____ Shortness of breath upon exertion
- ____ TB or TB exposure (tuberculosis)
- ____ Thrombophlebitis
- ____ Varicose veins

Infectious Diseases
- ____ Chicken pox (varicella)
- ____ German measles (rubella)
- ____ Gonorrhea
- ____ Measles (rubeola)
- ____ Mumps (parotitis)
- ____ Syphillis

Males
- ____ Difficulty starting stream
- ____ Prostate tumor
- ____ Sexual dissatisfaction
- ____ Sexual impotency
- ____ Sore on penis
- ____ Urethral infection

Nerve Disorders
- ____ Convulsive disorder
- ____ Difficulty with limb control
- ____ Extremities fall "asleep"
- ____ Head trauma
- ____ Headache
- ____ Memory problem
- ____ Muscle weakness
- ____ Speech problem
- ____ Stroke
- ____ Tremor (shaking)
- ____ Walking disorder

Nose
- ____ Deviated septum
- ____ Nosebleeds
- ____ Polyps
- ____ Runny nose
- ____ Sinusitis

Obstetrics & Gynecology
- ____ Abnormal Pap smear
- ____ Abnormal breast exam
- ____ Abnormal pelvic exam
- ____ Age began menstruating
- ____ Bleeding between periods
- ____ Menopause
- ____ Miscarriages
- ____ Painful intercourse
- ____ Painful menstruation
- ____ Post-menopause bleeding
- ____ Pregnancy
- ____ Sexual dissatisfaction
- ____ Tumors — breast, uterus, cervix, ovaries, etc.
- ____ Vaginal infections

Skin
- ____ Changes in wart, mole, etc.
- ____ Chronic skin infections/lesions
- ____ Common skin infections
- ____ Psoriasis
- ____ Skin rash
- ____ Skin sensitive to light
- ____ Skin tumors

Throat
- ____ Difficulty swallowing
- ____ Mouth infections
- ____ Persistent hoarseness
- ____ Recurrent sore throat
- ____ Sore tongue
- ____ Voice change

Family Medical History

	FATHER	MOTHER	BROTHERS/SISTERS		
Accident					
Alcoholism					
Allergies					
Anemia					
Cancer					
Diabetes					
Headaches					
Hearing Loss					
Heart Attack					
Hypertension					
Kidney					
Obesity					
Psychosis					
Rheumatoid Arthritis					
Stroke					
Tuberculosis					
Age Died					
Cause of Death					

Source: *Keeping Track: A Personal Health Record System*
(Santa Barbara, CA: Woodbridge Press, 1980).

PEOPLE'S MEDICAL SOCIETY®

Record of Your Individual Visits		
DATE	PROBLEMS / COMPLAINTS / SYMPTOMS	DIAGNOSIS AND TREATMENT

PEOPLE'S MEDICAL SOCIETY®

Record of Prescription Medications

DATE	MEDICATION	DOCTOR	PHARMACY	SIDE EFFECTS

Record of Over-the-Counter Medications–Include Vitamins and Minerals

DATE	MEDICATION	DATE	MEDICATION	DATE	MEDICATION

PEOPLE'S MEDICAL SOCIETY®

Record of Major Hospitalizations

DATE	HOSPITAL	DOCTOR	CONDITION / ILLNESS

Record and Results of Laboratory Tests

DATE	LAB TEST	RESULTS

PEOPLE'S MEDICAL SOCIETY®

Record of Dental Examinations

DATE	DENTIST	COMPLAINTS / PROBLEMS / TREATMENTS

Record of Eye Examinations

DATE	RESULTS OF EXAMINATION

PEOPLE'S MEDICAL SOCIETY®

DYING WITH DIGNITY; OR, AVOIDING THE HIGH COSTS OF DYING

Since the Karen Ann Quinlan case, national attention has been focused on such issues as "quality of life" and the "right to die," and the ethical questions of prolonging life in hopelessly ill people. Stories abound of people in comas with incurable diseases who are being kept alive "thanks" to the so-called marvels of modern technology. As Thomas and Colin Scully say in their book *Playing God: The New World of Medical Choices* (New York: Simon & Schuster, 1988), "For the first time in history, physicians have the ability, know-how, and sophisticated technology to sustain the physical life of patients beyond any reasonable quality of life they may want to endure."

Traditionally, the physician has been solely responsible for deciding when life is to be allowed to end and when further effort is to be expended to keep the person alive—an awesome power that too often has resulted in the overtreatment of the dying. But in recent years such medical practices have flown in the face of the burgeoning consumer movement and its attendant emphasis on patients' rights and patient autonomy. The consequence? Change is in the wind and, in many cases, states' laws.

The right-to-die movement, a movement away from impersonal technology to personal choices, is underway. If it is important to you to die with dignity, and to maintain autonomy over future legal and medical decisions made on your behalf, then you need to do some advance planning now. And that's what this section is all about. We will attempt to help you with this planning by explaining how you can use living wills and durable powers of attorney for health care to maintain your autonomy—and to ensure that the money you or your family spends on medical care is allocated according to your wishes. Not that these life-and-death decisions are made on the basis of economic considerations, but if spending lavish sums of money on life-sustaining technology is the *last* thing you want to do, then plan you must. Because without planning this just may end up being the last thing you ever do. But first you need to know the terms, starting with the most basic—and most complex.

Redefining Death

Death used to be simple. If you stopped breathing, your heart stopped, and your pupils dilated, you were dead. Not so today. No longer is the traditional heart-and-lungs concept of death applicable in every case. Therefore, if you are concerned about dying with dignity, it is important to understand how the medical and legal worlds are redefining what once was the most certain thing in life—death.

The changes in the definition of death have come about, according to the *Medico-Legal Journal*, thanks to what it calls the "revolution in intensive care technology, which now enables artificial ventilation and circulation, feeding by the intravenous route, and the elimination of waste products of metabolism by dialysis machine to be resorted to on bodies whose brains have been irreversibly destroyed." Organ transplantation has also changed the accepted definition of death.

As a result, the definition of death has been broadened to include the irreversible loss of all brain function—brain death. In a landmark report in 1968, the Harvard Medical School's Ad Hoc Committee to Examine the Definition of Brain Death laid down four characteristics of a permanently nonfunctioning brain:

1. Unreceptivity and unresponsivity (total unawareness to externally applied stimuli).

2. No movement or breathing (one hour's observation of spontaneous muscular movements, breathing, or response to stimuli). If the person is on a respirator, absence of breathing must be established by three minutes off the machine.

3. No reflexes present (fixed and dilated pupils, no eye movement or blinking, no contraction of muscles due to stimulation).

4. Flat electroencephalogram (EEG) after ten minutes of recording.

These tests, the report said, are to be done twice, twenty-four hours apart.

Either through laws or court decisions, most states recognize the concept of brain death, but have left the final determination to the doctor. The wording of most of the statutes conforms to what's called the Uniform Determination of Death Act: "An individual who has sustained either (1) irreversible cessation of circulatory and respiratory functions, or (2) irreversible cessation of all functions of the entire brain, including the brain stem, is dead. A determination must be made in accordance with accepted medical standards."

What about the states where there is no legislation? In their book *The Right to Die: Understanding Euthanasia* (New York: Harper & Row, 1986), Derek Humphry and Ann Wickett say that decisions on what constitutes death in those states are left up to physicians' own definitions. *Your state bar association can tell you what applies where you reside.*

Unfortunately, even a legal definition of brain death does not completely eliminate the uncertainty surrounding this issue. According to a 1985 report in *Washington Post Health,* the criteria for determining brain death vary slightly from hospital to hospital. So you may want to call your community hospitals—first try the office of the chief of the medical staff, then go on to the hospital administrators, if necessary—to find out what "standards" they use to determine brain death. (Remember, the criteria should always include total lack of movement, inability to breathe without a respirator, total unresponsiveness to stimuli, and total absence of reflexes.)

These are matters you may want to discuss with your physician, and perhaps with a lawyer knowledgeable in right-to-die issues, so that any advance directives you write encompass all the points about which you believe strongly. Any of the organizations concerned with death (which are listed later in this chapter) should be able to help you as well.

Basically, there are two legal routes to make your wishes regarding your death known and to help make sure your death—at least where life-sustaining technology is concerned—occurs on your terms: living wills and durable power of attorney.

Making Your Wishes Known: A Living Will

A living will is a written statement that you do not want life-prolonging medical procedures when your condition is hopeless and there is no chance of regaining a meaningful life. Living wills have been around since 1976, when California passed what is called the Natural Death Act. Although called "wills," they have nothing to do with property, but rather with one's self, and are intended to take effect when you are still alive. An outgrowth of concern over the loss of ability to direct medical care at the end of one's life, a living will is an advance directive and is operative only at the time you are terminally ill and are unconscious, or are otherwise incompetent to discuss and decide with your physician what treatment you wish.

Not only a tool to control the extent and type of medical care you receive at the end of your life, a living will can also help reduce the emotional stresses and strains felt by both your family and your doctor, who must decide whether to withhold, withdraw, or continue medical treatment that cannot cure or reverse your terminal condition.

By 1989 thirty-eight states and the District of Columbia had passed some form of law authorizing a person to make his or her own decisions about dying: "natural death acts," "death with dignity acts," "medical treatment decision acts," "right-to-die acts," and so on. The laws vary in detail from state to state, so be sure to find out the limitations of yours, including:

▶ Whether more than the standard two witnesses are required, and if notarization is mandatory

▶ Whether implementation of the living will is prohibited if you are pregnant

▶ Whether the withdrawal of life-sustaining treatment may include artificial feeding and hydration (This is one of the most controversial issues involved in the right-to-die movement. Many states' living-will laws specifically prohibit the withdrawal of food and water, others allow it, and some sidestep the issue entirely.)

▶ Whether you must follow a particular form or are permitted to add personalized instructions

▶ Whether your state's living will is valid in another state

If you reside in a state without a living-will statute, what can you do? Realize first and foremost, as Alice Mehling, former director of the Society for the Right to Die, says, "Even without a living will law, everyone has the common law right to refuse treatment." Her recommendation is to execute a general living will form as clear and convincing evidence of what you want.

Must your hospital and doctor accept your advance directive? In *The Right to Die* Humphry and Wickett say that some resist obeying living wills, a refusal that in many cases has led to litigation. In point of fact, Mehling tells us that the "growing body of legal opinion is that [failure to comply with a valid living will] is grounds for battery action."

For more information on the role of advance directives in the right-to-die issue; to obtain the appropriate living-will document to comply with your state's legislation, or the form you should use if your state lacks a living-will law; or to get answers to individual questions concerning living-will enforcement and many other issues, contact Concern for Dying or the Society for the Right to Die (see addresses on p. 342).

Making Your Wishes Known: Durable Power of Attorney for Health Care

The durable power of attorney for health care is an alternative form of advance directive, a written document that allows you to name someone as agent (also called proxy or "attorney-in-fact") with authority to make medical decisions for you (according to your previously expressed wishes) in the event you become incompetent and are unable to make those decisions for yourself.

You probably know durable power of attorney in its standard sense—that is, a way of authorizing another person to make decisions or take actions on your behalf in financial or property transactions. Indeed, all fifty states plus the District of Columbia have durable-power-of-attorney laws, and these laws have been used as the basis for directives regarding health care.

Despite that, however, some states have passed legislation creating a durable power of attorney specifically for health care decisions. This is to assure that health wishes are kept separate from other legal issues. But Concern for Dying says that even in states without a specific durable-power-of-attorney-for-health-care stat-

DOES YOUR STATE HAVE A LIVING-WILL LAW?

These are the thirty-nine jurisdictions with living-will laws:

Alabama	Mississippi
Alaska	Missouri
Arizona	Montana
Arkansas	Nevada
California	New Hampshire
Colorado	New Mexico
Connecticut	North Carolina
Delaware	Oklahoma
District of Columbia	Oregon
Florida	South Carolina
Georgia	Tennessee
Hawaii	Texas
Idaho	Utah
Illinois	Vermont
Indiana	Virginia
Iowa	Washington
Kansas	West Virginia
Louisiana	Wisconsin
Maine	Wyoming
Maryland	

ute, the courts generally have recognized such documents. *Check with your state bar association for details on the law.*

The most critical issue is deciding who is the appropriate decision-maker. Most experts recommend that you consider these factors: Who would you trust with life-and-death decisions? Who knows you best—your attitudes and values? Who would respect your wishes? Most people appoint spouses or close family members—good choices because they know you well—but if they are beneficiaries of your estate, there may be a conflict of interest.

The best strategy, some say, is to have both a living will and a durable power of attorney. A living will concerns only the final moments of life. Considered more flexible than a living will, a durable power of attorney can be drafted to include the authority to make decisions about several areas of medical treatment, not just the termination of life support, on behalf of people not capable of making their own decisions such as after a serious accident, a permanent loss of consciousness, or an incapacitating illness.

Concern for Dying and the Society for the Right to Die both have legal departments that will be able to give you more information. The National Hemlock Society also distributes copies of the durable power of attorney for health care.

Sources of Information on Death and Dying

Concern for Dying
250 West 57th Street
New York, NY 10107
212-246-6962

Elisabeth Kübler-Ross Center
South Route 616
Head Waters, VA 24442
703-396-3441

National Hemlock Society
P.O. Box 11830
Eugene, OR 97440
503-342-5748

National Hospice Organization
1901 North Moore Street, Suite 901
Arlington, VA 22209
703-243-5900

Society for the Right to Die
250 West 57th Street
New York, NY 10107
212-246-6973

SAMPLE*

"LIVING WILL" DECLARATION

Declaration made this ___ day of _____ , 19___
I,_____ , being of sound mind, willfully
and voluntarily make known my desire that my dying
shall not be artificially prolonged under the circumstances
set forth below, and do declare:

If at any time I should have an incurable injury, disease
or illness certified to be a terminal condition by two physi-
cians who have personally examined me, one of whom
shall be my attending physician, and the physicians have
determined that my death will occur whether or not life-
sustaining procedures are utilized and where the applica-
tion of life-sustaining procedures would serve only to arti-
ficially prolong the dying process, I direct that such proce-
dures be withheld or withdrawn, and that I be permitted to
die naturally with only the administration of medication
or the performance of any medical procedure deemed nec-
essary to provide me with comfort care.

In the absence of my ability to give directions regarding
the use of such life-sustaining procedures, it is my inten-
tion that this declaration shall be honored by my family
and physician(s) as the final expression of my legal right to
refuse medical or surgical treatment and accept the con-
sequences from such refusal.

I understand the full import of this declaration and I
am emotionally and mentally competent to make this dec-
laration.

Signed _____

Address _____

The declarant has been personally known to me and I be-
lieve him/her to be of sound mind.

Witness _____

Witness _____

Source: President's Commission for the Study of Ethical
Problems in Medicine and Behavioral Research, "Deciding
to Forego Life-Sustaining Treatment," U. S. Government
Printing Office, pp. 314-315.

*NOTE: This is just a sample and not to be taken as necessarily the
correct or legally binding form for your needs. Be sure to check the requirements of the statute in your state.

GLOSSARY OF LIFE-SUPPORT PROCEDURES

To help you make treatment decisions or to decide which specific instructions to add to your advance directive, Concern for Dying has assembled this glossary. It should help you learn the meaning and the treatment implications of the most commonly used of today's life-support measures. Be aware, however, that slightly different terms might be used at some institutions. Your personal physician should be able to answer any questions about the precise life-support terminology used in your community hospitals.

Cardiopulmonary Resuscitation (CPR). An attempt to restore heartbeat (cardio) and breathing (pulmonary) in someone whose heart has stopped— i.e., has suffered cardiac arrest. This involves mouth-to-mouth breathing and closed-chest compression of the heart. In a hospital setting it may also include intravenous medications, electrical shock to stimulate the heart, and intubation (an endotracheal tube is inserted into the trachea [windpipe] via the mouth to provide an airway) and ventilatory support (use of a respirator).

Code/No Code. "Code" means to institute CPR and call the cardiac-arrest team to make every effort to resuscitate someone whose heart has stopped. "No Code" means that no attempts will be made to resuscitate.

Intravenous (IV). Solutions that are given to patients through their veins. A needle or catheter is inserted into the vein and the solution administered through clear plastic tubing connected to the needle. An IV has many uses, two of which are to provide a route through which medications can be administered and to provide a source of hydration for a patient.

Respirator (Ventilator). A machine that assists a patient to breathe by providing artificial respiration. A respirator may be necessary after a patient has suffered cardiac arrest and has been resuscitated.

Gastrostomy Tube (GT); Jejunostomy Tube (JT). A gastrostomy is an operation to create an opening through the skin into the stomach. A jejunostomy is similar, but the opening is into a part of the small intestine called the jejunum. A GT or JT is a rubber tube or catheter inserted into the stomach or jejunum and sutured in place. The tube enables patients to be given blenderized or pureed food or special caloric supplements.

Nasogastric Tube (NG tube). A pliable plastic or rubber tube inserted through the nose into the stomach. NG tubes have many uses. After certain surgical procedures, a patient may have an NG tube connected to suctioning equipment to keep the stomach empty of secretions. An NG tube can be used to feed a patient who is unable to swallow and for whom TPN (see below) would not be medically appropriate. An NG tube can also be used to decompress the stomach and reduce pain and discomfort in a patient who has a bowel obstruction.

Total Parenteral Nutrition (TPN). Special intravenous solutions that contain vitamins, minerals, and calories to provide nourishment for a patient. TPN is used when the patient is unable to eat any food or sufficient food to maintain a good nutritional state.

Tracheostomy. Making an opening into the trachea (windpipe) through the neck so that a tube can be inserted to provide a passageway for air. A tracheostomy may be necessary if a patient will require mechanical ventilatory support for a protracted period of time. A tracheostomy also provides a passageway for suctioning if the lungs have copious secretions that the patient is unable to bring up because of a weak cough or an inability to cough.

Reprinted, by permission, from the *Concern for Dying Newsletter.*

SELF-CARE AND HOME TESTING

Consumers are doing more to keep the doctor away than just eating an apple a day. As the costs of medical care spiral higher and higher, people are taking more personal responsibility for their health and seeking to manage many of their health problems at home by learning the facts about how all of us can take better care of ourselves— *without the sometimes expensive and often potentially hazardous intervention of doctors and hospitals.* You could call this a movement *back* to earlier times, but it's certainly progress as well.

Self-care is what people do to treat their own health problems or those of their families, with or without help from health professionals. And it's based on certain proven assumptions, says noted self-care advocate Keith W. Sehnert, M.D., writing in *Consumers' Digest* (March-April 1987):

> Lay people supplied with clear, simple information can safely handle many uncomplicated ills, injuries, and emergencies earlier, cheaper, and sometimes better than health professionals.
>
> Those with little formal education can be trusted just as much as the highly educated to deal wisely and calmly with common health problems.
>
> Medical and nursing knowledge need not be the closed, guarded secrets of professionals, but can be shared safely with lay people. A little knowledge is not always a dangerous thing.

Self-care activities run the gamut from home treatment of a twisted ankle with ice and rest to preparing for major surgery or managing a terminal illness. And the program can start with something as simple as a well-stocked medicine cabinet and the knowledge to monitor signs and symptoms and treat injuries and illnesses.

TEN ESSENTIALS FOR A WELL-STOCKED MEDICINE CHEST

After you finish reading this, go in and open the door of your medicine chest. Take a look at what you've collected in there. When was the last time you took one of the pills in that prescription bottle from 1980? Do you dare open that half-empty bottle of patent medicine? Maybe it's time to clear things out and start fresh.

There's an art to stocking a medicine chest. While you might be tempted to keep something on hand for every conceivable complaint, a cabinet overcrowded with out-of-date or seldom-used medications is not in your best interest. Stick to the essentials: a thermometer, tweezers, and first-aid kit—plus a carefully chosen collection of basic healing aids to cope with minor aches, pains, and abrasions.

To save money and reduce clutter, look to items that have a variety of uses. Don't stock up with multisymptom cold concoctions, however. According to Arthur H. Kibbe, Ph.D., director of scientific affairs for the American Pharmaceutical Association, it's best to tailor treatment to your specific cold complaints—something you can't do until you're in the throes of a full-blown viral assault.

Here are 10 over-the-counter essentials to keep on hand for the most common minor health problems.

Petroleum Jelly

This universal healer is many dermatologists' number-one pick. Use it to protect and help heal dry, chafed, chapped, or wind-burned skin— from lips to elbows to heels. "Dry skin is a very common problem. It can become itchy, flaky, inflamed, and, if left untreated, develop painful cracks and fissures, opening the door for infection," says Bernett Johnson, M.D., vice chairman of the department of dermatology at the University of Pennsylvania School of Medicine. Petroleum jelly works by providing a physical barrier to evaporation. Johnson recommends applying it to damp skin after a shower or bath.

Petroleum jelly is also a useful treatment for hemorrhoids and can help protect and soothe minor burns or sunburned skin. If your clothes chafe when you walk or run, try applying some jelly to strategic points on your skin before exercise.

Antacids

Antacids can soothe heartburn, upset stomach, ulcers, indigestion, or gastritis. Stomach upset is commonly caused by excessive acid. A backup of acid into the esophagus can lead to the characteristic burning sensation of heartburn. Antacids neutralize excess acid, relieving the discomfort.

"The most commonly used and effective antacids are the aluminum and magnesium hydroxide compounds," says Samuel Klein, M.D., assistant professor in the division of gastroenterology at the University of Texas Medical Branch.

Aspirin

Few drugs can match the universal appeal of aspirin, a potent pain reliever for headaches, toothaches, fever, and muscle soreness. Because it reduces inflammation, aspirin is especially soothing for arthritis and injuries like strains and sprains. In a recent study at the University of Alabama, 20 women who were given two aspirin four times a day had less soreness and a greater range of motion two days after performing some unusual arm exercises than volunteers who didn't take aspirin. The researchers speculate that aspirin's anti-inflammatory effect was responsible for the reduction in "delayed muscle soreness."

If aspirin upsets your stomach or if you are allergic to it, acetaminophen is a good substitute. Acetaminophen also relieves pain and fever, but not inflammation. Ibuprofen relieves inflammation as well as pain and fever. Ultimately, however, your choice of pain reliever may simply come down to whatever works best for you. Just be aware that if you are allergic to aspirin, ibuprofen is generally off limits too.

Athlete's Foot Powder

The fungus that causes athlete's foot runs rampant on all kinds of feet. In fact, as many as 50 percent of people test positive for the infection at one time or another, according to Norman Klombers, D.P.M., executive director of the American Podiatric Medical Association. The fungus is so widespread that you can come in contact with it even if you never set foot on a locker room floor. And, once exposed, most people do an excellent job of growing the fungus. "That dark, warm, moist environment inside socks and shoes is a perfect incubator for athlete's foot fungus," says Klombers.

Daily care becomes essential to kill the fungus and prevent a serious outbreak. After a shower, be sure to dry your feet well, especially between the toes. Then apply a very light dusting of athlete's foot powder before dressing. And take note, more is *not* better; if you use too much powder, you'll clog the pores and moisture will accumulate—the very thing you're trying to avoid.

Antibiotic Ointment

These ointments use a "shotgun" approach to prevent infection in cuts and scrapes: they contain two or three different antibiotics, each effective against a different range of bacteria, to make sure that nothing grows in a wound except skin. According to a recent study, they're preferable to most traditional antiseptics.

Researchers at the University of Pennsylvania compared the effectiveness of triple-antibiotic ointment to that of double-antibiotic ointment as well as to a wide assortment of first-aid creams and antiseptic sprays and lotions. Old standbys, such as Mercurochrome, Merthiolate, hydrogen peroxide, and tincture of iodine, were also put to the test. Wounds treated with triple- and double-antibiotic ointment healed in about 9.2 and 8.8 days, respectively—faster and better than those treated with anything else. By comparison, wounds treated with hydrogen peroxide healed in 14.3 days, and iodine-treated cuts healed in 15.7 days. Interestingly, wounds receiving no treatment at all healed in 13.2 days, beating out some of the nonantibiotic preparations.

Why did the antiseptics fare so poorly compared to the antibiotic ointments?

"Antiseptics that hurt when you apply them to a wound do so because they're doing damage—actually injuring tissue," says Kibbe. Also, according to Johnson, some studies suggest that keeping a wound moist aids healing because the new cells can move into place more quickly. That may be another reason why the ointments were superior. The ingredients to look for are neomycin, polymyxin B, and bacitracin.

Just for the record, be sure to clean the wound with soap and water before applying the ointment. Cover with a bandage, if necessary. And, of course, if a cut is deep or too large to be closed with an adhesive bandage, seek medical help as soon as possible.

Salt

Salt is a natural antiseptic, and warm salt water is one of the most useful and natural healers around. Gargle with it to soothe a sore throat and kill germs. (The higher concentration of salt kills germs by dehydrating them through osmotic pressure.) You can also use warm salt water as a mouthwash to firm up gum tissue or to treat a mouth injury, or as nose drops to relieve congestion when you have a cold, or as an eyewash to treat eye inflammation.

To make an eyewash, use ½ teaspoon of salt in an 8-ounce glass of distilled warm water. Discard the leftover saline solution.

Hydrocortisone Cream

Available in low-dose over-the-counter preparations, hydrocortisone cream can relieve the itching and swelling of hemorrhoids. But it is most commonly used to soothe minor skin irritations—mild cases of contact dermatitis, insect bites, poison ivy or oak, and small patches of sunburn. Dab a little on, rub it in lightly, and leave the area unbandaged. "Heavy applications are unnecessary, since the drug will not diffuse from the top of a thick layer of cream," says Kibbe. "And don't use hydrocortisone on large areas or on broken skin without consulting a doctor."

Antidiarrheal

Most cases of simple diarrhea go away with or without treatment. All you have to do is hang in for about 24 hours. But why suffer? A diarrhea remedy can help soothe your gastrointestinal tract, stop the cramping, and ease the discomfort. Products containing the combination of kaolin and pectin are a good choice and are very safe, says Klein. But again, it comes down to personal preference; you may find that other products work better for you.

Check with your doctor before using antidiarrheal medication if you have a fever, or blood in your stool. And seek medical help if the diarrhea lasts more than 72 hours.

Ice Pack

Although this is technically not found in the medicine chest, it is a must in every home, especially for active people.

Cold treatment, or cryotherapy, is excellent first aid for acute injuries, such as muscle strains, sprains, and bruises. It helps stop internal bleeding from injured blood vessels by causing them to constrict. The less blood that collects around the injury, the shorter the healing time. Cold also reduces pain, swelling, and muscle spasm.

Choose any kind of ice pack that conforms to the contours of your body. A gel pack that's kept in the freezer is fine. So is a good old-fashioned rubberized ice bag. In a pinch you can even use a bag of frozen peas wrapped in a towel.

Apply the ice pack to your injury for 30 minutes, let the area warm for 15 minutes, then reapply the ice pack. You can repeat this for up to several hours.

You can even prevent pain by massaging an injury with ice before exercising. Applying an ice pack can also alleviate bursitis and reduce headache pain in some people. Ice can even take the itch out of insect bites and the sting out of minor burns.

Laxative

The best treatment for constipation is prevention—eating a high fiber diet, drinking plenty of water, and getting regular exercise. But occasionally, even the best of us faces a blockade. For those times, it's a good idea to have a laxative on hand. Just remember: The milder the product, the better, says Kibbe. Bulk-forming laxatives, especially those containing psyllium seeds, are the best choice.

Avoid stimulant-type laxatives. They can lead to laxative dependence, a condition that can result in permanent damage to your colon. Consult a pharmacist or physician for help in choosing the product that's safest for you.

SAVING MONEY ON
MEDICAL EQUIPMENT

At-home care certainly goes beyond the medicine cabinet. Simple medical equipment, such as hospital beds and wheelchairs, can be extremely valuable tools to aid you in caring for an ill person at home. This equipment is a great money-saver as well. Anything that enables a sick person to remain at home rather than in an institution saves you an incredible amount of money—*and* there are ways to save money on the equipment itself.

▶ Borrow medical equipment when possible. Most home health aids can be borrowed from various community organizations. Check the yellow pages under "Home Health Care" or "Visiting Nurse Association." If no such services are available in your area, you may be able to rent the required equipment from a local pharmacy, but before renting, check to see if your insurance policy will cover its purchase. If you need the equipment for a long period of time, you will probably have to purchase it.

▶ Save by owning medical self-care equipment. Simple devices such as thermometers, blood pressure cuffs, stethoscopes, and otoscopes can help you care for yourself and make informed choices concerning your need for a doctor's help.

▶ Check out the equipment's reliability before purchasing. Every piece of equipment you buy should come with literature that describes its reliability within a certain range. For instance, thermometers may be reliable within a range of one degree Fahrenheit, and some pieces of equipment will be more reliable than others. The accompanying literature should also describe the period of time the equipment can be expected to maintain this degree of reliability without servicing.

▶ Find out where servicing is available. Equipment such as blood pressure cuffs must be periodically serviced to maintain reliability. Make sure that you know how, where, and how often a piece of equipment must be serviced before you purchase it. You will save money if the equipment you buy can be serviced locally.

▶ Call the Better Business Bureau. For many health items—for example, hearing aids—it is wise to see if your local bureau has any complaints on file against the supplier from whom you are thinking of purchasing the equipment.

▶ Check for sales. With health and medical equipment, just as with most other consumer items, suppliers often offer sales.

▶ Only purchase equipment with a written warranty.
Manufacturers of high-quality equipment always offer a
warranty with their products.

SAVING MONEY
THROUGH PREVENTION

Preventive measures have the potential to save you more money on
health costs than anything you do. Anything that keeps you healthier in the long run will be a tremendous money-saver. We have
compiled a list of hints to help you prevent illness and injury. The
sooner you start, the healthier you will be.

▶ Learn stress-reduction techniques. There are some
techniques—some simple, others requiring professional
help—that can help you to lower your stress level. Strong
evidence suggests that people under stress, or those who
cope poorly with stress, are less healthy than others, and
that adds up to a lot of extra dollars spent on medical care.

▶ Quit smoking. Smoking increases a person's risk for a
number of major diseases: heart disease, stroke, and cancer.
But beyond that, smokers are more prone to illness in
general—and therefore lose more work time due to
illness—than nonsmokers. You must also consider the
increased risk at which you put your friends and family as
they breathe in your exhaled smoke.

▶ Don't do anything to excess. Excessive eating, drinking,
smoking, and even exercise can be harmful and expensive.

▶ Make your home injury-proof. Inspect your home for
safety. Check electrical cords, the condition of carpeting,
the placement of furniture, and so on. Improvements, such
as nonslip strips on bathtubs, are inexpensive ways to
ensure your safety and prevent the need for costly medical
care.

▶ Maintain desirable weight. This doesn't necessarily mean that you should weigh what those famous charts say you should weigh, but you will be healthier if you weigh what feels good for you. And you'll save money on medical care.

▶ Wear seat belts. This is a simple preventive method that not only saves lives each year, but also prevents tens of thousands of disabling injuries.

▶ Always properly restrain children in cars. You are responsible for the safety of children riding in your car. Aside from the emotional costs, injury prevention saves money.

▶ Avoid processed foods. Aside from the preservatives and other chemicals in them, processed foods usually contain more fat, more salt, and less fiber than unprocessed foods. The healthier you are, the more money you will save on medical care—so pass the bran.

▶ Have microwave emissions checked. Call the authorized repair service recommended in the literature accompanying your microwave, and ask someone to do a quick, low-cost emission check. Microwave emissions are potentially harmful, so a few dollars for a check may save you medical costs in the future.

▶ Plan fire escape routes—hold home drills. Simple fire safety measures, such as smoke alarms and fire drills, can prevent serious injury or worse in the event of a home fire.

▶ Exercise regularly. Regular exercise protects against heart disease, osteoporosis, and a variety of other common illnesses, and will also help you maintain a desirable weight. Joining a health club is cheaper than the costs associated with a chronic illness such as heart disease.

▶ Wear a lead apron for dental X rays. Always shield the parts of your body not being X-rayed. Excessive radiation is a definite health hazard.

► Keep current with immunizations. Adults need to be reimmunized periodically for tetanus, and in some areas of the country, other diseases as well. These immunizations often are given free or at very low cost through community agencies.

► Avoid too much exposure to the sun. Tans are not worth the risk of skin cancer.

► Wash your hands. Frequent hand washing will lower your chances of catching colds, flu, and other contagious illnesses.

► Take a vacation. Everyone needs and benefits from periodic breaks in the daily routine. Listen to yourself—and don't get too "burned out" before you give yourself a break. Hotels are cheaper than hospitals.

► Get enough sleep. Most people need seven to eight hours of sleep a day.

► Eat lots of fiber. Increasing the amount of fiber in your diet is the easiest way to lower your risk of colon cancer and will also help with constipation. Laxatives are much more expensive than an extra piece of whole wheat bread.

► Drink cranberry juice. Cheaper than antibiotics, cranberry juice can be protective against bladder infections. But be careful to avoid the juices with added sugar and corn syrups.

► Brush your teeth and floss daily.

► Contact a support group. A support group can be as helpful as a doctor in speeding a recovery from many illnesses.

► Purchase a pet. Studies have shown that an elderly person, in particular, is healthier with a pet to care for on a daily basis. Cat or dog food is cheaper than most prescription medications.

► Know the number for your local poison control center. Calling for help immediately if you suspect someone in your family has ingested a poisonous substance can make the difference between a minor digestive disturbance and a week in a hospital's intensive care unit. Prompt action saves lives and money.

▶ Read the popular press—including health magazines and the health section of your newspaper—for preventive tips. By doing just this, you'll usually stay way ahead of your doctor in general knowledge of prevention.

"LET'S PLAY DOCTOR": HOME TESTING

Sales of do-it-yourself medical tests a few years ago topped the $500-million-a-year mark, and the best predictions have sales climbing to $1.4 billion by 1992. Sold in drugstores, in supermarkets, and through catalogs, home tests make it possible for you to take your own blood pressure, check yourself for a urinary tract infection, determine whether you're pregnant, screen yourself for certain cancers, monitor your blood sugar levels, and even predict when you're ovulating. On the drawing board are home tests for cholesterol levels, sexually transmitted diseases, and yeast infections.

Home testing offers a low-cost, convenient—results are quick and private—alternative to the doctor's office, at least at the early stage of diagnosis. Clearly, it's an idea whose time has come as all of us look for ways to cut down on medical costs, save an unnecessary trip to the doctor or hospital, and maximize the value of every medical dollar spent. But aside from the cost-containment issue, such testing is becoming more popular as consumers involve themselves in self-care and take over aspects of their health care once exclusively the doctor's domain. Information once solely available to medical professionals is now available to almost anyone who wants to retrieve it.

In *The People's Book of Medical Tests* (New York: Summit Books, 1985), David S. Sobel, M.D., and Tom Ferguson, M.D., point out that home medical testing helps users in three specific ways:

1. *Screening* for hidden disorders before symptoms develop and to alert people to diseases at an early stage when prompt attention

may be invaluable. "I feel well, but is something wrong?" is how they characterize it.

2. *Diagnosis* to help a person decide whether professional help is called for—"I feel sick. What is it?"

3. *Monitoring* to help evaluate a continuing problem and determine the results and effects of various treatments—"I have a health problem. How well am I managing it?"

Do-it-yourself tests, however, are not without potential problems. No matter how careful you are, no test—not even the ones performed in hospitals and medical laboratories—is 100 percent accurate. All of them sometimes turn out false readings: false positives (abnormal readings even though you are healthy) and false negatives (failure to detect abnormalities). Sobel and Ferguson maintain that "for many home tests it is useful to have a health professional review with you the proper use and method the first time you do them," and they emphasize that home testing should not be a substitute for medical consultation. Many symptoms, they say, require immediate medical attention, such as blood in your stool or urine, or significant difficulty in breathing.

The bottom line here too is that there are times when the home test may be a waste of time and money. When you have a disturbing symptom that doesn't go away, a visit to a medical professional *is* necessary, and you will probably be wasting your money on a home test in the interim. A somewhat different scenario, however, is when a doctor repeats the test that you just took at home, the pregnancy test being the prime example of this. Even though you end up paying twice for possibly the same results, the value of the home pregnancy test is that, if positive, you can begin prenatal health care earlier, especially if you must wait a few weeks (a not uncommon phenomenon) for an appointment with a doctor.

Most experts agree that the objective of home medical tests is to enable you to *work together* with your health professional to ensure the best health for yourself. Home medical testing can be beneficial to your health and wallet, but a few cautionary notes are in order:

▶ Remember that the success of any home test depends on the user. The experts say a test's failure to reveal a condition that is indeed present—a false negative—is nearly always the result of carelessness.

▶ Ask your pharmacist or another health professional to help you anticipate and work out any difficulties you may have with a test.

▶ Note the manufacturer's name, address, and phone number. Most have toll-free numbers listed on the labels, so don't be shy about calling if you're confused by a test or its results.

▶ Check the expiration date for test kits that contain chemicals. Chemicals may lose potency and affect results if they go unused beyond the expiration date. Of course, don't buy the kit if the date is past.

▶ Comply with storage instructions, which may call for special storage to avoid heat or cold.

▶ Study the directions on the package insert. First read the insert in a general way, then scrutinize the directions step-by-step—before you begin the test. Check whether the test requires special dietary restrictions or specifies precautions relating to the user's physical activity before testing.

▶ Use a stop watch, digital watch, or watch with a sweep second hand, if necessary. Timing is critical in many tests, so heed any directions in this regard.

▶ Make sure you are clear on what the directions tell you to do if results are positive, negative, or uncertain.

▶ Use any containers provided in the kit. When collecting a urine specimen in your own container, however, make sure the container is clean and rinsed of all soap traces.

▶ Be sure you have normal color vision before trying to use any of the chemical tests that are read by color comparisons. Or get help from someone who does.

▶ Consult a doctor if a test is positive. If a test is negative but the symptoms persist or you're still concerned, see a doctor.

▶ Keep any chemicals out of reach of children and promptly discard any used test materials.

▶ Check around to see if you can get a test kit free. For starters, call your local cancer society, your county or municipal health department, etc.

▶ Remember—and we can't repeat this often enough—no test is 100 percent accurate.

▶ Remember too that not all home testing requires a kit. According to the American Cancer Society, every woman over twenty should examine her breasts monthly. Also, the most common type of cancer in humans, skin cancer, is largely curable if caught early, and you don't need a kit to check your skin for moles and suspicious and rapid changes in them.

HEALTH FAIRS: LEGITIMATE HEALTH SCREENING OR UNFAIR MARKETING?

You probably think you know all about health fairs, and you may even have gone to a few and taken "advantage" of the free services they offer: blood pressure screening, blood typing, screening for foot deformities and problems, vision testing, and on and on. They are usually sponsored by hospitals and feature a lot of giveaways, such as refrigerator magnets and brochures with the facility's logo emblazoned prominently. Along with the freebies you have the opportunity to schmooze with the health professionals distributing the brochures and doing the testing. A familiar scene—but not what it seems. Do you know that the reliability of the tests is questionable? And do you know that most health fairs are set up for the purpose of getting you to use (translate: *buy*) the services of the participating providers?

In the words of a top medical marketer, writing in the July 13, 1989 issue of *Medical Economics,* "Doctors looking for an inexpensive way to attract more patients frequently sign up with health fairs.

They figure the few hundred dollars it costs are well-spent in promoting their practices and generating good will. And a health fair is just the kind of low-key marketing that many physicians like best."

So the next time you find yourself at a health fair, stay low-key yourself. Make sure the promoters are providing a community service, not just an opportunity for doctors and hospitals to make a quick buck (or several hundred and more) off you.

You're Not Alone Out There

8

DIAL 800 FOR HEALTH

Many self-help and support groups operate toll-free telephone numbers to help you learn more about a medical condition, answer your questions, and help you to locate a local support group. And the good news is that much of the information is free.

Sponsored by a wide variety of organizations, these are some of the most popular health-related toll-free numbers. Some are operated by nonprofit groups; others are not. Some provide only information; others have products or publications to sell. Note that there are three types of numbers listed: national, regional, and state. Many organizations have national toll-free numbers that are accessible from every state, but there are exceptions, such as toll-free numbers limited to specific states or regions. We indicate the exceptions.

Every number listed here was checked to determine if it was operating, which it was as of June 1990. But should you encounter any problem with a number, we suggest that you contact the toll-free directory assistance operator at 800-555-1212.

We make no claims or guarantees for the groups listed here, nor do we endorse the groups or their recommendations. Use this as a reference directory, for informational purposes. As always, we encourage you to exercise your own good judgment when contacting any of these organizations.

AEROBIC EXERCISE

Aerobics and Fitness
  Association of America
800-BE-FIT-86
800-343-2584—California
  only
800-445-5950—8:30 A.M. to
  5 P.M. Pacific Time
  Provides basic information
on aerobic exercises, certified
instructors, and prevention
and treatment of
aerobic-related injuries.

National Dance-Exercise
  Instructors Training
  Association
Minneapolis, Minnesota
800-237-6242
612-340-1306—Minnesota
  only
  Provides information on
aerobics and seminars.

ALZHEIMER'S DISEASE

Alzheimer's Disease
  Association
800-621-0379
800-572-6037—Illinois only
  Provides information on
Alzheimer's disease and
referrals to local chapters.

AMYOTROPHIC LATERAL SCLEROSIS (LOU GEHRIG'S DISEASE)

ALS Associates
800-782-4747
  Provides information and
referrals to local support
groups.

ANEMIA

Cooley's Anemia Foundation
New York, New York
800-221-3571
800-522-7222—New York
  State only
  Provides information on
treatment, support groups,
and research.

National Association for
  Sickle Cell Diseases
Los Angeles, California
800-421-8453
  Provides information and
materials.

CANCER

AMC Cancer Information
American Medical Center
  Cancer Research Center
800-525-3777
303-233-6501—Colorado
  only

Provides the latest information on cancer prevention, detection, and treatment methods. Also offers counseling services.

American Cancer Society
800-227-2345—8:30 A.M. to
  4:30 P.M. Eastern Time
  Provides general information on cancer prevention, detection, and treatment. Also makes referrals to local ACS chapters.

American International
  Hospital Cancer Program
Zion, Illinois
800-FOR-HELP
  Provides information on cancer treatment programs.

Cancer Information Service
National Cancer Institute
  Department of Health and
  Human Services
800-4-CANCER
  Provides information on the prevention, detection, and treatment of cancer and information on treatment facilities.

Y-ME
Homewood, Illinois
800-221-2141—Monday–Friday, 9 A.M. to 5 P.M.
  Central Time
  Provides information and support to women who have had breast cancer.

CEREBRAL PALSY

United Cerebral Palsy
  Association
800-USA-1UCP
  Provides information on cerebral palsy and referrals to local support groups.

CHILDREN'S SERVICES

Child Abuse Hot Line
800-422-4453
  Provides general information, crisis counseling, and referrals on child abuse and related issues.

Child Care Information
  Service
Washington, D.C.
800-424-2460
  Provides information and referrals to accredited child care programs.

Childfind
800-IAM-LOST (426-5678)
  Operates an international service for locating missing children.

Covenant House
800-999-9999
  Provides 24-hour assistance to runaways and homeless youth. Also provides referrals.

Kevin Collins Foundation
   for Missing Children
800-272-0012
   Provides counseling and
education to the families of
missing or abducted
children.

Kid Watch
American Child Protective
   Association
800-543-9282
   Provides educational
materials, counseling, and
local referrals.

Missing Children Help
   Center
800-872-5437
   Provides assistance to
parents of missing children
by publicizing the children's
photographs.

National Council on Child
   Abuse
800-222-2000—referrals only
800-422-4453
   Operates a 24-hour crisis
line with trained therapists.

National Hot Line for
   Missing and
   Exploited Children
National Center for Missing
   and Exploited Children
800-843-5678—Monday–Fri-
   day, 7:30 A.M. to 11 P.M.
   Saturday, 10 A.M. to 6 P.M.
   Operates a hot line for
reporting sightings of
missing children as well as
those exploited by crime,

prostitution, and
pornography.

National Runaway
   Switchboard and
   Suicide Hot Line
800-621-4000
   Provides information and
counseling to teens who are
experiencing stressful
situations and may be
contemplating suicide.
Contacts families at the
request of the child.

Parents Anonymous
800-421-0353
800-352-0386—California
   only
   Provides referrals to
self-help groups for parents
involved in child abuse.

Runaway Hot Line
800-231-6946—24 hours
800-392-3352—Texas only
   Assists runaways and
contacts families at the
request of the child. Offers
information on, and referrals
to, counselors and shelters.

Vanished Children's Alliance
800-VANISHED
   Provides 24-hour
information on the
prevention and recovery of
missing children.

CLEFT PALATE

American Cleft Palate
  Educational Foundation
800-24-CLEFT
  Provides information on
where to obtain local
treatment and where to find
parent support groups.

CORNELIA DE LANGE SYNDROME

Cornelia De Lange
  Foundation
800-223-8355
  Provides general
information about the
syndrome.

CYSTIC FIBROSIS

Cystic Fibrosis Foundation
800-FIGHT-CF
  (344-4823)—8:30 A.M. to 5
  P.M. Eastern Time
301-951-4422—Maryland
  only
  Provides information on
cystic fibrosis and where to
find local services.

DIABETES

American Diabetes
  Association
800-232-3472—8:30 A.M. to
  5 P.M. Eastern Time
  Provides health education
information and referrals to

physicians and local support
groups.

Diabetes Center, Inc.
800-848-2793
  Provides a catalog on
educational materials
available for sale concerning
diabetes and other related
subjects.

Juvenile Diabetes
  Foundation Hot Line
800-223-1138
212-889-7575—New York
  City only
  Answers questions and
provides information on
juvenile diabetes. Also
makes referrals to physicians
and clinics.

DOMESTIC VIOLENCE

National Coalition Against
  Domestic Violence
800-333-SAFE
  Provides assistance and
information on domestic
violence. Also makes
referrals to shelters.

DOWN'S SYNDROME

National Down's Syndrome
  Congress
800-232-6372
  Provides information on
Down's syndrome, including
educational materials and

newsletter. Makes referrals to parent support groups in the callers' local areas.

National Down's Syndrome
  Society
800-221-4602
212-460-9330—New York
  City only
  Provides information and referrals to local programs where available.

DRINKING WATER

Drinking Water Hot Line
800-426-4791—Monday–Friday, 8 A.M. to 4:30 P.M.
  Eastern Time
202-382-5533—Washington,
  D.C. only
  Provides information on Environmental Protection Agency regulations affecting drinking-water supplies.

DRUG USE AND ABUSE

See Substance Abuse.

DYSLEXIA

Orton Dyslexia Society
800-ABCD-123—Monday–
  Friday, 9 A.M. to 5 P.M.
  Eastern Time
  Provides information on overcoming dyslexia and refers to support groups.

EATING DISORDERS

BASH, Inc.
Bulimia-Anorexia Self-Help
800-762-3334
  Provides 24-hour information and counseling on eating disorders.

Mercy Hospital Eating
  Disorder Unit
800-332-2832
  Provides information on anorexia and bulimia, and referrals to physicians and support groups.

EMERGENCY COMMUNICATION SYSTEMS

American Medical Alert
  Company
800-645-3244
800-632-6729—New York
  State only
  Provides information on telecommunications devices that may be used to summon help in the event of a personal emergency.

Lifeline Systems
800-451-0525
617-923-4141—Alaska,
  Hawaii, and
  Massachusetts only
  Provides information on emergency communication systems that enable the elderly and handicapped to

have a direct line to hospitals.

EPILEPSY

Epilepsy Foundation of
  America
800-EFA-1000—Monday–
  Friday, 9 A.M. to 6 P.M.
  Eastern Time
  Provides referrals to
physician and state
organizations, and sends
information packets to
callers.

HANDICAPPED

See also Hearing-Impaired;
  Visually Impaired.

AT&T National Special
  Needs Center
800-233-1222
  Provides services and
equipment to hearing-,
speech-, motion-, and
vision-impaired individuals.

American Paralysis
  Association
800-225-0292
  Provides information on
spinal cord injury and other
central nervous system
disorders.

Jobs Accommodation
  Network
800-526-7234—Monday–Fri-
  day, 8:30 A.M. to 4:30 P.M.
  Eastern Time

800-526-4698—West
  Virginia only
  Provides information on
how handicapped workers
can be accommodated in the
workplace.

National Clearinghouse on
  Postsecondary Education
  for the Handicapped
800-544-3284
  Provides information on
postsecondary educational
opportunities for
handicapped people.

National Organization of the
  Disabled
Special Projects
800-248-ABLE—9 A.M. to
  5:30 P.M. Eastern Time
  Provides information on
community, corporate, and
national human-service-
organization projects to aid
the handicapped.

National Rehabilitation
  Information Center
800-34-NARIC
  (voice/TDD)—8 A.M. to 6
  P.M. Eastern Time
  Provides information on
rehabilitation, disabilities,
and related issues.

Youth With Disabilities
800-333-6293
  Provides information on
programs open to young
people with disabilities.

HANSON'S DISEASE

American Leprosy Missions
800-543-3131
Provides information on the modern treatment of leprosy.

HEAD INJURY

National Head Injury
Foundation
800-444-NHIF
Provides information and referrals to local support groups. Also runs support groups for state associations.

HEADACHE

National Headache
Foundation
800-843-2256
Provides information on the causes, symptoms, and treatment of headaches. Provides names of physician-members who treat headache patients.

HEALTH INFORMATION

American Medical
Association
American Medical Radio
News
800-448-9384
Provides a recorded message on a current health topic or a feature story on medicine.

American Osteopathic
Association
800-621-1773
Provides information about osteopathic physicians.

American Trauma Society
800-556-7890
Provides professional and public education materials on trauma.

Doctor Referral Service
Mt. Sinai Medical Center
800-MD-SINAI
Provides referrals in the New York City area.

National Library of
Medicine
800-272-4787—general
information
800-638-8480
Provides computer access to medical literature.

Office of Disease Prevention
and Health Promotion
National Health Information
Center
800-336-4797
Provides an information-and-referral service on a variety of health-related topics.

Total Health Foundation
800-348-0120
Provides information on becoming a patient for life-

style-related health
problems.

HEARING-IMPAIRED

Better Hearing Institute
800-424-8576
800-EAR-WELL—Monday–
    Friday, 9 A.M. to 5 P.M.
    Eastern Time
703-642-0580 Virginia only
    Provides information on
hearing disorders, hearing
aids, and specialists.

Captioned Films and Videos
    for the Deaf
U.S. Department of
    Education
800-237-6213
    Provides free loan of films
and videotapes for the
hearing-impaired.

Deafness Research
    Foundation
800-535-3323
    Provides information and
refers callers to local
organizations.

Hearing Aid Help Line
800-521-5247—9 A.M. to
    5 P.M. Eastern Time
Or write:
Hearing Aid Help Line
20361 Middlebelt
Livonia, MI 48152
    Provides information on
hearing aids and a list of
certified hearing specialists.

Hearing Screening Test
800-222-EARS—Monday–
    Friday, 9 A.M. to 6 P.M.
    Eastern Time
800-345-3277—Pennsylvania
    only
    Provides an on-line
hearing test that can be
taken in two minutes, and
information on local hearing
specialists.

National Association for
    Hearing and Speech
800-638-8255
301-897-8682—Maryland
    only (call collect)
    Provides information on
hearing and speech problems
and a list of audiologists and
speech pathologists certified
by the American Speech-
Language Hearing
Association.

TRIPOD Grapevine
800-352-8888—8:00 A.M. to
    6 P.M. Pacific Time
    Provides information,
reassurance, and support to
the families of deaf children.

HOSPICE

Children's Hospital
    International
800-24-CHILD
    Provides information and
referrals to children's
hospice services, and
provides support for

children with life-
threatening conditions, their
families, and health
professionals.

Hospice Education Institute
800-331-1620—9 A.M. to
    4 P.M. Eastern Time
203-767-1620—Alaska and
    Connecticut only
    Provides information on
hospice care and referrals to
hospice centers.

HOSPITAL CARE

St. Jude Children's Research
    Hospital
800-621-5359—Chicago only
800-654-8563—Georgia only
    Provides information on
treatment for children with
serious illnesses.

Shriners Hospital Referral
    Line
800-237-5055—8 A.M. to
    5 P.M. Eastern Time
800-282-9161—Florida only
    Provides information on
the children's services
available at the Shriners'
hospitals.

U.S. Public Health Service
Hill-Burton Hospital Free
    Care Program
800-638-0742
800-492-0359—Maryland
    only

Provides information on
hospitals that are
participating in the
Hill-Burton Free Care
Program.

HUNTINGTON'S DISEASE

Huntington's Disease
    Society of America
800-345-4372
212-242-1968—New York
    City only
    Provides information and
referrals to support groups.

INCONTINENCE

Simon Foundation
800-23-SIMON
    Provides information on
incontinence and makes
referrals to local support
groups.

INSURANCE

American Council of Life
    Insurance
800-423-8000
202-862-4054—Washington,
    D.C. only
    Provides information on
various types of insurance.

Co-op America
800-424-9711
202-872-5307 Washington,
    D.C. only

Provides information on worker-owned and cooperatively structured health insurance plans.

Insurance Information
   Institute
800-221-4954
   Provides information on how to shop for and purchase various types of insurance. Does not provide specific information on policies or companies.

Life and Health Insurance
   Information House
800-423-8000
   Provides answers to questions about life and health insurance.

KIDNEY DISEASE

American Kidney Fund
800-638-8299
800-492-8361—Maryland
   only
   Provides financial assistance to kidney patients and also provides information on kidney diseases and organ donor programs.

Kidney Stones
800-333-3032
   Provides material on the treatment of kidney stones.

LIVER DISEASE

American Liver Foundation
800-223-0179—Monday–Friday, 8:30 A.M. to 4:30 P.M. Eastern Time
201-256-2550—New Jersey
   Provides information and assistance to children and adults with liver diseases, and refers to specialists and support groups.

LUNG DISEASES

National Jewish Center for
   Immunology and
   Respiratory Medicine
800-222-5864
303-355-5864—Colorado
   only
   Answers questions about asthma, emphysema, chronic bronchitis, and other respiratory diseases.

LUPUS

Lupus Hot Line
Lupus Foundation of
   America
800-558-0121
   Provides information on books written by doctors and patients who have lupus, and refers to local chapters.

MEDIC ALERT

Medic Alert Foundation
800-ID-ALERT (344-3226)
Provides emergency
telephone numbers and ID
bracelets and cards to people
with serious medical
conditions. Also maintains
copies of medical records
and other pertinent
information.

MEDICARE AND MEDICAID

Department of Health and
 Human Services
Inspector General's Hot Line
800-368-5779
800-638-3986—Maryland
 only
Handles complaints from
recipients relating to
overcharges, and possible
fraud and waste of funds.

MEN'S HEALTH

Impotence Foundation
800-221-5517—9 A.M. to
 5 P.M. Pacific Time
Provides information on
the treatment of impotence.

Impotence Information
 Center
800-843-4315
Provides free information
on the causes and treatments
of impotence.

Potency Plus Hot Line
800-227-6836
213-277-1444—Los Angeles
 only
Provides information on
impotency and available
treatments.

Recovery of Male Potency
Grace Hospital
Detroit, MI
800-835-7667
Provides information,
referrals, and recorded
messages.

MENTAL HEALTH

American Mental Health
 Fund
800-433-5959
Provides information on a
variety of mental health
issues.

American Schizophrenic
 Association
800-847-3802
Provides information and
educational materials about
mental illnesses and learning
disabilities.

MENTAL RETARDATION

American Association of
   Mentally Retarded
800-424-3688
   Provides general
information on retardation.

MULTIPLE SCLEROSIS

National Multiple Sclerosis
   Society
800-624-8236
   Provides information and
referrals to local groups.

NEUROFIBROMATOSIS

National Neurofibromatosis
   Foundation
800-323-7938
   Provides information and
assistance to
neurofibromatosis patients
and their families.

NUTRITION
INFORMATION

Beech-Nut Nutrition Hot
   Line
800-523-6633—9 A.M. to
   5 P.M. Eastern Time
   Provides information on
nutritional content of baby
food and answers
food-related questions.

Gerber Products Company
800-443-7237

Provides information on
caring for and feeding your
baby.

Lactaid
Pleasantville, New York
800-257-8650
   Provides information on
lactose-intolerance
conditions.

Sodium Information Hot
   Line
Mrs. Dash's Foods
800-622-DASH—9 A.M. to
   5 P.M. Eastern Time
   Provides information on
the sodium content of foods
for people on
sodium-restricted diets.

Vitamin Hot Line
Your Life Vitamins
800-533-VITA
   Provides nutritional advice
on school-age children.

ORGAN DONOR
PROGRAMS

The Living Bank
800-528-2971
   Operates a registry and
referral program for people
wishing to donate their vital
organs or bodies to research.

Organ Donor Hot Line
North American Transplant
   Coordinator Organization
800-24-DONOR

Provides information on how to become a donor.

ORPHAN DRUGS

National Information Center
  for Orphan Drugs and
  Rare Diseases
800-456-3505
  Provides information on how to locate a source for orphan drugs. (Orphan drugs, for which there is only a small market, are used to treat rare illnesses.)

PARENTING

A Way Out
800-A-WAY-OUT
  Provides 24-hour assistance to parents who are considering abducting their children or have taken their children.

Parents Without Partners
800-637-7974
301-588-9356—Maryland
  only
  Provides information on area support groups for single parents.

PARKINSON'S DISEASE

American Parkinson's
  Disease Association
800-223-2732

Provides brochures and sends information on medicines and the nearest referral center.

National Parkinson's
  Foundation
800-327-4545
800-433-7022—Florida only
305-547-6666—Miami area
  Provides information on Parkinson's disease and makes referrals to physicians.

Parkinson's Education
  Program
800-344-7872
714-640-0218—California
  Provides written materials including definition of terms, newsletters, and other publications. Also makes referrals to support groups.

PESTICIDES

National Pesticide
  Telecommunications
  Network
800-858-7378
  Provides information around-the-clock on various pesticides.

POISON CONTROL

See also Pesticides; Toxic
  Substances.

Poison Control Hot Lines
800-843-0505—Iowa,
Minnesota, North Dakota,
Nebraska, and Wyoming
only
800-282-5846—Georgia only
800-762-0727—Ohio only
800-952-0123—South
Dakota only
800-462-6642—Michigan
only
Provides information
about dangerous and toxic
chemicals that are found in
the home and how to deal
with accidental poisonings.
NOTE: If a number is not
listed for your state, contact
the hospital closest to your
area.

PREGNANCY SERVICES

ASPO/Lamaze
800-368-4404
Provides information on
the Lamaze technique and
makes referrals to local
centers.

Abortion Information
Service
800-321-0575
800-362-1205—Ohio only
Provides information on
abortion services and makes
referrals to participating
clinics. Serves the eastern
U.S. from Michigan through
Georgia.

American Academy of
Husband-Coached
Childbirth
800-423-2397
800-42-BIRTH
Provides information on
the Bradley method of
childbirth and makes local
referrals.

Birthright
800-848-5683—8 A.M. to
Midnight Eastern Time
Provides counseling on
pregnancy and free
pregnancy tests.

Edna Gladney Center
Pregnancy Hot Line
800-433-2922
817-926-3304—Texas only
Provides information on
adoption services and
provides pregnancy
counseling.

National Abortion
Federation
800-772-9100
202-667-5881—Washington,
D.C.
Answers questions on
pregnancy and abortion
procedures. Makes referrals
to affiliated clinics.

National Adoption Center
800-TO-ADOPT
Provides referrals and
adoption information and
specializes in special-needs
adoptions (children with

handicaps and older children).

National Pregnancy Hot
   Line
800-852-5683
   Provides referrals on crisis
pregnancies.

Pregnancy Crisis Center
800-368-3336
   Provides 24-hour hot line
and nationwide outreach for
starting new pregnancy
centers.

PREMENSTRUAL SYNDROME

Madison Pharmacy
   Associates, Inc.
PMS Access
800-222-4PMS
   Provides information on
all aspects of PMS. Provides
referrals to physicians (for a
fee) in the callers' areas.

PRODUCT SAFETY

Consumer Product Safety
   Commission
800-638-CPSC
800-638-8270 (teletype line)
800-492-8104 (teletype line
   for Maryland)

RETINITIS PIGMENTOSA

National Retinitis
   Pigmentosa Foundation
800-638-2300
301-225-9400—Maryland
   only
   Provides information on
the latest developments in
the treatment of RP and
answers questions.

REYE'S SYNDROME

National Reye's Syndrome
   Foundation
800-233-7393
   Provides information on
symptoms of Reye's and
also treatment and support
networks.

SENIOR CITIZEN SERVICES

Alcohol Rehabilitation for
   the Elderly
800-354-7089
800-344-0824—Illinois only
   Provides information and
referrals to treatment
programs for those over age
fifty.

American Association of
   Retired Persons
800-453-5800
   Provides information on
issues of interest to senior
citizens.

Healthy Older People
National Health Information
  Center
800-336-4797
  Provides educational
materials on health for older
people.

Life Extension Foundation
800-327-6110
  Provides information on
anti-aging research and
makes referrals.

National Council on Aging
800-424-9046
  Provides information on
aging and makes referrals to
local agencies.

National Eye Care Project
  Hot Line
800-222-EYES
  Provides information on
eye diseases and makes
referrals to physicians for
those sixty-five or over who
cannot afford the care they
need.

SEXUALLY TRANSMITTED DISEASES

AIDS Information Hot Line
Public Health Service
800-342-AIDS—24 hours
202-245-6887—Alaska and
  Hawaii only (call collect)
800-344-SIDA (Spanish line)

  Provides information on
the symptoms and possible
causes of AIDS, and
recommended preventive
measures. Also provides
referrals to AIDS clinics and
limited information on
symptoms and transmission
of HIV and possible sources
of help.

AIDS Clinical Trials
  Information Service
800-874-2572
  NYAD studies—provides
purpose of study and a
printout of names and
phone numbers.

Gay and Lesbian Crisis Hot
  Line
800-767-4297—Monday–
  Friday, 3 P.M. to 9 P.M.
  Eastern Time
  Provides information and
counseling on AIDS and
makes referrals to local
groups.

STD National Hot Line
American Social Health
  Association
800-227-8922
  Provides free and
confidential information on
sexually transmitted
diseases. Also provides
referrals for diagnosis and
treatment.

Teen AIDS Information
800-234-TEEN—Monday–

Friday, 4 P.M. to 8 P.M.
Central Time
Provides confidential
AIDS information to teens.

SKIN DISORDERS

Poison Ivy
Interpro, Inc.
Haverhill, Massachusetts
800-45-NO-IVY
Provides information on
skin creams that prevent
poison ivy and oak
dermatitis.

United Scleroderma
   Foundation
Watsonville, California
800-722-4673
Provides information on
the skin disease scleroderma
and makes referrals to local
support groups and referrals
to treatment.

SLEEP DISORDERS

American Narcolepsy
   Association
San Carlos, California
800-222-6085
Provides information and
makes local referrals.

SOCIAL SECURITY

National Association for
   Social Security

Claimants Representatives
800-431-2804
Provides the names of
attorneys who specialize in
Social Security disability
cases.

Social Security
   Administration
Washington, D.C.
Social Security Hot Line
800-234-5772
Provides information on
claims and problems
between 8 A.M. and 7 P.M.

SPINA BIFIDA

Spina Bifida Association of
   America
Spina Bifida Information and
   Referral
800-621-3141
301-770-7222—Washington,
   D.C. area only
Provides information, and
referrals to local chapters.

SPINAL CORD INJURY

National Spinal Cord Injury
   Association
Woburn, Massachusetts
800-962-9629
Provides information on
starting a local support
group and information on
spinal cord injury and
advocacy.

Spinal Cord Injury National
   Hot Line
800-526-3456—Monday–
   Friday, 8 A.M. to 4 P.M.
   Provides information,
referrals, and peer support
for families and individuals.

SPORTS MEDICINE

Women's Sports Foundation
800-227-3988—9 A.M. to
   5 P.M. Eastern Time
212-972-9170—Alaska,
   Hawaii only
   Provides phone numbers
for related health
organizations.

STROKE

Courage Stroke Network
800-553-6321
   Provides consultation,
information, public
education, and referrals to
local support groups.

STUTTERING

National Center for
   Stuttering
Stuttering Hot Line
800-221-2483
212-532-1460—New York
   City only
   Provides information on
the various treatment

programs available for
young children, adolescents,
and adults.

SUBSTANCE ABUSE

Alcohol Abuse Emergency
   24-Hour Hot Line
800-252-6465
   Provides basic information
on alcohol treatment and
referrals to local treatment
facilities.

Alcohol and Drug Helpline
800-821-4357
   Provides referrals to
alcohol and drug
dependency units and
Alcoholics Anonymous
groups. Also provides
treatment and intervention.

Alcoholism and Drug
   Addiction Treatment
   Center
Scripps-Memorial Hospital
800-382-4357
   Provides treatment referral
service for adults and
adolescents.

Cottage Program
   International
800-752-6100
   Provides some counseling
and seminars on substance
abuse. Also provides local
referrals.

Just Dial No
U.S. Man of the Year, Inc.
800-USA-1-MAN
    Provides information and counseling for elementary school students who want to say no to drugs.

Just Say No Foundation
800-258-2766
    Provides assistance in establishing Just Say No clubs.

Mothers Against Drunk
    Driving
800-438-6233
    Provides counseling, victim hot line, and newest chapter referrals.

National Cocaine Hot Line
800-COC-AINE
    Provides information on the risks of cocaine addiction and provides referrals to counseling services.

National Drug Information
    Referral Line
800-662-HELP
    Provides information on local treatment programs.

National Parents' Resource
    Institute for Drug
    Education
800-677-7433
    Provides information on street drugs and a list of hot line numbers.

Sedona Villa (Drugs)
800-548-3008
800-874-9070—Arizona only
    Provides information about cocaine, alcohol, and prescription drug dependency and makes referrals.

Target National Resource
    Center Hot Line
800-366-6667
    Provides films and publications on substance abuse.

United States Athlete's
    Association
St. Paul, Minnesota
800-342-8722
    Provides information on establishing sports programs with an antidrug message.

SUDDEN INFANT DEATH SYNDROME (SIDS)

SIDS National Headquarters
800-638-7437—24 hours
    Provides information on the prevention of SIDS. Also provides referrals.

National SIDS Foundation
800-221-SIDS
    Provides written information pertaining to SIDS as well as referrals to specialists and support groups.

SURGERY SERVICES

American Association of
   Oral and Maxillofacial
   Surgeons
800-822-6637
   Provides information on
and referrals to oral
surgeons.

American Society for Plastic
   and Reconstructive
   Surgeons
800-635-0635
   Provides referrals to
specialists and information
on plastic surgical
procedures.

Associates Plastic Aesthetic
   Surgery
800-331-2863—8 A.M. to
   4:30 P.M. Eastern Time
   Provides information
about various plastic surgery
procedures, including cost
estimates. Also makes local
referrals.

Cosmetic Surgery
   Information Services
800-221-9808—8 A.M. to
   5 P.M. Eastern Time
   Provides information on
cosmetic surgery and
provides a physician referral
list.

Eyesight Information Center
   of America
800-CATARAC
800-228-2722

Provides information on
cataract surgery and referrals
to cataract centers.

Facial Plastic and
   Reconstructive Surgery
800-332-FACE
800-523-FACE—Canada
   Provides information on
specialists and the various
types of surgery available.
The hot line is sponsored by
the American Academy of
Facial Plastic and
Reconstructive Surgery.

International Craniofacial
   Foundation
800-535-3643
   Provides information and
educational materials to
victims of facial deformities
and makes referrals to
qualified centers and support
groups.

National Second Opinion
   Surgical Program
Department of Health and
   Human Services
800-638-6833
800-492-6603—Maryland
   only
   Provides assistance in
locating a specialist for a
second opinion when
surgery has been
recommended.

TOURETTE SYNDROME

Tourette Syndrome
  Association
800-237-0717
  Provides information on
the syndrome. Also provides
a physician referral list for
each state.

TOXIC SUBSTANCES

Chemical Referral Center
Chemical Manufacturers
  Association
800-CMA-8200—9 A.M. to
  6 P.M. Eastern Time
  Provides information on
the hazards of household
and commercial chemicals.

Environmental Protection
  Agency
National Pesticide
  Information Clearinghouse
800-858-7378
806-743-3091—Texas only
  Provides information
about the health effects of
pesticides and referrals to
poison control centers.

Radon Technical
  Information Services
800-334-8571 (Ext. 7131)—
  9 A.M. to 5 P.M. Eastern
  Time
  Provides free material on
the hazards of radon.

VIETNAM VETERANS

Agent Orange Veteran
  Payment Program
800-225-4712
  Provides counseling and
information packets to
veterans wishing to file
claims for the Agent Orange
Veteran Payment Program.

VISUALLY IMPAIRED

See also Retinitis
  Pigmentosa.

American Council of the
  Blind
800-424-8666—3 P.M. to 5:30
  P.M. Eastern Time
202-393-3666—Washington,
  D.C. only
  Provides information and
referrals to clinics,
organizations, and
government agencies that
provide services to the blind.

American Foundation for the
  Blind
800-232-5463
  Provides answers to
nonmedical questions
concerning vision loss and
blindness.

Association of Radio
  Reading Services
800-255-2777—24 hours
  Provides information on
reading services for the
blind.

Blind Children's Center
800-222-3566
Provides information on
blindness and family
counselors.

Guide Dog Foundation for
the Blind
800-548-4337
Provides information on
guide dogs.

Job Opportunities for the
Blind
800-638-7518—8 A.M. to
5 P.M. Eastern Time
Provides career
counseling, job listings, and
referrals to blind people
seeking employment.

Library of Congress Services
for the Blind
Talking Books
800-424-8567
Provides information on
libraries that offer talking
books and books in Braille.

National Society to Prevent
Blindness
National Center for Sight
800-221-3004
Provides literature on
specific problems and
conditions.

Recordings for the Blind
800-221-4792
Provides cassette tapes.

WOMEN'S HEALTH

Johnson & Johnson, Inc.
Personal Products Consumer
Information Center
800-526-3967
Provides information on a
wide range of women's
health concerns, including
toxic shock syndrome.

Women's Center
800-544-8293—Pennsylvania
only
Provides referrals for
family planning.

MORE INFORMATION AS CLOSE AS YOUR TELEPHONE

While you're reaching out and calling someone, you might want to
take advantage of other telephone services that offer medical and
health information.

One such service, Tel-Med, Inc., is among the oldest. A nonprofit
California corporation founded in 1971 by the San Bernardino

County Medical Society, Tel-Med maintains a library of approximately 550 taped messages on subjects ranging from alcoholism to venereal warts, and including more than 50 tapes by the psychologist Dr. Joyce Brothers on such topics as loneliness and parent-teenager relationships. The entire concept of "dial access," as it's sometimes called, is tremendously popular, in part because even the most sensitive subjects, such as birth control or drug abuse, are covered.

How do *you* access this service? Various hospitals across the country—in more than 350 communities, says Tel-Med's executive director—sponsor the service, which since its inception is reported to have dispensed more than 100 million messages. Call around to your local hospitals to find out if any offer the service, and what the topics and hours of operation are.

One of the newest telephone programs is Ask-A-Nurse. It was developed by the Adventist Health System to provide health information *and* referrals to community resources and hospital services. Hospitals in more than fifty communities in twenty states—excluding Connecticut, New Jersey, and New York—and the District of Columbia are now licensed to provide the service, which puts registered nurses on the telephone, sometimes twenty-four hours a day, to answer questions about hundreds of topics (*New York Times,* January 5, 1989). And by the way, the nurses also furnish information on the services and staff of the sponsoring hospital or hospitals.

Our best advice here? Take advantage of all the free information you can, but keep a wary attitude about any marketing tactics that may creep into the communication. Telephone information certainly can be convenient and serve a legitimate health need; however, it can *also be a good promotional tool for the sponsors.*

SELF-HELP
CLEARINGHOUSES

Mutual-aid self-help groups exist for just about every medical condition, dilemma, or illness that you can think of, from Addison's disease to Zellweger syndrome. For people looking to get the most for their medical dollars, these groups can be immensely valuable—particularly since the purpose of a self-help group is to get people together who share a common experience or situation. Self-help groups do not replace professional services; they go one very necessary step further: they lend mutual support and help people deal creatively with a wide variety of problems, something the medical professionals cannot do.

The first place to start to find a mutual-aid self-help group for your concern is the list of national and state clearinghouses. These clearinghouses can point you to the groups in their areas and, in many cases, provide you with information and resources. Be sure to enclose a stamped self-addressed envelope to make it easier for the group to respond.

State Clearinghouses

CALIFORNIA

California Self-Help Center
UCLA
405 Hilgard Avenue
Los Angeles, CA 90024
800-222-LINK—California
  only
213-825-1799

Bay Area Self-Help Center
Mental Health Association
2398 Pine Street
San Francisco, CA 94115
415-921-4401

Central Region Self-Help
  Center
Mental Health Association
  of Merced County
P.O. Box 839
Merced, CA 95341
209-385-6937

Northern Region Self-Help
  Center

Mental Health Association
  of Sacramento
5370 Elvos Avenue, Suite B
Sacramento, CA 95819
916-456-2070

Self-Help Clearinghouse of
  Yolo County
Mental Health Association
P.O. Box 447
Davis, CA 95617
916-756-8181

Southern Region Self-Help
  Center
Mental Health Association
  of San Diego
3958 Third Avenue
San Diego, CA 92103

CONNECTICUT

Connecticut Self-Help/
  Mutual Support Network

Consultation Center
19 Howe Street
New Haven, CT 06511
203-789-7645

ILLINOIS

Illinois Self-Help Center
1600 Dodge Avenue, Suite
  S-122
Evanston, IL 60201
800-322-MASH—Illinois
  only
312-328-0470

Self-Help Center
Family Service of
  Champaign County
405 South State Street
Champaign, IL 61820
217-352-0092

IOWA

Iowa Self-Help
  Clearinghouse
Iowa Pilot Parents, Inc.
33 North 12th Street
Fort Dodge, IA 50501
800-383-4777—Iowa only
515-576-5870

KANSAS

Kansas Self-Help Network
Campus Box 34
Wichita State University
Wichita, KS 67208-1595
316-689-3170

MASSACHUSETTS

Massachusetts Clearinghouse
  of Mutual Help Groups
Massachusetts Cooperative
  Extension
113 Skinner Hall
University of Massachusetts
Amherst, MA 01003
413-545-2313

MICHIGAN

Center for Self-Help
Riverwood Center
1485 Highway M-139
Benton Harbor, MI 49022
616-925-0594

Michigan Self-Help
  Clearinghouse
Michigan Protection and
  Advocacy Service
109 West Michigan Avenue,
  Suite 900
Lansing, MI 48933
800-752-5858—Michigan
  only
517-484-7373

MINNESOTA

Minnesota Mutual Help
  Resource Center
Wilder Foundation
  Community Care Unit
919 Lafond Avenue
St. Paul, MN 55104
612-642-4060

MISSOURI

Support Group
  Clearinghouse
Kansas City Association for
  Mental Health
706 West 42nd Street
Kansas City, MO 64111
816-561-HELP

NEBRASKA

Self-Help Information
  Services
1601 Euclid Avenue
Lincoln, NE 68502
402-476-9668

NEW JERSEY

New Jersey Self-Help
  Clearinghouse
St. Clares-Riverside Medical
  Center
Pocono Road
Denville, NJ 07834
800-FOR-MASH—New
  Jersey only
201-625-9565
TDD 201-625-9053

NEW YORK

Brooklyn Self-Help
  Clearinghouse
Heights Hills Mental Health
  Service
30 Third Avenue
Brooklyn, NY 11217
718-834-7341 or 834-7332

Long Island Self-Help
  Clearinghouse
New York Institute of
  Technology
Central Islip Campus
Central Islip, NY 11722
516-348-3030

New York City Self-Help
  Clearinghouse
P.O. Box 022812
Brooklyn, NY 11202
718-596-6000

New York State Self-Help
  Clearinghouse
N.Y. Council on Children
  and Families
Empire State Plaza, Tower 2
Albany, NY 12224
518-474-6293

Westchester Self-Help
  Clearinghouse
Westchester Community
  College
75 Grasslands Road
Valhalla, NY 10595
914-347-3620

OREGON

Northwest Regional
  Self-Help Clearinghouse
718 West Burnside Avenue
Portland, OR 97209
503-222-5555

PENNSYLVANIA

Pennsylvania Self-Help
  Information and
  Networking Exchange
Voluntary Action Center of
  Northeast Pennsylvania
225 North Washington
  Avenue
Park Plaza, Lower Level
Scranton, PA 18503
717-961-1234

Self-Help Group Network of
  the Pittsburgh Area
710½ South Avenue
Pittsburgh, PA 15221
412-247-5400

RHODE ISLAND

Support Group Helpline
Rhode Island Department of
  Health
Cannon Building
Davis Street
Providence, RI 02908
401-277-2231

SOUTH CAROLINA

Midland Area Support
  Group Network
Lexington Medical Center
2720 Sunset Boulevard
West Columbia, SC 29169
803-791-9227

TENNESSEE

Support Group
  Clearinghouse
Mental Health Association
  of Knox County
6712 Kingston Pike, No. 203
Knoxville, TN 37919
615-584-6736

TEXAS

Dallas Self-Help
  Clearinghouse
Mental Health Association
  of Dallas County
2500 Maple Avenue
Dallas, TX 75201-1998
214-871-2420

Greater San Antonio
  Self-Help Clearinghouse
Mental Health Association
  in Greater San Antonio
901 Northeast Loop 410,
  Suite 500
San Antonio, TX 78209
512-826-2288

Self-Help Clearinghouse
Mental Health Association
  in Houston and Harris
  County
2211 Norfolk, Suite 810
Houston, TX 77098
713-523-8963

Tarrant County Self-Help
  Clearinghouse
Mental Health Association
  of Tarrant County
3136 West 4th Street

Fort Worth, TX 76107-2113
817-335-5405

Texas Self-Help
  Clearinghouse
Mental Health Association
  in Texas
8401 Shoal Creek Boulevard
Austin, TX 78758-7544
512-454-3706

VERMONT

Vermont Self-Help
  Clearinghouse
c/o Parents Assistance Line
103 South Main Street
Waterbury, VT 05676
800-442-5356—Vermont
  only
802-241-2249

WASHINGTON, D.C.

Self-Help Clearinghouse of
  Greater Washington
Mental Health Association
  of Northern Virginia
100 North Washington
  Street, Suite 232
Falls Church, VA 22046
703-536-4100

NATIONAL CLEARINGHOUSES

National Self-Help
  Clearinghouse
25 West 43rd Street,
  Room 620
New York, NY 10036
212-642-2944

Self-Help Clearinghouse
St. Clare's–Riverside Medical
  Center
Pocono Road
Denville, NJ 07834
201-625-9565
TDD 201-625-9053
  This clearinghouse
publishes an excellent book
on the subject of finding
and forming mutual-aid
self-help groups.

Self-Help Center
1600 Dodge Avenue, Suite
  S-122
Evanston, IL 60201
312-328-0470

SOURCE: Self-Help Clearinghouse, St. Clares-Riverside Medical Center, Denville, N.J.

BOOKS FOR A PEOPLE'S
MEDICAL LIBRARY

So much of the medical world is shrouded in myth. Think about it. How many times have you been given a prescription by your doctor and not been told the potential side effects? Have you ever had surgery performed, only to discover afterward that you now suffer from an aftereffect that you were not advised about prior to the operation? Have you ever been told that you had a particular condition and didn't really understand what it was? But in all these instances and more, you were expected to foot the bill, to pay for being kept in the dark.

This is why the thrust throughout *Getting the Most for Your Medical Dollar* is to demystify medicine and the way health professionals treat you. It's a very simple notion: Know how the system works (or doesn't work, whatever the case may be) and bills for its services, ask the logical and informed questions, and you will be able to be a major partner in making your health decisions.

Throughout the book, we have suggested the questions that will invariably set you on the road to active and aware consumerism, but we haven't been able to cover it all. Now you may want to do some homework on your own. Where do you start? The explosion of medical and health care books certainly makes it difficult to decide which ones should compose a list of "must-see" books, but the following is a sampling of books on various medical and health topics.

Advanced First Aid and Emergency Care. American Red Cross. New York: Doubleday, 1986.

Advice for the Patient: Drug Information in Lay Language (9th ed.). Rockville, Md.: United States Pharmacopeial Convention, 1989.

Alternative Medicine: A Guide to Natural Therapies. Andrew Stanway. New York: Penguin, 1982.

American Medical Directory (30th ed.) Chicago: American Medical Association, 1988.

Anatomy of an Illness as Perceived by the Patient. Norman Cousins. New York: Norton, 1979.

Arthritis: What Works. Dava Sobel and Arthur C. Klein. New York: St. Martin, 1989.

Avoiding the Medicaid Trap. Armond D. Budish. New York: Henry Holt & Co., 1989.

Cancer: Principles and Practice of Oncology (2nd ed., rev.). Edited by Vincent T. Devita, Jr., et al. Philadelphia: Lippincott, 1985.

Cancer Book. The American Cancer Society. Garden City, N.Y.: Doubleday, 1986.

Cecil Textbook of Medicine (17th ed.). Edited by James Wyngaarden and Lloyd Smith. Philadelphia: W. B. Saunders, 1985.

Chemotherapy and You. National Cancer Institute. Bethesda, Md.: U.S. Department of Health and Human Services, 1987.

Choices: Realistic Alternatives in Cancer Treatment. Revised and updated by Marion Morra and Eve Potts. New York: Avon, 1987.

Coming Back: A Guide to Recovering from Heart Attack. Keith Cohn and Darby Duke. Reading, Mass.: Addison-Wesley, 1987.

Complete Book of Vitamins and Minerals for Health. The editors of **Prevention** magazine. Emmaus, Pa.: Rodale Press, 1988.

Complete Guide to Healing Your Body Naturally. Gary Null. New York: McGraw-Hill, 1988.

Consumerism in Medicine: Challenging Physician Authority. Marie Haug and Bebe Lavin. Beverly Hills, Calif.: Sage Publications, 1983.

Current Medical Diagnosis and Treatment (26th ed.). Marcus Krupp and Milton L. Chatton. Los Altos, Calif.: Appleton-Lange, 1987.

Current Obstetric and Gynecologic Treatment (6th ed.). Ralph C. Benson and Martin Pernoll. Los Altos, Calif.: Appleton-Lange, 1987.

Current Surgical Diagnosis and Treatment (7th ed.). L. W. Way. Los Altos, Calif.: Appleton-Lange, 1985.

Dermatology (2nd ed.). Samuel L. Moschella et al. Philadelphia: Saunders, 1985.

Directory of Medical Specialists (23rd ed.). Chicago: Marquis Who's Who, 1987.

Do-It-Yourself Medical Testing (3rd ed.). Cathey Pinckney and Edward Pinckney. New York: Facts on File, 1989.

Dorland's Illustrated Medical Dictionary (26th ed.). Philadelphia: W. B. Saunders, 1985.

Drug Information for the Consumer. Mount Vernon, N.Y.: Consumer Reports Books, 1987.

Fifty Plus: The Graedons' People's Pharmacy for Older Adults. Joe Graedon and Teresa Graedon. New York: Bantam, 1988.

Fighting Disease. Ellen Michaud and Alice Feinstein. Emmaus, Pa.: Rodale Press, 1989.

General Ophthalmology (11th ed.). Daniel Vaughn and Taylor Asbury. Los Altos, Calif.: Appleton-Lange, 1986.

Harrison's Principles of Internal Medicine (11th ed.). Edited by Eugene Braunwald, M.D., et al. New York: McGraw-Hill, 1987.

Health Care U.S.A.: Where to Find the Best Answers to Your Family Medical Health Problems. Jean Carper. New York: Prentice-Hall, 1987.

Heart Disease: A Textbook of Cardiovascular Medicine. Edited by Eugene Braunwald, M.D. Philadelphia: W. B. Saunders, 1988.

Hospital Infections (2nd ed.). Edited by John V. Bennett and Philip S. Brachman. Boston: Little, Brown, 1985.

How to Avoid a Hysterectomy. Lynn Payer. New York: Pantheon, 1987.

How to Evaluate and Select a Nursing Home. R. Barker Bausell, Michael A. Rooney, and Charles B. Inlander. Reading, Mass.: Addison-Wesley, 1988.

How to Keep Your Child Fit from Birth to Six. Bonnie Prudden. New York: Ballantine Books, 1986.

Let Me Die Before I Wake. Derek Humphry. Los Angeles: Hemlock Society, 1984.

Mastering Pain: A Twelve-Step Program for Coping with Chronic Pain. Richard A. Sternbach. New York: Putnam Publishing Group, 1987.

Matters of Life and Death. Eugene D. Robin. New York: W. H. Freeman & Co., 1984.

Mayo Clinic Diet Manual: A Handbook of Dietary Practices (5th ed.). Philadelphia: W. B. Saunders, 1981.

Medical Self-Care Book of Women's Health. Sadja Greenwood and Michael Castleman. Garden City, N.Y.: Doubleday, 1987.

Medicare Made Easy. Charles B. Inlander and Charles MacKay. Reading, Mass.: Addison-Wesley, 1989.

Medicine and Culture: Varieties of Treatments in the United States, England, West Germany, and France. Lynn Payer. New York: Henry Holt & Co., 1988.

Medicine on Trial. Charles B. Inlander, Lowell Levin, and Ed Weiner. New York: Prentice-Hall, 1988.

Merck Manual of Diagnosis and Treatment (15th ed.). Edited by Robert Berkow, M.D., et al., Rahway, N.J.: Merck, Sharp & Dohme, 1987.

No Housecalls: Irreverent Notes on the Practice of Medicine. Peter Gott, M.D. New York: Poseidon Press, 1986.

Nursing a Loved One at Home. Susan Golden, R.N. Philadelphia: Running Press, 1988.

Ourselves Growing Older: Women Aging with Knowledge and Power. Boston Women's Healthbook Collective. New York: Simon & Schuster, 1987.

Over-the-Counter Pills That Don't Work. Joel Kaufman et al. Washington, D.C.: Public Citizen Health Research Group, 1983.

Patient Beware. Cynthia Carver. Scarborough, Ont.: Prentice-Hall, 1984.

Peace, Love, and Healing. Bernie S. Siegel, M.D. New York: Harper & Row, 1989.

Playing God: The New World of Medical Choices. Thomas Scully and Colin Scully. New York: Simon & Schuster, 1988.

Rodale's Encyclopedia of Natural Home Remedies. Mark Bricklin. Emmaus, Pa: Rodale Press, 1982.

So You're Having an Operation: A Step-by-Step Guide to Controlling Your Hospital Stay. Karen R. Williams and Janet K. Stensaas. Englewood Cliffs, N.J.: Prentice-Hall, 1986.

Springhouse Drug Reference. Springhouse, Pa.: Springhouse Corporation, 1988.

Standard First Aid and Personal Safety. American Red Cross. Garden City, N.Y.: Doubleday, 1986.

Staying Healthy Without Medicine. Daniel P. Marshall, J. Gregory Rabold, and Edgar S. Wilson. Chicago: Nelson-Hall, 1983.

Take Care of Yourself: A Consumer's Guide to Medical Care (3rd ed.). Donald M. Vickery, M.D., and James F. Fries, M.D. Reading, Mass.: Addison-Wesley, 1986.

Take This Book to the Hospital with You (rev. ed.). Charles B. Inlander and Ed Weiner. New York: Pantheon, 1991.

The American Medical Association Family Medical Guide (rev. ed.). Edited by Jeffery R. Kuntz, M.D., and Asher J. Finkel, M.D. New York: Random House, 1987.

The American Medical Association Home Medical Adviser. Edited by Charles Clayman, M.D., et al. New York: Random House, 1988.

The Best Hospitals in America. Linda Sunshine and John W. Wright. New York: Henry Holt & Co., 1987.

The Clay Pedestal: A Re-examination of the Doctor-Patient Relationship. Thomas Preston, M.D. Seattle: Madrona Publishers, 1981.

The Columbia University College of Physicians and Surgeons Complete Home Medical Guide. Edited by Donald F. Tapley, M.D., et al. New York: Crown, 1985.

The Consumer's Guide to Successful Surgery. Seymour Isenberg and L. M. Elting. New York: St. Martin, 1976.

The Diabetic's Total Health Book. June Biermann and Barbara Toohey. Los Angeles: Jeremy P. Tarcher, 1988.

The Endometriosis Answer Book: New Hope, New Help. Niels H. Lauersen, M.D., and Constance DeSwann. New York: Macmillan, 1988.

The Essential Guide to Prescription Drugs (6th ed.). James W. Long. New York: Harper & Row, 1988.

The Food and Drug Interaction Books. Brian L. Morgan. New York: Simon & Schuster, 1986.

The Healing Heart. Norman Cousins. New York: Avon, 1984.

The Home Medical Handbook. Jack I. Stern, M.D., and David L. Carroll. New York: Morrow, 1987.

The Layman's Guide to Acupuncture. Yoshio Manaka and Ian Urguahart. New York: Weatherhill Press, 1986.

The New Good Housekeeping Family Health and Medical Guide. New York: Hearst Books, 1989.

The New Our Bodies, Ourselves. Boston Women's Healthbook Collective. New York: Simon & Schuster, 1984.

The New People's Pharmacy Book: A Guide to Prescription Drugs. Joe Graedon. New York: Bantam, 1985.

The Patient's Advocate. Barbara Huttman. New York: Penguin, 1981.

The Patient's Guide to Medical Tests (3rd ed., rev. and enl.). Cathey Pinckney and Edward Pinckney. New York: Facts on File, 1987.

The People's Book of Medical Tests. Tom Ferguson, M.D., and David Sobel, M.D. New York: Summit Books, 1985.

The People's Medical Manual. Howard R. Lewis and Martha E. Lewis. Garden City, N.Y.: Doubleday, 1986.

The Pharmacist's Prescription: Your Complete Guide to Over-the-Counter Remedies. F. James Grogan. Riverside, N.J.: Rawson Associates, 1987.

The Physician and the Hopelessly Ill Patient: Legal, Medical, and Ethical Guidelines. New York: Society for the Right to Die, 1985.

The Practical Encyclopedia of Natural Healing (rev. ed.). Mark Bricklin. Emmaus, Pa.: Rodale Press, 1987.

The Right to Die: Understanding Euthanasia. Derek Humphry and Ann Wickett. New York: Harper & Row, 1986.

The Rights of Patients: The Basic ACLU Guide to Patient Rights (2nd ed.). George J. Annas. Carbondale, Ill.: Southern Illinois University Press, 1989.

The Social Transformation of American Medicine. Paul Starr. New York: Basic Books, 1982.

Third Opinion. John M. Fink. Garden City, N.Y.: Avery Publishing Group, 1988.

What Your Doctor Didn't Learn in Medical School. Stuart M. Berger, M.D. New York: Morrow, 1988.

When to Say No to Surgery. Robert G. Schneider, M.D. Englewood Cliffs, N.J.: Prentice-Hall, 1982.

Womancare: A Gynecological Guide to Your Body. Linda Madras and Jane Patterson. New York: Avon, 1984.

Worst Pills, Best Pills. Sidney Wolfe, M.D., et al. Washington, D.C.: Public Citizen Health Research Group, 1988.

Your Medical Rights. Charles B. Inlander and Eugene Pavalon. Boston: Little, Brown, 1990.

USE YOUR LIBRARY
RESOURCES

Can't find the book in the bookstore? Don't neglect to take advantage of a free service right there in your own community: your local public library. If you have not discovered the resources, ingenuity, and helpfulness that a reference librarian has to offer, then by all means do so. Even if you live in a small community with a modest library, one with a limited catalog of medical and health books, there's always interlibrary loan.

Although the policies may vary, most libraries do offer this service. And all you have to do is know the title of the book you desire and the author. Preferably, furnish *both* to the librarian in order to prevent confusion, since it's not unusual for different authors to use similar titles. But if you know only the book title or only the author, as one librarian told us, "When in doubt, try! The librarian will always tell you if the information is inadequate." Of course, any additional information you can supply—the publisher and the date of publication—will only help and just may speed up the process.

Speaking of speed—there are some minor quirks regarding interlibrary loan that you should keep in mind. Depending upon where you live and how far the loaning library (the library that has the book) is from the borrowing library (your local library), you may have to wait a few weeks or longer for the book to arrive. So if you need the book immediately—a family member is scheduled for hospitalization tomorrow, or whatever—this service is not the way to go. And once you get the book, take special note of the due date, which is generally set by the loaning library and may vary anywhere from a few weeks to longer. If you think the time limit is not adequate for your needs, let your librarian know *ahead of the due date* that you may want to renew. That way the wheels can be set in motion, and you can continue to take advantage of a valuable resource while you wait.

Happy reading.

MEDICAL LICENSING BOARDS: M.D.'S

(In alphabetical order by state)

Alabama Medical Licensure
  Commission
P.O. Box 887
Montgomery, AL 36101
205-261-4116

Alaska Department of
  Commerce and Economic
  Development
State Medical Board
P.O. Box D-LIC
Juneau, AK 99811
907-465-2541

Arizona Board of Medical
  Examiners
2001 West Camelback Road,
  Suite 300
Phoenix, AZ 85015
602-255-3751

Arkansas Board of Medical
  Examiners
P.O. Box 102

Harrisburg, AR 72432
501-578-2448

California Board of Medical
  Quality Assurance
1430 Howe Avenue
Sacramento, CA 95825
916-920-6393

Colorado Board of Medical
  Examiners
1525 Sherman Street, No.
  132
Denver, CO 80203
303-866-2468

Connecticut Board of
  Medical Examiners
150 Washington Street
Hartford, CT 06106
203-566-1035

Delaware Board of Medical
  Practice

Margaret O'Neill Building,
2nd Floor
Dover, DE 19903
302-736-4522

District of Columbia
Occupational and
Professional Licensing
Division
614 H Street, N.W., Room
904
Washington, DC. 20001
202-727-7480

Florida Board of Medical
Examiners
1940 North Monroe Street
Tallahassee, FL 32399-0750
904-488-0595

Georgia Composite State
Board of Medical
Examiners
166 Pryor Street, S.W.
Atlanta, GA 30303
404-656-3913

Hawaii Board of Medical
Examiners
P.O. Box 3469
Honolulu, HI 96801
808-548-4100

Idaho State Board of
Medicine
500 South 10th Street, Suite
103
Boise, ID 83720
208-334-2822

Illinois Department of
Registration and Education

320 West Washington Street
Springfield, IL 62786
217-785-0800

Indiana Consumer Protection
Division
219 State House
Indianapolis, IN 46204
317-232-6330
800-382-5516

Iowa State Board of Medical
Examiners
Executive Hills West
1209 East Court Avenue
Des Moines, IA 50319
515-281-5171

Kansas State Board of
Healing Arts
900 Southwest Jackson,
Suite 553
Topeka, KA 66612
913-296-7413

Kentucky Board of Medical
Licensure
400 Sherburn Lane, Suite
2222
Louisville, KY 40207
502-896-1516

Louisiana State Board of
Medical Examiners
830 Union Street, Suite 100
New Orleans, LA 70112
504-524-6763

Maine Board of Registration
in Medicine
State House Station 137

Augusta, ME 04333
207-289-3601

Maryland Physician Quality
   Assurance
P.O. Box 2571
Baltimore, MD 21215-0095
301-764-4777

Massachusetts Board of
   Registration in Medicine
10 West Street
Boston, MA 02111
617-727-3086

Michigan Board of Medicine
P.O. Box 30192
Lansing, MI 48909
517-373-1870

Minnesota State Board of
   Medical Examiners
2700 University Avenue, W.,
   Suite 106
St. Paul, MN 55114
612-642-0538

Mississippi State Board of
   Medical Licensure
2688-D Insurance Center
   Drive
Jackson, MS 39216
601-354-6645

Missouri State Board of
   Registration for the
   Healing Arts
P.O. Box 4
Jefferson City, MO 65102
314-751-2334 (Ext. 151)

Montana Board of Medical
   Examiners
1424 9th Avenue
Helena, MT 59620
406-444-4284

Nebraska Board of Medical
   Examiners
301 Centennial Mall, South
Box 95007
Lincoln, NE 68509
402-471-2115

Nevada State Board of
   Medical Examiners
P.O. Box 7238
Reno, NV 89510
702-329-2559

New Hampshire Board of
   Registration in Medicine
Health and Welfare Building
6 Hazen Drive
Concord, NH 03301
603-271-1203

New Jersey State Board of
   Medical Examiners
28 West State Street
Trenton, NJ 08608
609-292-4843

New Mexico Board of
   Medical Examiners
P.O. Box 20001
Santa Fe, NM 87504
505-827-9933

New York State Department
   of Health
Office of Professional
   Medical Conduct

Corning Tower Building
Empire State Plaza
Albany, NY 12237
518-474-8357

North Carolina Board of
Medical Examiners
P.O. Box 26808
Raleigh, NC 27611
919-876-3885

North Dakota State Board of
Medical Examiners
City Center Plaza, Suite
C-10
418 East Broadway Avenue
Bismarck, ND 58501
701-223-9485

Ohio State Medical Board
77 South High Street, 17th
Floor
Columbus, OH 43215
614-466-3938

Oklahoma State Board of
Medical Examiners
5104 North Francis, Suite C
Oklahoma City, OK 73118
405-848-6841

Oregon State Board of
Medical Examiners
1500 Southwest 1st Avenue,
Room 620
Portland, OR 97201
503-229-5770

Pennsylvania State Board of
Medical Education and
Licensure
P.O. Box 2649

Harrisburg, PA 17105
717-787-2381

Puerto Rico Board of
Medical Examiners
Call Box 10200
Santurce, PR 00908
809-725-7903

Rhode Island Division of
Professional Regulation
3 Capitol Hill
Providence, RI 02908
401-277-2827

South Carolina State Board
of Medical Examiners
1220 Pickens Street
Columbia, SC 29201
803-734-8901

South Dakota State Board of
Medical and Osteopathic
Examiners
1323 South Minnesota
Avenue
Sioux Falls, SD 57105
605-336-1965

Tennessee Board of Medical
Examiners
283 Plus Park Boulevard
Nashville, TN 37217
615-367-6231

Texas Board of Medical
Examiners
P.O. Box 13562
Capitol Station
Austin, TX 78711
512-452-1078

Utah Department of
  Commerce
Medical Licensing
160 East 300 South, 4th
  Floor
P.O. Box 45802
Salt Lake City, UT 84145
801-530-6628

Vermont Board of Medical
  Practice
Secretary of State's Office
Pavilion Office Building
Montpelier, VT 05602
802-828-2673

Virgin Islands Department
  of Health
Attn: Licensure
St. Thomas Hospital
St. Thomas, VI 00801
809-774-0117

Virginia State Board of
  Medicine
1601 Rolling Hills Drive
Richmond, VA 23229
804-662-9908

Washington State Medical
  Boards
Division of Professional
  Licensing
P.O. Box 9012
Olympia, WA 98504
206-753-2205

West Virginia Board of
  Medicine
101 Dee Drive
Charleston, WV 25311
304-348-2921

Wisconsin Medical
  Examining Board
1400 East Washington
  Avenue
P.O. Box 8935
Madison, WI 53708-8935
608-266-2811

Wyoming Board of Medical
  Examiners
Barrett Building, 3rd Floor
Cheyenne, WY 82002
307-777-6463

MEDICAL LICENSING BOARDS: D.O.'S

(In alphabetical order by state)

Alabama Medical Licensure
  Commission
P.O. Box 887
Montgomery, AL 36101
205-261-4153

Alaska Osteopathic Medical
  Board
Department of Commerce
  and Economic
  Development
Division of Occupational
  Licensing
P.O. Box D
Juneau, AK 99811
907-465-2541

Arizona Osteopathic
  Examiners in Medicine
  and Surgery
1830 West Colter Street,
  Suite 104
Phoenix, AZ 85015
602-255-1747

Arkansas Board of Medical
  Examiners
P.O. Box 102
Harrisburg, AR 72432
501-578-2448

California Board of
  Osteopathic Examiners
921 11th Street, Suite 1201
Sacramento, CA 95814
916-322-4306

Colorado Board of Medical
  Examiners
1525 Sherman Street
Denver, CO 80203
303-866-2468

Connecticut Osteopathic
  Medical Board
Department of Health
  Services
Division of Medical Quality
  Assurance
79 Elm Street

402 APPENDIX B

Hartford, CT 06106
203-566-1039

Delaware Board of Medical
  Practice
O'Neill Building
P.O. Box 1401
Dover, DE 19903
302-736-4522

District of Columbia
  Commission on Licensure
  to Practice the Healing Art
605 G Street, N.W.
Washington, DC 20001
201-727-5365

Florida Board of Osteopathic
  Medical Examiners
1940 North Monroe Street
Tallahassee, FL 32399-0775
904-488-7546

Georgia Composite State
  Board of Medical
  Examiners
166 Pryor Street, S.W.
Atlanta, GA 30303
404-656-3913

Hawaii Board of
  Osteopathic Examiners
P.O. Box 3469
Honolulu, HI 96801
808-548-3952

Idaho State Board of
  Medicine
State House
Boise, ID 83720
208-334-2822

Illinois Department of
  Professional Regulation
320 West Washington, 3rd
  Floor
Springfield, IL 62786
217-782-0458

Indiana Medical Licensing
  Board
1 American Square, Suite
  1020
Box 82067
Indianapolis, IN 46282
317-232-2960

Iowa State Board of Medical
  Examiners
Executive Hills West
1209 East Court Avenue
Des Moines, IA 50319
515-281-5171

Kansas Board of Healing
  Arts
900 Southwest Jackson,
  Suite 553
Topeka, KS 66612
913-296-7413

Kentucky Board of Medical
  Licensure
400 Sherburn Lane, Suite
  222
Louisville, KY 40207
502-896-1516

Louisiana State Board of
  Medical Examiners
830 Union Street
New Orleans, LA 70112
504-524-6763

Maine Board of Osteopathic
Examination and
Registration
State House Station 142
Augusta, ME 04333
207-289-2480

Maryland Physician Quality
Assurance
4201 Patterson Avenue
P.O. Box 2571
Baltimore, MD 21215-0002
301-764-4777

Massachusetts Board of
Registration in Medicine
10 West Street
Boston, MA 02111
617-727-3086

Michigan Board of
Osteopathic Medicine and
Surgery
P.O. Box 30018
Lansing, MI 48909
517-373-6650

Minnesota State Board of
Medical Examiners
2700 University Avenue, W.,
Suite 106
St. Paul, MN 55114-1080
612-642-0538

Mississippi State Board of
Medical Licensure
2688-D Insurance Center
Drive
Jackson, MS 39216
601-354-6645

Missouri Board of
Registration for the
Healing Arts
P.O. Box 4
Jefferson City, MO 65102
314-751-2334

Montana Board of Medical
Examiners
1424 9th Avenue
Helena, MT 59620-0407
406-444-4284

Nebraska Board of
Examiners in Medicine
and Surgery
P.O. Box 95007
Lincoln, NE 68509
402-471-2115

Nevada Board of
Osteopathic Examiners
1198 Sweetwater Drive
Reno, NV 89509
702-826-8383

New Hampshire Board of
Registration in Medicine
Health and Welfare Building
Hazen Drive
Concord, NH 03301
603-271-1203

New Jersey Board of
Medical Examiners
28 West State Street, Room
602
Trenton, NJ 08608
609-292-4843

New Mexico Board of
Osteopathic Medical
Examiners
725 St. Michael's Drive
P.O. Box 25101
Santa Fe, NM 87504
505-827-7171

New York Board for
Medicine
New York State Education
Department
Cultural Education Center
Room 3023
New York State Plaza
Albany, NY 12230
518-474-3841

North Carolina Board of
Medical Examiners
1313 Navaho Drive
Raleigh, NC 27609
919-876-3885

North Dakota Board of
Medical Examiners
City Center Plaza, Suite
C-10
418 East Broad Way
Bismarck, ND 58501
701-223-9485

Ohio State Medical Board
77 South High Street, 17th
Floor
Columbus, OH 43266-0315
614-466-3934

Oklahoma Board of
Osteopathic Examiners
Suite 100
4848 North Lincoln
Boulevard

Oklahoma City, OK 73105
405-528-8625

Oregon State Board of
Medical Examiners
1500 Southwest 1st Avenue,
Room 620
Portland, OR 97201
503-229-5770

Pennsylvania Board of
Osteopathic Medical
Examiners
P.O. Box 2649
Harrisburg, PA 17105
717-783-7156

Puerto Rico Board of
Medical Examiners
Call Box 10200
Santurce, PR 00908
809-725-7903

Rhode Island Board of
Medical Licensure and
Discipline
Department of Health
Cannon Building, Room 205
3 Capitol Hill
Providence, RI 20908-5097
401-277-3855

South Carolina Board of
Medical Examiners
1220 Pickens Street
P.O. Box 12245
Columbia, SC 29201
803-734-8901

South Dakota Board of
Medical and Osteopathic
Examiners

1323 South Minnesota
Avenue
Sioux Falls, SD 57105
605-336-1965

Tennessee Board of
Osteopathic Examination
283 Plus Park Boulevard
Nashville, TN 37219-5407
615-367-6393

Texas Board of Medical
Examiners
P.O. Box 13562
Capitol Station
Austin, TX 78711
512-452-1078

Utah Department of
Commerce
Division of Occupational
and Professional Licensure
160 East 300 South
P.O. Box 45802
Salt Lake City, UT 84145-
0802
801-530-6628

Vermont Board of Osteo-
pathic Examination and
Registration
Secretary of State's Office
Pavilion Office Building
Montpelier, VT 05602
802-828-2673

Virgin Islands Department of
Health
Attn: Licensing
St. Thomas Hospital
St. Thomas, VI 00801
809-774-0117

Virginia State Board of Medicine
Department of Health Professionals
1601 Rolling Hills Drive
Richmond, VA 23229-5005
804-662-9908

Washington Division of Professional Licensing
P.O. Box 9012
Olympia, WA 98504
206-753-3095

West Virginia Board of Osteopathy
334 Penco Road
Weirton, WV 26062
304-723-4638

Wisconsin Medical Examin-
ing Board
P.O. Box 8935
Madison, WI 53708
608-266-2811

Wyoming Board of Medical
Examiners
Barrett Building, 3rd Floor
Cheyenne, WY 82002
307-777-6463

DENTAL LICENSING BOARDS

(In alphabetical order by state)

Alabama State Board of
 Dental Examiners
2308-B Starmount Circle
Huntsville, AL 35801
205-533-4638

Alaska State Board of
 Dental Examiners
Department of Commerce
Division of Occupational
 Licensing
P.O. Box D-LIC
Juneau, AK 99811-0800
907-465-2544

Arizona State Board of
 Dental Examiners
5060 North 19th Avenue,
 Suite 406
Phoenix, AZ 85015
602-255-3696

Arkansas State Board of
 Dental Examiners
Tower Building, Suite 1200

4th and Center Streets
Little Rock, AR 72201
501-682-2085

California State Board of
 Dental Examiners
1430 Howe Avenue, Suite
 85B
Sacramento, CA 95825
916-920-7451

Colorado State Board of
 Dental Examiners
1525 Sherman, Room 132
Denver, CO 80203
303-866-5807

Connecticut Department of
 Health Services
Medical Quality
 Assurance—Dental
150 Washington Street
Hartford, CT 06106
203-566-1027

Delaware State Board of
Dental Examiners
P.O. Box 1401
O'Neill Building
Dover, DE 19903
302-736-3029

District of Columbia
Department of Consumer
and Regulatory Affairs
614 H Street, N.W., Room
910
Washington, DC 20001
202-727-7823

Florida Department of
Professional Regulation
1940 North Monroe Street
Tallahassee, FL 32399-0750
904-488-6015

Georgia Board of Dentistry
166 Pryor Street, S.W.
Atlanta, GA 30303
404-656-3925

Hawaii State Professional
and Vocational Licensing
P.O. Box 3469
Honolulu, HI 96801
808-548-4100

Idaho State Board of
Dentistry
State House
Boise, ID 83720
208-334-2369

Illinois State Department of
Professional Regulation
Attn: Dental Unit
100 West Randolph Street,
Suite 9-300

Chicago, IL 60601
312-917-4481

Indiana Consumer Protection
Division
Health Professions Bureau
1 American Square, Suite
1020
Box 82067
Indianapolis, IN 46282
317-232-2960

Iowa State Board of Dental
Examiners
Executive Hills West
1209 East Court
Des Moines, IA 50319
515-281-5157

Kansas State Board of
Dental Examiners
Lower Level
4301 Huntoon, Suite 4
Topeka, KS 66604
913-273-0780

Kentucky State Board of
Dentistry
2106 Bardstown Road
Louisville, KY 40205
502-451-6832

Louisiana State Board of
Dental Examiners
1515 Poydras Street, Suite
2240
New Orleans, LA 70112
504-568-8574

Maine State Board of Dental
Examiners
State House Station 143

Augusta, ME 04333
207-289-3333

Maryland State Board of
   Dental Examiners
4201 Patterson Avenue
Baltimore, MD 21215-2299
301-764-4730

Massachusetts State Board
   of Registration in
   Dentistry
Investigative Unit
100 Cambridge Street, Room
   1509
Boston, MA 02202
617-727-7406

Michigan Department of
   Licensing and Regulation
Bureau of Health Services
Licensing Division
P.O. Box 30018
Lansing, MI 48909
517-373-6650
517-373-9196 (To file a
   complaint)

Minnesota Board of
   Dentistry
2700 University Avenue, W.,
   Suite 109
St. Paul, MN 55114
612-642-0579

Mississippi State Board of
   Dental Examiners
P.O. Box 1960
Clinton, MS 39060
601-924-9622

Missouri Dental Board
P.O. Box 1367

Jefferson City, MO 65102
314-751-2334

Montana Department of
   Commerce
1424 9th Avenue
Helena, MT 59620-0407
406-444-3745

Nebraska State Board of
   Dental Examiners
Bureau of Examining Boards
P.O. Box 95007
Lincoln, NE 68509-5007
402-471-2115

Nevada State Board of
   Dental Examiners
P.O. Box 80360
Las Vegas, NV 89180
702-258-4230

New Hampshire State Board
   of Dental Examiners
Health and Welfare Building
6 Hazen Drive
Concord, NH 03301
603-271-4561

New Jersey State Board of
   Dental Examiners
1100 Raymond Boulevard,
   Room 321
Newark, NJ 07102
201-648-7087

New Mexico State Board of
   Dental Examiners
P.O. Box 25101
Santa Fe, NM 87504
505-827-6207

New York State Education
Department
Office of Professional
Discipline
622 Third Avenue
New York, NY 10017
212-557-2100
800-442-8106

North Carolina State Board
of Dental Examiners
P.O. Box 32270
Raleigh, NC 27622
919-781-4901

North Dakota State Board of
Dental Examiners
P.O. Box 179
Valley City, ND 58072
701-845-3708

Ohio State Dental Board
77 South High Street, 18th
Floor
Columbus, OH 43266-0306
614-466-2580

Oklahoma State Board of
Governors of Registered
Dentists
2726 North Oklahoma
Oklahoma City, OK 73105
405-521-2350

Oregon Board of Dentistry
1515 Southwest 5th Avenue,
Suite 400
Portland, OR 97201
503-229-5520

Pennsylvania Department of
State

Bureau of Professional
Occupational Affairs
Dental Board, Complaint
Department
P.O. Box 2649
Harrisburg, PA 17105
717-787-8503
800-922-2113

Puerto Rico Board of Dental
Examiners
Department of Health
Call Box 10200
Santurce, PR 00908
809-723-1617

Rhode Island Department of
Health
Division of Professional
Regulation
3 Capitol Hill
Providence, RI 02908
401-277-2827

South Carolina State Board
of Dental Examiners
1315 Blanding Street
Columbia, SC 29201
803-734-8904

South Dakota State Board of
Dentistry
1708 Space Court
Rapid City, SD 57702
605-342-3026

Tennessee State Board of
Dental Examiners
283 Plus Park Boulevard
Nashville, TN 37219-5407
615-367-6228

Texas State Board of Dental
  Examiners
P.O. Box 13165
Capitol Station
Austin, TX 78711
512-834-6021

Utah Department of
  Commerce
160 East 300 South
P.O. Box 45802
Salt Lake City, UT 84145
801-530-6628

Vermont Secretary of State
  Office
Attn: Complaint Department
Pavilion Office Building
Montpelier, VT 05602
802-828-2390

Virgin Islands Department
  of Health
48 Sugar Estates
St. Thomas, VI 00802
809-774-0117

Virginia State Board of
  Dental Examiners
1601 Rolling Hills Drive
Richmond, VA 23229
804-662-9906

Washington State Dental
  Disciplinary Board
Department of Licensing
Program Management
  Division
P.O. Box 9012
Olympia, WA 98504-8001
206-753-1156

West Virginia Board of
  Dental Examiners
P.O. Drawer 1459
Beckley, WV 25802-1459
304-252-8266

Wisconsin State Board of
  Dental Examiners
Department of Regulation
  and Licensing
P.O. Box 8935
Madison, WI 53708
608-266-1396

Wyoming State Board of
  Dental Examiners
P.O. Box 1024
Powell, WY 82435
307-754-3476

MEDICAL SPECIALTY BOARDS: M.D.'S

Allergy and Immunology,
American Board of
University City Science
Center
3624 Market Street
Philadelphia, PA 19104
215-349-9466

Anesthesiology, American
Board of
100 Constitution Plaza,
Room 1668
Hartford, CT 06103
203-522-9857

Colon and Rectal Surgery,
American Board of
8750 Telegraph Road, Suite
410
Taylor, MI 48180
313-295-1740

Dermatology, American
Board of
Henry Ford Hospital

Detroit, MI 48202
313-871-8739

Emergency Medicine,
American Board of
200 Woodland Pass, Suite D
East Lansing, MI 48823
517-332-4800

Family Practice, American
Board of
2228 Young Drive
Lexington, KY 40505
606-269-5626

Internal Medicine, American
Board of
University City Science
Center
3624 Market Street
Philadelphia, PA 19104
215-243-1500

Neurological Surgery,
American Board of

Smith Tower
6550 Fannin Street, Suite
  2139
Houston, TX 77030-2701
713-790-6015

Nuclear Medicine, American
  Board of
900 Veteran Avenue, Room
  12-200
Los Angeles, CA 90024
213-825-6787

Obstetrics and Gynecology,
  American Board of
4225 Roosevelt Way, N.E.,
  Suite 305
Seattle, WA 98105
206-547-4884

Ophthalmology, American
  Board of
111 Presidential Boulevard,
  Suite 241
Bala Cynwyd, PA 19004
215-664-1175

Orthopedic Surgery,
  American Board of
737 North Michigan
  Avenue, Suite 1150
Chicago, IL 60611
312-664-9444

Otolaryngology, American
  Board of
5615 Kirby Drive, Suite 936
Houston, TX 77005
713-528-6200

Pathology, American Board
  of

5401 West Kennedy
  Boulevard, Suite 780
P.O. Box 25915
Tampa, FL 33622
813-286-2444

Pediatrics, American Board
  of
111 Silver Cedar Court
Chapel Hill, NC 27514
919-929-0461

Physical Medicine and
  Rehabilitation, American
  Board of
Nor'west Center, Suite 674
21 First Street, S.W.
Rochester, MN 55902
507-282-1776

Plastic Surgery, American
  Board of
7 Penn Center
1635 Market Street
Philadelphia, PA 19103-2204
215-587-9322

Preventive Medicine,
  American Board of
Department of Community
  Medicine
Wright State University
  School of Medicine
P.O. Box 927
Dayton, OH 45401
513-278-6915

Psychiatry and Neurology,
  American Board of
500 Lake Cook Road, Suite
  335
Deerfield, IL 60015
312-945-7900

Radiology, American Board
  of
300 Park, Suite 440
Birmingham, MI 48009
313-645-0600

Surgery, American Board of
1617 John F. Kennedy
  Boulevard, Suite 860
Philadelphia, PA 19103-1847
215-568-4000

Thoracic Surgery, American
  Board of
1 Rotary Center, Suite 803
Evanston, IL 60201
312-475-1520

Urology, American Board of
31700 Telegraph Road, Suite
  150
Birmingham, MI 48010
313-646-9720

Appendix E

MEDICAL SPECIALTY BOARDS: D.O.'S

Anesthesiology, American
Osteopathic Board of
17201 East 40 Highway,
Suite 204
Independence, MO 64055
816-373-4700

Dermatology, American
Osteopathic Board of
25510 Plymouth Road
Detroit, MI 48239
313-937-1200

Emergency Medicine,
American Osteopathic
Board of
Philadelphia Osteopathic
Medical Center
4190 City Avenue
Philadelphia, PA 19131
215-871-2811

General Practice, American
Osteopathic Board of

2474 Dempster Street, Suite
217
Des Plaines, IL 60016
312-635-8477

Internal Medicine, American
Osteopathic Board of
5200 South Ellis Avenue
Chicago, IL 60615
312-947-4880

Neurology and Psychiatry,
American Osteopathic
Board of
Department of Psychiatry
401 Haddon Avenue
Camden, NJ 08103-1505
609-757-7765

Nuclear Medicine, American
Osteopathic Board of
5200 South Ellis Avenue
Chicago, IL 60615
312-947-4490

Obstetrics and Gynecology,
American Osteopathic
Board of
Ohio University College of
Osteopathic Medicine
Grosvenor Hall, West 064
Athens, OH 45701
614-593-2239

Ophthalmology and
Otorhinolaryngology,
American Osteopathic
Board of
405 Grand Avenue
Dayton, OH 45405
513-222-4213

Orthopedic Surgery,
American Osteopathic
Board of
5155 Raytown Road, Suite
103
Kansas City, MO 64133
816-353-6400

Pathology, American
Osteopathic Board of
13355 East Ten Mile Road
Warren, MI 48089
313-759-7565

Pediatrics, American
Osteopathic Board of
2700 River Road, Suite 407
Des Plaines, IL 60018
312-635-0201

Preventive Medicine,
American Osteopathic
Board of
12535 Lt. Nichols Road
Fairfax, VA 22033
703-648-3834

Proctology, American
Osteopathic Board of
75 Skylark Road
Springfield, NJ 07081
201-687-2062

Radiology, American
Osteopathic Board of
Route 2, Box 75
Milan, MO 63556
816-265-4991

Rehabilitation Medicine,
American Osteopathic
Board of
9058 West Church
Des Plaines, IL 60016
312-699-0048

Surgery, American
Osteopathic Board of
405 Grand Avenue
Dayton, OH 45405
513-226-2656

DENTAL SPECIALTY BOARDS

Endodontics, American
  Board of
211 East Chicago Avenue,
  Suite 1501
Chicago, IL 60611
312-266-7310

Oral and Maxillofacial
  Surgery, American Board of
625 North Michigan
  Avenue, Suite 1820
Chicago, IL 60611
312-642-0070

Oral Pathology, American
  Board of
5401 West Kennedy
  Boulevard
P.O. Box 25915
Tampa, FL 33622
813-286-2444

Orthodontics, American
  Board of
225 South Meramec Avenue,
  Room 310

St. Louis, MO 63105
314-727-5039

Pediatric Dentistry,
  American Board of
Indiana University
School of Dentistry
1193 Woodgate Drive
Carmel, IN 46032
317-573-0877

Periodontology, American
  Board of
University of Southern
  California
School of Dentistry
925 West 34th Street
Los Angeles, CA 90089
213-743-2800

Prosthodontics, American
  Board of
4707 Olley Lane
Fairfax, VA 22032
703-273-7323

Nursing Home Licensing Offices

(In alphabetical order by state)

Alabama Nursing Home
  Licensure Office
Division of Licensure and
  Certification
Alabama Department of
  Health
434 Monroe Street
Montgomery, AL
  36130-1701
205-261-5113

Alaska Nursing Home
  Licensure Office
Department of Health and
  Social Services
Health Facilities Certification
  and Licensing
4433 Business Park
  Boulevard, Building M
Anchorage, AK 99503
907-561-2171

Arizona Department of
  Health Services

Office of Health Care
  Licensure
701 East Jefferson Street,
  Suite 300
Phoenix, AZ 85034
602-255-1177

Arkansas Department of
  Health
Certification and Licensure
  Section
Office of Long Term Care
P.O. Box 8059
Little Rock, AR 72203-8059
501-682-8430

California Nursing Home
  Licensure Office
Licensure and Certification
  Unit
714-744 P Street
Sacramento, CA 95814
916-445-3281

Colorado Nursing Home
  Licensure Office
Colorado Department of
  Health
Health Facilities Division
Evaluation and Licensure
  Section
4210 East 11th Avenue,
  Room 254
Denver, CO 80220
303-331-4930

Connecticut Nursing Home
  Licensure Office
Connecticut State
  Department of Health
Division of Hospital and
  Medical Care
150 Washington Street
Hartford, CT 06106
203-566-5758

Delaware Office of Health
  Facility Licensing and
  Certification
Nursing Home Division
Division of Public Health
3000 Newport Gap Pike
Wilmington, DE 19808
302-571-3499

District of Columbia Office
  of Licensing and
  Certification
Nursing Home Division
Department of Consumer
  Regulatory Affairs
Service Facility Regulation
614 H Street, N.W., Suite
  1014
Washington, DC 20001
202-727-7190

Florida Nursing Home
  Licensure Office
Licensure and Certification
  Branch
Division of Health
Department of
  Rehabilitation Services
2727 Mahan Drive
Tallahassee, FL 32308
904-487-3513

Georgia Nursing Home
  Licensure Office
Standards and Licensure
  Unit
Office of Regulatory Services
878 Peachtree Street, N.E.,
  Suite 803
Atlanta, GA 30309
404-894-5137

Hawaii Nursing Home
  Licensure Office
Hospital and Medical
  Facility Branch
Hawaii State Department of
  Health
P.O. Box 3378
Honolulu, HI 96801
808-548-5935

Idaho Nursing Home
  Licensure Office
Facilities Standards and
  Development
Idaho Department of Health
  and Welfare
450 West State Street, 2nd
  Floor
Boise, ID 83720
208-334-6626

Illinois Nursing Home
  Licensure Office
Illinois Department of Public
  Health
Long Term Care Quality
  Assurance
525 West Jefferson, 5th
  Floor
Springfield, IL 62761
217-782-5180

Indiana Nursing Home
  Licensure Office
Division of Health Facilities
Indiana State Board of
  Health
1330 West Michigan Street
P.O. Box 1964
Indianapolis, IN 46206-1964
317-633-8442

Iowa Nursing Home
  Licensure Office
Division of Health Facilities
Lucas State Office Building
Des Moines, IA 50319
515-281-4115
800-523-3213

Kansas Department of
  Health and Environment
Bureau of Adult and Child
  Care
Landon State Office Building
900 Southwest Jackson,
  Suite 1001
Topeka, KS 66612-1290
913-296-1240

Kentucky Office of the
  Inspector General
Division for Licensing and
  Regulation

CHR Building, 4th Floor
  East
275 East Main Street
Frankfort, KY 40621
502-564-2800

Louisiana Nursing Home
  Licensure Office
DHH Department of Health
  and Human Resources
Bureau of Health Services
Financing Health Standards
  Section
P.O. Box 3767
Baton Rouge, LA
  70821-3767
504-342-5774

Maine Nursing Home
  Licensure Office
Division of Licensure and
  Certification
249 Western Avenue
State House Station 11
Augusta, ME 04333
207-289-2606

Maryland Department of
  Health and Mental
  Hygiene
Office of Licensing and
  Certification Program
Metro Executive Center
4201 Patterson Avenue
Baltimore, MD 21215
301-764-2770

Massachusetts Nursing
  Home Licensure Office
Long-Term Care Facilities
  Program
Department of Public Health

80 Boylston Street, 11th
Floor
Boston, MA 02116
617-727-5864

Michigan Home Licensure
Office
Bureau of Health Facilities
Department of Public Health
3423 North Logan Street
P.O. Box 30195
Lansing, MI 48909
517-335-8505

Minnesota Nursing Home
Licensure Office
Minnesota Department of
Health
Survey and Compliance
Section
393 North Dunlap Street
P.O. Box 64900
St. Paul, MN 55164-0900
612-643-2101

Mississippi Nursing Home
Licensure Office
Health Facilities Certification
and Licensure
Mississippi State Board of
Health
P.O. Box 1700
Jackson, MS 39215
601-960-7769

Missouri Department of
Social Services
Division of Aging
P.O. Box 1337
1440 Aaron Court
Jefferson City, MO 65102
314-751-2712

Montana Department of
Health and Environmental
Sciences
Licensing and Certification
Bureau
Health Services Division
Cogswell Building
Helena, MT 59620
406-444-2037

Nebraska Department of
Health
Bureau of Health Facility
Standards
301 Centennial Mall South
P.O. Box 95007
Lincoln, NE 68509
402-471-2946

Nevada Bureau of
Regulatory Health
Services
505 East King Street, Room
202
Carson City, NV 89710
702-885-4475

New Hampshire Department
of Health and Human
Services
Division of Public Health
Bureau of Health Facilities
Administration
6 Hazen Drive
Concord, NH 03301
603-271-4592

New Jersey Nursing Home
Licensure Office
New Jersey State
Department of Health
Licensing Certification and
Standards

CN 367
Trenton, NJ 08625-0367
609-588-7726

New Mexico Nursing Home
    Licensure Office
Health and Environment
    Department
Public Health Division
Licensing and Certification
    Bureau
Harold Runnels Building,
    North 1300
1190 St. Francis Drive
Santa Fe, NM 87503
505-827-2434

New York State Department
    of Health
Bureau of Long Term Care
    Services
Corning, Second Tower,
    Room 1882
Empire State Plaza
Albany, NY 12237
518-473-1564

North Carolina Nursing
    Home Licensure Office
Licensure and Certification
    Section
Health Care Facilities Branch
701 Barbour Drive
Raleigh, NC 27603
919-733-2786

North Dakota Division of
    Health Facilities
State Department of Health
    and Consolidated
    Laboratories
Judicial Wing, 2nd Floor

600 East Boulevard
Bismarck, ND 58505-0200
701-224-2352

Ohio Nursing Home
    Licensure Office
Bureau of Medical Services
Licensing and Certification
    Division
Ohio Department of Health,
    8th Floor
246 North High Street, Box
    118
Columbus, OH 43266-0118
614-466-2070

Oklahoma Nursing Home
    Licensure Office
Special Health Services
Oklahoma State Department
    of Health
P.O. Box 53551
Oklahoma City, OK 73152
405-271-6868

Oregon Senior Services
    Division
Long Term Care Licensing
Licensing and Certification
313 Public Service Building
Salem, OR 97310
503-378-3751

Pennsylvania Nursing Home
    Licensure Office
Commonwealth of
    Pennsylvania
Division of Long-Term Care
Health and Welfare
    Building, Room 526
Harrisburg, PA 17120
717-787-1816

Rhode Island Nursing Home
  Licensure Office
Rhode Island Department of
  Health
Division of Facilities
  Regulation
3 Capitol Hill
Providence, RI 02908
401-277-2566

South Carolina Nursing
  Home Licensure Office
Division of Health Facilities
  and Services
Department of Health
  Licensing
2600 Bull Street
Columbia, SC 29201
803-734-4680

South Dakota Department
  of Health
Division of Public Health
Division of Licensure and
  Certification
523 East Capitol Street
Pierre, SD 57501
605-773-3364

Tennessee Department of
  Health and Environment
Board of Licensing Health
  Care Facilities
283 Plus Park Boulevard
Nashville, TN 37219-5407
615-367-6303

Texas Nursing Home
  Licensure Office
Texas Department of Health
Licensing Division
1100 West 49th Street,
  Room T201

Austin, TX 78756-3188
512-458-7490

Utah Nursing Home
  Licensure Office
Utah Department of Health
Bureau of Health Facilities
  Licensing
P.O. Box 16660
Salt Lake City, UT
  84116-0660
801-538-6152

Vermont Nursing Home
  Licensure Office
Vermont Department of
  Rehabilitation and Aging
Medical Care Regulations
P.O. Box 70
Burlington, VT 05402
802-863-7250

Virginia Nursing Home
  Licensure Office
Division of Licensure and
  Certification
1013 Madison Building
109 Governor Street
Richmond, VA 23219
804-786-2081

Washington Nursing Home
  Licensure Office
DSHS-Health Services
  Division
Aging and Adult Services
  Administration
623 8th Avenue, S.E.
Mail Stop HB-11
Olympia, WA 98504-0095
206-753-5840

West Virginia Nursing
   Home Licensure Office
Health Facilities and
   Licensure Certification
   Section
1900 Kanawha Boulevard
Building 3, Room 535
Charleston, WV 25305
304-348-0050

Wisconsin Department of
   Health and Social Services
Division of Health
Bureau of Quality
   Compliance
1 West Wilson Street, Room
   150
P.O. Box 309
Madison, WI 53701
608-266-3024

Wyoming Department of
   Health and Social Services
Division of Health and
   Medical Services
Medical Facilities
Hathaway Building, 4th
   Floor
Cheyenne, WY 82002-0710
307-777-7121

NURSING HOME OMBUDSMAN OFFICES

(In alphabetical order by state)

Alabama Commission on
  Aging
136 Cotoma Street
Montgomery, AL 36130
205-261-5743

Alaska Older Alaskan's
  Commission
Department of
  Administration
2600 Denali Street, Suite 403
Anchorage, AK 99503
907-279-2232

Arizona Aging and Adult
  Administration
Department of Economic
  Security
1400 West Washington
  Street
Phoenix, AZ 85007
602-542-4446

Arkansas Division of Aging
  and Adult Services
Department of Human
  Services
Donaghey Building
7th and Main Streets
Little Rock, AR 72201
501-682-2441

California Department of
  Aging
Office of the Long-Term
  Care Ombudsman
1600 K Street
Sacramento, CA 95814
916-322-3887
800-231-4024

Colorado Long-Term Care
  Ombudsman
455 Sherman Street, Suite
  130
Denver, CO 80203
303-722-0300

Connecticut Department on
Aging
175 Main Street
Hartford, CT 06106
203-566-7770

Delaware Division of Aging
(North)
Delaware State Hospital
1901 North Dupont
Highway
C.T. Building, 2nd Floor
New Castle, DE 19720
302-421-6791

Delaware Division of Aging
(South)
Milford State Services
Center
11–13 Church Street
Milford, DE 19963
302-422-1386

District of Columbia Office
of Aging
1424 K Street, N.W., 2nd
Floor
Washington, DC 20005
202-724-5622

Florida State Long-Term
Care Ombudsman Council
1317 Winewood Boulevard
Building 1, Room 308
Tallahassee, FL 32399-0700
904-488-6190

Georgia Office of Aging
Department of Human
Resources
878 Peachtree Street, N.E.,
Room 642

Atlanta, GA 30309
404-894-5336

Hawaii Executive Office on
Aging
Office of the Governor
335 Merchant Street, Room
241
Honolulu, HI 96813
808-548-2593

Idaho Office on Aging
Statehouse, Room 108
Boise, ID 83720
208-334-3833

Illinois Department on
Aging
421 East Capitol Avenue
Springfield, IL 62701
217-785-3140

Indiana Department of
Human Services
251 North Illinois
P.O. Box 7083
Indianapolis, IN 46207-7083
317-232-1223
800-622-4484

Iowa Department of Elder
Affairs
914 Grand Avenue
236 Jewett Building
Des Moines, IA 50319
515-281-5187

Kansas Department on
Aging
Docking State Office
Building

915 Southwest Harrison,
  Room 122-S
Topeka, KS 66612-1500
913-296-4986

Kentucky Department of
  Social Services
Division of Aging Services
CHR Building, 6 West
275 East Main Street
Frankfort, KY 40621
502-564-6930

Louisiana Governor's Office
  of Elderly Affairs
4550 North Boulevard
P.O. Box 80374
Baton Rouge, LA
  70898-0374
504-925-1700

Maine Long-Term Care
  Ombudsman Program
Maine Committee on Aging
State House Station 127
Augusta, ME 04333
207-289-3658

Maryland Office on Aging
301 West Preston Street,
  Room 1004
Baltimore, MD 21201
301-225-1083

Massachusetts Executive
  Offices Elder Affairs
38 Chauncy Street
Boston, MA 02111
617-727-7750

Michigan Citizens for Better
  Care

David Whitney Building,
  Suite 525
1553 Woodward
Detroit, MI 48226
313-962-5968

Minnesota Board on Aging
Human Services Building
444 Lafayette Road
St. Paul, MN 55155-3843
612-296-2770

Mississippi Aging and Adult
  Services
421 West Pascagoula Street
Jackson, MS 89203-3524
601-949-2029

Missouri Division of Aging
Department of Social
  Services
2701 West Main Street
Jefferson City, MO 65102
314-751-3082

Montana Seniors Office
Legal and Ombudsman
  Services
P.O. Box 232
Capitol Station
Helena, MT 59620
406-444-4676

Nebraska Department on
  Aging
P.O. Box 95044
Lincoln, NE 68509
402-471-2307

Nevada Division for Aging
  Services
505 East King Street, Room
  101

Carson City, NV 89710
702-885-4210

New Hampshire Long-Term
 Care Ombudsman
 Program
Department of Elderly and
 Adult Services
6 Hazen Drive, 3rd Floor
 East
Concord, NH 03301-6508
603-271-4375

New Jersey Ombudsman for
 the Institutionalized
 Elderly
28 West State Street, Room
 305
Trenton, NJ 08625
609-292-8016

New Mexico State Agency
 on Aging
224 East Palace Avenue, 4th
 Floor
Santa Fe, NM 87501
505-827-7640

New York State Office for
 Aging
Agency Building Number 2,
 2nd Floor
Empire State Plaza
Albany, NY 12223
518-474-7329

North Carolina Division of
 Aging
1985 Umstead Drive
Raleigh, NC 27603
919-733-3983

North Dakota Long-Term
 Care Ombudsman
Aging Services Division
State Capitol
600 East Boulevard
Bismarck, ND 58505-0250
701-224-2577

Ohio Department on Aging
State Ombudsman
50 West Broad Street, 9th
 Floor
Columbus, OH 43266-0501
614-466-1220

Oklahoma Department of
 Human Services
Long-Term Care
 Ombudsman
312 Northeast 28th
Oklahoma City, OK 73125
405-521-2281

Oregon Long-Term Care
 Ombudsman's Office
Building B, Suite 9
2475 Lancaster Drive, N.E.
Salem, OR 97310
503-378-6533

Pennsylvania Department of
 Aging
Bureau of Program and Field
 Operations
231 State Street
Harrisburg, PA 17101
717-783-7247

Rhode Island Department of
 Elderly Affairs
160 Pine Street
Providence, RI 02903
401-277-2894

South Carolina Governor's
Office Ombudsman
Division
Edgar A. Brown Building
1205 Pendleton Street
Columbia, SC 29201
803-734-0457

South Dakota Office of
Adult Services and Aging
State Ombudsman
700 Governor's Drive
Pierre, SD 57501-2291
605-773-3656

Tennessee Commission on
Aging
706 Church Street, Suite 201
Nashville, TN 37219
615-741-2056

Texas Department on Aging
P.O. Box 12786
Austin, TX 78711
512-444-2727

Utah State Division of
Aging and Adult Services
Long-Term Care Ombudsman
120 North 200 West, Room
401
Salt Lake City, UT 84103
801-538-3929

Vermont Department of
Rehabilitation and Aging
Long-Term Care
Ombudsman Program
103 South Main Street
Waterbury, VT 05676
802-241-2400
800-642-5119

Virginia Department for the
Aging
700 Center, 10th Floor
700 East Franklin Street
Richmond, VA 23219-2327
804-225-2271
800-552-3402

Washington State
Long-Term Care
Ombudsman
1200 South 336th Street
Federal Way, WA 98003
206-838-6810

West Virginia Commission
on Aging
State Capitol Complex
Charleston, WV 25305
304-348-3317

Wisconsin Governor's
Ombudsman Program for
the Aging and Disabled
819 North 6th, Room 619
Milwaukee, WI 53203
414-227-4386

Wyoming Long-Term Care
Ombudsman
P.O. Box 94
Wheatlyn, WY 82201
307-322-5553

Appendix I

STATE HEALTH DEPARTMENTS

(In alphabetical order by state)

Alabama Department of
  Public Health
State Office Building
501 Dexter Avenue
Mail to: 434 Monroe Street
Montgomery, AL
  36130-1701
205-242-5095

Alaska Department of
  Health and Social Services
Alaska Office Building,
  Room 503
350 Main Street
Pouch H-06
Juneau, AK 99811-0610
907-465-3030

Arizona Department of
  Health Services
1740 West Adams Street
Phoenix, AZ 85007
602-542-1024

Arkansas Department of
  Health
State Health Building
4815 West Markham Street
Little Rock, AR 72205-3867
501-661-2112

California Department of
  Health Services
714 P Street, Room 1253
Sacramento, CA 95814
916-445-1248

Colorado Department of
  Health
4210 East 11th Avenue
Denver, CO 80220
303-331-4602

Connecticut Department of
  Health Services
150 Washington Street
Hartford, CT 06106
203-566-2038

Delaware Division of Public
    Health
Department of Health and
    Social Services
Jessie S. Cooper Building
P.O. Box 637
Dover, DE 19901
302-736-4701

District of Columbia
    Department of Human
    Services
Commission of Public
    Health
1660 L Street, N.W., 12th
    Floor
Washington, DC 20036
202-673-7700

Florida Health Program
    Office
Department of Health and
    Rehabilitative Services
1323 Winewood Boulevard,
    Building 1, Room 115
Tallahassee, FL 32399-0700
904-488-4115

Georgia Division of Public
    Health
Department of Human
    Resources
878 Peachtree Street, N.E.,
    Suite 201
Atlanta, GA 30309
404-894-7505

Hawaii Department of
    Health
Kinau Hale
1250 Punchbowl Street
P.O. Box 3378

Honolulu, HI 96801
808-548-6505

Idaho Bureau of Preventive
    Medicine
Division of Health
Department of Health and
    Welfare
Towers Building, 4th Floor
450 West State Street
Boise, ID 83720
208-334-5930

Illinois Department of Public
    Health
535 West Jefferson Street
Springfield, IL 62761
217-782-4977

Indiana State Board of
    Health
1330 West Michigan Street
P.O. Box 1964
Indianapolis, IN 46206-1964
317-633-8400

Iowa Department of Public
    Health
Lucas State Office Building
East 12th and Walnut
    Streets
Des Moines, IA 50319
515-281-5605

Kansas Division of Health
Department of Health and
    Environment
Forbes Field, Building 740
Topeka, KS 66620
913-296-1500

Kentucky Department for
    Health Services

Cabinet for Human
Resources
Health Services Building, 1st
Floor
275 East Main Street
Frankfort, KY 40621
502-564-3970

Louisiana Department of
Hospitals
Department of Health and
Human Resources
Office of Public Health
Services
325 Loyola Avenue
P.O. Box 60630
New Orleans, LA 70160
504-568-5052

Maine Bureau of Health
Department of Human
Services
157 Capitol Street
State House Station 11
Augusta, ME 04333
207-289-3201

Maryland Department of
Health and Mental
Hygiene
Herbert R. O'Conor State
Office Building
201 West Preston Street
Baltimore, MD 21201
301-225-6500

Massachusetts Department
of Public Health
150 Tremont Street
Boston, MA 02111
617-727-0201

Michigan Department of
Public Health
Baker-Olin West Building
3423 North Logan Street
P.O. Box 30195
Lansing, MI 48909
517-335-8000

Minnesota Department of
Health
717 Delaware Street, S.E.
P.O. Box 9441
Minneapolis, MN 55440
612-623-5460

Mississippi Department of
Health
2423 North State Street
P.O. Box 1700
Jackson, MS 39215-1700
601-960-7400

Missouri Department of
Health
P.O. Box 570
Jefferson City, MO 65102
314-751-6001

Montana Department of
Health and Environmental
Sciences
Cogswell Building, Room
C108
Helena, MT 59620
406-444-2544

Nebraska Department of
Health
State Office Building
301 Centennial Mall, South
P.O. Box 95007

Lincoln, NE 68509
402-471-2133

Nevada Health Division
Department of Human
  Resources
Kinkead Building
505 East King Street
Carson City, NV 89710
702-885-4740

New Hampshire Division of
  Public Health Services
Department of Health and
  Human Services
Health and Welfare Services
  Building
6 Hazen Drive
Concord, NH 03301-6527
603-271-4501

New Jersey Department of
  Health
Health and Agriculture
  Building
John Fitch Plaza
CN 360
Trenton, NJ 08625
609-292-7837

New Mexico Division of
  Public Health
Health and Environment
  Department
Harold Runnels Building
1190 St. Francis Drive
Santa Fe, NM 87503
505-827-0020

New York Department of
  Health
Corning Tower, Room 1408
Empire State Plaza

Albany, NY 12237
518-474-2011

North Carolina Department
  of Environmental Health
  and Natural Resources
Office of the State Health
  Director
Archdale Building
512 North Salisbury Street
P.O. Box 27687
Raleigh, NC 27611
919-733-3446

North Dakota Department
  of Health
State Capitol
600 East Boulevard Avenue
Bismarck, ND 58505-0200
701-224-2372

Ohio Department of Health
246 North High Street
Columbus, OH 43226-0588
614-466-3543

Oklahoma Department of
  Health
1000 Northeast 10th Street
P.O. Box 53551
Oklahoma City, OK 73152
405-271-4200

Oregon Health Division
Department of Human
  Resources
State Office Building, Room
  811
1400 Southwest 5th Avenue
P.O. Box 231
Portland, OR 97207
503-229-5032

Pennsylvania Department of
Health
Health and Welfare
Building, Room 802
Commonwealth Avenue and
Forster Street
P.O. Box 90
Harrisburg, PA 17108
717-787-6436

Puerto Rico Department of
Health
Call Box 70184
San Juan, PR 00936
809-250-7227

Rhode Island Department of
Health
Cannon Building, Room 401
3 Capitol Hill
Providence, RI 02908
401-277-2231

South Carolina Department
of Health and
Environmental Control
2600 Bull Street
Columbia, SC 29201
803-734-4880

South Dakota Department
of Health
Joe Foss Building
523 East Capitol Avenue
Pierre, SD 57501
605-773-3361

Tennessee Department of
Health and Environment
Cordell Hull Building, Room
344
Nashville, TN 37219
615-741-3111

Texas Department of Health
1100 West 49th Street
Austin, TX 78756-3199
512-458-7375

Utah Department of Health
288 North 1460 West
Salt Lake City, UT
84116-0700
801-538-6101

Vermont Department of
Health
Agency of Human Services
60 Main Street
P.O. Box 70
Burlington, VT 05402
802-863-7280

Department of Health
James Madison Building
109 Governor Street
Richmond, VA 23219
804-786-3561

Virgin Islands Department
of Health
St. Thomas Hospital
Charlotte Amalie
St. Thomas, VI 00802
809-774-0117

Washington Division of
Health
Department of Health
1112 South Quince Street
Mail Stop ET-21
Olympia, WA 98504
206-753-5871

West Virginia Department
of Health

State Office Building 3,
  Room 206
1800 Washington Street, E.
Charleston, WV 25305
304-348-2971

Wisconsin Division of
  Health
Department of Health and
  Social Services
Wilson Street State Office
  Building
1 West Wilson Street
P.O. Box 309
Madison, WI 53701-0309
608-266-7568

Wyoming Department of
  Health and Social Services
Hathaway Building
2300 Capitol Avenue
Cheyenne, WY 82002-0710
307-777-7656

Appendix J

STATE INSURANCE DEPARTMENTS

(In alphabetical order by state)

Alabama Insurance
  Department
Retirement Systems Building
135 South Union Street
Montgomery, AL
  36130-3401
205-269-3550

Alaska Division of Insurance
Department of Commerce
  and Economic
  Development
State Office Building, 9th
  Floor
333 Willoughby Avenue
P.O. Box D
Juneau, AK 99801-0800
907-465-2515

Arizona Insurance
  Department
3030 North 3rd Street
Phoenix, AZ 85012
602-255-5400

Arkansas Insurance
  Commissioner's Office
University Tower Building,
  Room 400
12th Street and University
  Avenue
Little Rock, AR 72204
501-371-1325

California Department of
  Insurance
3450 Wilshire Boulevard
Los Angeles, CA 90010
213-736-2551

Colorado Division of
  Insurance
Department of Regulatory
  Agencies
First Western Plaza Building,
  Room 500
303 West Colfax Avenue
Denver, CO 80204
303-866-6400

Connecticut Insurance
  Department
State Office Building, Room
  425
165 Capitol Avenue
Hartford, CT 06106
203-297-3800

Delaware Insurance
  Department
Rodney Building, Suite 100
841 Silver Lake Boulevard
Dover, DE 19901
302-739-4251
800-282-8611

District of Columbia
  Insurance Administration
Department of Consumer
  and Regulatory Affairs
P.O. Box 37200
Washington, DC 20013-7200
202-727-8001

Florida Department of
  Insurance
The Capitol, Plaza Level 11
Tallahassee, FL 32399-0300
202-727-7424

Georgia Office of
  Commissioner of
  Insurance
716 West Tower, Floyd
  Building
2 Martin Luther King, Jr.
  Drive
Atlanta, GA 30334
404-656-2056

Hawaii Insurance Division
Department of Commerce
  and Consumer Affairs

250 South King Street
P.O. Box 3614
Honolulu, HI 96811
808-586-2790

Idaho Department of
  Insurance
State Capitol Building
500 South 10th Street
Boise, ID 83720
208-334-2250

Illinois Department of
  Insurance
Bicentennial Building
320 West Washington Street
Springfield, IL 62767
217-782-4515

Indiana Department of
  Insurance
311 West Washington
  Street, Suite 300
Indianapolis, IN 46204
317-232-2385

Iowa Division of Insurance
Department of Commerce
Lucas State Office Building
East 12th and Grand Avenue
Des Moines, IA 50319
515-281-5705

Kansas Insurance
  Department
420 West 9th Street
Topeka, KS 66612
913-296-7801

Kentucky Department of
  Insurance
Fitzgerald Building
229 West Main Street

P.O. Box 517
Frankfort, KY 40602
502-564-3630

Louisiana Department of
Insurance
Insurance Building
950 North 5th Street
P.O. Box 94214
Baton Rouge, LA
    70804-9214
504-342-5900

Maine Bureau of Insurance
Department of Professional
    and Financial Regulation
State House Station 34
Augusta, ME 04333
207-582-8707

Maryland Insurance Division
Department of Licensing and
    Regulation
Stanbalt Building
501 St. Paul Place
Baltimore, MD 21202
410-333-2520

Massachusetts Division of
    Insurance
280 Friend Street
Boston, MA 02114
617-727-7189

Michigan Insurance Bureau
Department of Licensing and
    Regulation
Ottawa Building North
611 West Ottawa Street
P.O. Box 30220
Lansing, MI 48909
517-373-9273

Minnesota Department of
    Commerce
Metro Square Building,
    Room 500
7th and Robert Streets
St. Paul, MN 55101
612-296-2488

Mississippi Insurance
    Department
1804 Sillers Building
550 High Street
P.O. Box 79
Jackson, MS 39205
601-359-3569

Missouri Company
    Regulation
Division of Insurance
Department of Economic
    Development
Harry S. Truman State
    Office Building, Room 630
301 West High Street
P.O. Box 690
Jefferson City, MO 65102
314-751-4126

Montana State Auditor
    Office
P.O. Box 4009
Helena, MT 59604-4009
406-444-2040

Nebraska Department of
    Insurance
State Office Building
941 O Street, Suite 400
Lincoln, NE 68508
402-471-2201

Nevada Insurance Division
Department of Commerce
1665 Hotsprings Road
Carson City, NV 89710
702-687-4270

New Hampshire Insurance
   Department
169 Manchester Street
Concord, NH 03301
603-271-2261

New Jersey Division of
   Administration
Department of Insurance
Arnold Constable Building,
   Room 307
20 West State Street
Trenton, NJ 08625
609-292-5363

New Mexico Department of
   Insurance
495 Old Santa Fe Trail
Paseo de Peralta
P.O. Drawer 1269
Santa Fe, NM 87504-1269
505-827-4500

New York Insurance
   Department
160 West Broadway
New York, NY 10013
212-602-0429

North Carolina Agent
   Services and Consumer
   Division
Department of Insurance
Dobbs Building
430 North Salisbury Street
P.O. Box 26387

Raleigh, NC 27611
919-733-7343

North Dakota Insurance
   Department
State Capitol, 5th Floor
Bismarck, ND 58505
701-224-2440

Ohio Department of
   Insurance
2100 Stella Court
Columbus, OH 43266-0566
614-644-2651

Oklahoma Insurance
   Department
State Insurance Building
1901 North Walnut
   Boulevard
P.O. Box 53408
Oklahoma City, OK
   73152-3408
405-521-2828

Oregon Insurance and
   Finance Division
21 Labor and Industry
   Building
Salem, OR 97310
503-378-4271

Pennsylvania Division of
   Consumer Affairs and
   Enforcement
Department of Insurance
1321 Strawberry Square
Harrisburg, PA 17120
717-787-5173

Puerto Rico Office of the
   Insurance Commissioner

Cobian's Plaza
1607 Ponce de Leon Avenue,
    Stop 23
P.O. Box 8330
Fernandez Juncos Station
Santurce, PR 00910
809-722-8686

Rhode Island Department of
    Business Regulation
Director and Insurance
    Commissioner
233 Richmond Street, Suite
    233
Providence, RI 02903
401-277-2246

South Carolina Department
    of Insurance
1612 Marion Street
P.O. Box 100105
Columbia, SC 29202-3105
803-737-6117

South Dakota Division of
    Insurance
910 East Sioux Avenue
Pierre, SD 57501-3940
605-773-3563

Tennessee Department of
    Commerce and Insurance
500 James Robertson
    Parkway
Nashville, TN 37243-0565
615-741-2241

Texas State Board of
    Insurance
1110 San Jacinto Boulevard
Austin, TX 78701-1998
512-463-6501

Utah Insurance Department
Heber M. Wells Building
160 East 300 South
P.O. Box 45803
Salt Lake City, UT 84145
801-530-6400

Vermont Department of
    Banking and Insurance
State Office Building
120 State Street
Montpelier, VT 05602
802-828-3301

Virgin Islands Office of the
    Lieutenant Governor
Lieutenant Governor's Office
    Building
18 Kongen Gade
Charlotte Amalie
St. Thomas, VI 00801
809-774-2991

Virginia Bureau of Insurance
State Corporation
    Commission
Jefferson Building
1220 Bank Street
P.O. Box 1157
Richmond, VA 23209
804-786-3741

Washington Office of the
    Insurance Commissioner
Insurance Building, Room
    200
Mail Stop AQ-21
Olympia, WA 98504
206-753-7301

West Virginia Department
    of Insurance

2019 Washington Street, E.
Charleston, WV 25305
304-348-3394

Wisconsin Office of the
  Commissioner of
  Insurance
Loraine Building
123 West Washington
  Avenue
P.O. Box 7873
Madison, WI 53707
608-266-3585

Wyoming Insurance
  Department
Herschler Building, 3rd Floor
122 West 25th Street
Cheyenne, WY 82002
307-777-7401

Appendix K

STATE MEDICAID OFFICES

(In alphabetical order by state)

Alabama Medicaid Director
Alabama Medicaid Agency
2500 Fairlane Drive
Montgomery, AL 36110
205-277-2710

Alaska Medicaid Director
Division of Medical
  Assistance
Department of Health and
  Social Services
P.O. Box H-07
Juneau, AK 99811-0601

Arizona Medicaid Director
Arizona Health Care Cost
  Containment System
  (AHCCCS)
801 East Jefferson
Phoenix, AZ 85034
602-234-3655 (Ext. 4053)

Arkansas Medicaid Director
Office of Medical Services

Arkansas Department of
  Human Services
P.O. Box 1437, Slot 1100
Little Rock, AR 72203-1437
501-682-8292

California Medicaid Director
Medical Care Services
Department of Health
  Services
714 P Street, Room 1253
Sacramento, CA 95814
916-322-5824

Colorado Medicaid Director
Bureau of Medical Services
Department of Social
  Services
1575 Sherman, 6th Floor
Denver, CO 80203-1714
303-866-5901

Connecticut Medicaid
  Director
Medical Care Administration

Department of Income
  Maintenance
110 Bartholomew Avenue
Hartford, CT 06106
203-566-2934

Delaware Medicaid Director
Department of Health and
  Social Services
Delaware State Hospital
New Castle, DE 19720
302-421-6139

District of Columbia
Washington, D.C. Medicaid
  Director
Office of Health Care
  Financing
D.C. Department of Human
  Services
1331 H. Street, N.W., Suite
  500
Washington, DC 20005
202-727-0735

Florida Medicaid Director
Assistant Secretary for
  Medicaid
Department of Health and
  Rehabilitative Services
Building 6, Room 233
1317 Winewood Boulevard
Tallahassee, FL 32399-0700
904-488-3560

Georgia Medicaid Director
Georgia Department of
  Medical Assistance
1220-C West Tower
2 Martin Luther King, Jr.
  Drive, S.E.
Atlanta, GA 30334
404-656-4479

Hawaii Medicaid Director
Health Care Administration
  Division
Department of Social
  Services and Housing
P.O. Box 339
Honolulu, HI 96809
808-548-6584

Idaho Medicaid Director
Bureau of Medical
  Assistance
Department of Health and
  Welfare
450 West State Street
Statehouse Mail
Boise, ID 83720
208-334-5794

Illinois Medicaid Director
Division of Medical
  Programs
Illinois Department of Public
  Aid
201 South Grand Avenue, E.
Springfield, IL 62743-0001
217-782-2570

Indiana Medicaid Director
Medicaid Division
Indiana State Department of
  Public Welfare
State Office Building, Room
  702
Indianapolis, IN 46204
317-232-4333

Iowa Medicaid Director
Bureau of Medical Services
Department of Human
  Services
Hoover State Office Building,
  5th Floor

Des Moines, IA 50319
515-281-8794

Kansas Medicaid Director
Medical Services Division
Department of Social and
  Rehabilitative Services
Docking State Office
  Building, Room 628-S
Topeka, KS 66612
913-296-3981

Kentucky Medicaid Director
Department of Medicaid
  Services
275 East Main Street
Frankfort, KY 40621
502-564-4321

Louisiana Medicaid Director
Bureau of Health Service
  Finance
P.O. Box 91030
Baton Rouge, LA
  70821-9030
504-342-3891

Maine Medicaid Director
Bureau of Medical Services
Department of Human
  Services
State House Station 11
Augusta, ME 04333
207-289-2674

Maryland Medicaid Director
Health Care Policy, Finance
  and Regulation
Department of Health and
  Mental Hygiene
201 West Preston Street,
  Room 525

Baltimore, MD 21201
301-225-6535

Massachusetts Medicaid
  Director
Department of Public
  Welfare
180 Tremont Street, 13th
  Floor
Boston, MA 02111
617-574-0211

Michigan Medicaid Director
Medical Services
  Administration
Department of Social
  Services
P.O. Box 30037
Lansing, MI 48910
517-334-7262

Minnesota Medicaid
  Director
Health Care Programs
  Division
Department of Human
  Services
444 Lafayette Road, 6th
  Floor
St. Paul, MN 55155-3848
612-296-2766

Mississippi Medicaid
  Director
Division of Medicaid
Office of the Governor
Robert E. Lee Building
239 North Lamar Street,
  Suite 801
Jackson, MS 39201-1311
601-359-6050

Missouri Medicaid Director
Division of Medical Services
Department of Social
  Services
P.O. Box 6500
Jefferson City, MO 65102
314-751-6529

Montana Medicaid Director
Economic Assistance
  Division
Department of Social and
  Rehabilitation Services
P.O. Box 4210
Helena, MT 59604
406-444-4540

Nebraska Medicaid Director
Medical Services Division
Department of Social
  Services
301 Centennial Mall South,
  5th Floor
Lincoln, NE 68509
402-471-9330

Nevada Medicaid Director
Deputy Administrator
Nevada Medicaid
Welfare Division,
  Department of Human
  Resources
2527 North Carson Street
Carson City, NV 89710
702-885-4378

New Hampshire Medicaid
  Director
Office of Medical Services
New Hampshire Division of
  Human Services
Department of Health and
  Human Services

6 Hazen Drive
Concord, NH 03301-6521
603-271-4353

New Jersey Medicaid
  Director
Division of Medical
  Assistance and Health
  Services
Department of Human
  Services
CN-712, 7 Quakerbridge
  Plaza
Trenton, NJ 08625
609-588-2602

New Mexico Medicaid
  Director
Chief, Program Support
  Bureau
Department of Human
  Services
P.O. Box 2348
Santa Fe, NM 87504-2348
505-827-4315

New York Medicaid
  Director
Division of Medical
  Assistance
State Department of Social
  Services
Ten Eyck Office Building
40 North Pearl Street
Albany, NY 12243-0001
518-474-9132

North Carolina Medicaid
  Director
Division of Medical
  Assistance
Department of Human
  Resources

1985 Umstead Drive
Raleigh, NC 27603
919-733-2060

North Dakota Medicaid
  Director
Medical Services
North Dakota Department
  of Human Services
State Capitol, Judicial Wing
600 East Boulevard
Bismarck, ND 58505-0251
701-224-2321

Ohio Medicaid Director
Benefits Administration
Medicaid Administration
Department of Human
  Services
30 East Broad Street, 31st
  Floor
Columbus, OH 43266-0423
614-466-3196

Oklahoma Medicaid
  Director
Assistant Director
Division of Medical Services
Department of Human
  Services
P.O. Box 25352
Oklahoma City, OK 73125
405-557-2539

Oregon Medicaid Director
Adult and Family Services
  Division
Department of Human
  Resources
203 Public Service Building
Salem, OR 97310
503-378-2263

Pennsylvania Medicaid
  Director
Deputy Secretary for
  Medical Assistance
  Programs
Department of Public
  Welfare
Health and Welfare
  Building, Room 515
Harrisburg, PA 17120
717-787-1870

Puerto Rico Medicaid
  Director
Office of Economic
  Assistance to the
  Medically Indigent
Building A, Call Box 70184
San Juan, PR 00936
809-765-9941

Rhode Island Medicaid
  Director
Division of Medical Services
Department of Human
  Services
Aime J. Forand Building
600 New London Avenue
Cranston, RI 02920
401-464-3575

South Carolina Medicaid
  Director
Deputy Executive Director
  for Programs
Health and Human Services
  Finance Commission
P.O. Box 8206
Columbia, SC 29202-8206
803-253-6100

South Dakota Medicaid
  Director

Program Administrator
Medical Services
Department of Social
   Services
Kneip Building
700 Governor's Drive
Pierre, SD 57501-2291
605-773-3495

Tennessee Medicaid Director
Director, Bureau of
   Medicaid
Department of Health and
   Environment
729 Church Street
Nashville, TN 37219
615-741-0213

Texas Medicaid Director
Deputy Commissioner for
   Services to the Aged and
   Disabled
Department of Human
   Services
P.O. Box 149030
Austin, TX 78714-9030
512-450-3192

Utah Medicaid Director
Division of Health Care
   Financing
Utah Department of Health
P.O. Box 16580
Salt Lake City, UT
   84116-0580
801-538-6151

Vermont Medicaid Director
Department of Social
   Welfare
Vermont Agency of Human
   Services

103 South Main Street
Waterbury, VT 05676
802-241-2880

Virgin Islands Medicaid
   Director
Bureau of Health Insurance
   and Medical Assistance
Knud Hansen Complex
Charlotte Amalie
St. Thomas, VI 00802
809-774-4624

Virginia Medicaid Director
Virginia Department of
   Medical Assistance
   Services
600 East Broad Street, Room
   1300
Richmond, VA 23219
804-786-7933

Washington Medicaid
   Director
Division of Medical
   Assistance
Department of Social and
   Health Services
12th and Franklin
Mail Stop HB-41
Olympia, WA 98504
206-753-1777

West Virginia Medicaid
   Director
Division of Medical Care
West Virginia Department
   of Human Services
1900 Washington Street, E.
Charleston, WV 25305
304-348-8990

Wisconsin Medicaid Director
Bureau of Health Care
  Financing
Division of Health
Wisconsin Department of
  Health and Social Services
P.O. Box 309
Madison, WI 53701
608-266-2522

Wyoming Medicaid Director
Medical Assistance Services
Department of Health and
  Social Services
Hathaway Building, 4th
  Floor
Cheyenne, WY 82002
307-777-7531

Appendix L
MEDICARE CARRIERS

ALABAMA

Medicare/Blue Cross–Blue
  Shield of Alabama
P.O. Box C-140
Birmingham, AL 35283
205-988-2244
800-292-8855

ALASKA

Medicare/Aetna Life and
  Casualty
200 Southwest Market Street
P.O. Box 1998
Portland, OR 97207-1998
800-547-6333

ARIZONA

Medicare/Aetna Life and
  Casualty

P.O. Box 37200
Phoenix, AZ 85069
602-861-1968
800-352-0411

ARKANSAS

Medicare/Arkansas Blue
  Cross and Blue Shield
P.O. Box 1418
Little Rock, AR 72203
501-378-2320
800-482-5525

CALIFORNIA

Medicare/Transamerica
  Occidental Life Insurance
  Company
Box 50061
Upland, CA 91785-0061
213-748-2311
800-252-9020

(In Los Angeles, Orange,
San Diego, Ventura,
  Imperial, San Luis Obispo,
  and Santa Barbara
  counties)

Medicare Claims
  Department
Blue Shield of California
Chico, CA 95976
916-743-1583
800-952-8627
(In Area Codes 209, 408,
  415, 707, 916)
714-824-0900
800-848-7713
(In Area Codes 213, 619,
  714, 805, and 818)

COLORADO

Medicare/Blue Shield of
  Colorado
700 Broadway
Denver, CO 80273
303-831-2661
800-332-6681

CONNECTICUT

Medicare/Travelers
  Insurance Company
P.O. Box 5005
Wallingford, CT 06493-5005
800-982-6819
203-728-6783 (In Hartford)

DELAWARE

Medicare/Pennsylvania Blue
  Shield
P.O. Box 890200
Camp Hill, PA 17089-0200
800-851-3535

DISTRICT OF COLUMBIA

Medicare/Pennsylvania Blue
  Shield
P.O. Box 890100
Camp Hill, PA 17089-0100
800-233-1124

FLORIDA

Medicare/Blue Shield of
  Florida, Inc.
P.O. Box 2525
Jacksonville, FL 32231
904-355-3680
800-333-7586

GEORGIA

Medicare/Aetna Life and
  Casualty
Medicare Administration
12052 Middleground Road,
  Suite A
Savannah, GA 31419-1699
912-927-0934

IDAHO

Equicor, Inc.
P.O. Box 8048
Boise, ID 83707
208-342-7763
800-632-6574

ILLINOIS

Medicare Claims
Blue Cross and Blue Shield
  of Illinois
P.O. Box 4422
Marion, IL 62959
312-938-8000
800-642-6930

INDIANA

Medicare Part B
Associated Insurance
  Companies, Inc.
P.O. Box 7073
Indianapolis, IN 46207
317-842-4151
800-622-4792

IOWA

Medicare/Blue Shield of
  Iowa
636 Grand Avenue
Des Moines, IA 50309
515-245-4785
800-532-1285

KANSAS

Medicare/Blue Shield of
  Kansas City
P.O. Box 169
Kansas City, MO 64141
816-561-0900
800-892-5900
(In Johnson and Wyandotte
  counties)

Medicare/Blue Shield of
  Kansas
P.O. Box 239
Topeka, KS 66601
913-232-3773
800-432-3531
(In the rest of the state)

KENTUCKY

Medicare Part B
Blue Cross and Blue Shield
  of Kentucky
100 East Vine Street
Lexington, KY 40507
606-233-1441
800-432-9255

LOUISIANA

Blue Cross and Blue Shield
  of Louisiana
Medicare Administration
P.O. Box 95024
Baton Rouge, LA
  70895-9024

MEDICARE CARRIERS 451

800-462-9666
504-529-1494 (In New
  Orleans)
504-272-1242 (In Baton
  Rouge)

MAINE

Medicare/Blue Shield of
  Massachusetts/Tri-State
P.O. Box 1010
Biddeford, ME 04005
800-492-0919

MARYLAND

Medicare/Pennsylvania Blue
  Shield
P.O. Box 890100
Camp Hill, PA 17089-0100
800-233-1124
(In Montgomery and Prince
  Georges counties)

Maryland Blue Shield, Inc.
700 East Joppa Road
Towson, MD 21204
800-492-4795
301-561-4160
(In the rest of the state)

MASSACHUSETTS

Medicare/Blue Shield of
  Massachusetts, Inc.
55 Accord Park Drive
Rockland, MA 02371
800-882-1228

MICHIGAN

Medicare Part B
Michigan Blue Cross and
  Blue Shield
P.O. Box 2201
Detroit, MI 48231-2201
800-482-4045 (In Area Code
  313)
800-322-0607 (In Area Code
  517)
800-442-8020 (In Area Code
  616)
800-562-7802 (In Area Code
  906)
313-225-8200 (In Detroit)

MINNESOTA

Medicare/The Travelers
  Insurance Company
8120 Penn Avenue
South Bloomington, MN
  55431
800-352-2762
612-884-7171 (In Anoka,
  Dakota, Filmore,
  Goodhue, Hennepin,
  Houston, Olmstead,
  Ramsey, Wabasha,
  Washington, and Winona
  counties)

Medicare/Blue Shield of
  Minnesota
P.O. Box 64357
St. Paul, MN 55164
800-392-0343
612-456-5070
(In the rest of the state)

MISSISSIPPI

Medicare/The Travelers
  Insurance Company
P.O. Box 22545
Jackson, MS 39225-2545
800-682-5417
601-956-0372

MISSOURI

Medicare/Blue Shield of
  Kansas City
P.O. Box 169
Kansas City, MO 64141
800-892-5900
816-561-0900
(In Andrew, Atchison, Bates,
  Benton, Buchanan,
  Caldwell, Carroll, Cass,
  Clay, Clinton, Daviess,
  DeKalb, Gentry, Grundy,
  Harrison, Henry, Holt,
  Jackson, Johnson,
  Lafayette, Livingston,
  Mercer, Nodaway, Pettis,
  Platte, Ray, St. Clair,
  Saline, Vernon, and Worth
  counties)

Medicare/General American
  Life Insurance Company
P.O. Box 505
St. Louis, MO 63166
800-392-3070
314-843-8880
(In the rest of the state)

MONTANA

Medicare/Blue Shield of
  Montana, Inc.

2501 Beltview
P.O. Box 4310
Helena, MT 59604
800-332-6146
406-444-8350

NEBRASKA

Medicare Part B
Blue Cross and Blue Shield
  of Nebraska
P.O. Box 3106
Omaha, NE 68103-0106
800-633-1113

NEVADA

Medicare/Aetna Life and
  Casualty
P.O. Box 37230
Phoenix, AZ 85069
800-528-0311

NEW HAMPSHIRE

Medicare/Blue Shield of
  Massachusetts/Tri-State
P.O. Box 1010
Biddeford, ME 04005
800-447-1142

NEW JERSEY

Medicare/Pennsylvania Blue
  Shield
Box 4000100
Camp Hill, PA 17140-0100
800-462-9306

NEW YORK

Medicare/Empire Blue Cross
  and Blue Shield
P.O. Box 100
Yorktown Heights, NY
  10598
212-490-4444
(In Bronx, Kings, New York,
  and Richmond counties)

Medicare/Empire Blue Cross
  and Blue Shield
P.O. Box 100
Yorktown Heights, NY
  10598
800-442-8430
(In Columbia, Delaware,
  Dutchess, Greene, Nassau,
  Orange, Putnam,
  Rockland, Suffolk,
  Sullivan, Ulster, and
  Westchester counties)

Medicare/Group Health, Inc.
P.O. Box 1608
Ansonia Station
New York, NY 10023
212-712-1770
(In Queens County)

Medicare/Blue Shield of
  Western New York
P.O. Box 5600
Binghamton, NY 13902-0600
607-772-6906
800-252-6550
(In the rest of the state)

NORTH CAROLINA

Equicor, Inc.
Medicare Administration
1 Triad Center, Suite 240
7736 McClould Road
Greensboro, NC 27409
919-665-0341
919-665-0348
800-672-3071

NORTH DAKOTA

Medicare/Blue Shield of
  North Dakota
4510 13th Avenue, S.W.
Fargo, ND 58121-0001
800-247-2267
701-282-1100

OHIO

Medicare/Nationwide
  Mutual Insurance
  Company
P.O. Box 57
Columbus, OH 43216
800-282-0530
614-249-7157

OKLAHOMA

Medicare/Aetna Life and
  Casualty
701 Northwest 63rd Street,
  Suite 100
Oklahoma City, OK
  73116-7693
800-522-9079
405-848-7711

OREGON

Medicare/Aetna Life and
  Casualty
200 Southwest Market Street
P.O. Box 1997
Portland, OR 97207-1997
800-452-0125
503-222-6831

PENNSYLVANIA

Medicare/Pennsylvania Blue
  Shield
Box 890065
Camp Hill, PA 17089-0065
800-382-1274

PUERTO RICO

Medicare/Seguros de
  Servicio de Salud de
  Puerto Rico
Call Box 71391
San Juan, PR 00936
137-800-462-2970
809-759-9191

RHODE ISLAND

Medicare/Blue Shield of
  Rhode Island
444 Westminster Mall
Providence, RI 02901
800-662-5170
401-861-2273

SOUTH CAROLINA

Medicare Part B
Blue Cross and Blue Shield
  of South Carolina
Fontaine Road Business
  Center
300 Arbor Lake Drive, Suite
  1300
Columbia, SC 29223
800-922-2340
803-754-0639

SOUTH DAKOTA

Medicare Part B
Blue Shield of North Dakota
4510 13th Avenue, S.W.
Fargo, ND 58121-0001
800-437-4762

TENNESSEE

Equicor, Inc.
P.O. Box 1465
Nashville, TN 37202
800-342-8900
615-244-5650

TEXAS

Medicare/Blue Cross and
  Blue Shield of Texas, Inc.
P.O. Box 660031
Dallas, TX 75266-0031
800-442-2620

UTAH

Medicare/Blue Shield of
  Utah
2455 Parley's Way
P.O. Box 30269
Salt Lake City, UT
  84130-0269
800-426-3477
801-481-6196

VERMONT

Medicare/Blue Shield of
  Massachusetts/Tri-State
P.O. Box 1010
Biddeford, ME 04005
800-447-1142

VIRGIN ISLANDS

Medicare/Seguros de
  Servicio de Salud de
  Puerto Rico
Call Box 71391
San Juan, PR 00936
137-800-462-2970
809-759-9191

VIRGINIA

Medicare/Pennsylvania Blue
  Shield
P.O. Box 890100
Camp Hill, PA 17089-0100
800-233-1124
(In Arlington, and Fairfax
  counties, and the cities of

Alexandria, Falls Church,
  and Fairfax)

Medicare/The Travelers
  Insurance Company
P.O. Box 26463
Richmond, VA 23261
800-552-3423
804-254-4130 (In the rest of
  the state)

WASHINGTON

Medicare/Washington
  Physician's Service
Mail to your local medical
  service bureau. If you do
  not know which bureau
  handles your claim, mail
  to:
Medicare/Washington
  Physician's Service
4th and Battery Building,
  6th Floor
2401 4th Avenue
Seattle, WA 98121
800-422-4087 (In King
  County)
206-464-3711
800-572-5256 (In Spokane)
509-536-4550
800-552-7114 (In Kitsap
  County)
206-377-5576
206-597-6530 (In Pierce
  County)

WEST VIRGINIA

Medicare/Nationwide
  Mutual Insurance
  Company
P.O. Box 57
Columbus, OH 43216
800-848-0106

WISCONSIN

Medicare/WPS
Box 1787
Madison, WI 53701
800-362-7221
608-221-3330 (In Madison)
414-931-1071 (In
  Milwaukee)

WYOMING

North Dakota Blue Shield
4000 House Avenue
P.O. Box 628
Cheyenne, WY 82003
800-442-2371

INDEX

ABOUT THE AUTHORS

CHARLES B. INLANDER is president of the People's Medical
Society and has been its executive officer since its founding
in early 1983. He is the co-author of six books on health
care, with four more to be published in 1991. Mr. Inlander is
a faculty lecturer at the Yale University School of Medicine,
and his articles have appeared in scores of publications. Prior
to joining the People's Medical Society, he was an advocate
for the rights of handicapped citizens and the mentally
retarded. A native of Chicago, he is a graduate of American
University in Washington, D.C.

KARLA MORALES is director of communications at the People's
Medical Society, and co-author of the forthcoming book
Take This Book to the Obstetrician with You. A native of Baton
Rouge, she is a graduate of Louisiana State University.